THE SHOW MUST GO ON

ALSO BY ELMER RICE

PLAYS

On Trial

The Adding Machine

Wake Up Jonathan
(with Hatcher Hughes)

The Lady Next Door
(with Dorothy Parker)

Cock Robin
(with Philip Barry)

Street Scene

The Subway

See Naples and Die

The Left Bank

Counsellor-at-Law

The House in Blind Alley

We the People

Judgment Day

Between Two Worlds

Not for Children

Black Sheep

American Landscape

Two on An Island

Flight to the West

A New Life

Dream Girl

NOVELS

On Trial *(novelization)*

A Voyage to Purilia

Imperial City

THE
SHOW
MUST
GO ON

a novel by

ELMER RICE

New York · 1949

THE VIKING PRESS

PRINTED IN U.S.A. BY AMERICAN BOOK—STRATFORD PRESS, INC.

To my associates

in the Playwrights' Company

and to the memory

of Sidney Howard

THE SHOW MUST GO ON

I.

Among the thousands, the tens of thousands, who daily and nightly tramp through the streets that lead to Times Square, very few are observant enough to notice the narrow alleys alongside certain of the playhouses; and even fewer ever enter them. Vestiges of a more spacious era, these alleys are gradually disappearing from the metropolitan scene, as, one by one, the older theaters are swept away by the relentless tide of commerce.

For real estate, in New York's theatrical district, is valued by the foot; and, at best, a building that can be used for only a few hours a day is economically wasteful. Alleys serving only as a means of access to the region that lies behind the curtain or of egress for the departing audience merely increase the landowner's tax burden without adding a penny to his revenue. In the great theater-building boom of the twenties, when land values soared to unprecedented figures, resourceful architects devised means of eliminating the traditional alleys. Sometimes, when several theaters were built in a cluster, a common passageway, twisting beneath the complex of buildings from the sidewalk to the backstage areas was contrived. But in most modern theaters even this waste of space is not tolerated, and in these tightly constructed buildings, the stage door, the numerous exit doors of the auditorium, and the great scene doors of the stage itself open directly upon the street, and only the outer wall of the theater deadens the sound of the traffic that roars and honks incessantly through these narrow thoroughfares. Actors and auditors suffer alike from this distracting din, but comfort and convenience must yield to the inexorable operation of economic laws.

Yet the disappearance of the old alleys hardly calls for a nostalgic sigh. The few that survive are no ornament to the city. Narrow,

3

dank, dark, flanked by gloomy, windowless walls hung with fire escapes, exposed to rain, sleet and snow, reeking with stale odors and foul with debris, they are an offense to the senses and, in bad weather, a trial and a hazard to those who must traverse them. During intermissions some of the spectators step out for a cigarette or a breath of air (though its quality is not noticeably better than that in the auditorium); and at the end of the performance the alley is briefly flooded by the outgoing surge. Occasionally some members of the unruly crowd of adolescents that congregates on the sidewalk to gape at the actors or clamor for their autographs escape the vigilance of the police or the house manager and penetrate the alley. And, on opening nights, there is usually a swarm of backstage visitors after the final curtain.

But, for the most part, only those who make their living in the theater ever use the alley. To them it is the habitual path of arrival and departure. Of all the theater's many unwritten laws, none is more firmly established than the rule that no person who works behind the proscenium—or, more accurately, behind the rail of the orchestra pit—enters or leaves through the "front of the house." This applies even during rehearsals or when the theater is empty. Only some special circumstance warrants its breach, and the most celebrated and self-willed stars seldom violate it. Indeed, the artists and artisans of the theater who customarily tread the unlovely lane that leads to the stage door would give up almost anything rather than that right of way, which is especially theirs.

"Pull up there, by the alley," said Leroy Thompson, as the taxi slowed down in front of the Farow Theater. The cab rolled along for another ten yards and came to a stop. Thompson and Claire Weir got out, and he offered the driver a five-dollar bill.

"Geez, Mac," grumbled the driver, "ain't you got somethin' smaller? All I been gettin' all day is big bills."

"We're living in boom times," said Thompson.

"Yeah? Ever try to make a fast buck drivin' a hack?"

"Not recently. Sorry, but I'm afraid that's the smallest I've got."

"Wait, I may have it," said Claire, fumbling in her handbag. "No, I haven't."

"They'll break it for you over at O'Leary's," said Thompson, pointing to a little bar-restaurant opposite the theater. With a muttered obscenity the driver got out of the cab and dodged across the street through the traffic.

4

"Let's get out of this heat!" exclaimed Claire. They stepped under the marquee of the theater, which offered a refuge from the searing June sun. The glass-paneled lobby doors of the untenanted theater bore a thick coating of grime and dust, upon which childish fore-fingers had traced shaky inscriptions. Thompson tried to peer into the lobby, then burst into laughter as he noticed the gilt-lettered scarlet houseboards, which the last occupant had not taken the trouble to remove.

"It must be good," said Claire, slightly irritated. She wished that she had had the courage to leave off her girdle.

Thompson pointed to the flaking gold title on the houseboards: Forever and A Day. "They went a little overboard on that title," he said. "That was that little number of Dave Bloomfield's that closed the second night."

"I had a chance to buy a piece of it."

"Well, you could have taken a nice clean tax loss." He walked back to the cab as the driver returned. "How much is it?"

"Sixty," said the driver surlily.

"Give me four bucks."

"Okay," said the driver, somewhat mollified by the forty-cent tip.

The rusty iron gate at the alley's entrance creaked harshly when Thompson pushed it open. They entered, and Thompson closed the gate behind him. He noticed, with faint distaste, Claire's beaded mustache of perspiration.

"Don't they ever clean this place?" she asked as they picked their way down the littered alley.

"Every time the Senators win a pennant. I remember some of this dirt from the last time I played here, and that was fourteen years ago."

"Yes, you always did have a good memory for dirt."

"Love-fifteen," said Thompson.

He opened the wooden stage door. Inside it was cool, almost chilly. Claire breathed a grateful sigh. "Ooh, what a relief!"

An elderly man, who was reading a newspaper by the light of a swaying, naked electric bulb in the stage-doorman's cubicle, hobbled forward to greet them, slipping his steel-rimmed spectacles into the pocket of his faded overalls.

"Hi, Harry," said Thompson, shaking hands warmly. "How you been?"

5

"Well, pretty good, Mr. Thompson, takin' everything into consideration. Only I guess maybe I ain't quite as young as I used to be."

"I don't notice it. And where do you get that mister stuff? Tommy to you! I'm the guy that used to work around here."

"That was quite a good many years ago," said Harry, flattered. "You've come up a mighty long ways since them days."

"Listen, I'm still the best goddam assistant stage manager in the business! You know Mrs. Weir, don't you? This is Harry Baumrucker. He's been house carpenter here ever since—how long is it, Harry?"

"Ever since the Old Man built the house, and that's a good thirty-nine years."

"Why, that's about the time I was giving my mother morning sickness."

Harry shifted his feet in embarrassment. "Oh, almost forgot to tell you. Mr. Anthony Weir phoned to say he'll be a little late and for you folks to go right ahead without him."

Claire was annoyed, not only by this message, but by the way Harry seemed to be staring at her. "Tony can never be anywhere on time," she said. "I don't know how he manages to keep his clients. Well, since there's no telling when he'll show up, we may as well not wait, I suppose."

"I guess you'll want to see the whole plant?"

"Yes, while we're at it," said Thompson.

"Well, if you don't mind waitin' a minute while I throw on some lights." Harry found a flashlight and hobbled off into the darkness.

"Looks like the old fellow's arthritis is getting him down," said Thompson. "But he's still quite a character."

Claire wiped and powdered her face. "It's no wonder he has arthritis, sitting around here."

"He wouldn't know where else to sit. There go the stage lights. All right, let's have a look at the old firetrap." He had decided that the best line to take with Claire was a general attitude of depreciation.

The illumination increased progressively as Harry pulled the several switches that controlled the house lights. Claire and Thompson walked to the center of the stage and stood looking out. The ornate auditorium was heavy with carvings, gilt reliefs, crystal chandeliers, and brocade draperies—the nondescript tastelessness and lavishness of the whole accentuated by the beige cotton dust-covers

6

protecting the crimson upholstery of the seats. Harry watched them anxiously as their eyes roved over the empty theater.

"Funny how different it looks from this angle," said Claire with an almost girlish excitement. "I've sat out front dozens of times, but it doesn't give you the same feeling at all." Shrewd and businesslike though she was, and well accustomed to the inner workings of theaters, the prospect of making all this her own—this famous, almost historic playhouse, with its rich aura of association and legend—filled her with romantic anticipation.

"It's a beautiful house," said Harry. "The Old Man put his heart and soul into it, and he loved it like it was his own flesh and blood."

"It's so intimate, that's what I like about it," said Claire. "They're all right there, almost as though you could take them in your arms." She stretched out her arms, for the moment a great star acknowledging the acclaim of a crowded house.

"I could do without all those boxes," said Thompson. "And unless you've got a sell-out, that second balcony is just a headache."

"The Old Man used to say," said Harry wistfully, "that that's where you'd find the real theayter lovers."

"That was before Eli Whitney dreamed up the movie camera. Who wants to climb up eighteen flights and sit in those funeral-parlor chairs when for an extra quarter you can buy yourself an overstuffed divan at the Music Hall, with hot and cold Rockettes thrown in?"

"You know it isn't the same thing! Not for anybody who really cares!" said Claire indignantly.

Secretly Thompson, who had grown up under the spell of the Farow legend, agreed with her. From the beginning of the century until his death on the eve of the Second World War, Oscar Farow had been a dominant figure in the American theater. His fame as a showman had been enhanced by the atmosphere of mystery in which he deliberately enveloped himself. No one really ever got to know him; no one even knew his real name or his origin. In appearance he was a Levantine, but there were a dozen conflicting stories about his ancestry—and at various stages of his career he had corroborated them all. He first appeared in the theater as a candy vendor in a Boston vaudeville house; then, in rapid succession, worked as usher, box-office assistant, advance man, house manager, and theater lessee, until at thirty-five he became a director-producer, whose genius won almost instant recognition. With the opening of

7

his own theater his position and influence became secure, and the playhouse had been the scene of an almost unbroken series of triumphs. Except for an occasional revival of Sheridan or Shakespeare, the plays he produced were for the most part trivial: obvious melodramas, sentimental comedies, sirupy romances, risqué farces and creampuffs from Budapest, Vienna, and the boulevards of Paris. But no matter how shoddy or ephemeral the manuscript, it was always so lavishly mounted, so cunningly produced, and so skillfully acted that it was generally accepted (for the moment, at least) as a masterpiece.

It had been every actor's ambition to work for Oscar Farow, and everyone who was associated with him adored him. He was a stern, even a harsh, taskmaster, but he tempered the severity of a martinet with a patriarchal benignity and was universally referred to—sometimes in his presence—as the Old Man. Aloof and unapproachable though he was, his charming little compliments and remembrances had endeared him to the people of the theater, to whom a word of praise or a gesture of affection are gifts without price.

Claire had never known Oscar Farow but, gazing out at the empty house, she could almost feel the Old Man's spirit hovering over her and blessing her successorship. Thompson's emotion was more genuine. He had actually worked for Farow, and the ghosts that haunted the old playhouse were his spiritual forebears.

"Curtain in pretty good condition?" he asked.

"Perfect!" said Harry. "You couldn't buy the like of it today for love nor money. And good for another twenty years if it gets the right care."

Thompson stepped back and craned his neck. "Grid all right?"

"Couldn't be better. Two or three of the lines need overhaulin', but that don't amount to nothin'."

"Any leaks in the roof? I had a brand-new set ruined at the Clinton couple of years ago."

"You don't need to worry about that. It's as tight as a drum. Some buildin' feller from the bank was here, last month, and he went over the house from top to toe. I guess Mr. Weir could get hold of his report for you."

"He's seen it," said Claire. "And he says that very little needs to be done."

Thompson pursued his inquiries as though he had not heard her. "How's the switchboard?"

8

"Well, that's somethin' you know about firsthand. And Charlie keeps it right up to scratch. You wouldn't want a better board. The Old Man was always way ahead of his time when it came to lightin'. You know that."

"Well, there are two schools of thought about that, Harry," said Thompson. Then, as he saw the troubled look on the carpenter's face, "But I guess you're right at that. He knew his way around."

"He was a wizard," said Harry with finality. "Where are you gonna find another stage like this, Mr. Thom—Tommy, that is? You got depth here. Thirty-two feet to the back wall, and that's not countin' the apron. You could stack a Ben Hur production and not even know it was there. And miles of offstage space. No light bridges or anythin' to louse up a platform show. And a fine, big orchestra pit. Why, we've had musicals here!"

"Yes," said Thompson dryly, "I've seen some of them." He hastened to dispel another cloud from Harry's face. "But, what the hell, they can't all be hits."

"You're right, they can't! I want to tell you, some of the ones we had in here lately! I could hear the Old Man turnin' over in his grave!"

"With plenty of good sound effects, I'll bet." He walked around, testing the floorboards with his feet. "Stage is a little warped."

"Well, now, that's somethin' you can't help," said Harry, worried. "You take a buildin' as old as this, and it's bound to settle a little, specially with all them trucks poundin' by. And that new subway don't help either. But once you get a ground-cloth down, you don't have no trouble."

"What about platforms?"

"Well, then you got to put down tracks, anyhow. An' it's just a matter of gettin' them level. I always take care of that myself, to make sure it's done right."

"All right, let's shove on," said Thompson. He paused and added solicitously, "Unless you want to look at the switchboard, Claire."

"Wouldn't mean a thing to me," she said, too deep in her dreams of possession to detect his malice.

They followed Harry off beyond the proscenium. He lifted the bar of the heavy iron pass-door and clanked it open. "Watch them two little steps," he said. They went down the steps and through the little passage behind the stage boxes to the side aisle of the theater.

Claire stopped to lift the dust-covers of three or four of the orchestra chairs. "The upholstery's beginning to wear a little, isn't it?"

"Well, ma'am," said Harry, "them chairs ain't been empty much—at least not in the Old Man's day. But there ain't many bad ones—a dozen or so, maybe, and we got 'em all spotted."

They moved along slowly to the back of the auditorium. "Here's the box-office," said Harry. "Oh, say, I don't think I got that key on this ring. If you'll wait just a minute I'll run back and get it."

"Never mind it," said Thompson. "All a box-office needs is a good deep cash-drawer."

"I *would* like to see the lounge," said Claire. "Of course, I've been in it, dozens of times, but still—"

"Yes, ma'am, just let me switch on the lights." He opened a door and preceded them down a wide staircase, turning on the lights as he went along.

"This carpet's pretty bad," said Thompson.

"Carpet runs into money," Claire replied.

"Not as much as a few broken legs and fractured skulls."

The lounge, which was under the lobby, ran almost the entire width of the theater. The men's lavatory was at one end and the women's at the other. Claire sat on one of the long sofas and looked around. "This does look a little dingy. Tommy, do you think—"

"Back in a minute," he said, striding to the men's room.

"Of course, it's in absolutely filthy condition," said Claire petulantly. She was annoyed at Thompson because she did not have the courage to follow his example and flustered by the persistence of Harry's stare.

"Well, we had it all cleaned up, spick and span, when that last one folded," said Harry. "And the place has been shut up tight ever since. I don't know where all the muck comes from, but I never yet saw the theayter that you could keep the dirt out of."

"Well, it's something we'll have to think about."

"Do you want to take a look at the balconies?" asked Harry as Thompson rejoined them and they went up the stairs at the other end of the lounge.

"No," said Thompson before Claire could answer.

"How about the apartment and all that?"

"Oh, definitely!" said Claire.

"Well, this way, please." He pushed against the bar of one of the emergency exit doors, and as it opened they felt a blast of heat.

"Whoo, I'd forgotten how hot it is!" said Claire. They stepped out into the alley that was used for the transit of scenery and that paralleled the stage-door alley on the other side of the house. "Where are we going?"

"Just back to the elevator, ma'am," said Harry, making sure that the auditorium door was tightly shut. At the back of the alley he unlocked the door of a tiny foyer, which gave access to a small automatic elevator. "It's a kinder tight fit for three but I guess we can make it." Claire and Thompson squeezed against the rear wall of the elevator to make room for Harry, who barely managed to get the door closed. He pushed a button, and the elevator began to ascend slowly, shaking and wheezing.

"Is it safe?" asked Claire.

"Nothin' to be scared of. She always shimmies like that, but she always gets you there." He turned his head to give her a reassuring look, his face not three inches from hers, and she almost gasped as she discovered the reason for his fixed stare: his left eye was glass. He did not appear to notice her involuntary reaction, and she felt relieved; but Thompson, with his morbid hypersensitivity, was quick to see the slight movement of Harry's lower jaw.

The elevator stopped with a bump. "Well, for heaven's sake!" Claire exclaimed when Harry opened the door. Confronting them was a wide doorway flanked by two large polychrome columns whose capitals represented lotus buds. Harry led the way, between the columns, into an enormous duplex studio. The walls were covered, from floor to ceiling, with hieroglyphs and Egyptian wall paintings. "What's the idea of all this?" asked Claire in amazement.

"A tribute to his ancestors," said Thompson.

"What do you mean?"

"Oh, don't you know about that? Some shrewd cookie sold the Old Man the idea that he was descended from the kings of Egypt. Farow, Pharaoh—get it? Just a slight difference in spelling."

"You mean he really believed he was descended from—from King Tut?" asked Claire, probing her memory for the name of an Egyptian potentate.

Thompson nodded. "Tut was his great-granddaddy. I don't know if he really believed it, but he certainly backed the idea with a lot of coin. You should have seen this place when it was furnished. It was strictly a De Mille production."

"I wish I *had* seen it! What became of it all?"

"It went under the hammer," said Harry. "And for the price of junk. I wisht I had what it cost!"

"Why it's absolutely fascinating," said Claire, staring at the hieroglyphs. "It would be wonderful to know what all this means."

"Probably just some of Cleopatra's old box-office statements," said Thompson.

"Oh, and look, there's a whaddye-call-it!" As excited as a child in a toy shop, she pointed to a low shelf that held a small model of the Giza sphinx.

"Spinx," said Harry. "Open it."

"Open it?"

"Yes, ma'am. The head is on hinges."

A little uncertainly Claire took hold of the sphinx's head and pulled. It swung back. Inside was a telephone.

"Well, now I ask you!" she said. Harry laughed.

"A clever people, the Egyptians," said Thompson. "Now for the love nest." He walked over to a small wooden staircase that led to a railed narrow balcony. "They tell me, Harry," he said, stopping at the foot of the stairs, "that the Old Man used to lie down here on an Egyptian studio couch, while a certain leading lady made an entrance down these stairs, modeling a chiffon veil."

Harry shifted uncomfortably. "Well, I couldn't say about that. That wasn't in my department."

"You mustn't believe everything you hear, Tommy," said Claire. "Maybe that's just the way she would have liked it to be."

Opening off the balcony were a bedroom, a bathroom, and a tiny kitchen. Except for the kitchen, which was strictly utilitarian, the Egyptian motif was sustained throughout. Three walls of the bedroom were covered with fine parchment, painted in imitation of dynastic papyri. The fourth wall and the ceiling were all mirror.

"What beautiful wallpaper!" said Claire. "But I don't know how much I'd like to live with it."

"Beautiful mirrors too," said Thompson casually.

She threw him an angry look. "Disgusting!" she said under her breath.

The bathroom was a replica of a royal burial chamber, the walls decorated with tomb paintings and the porcelain tub shaped and painted to represent the lower half of a mummy case.

12

"Well, now, really!" said Claire. "Have you seen this before, Tommy?"

"No, I never got this far. I can't wait to tell my mummy about it."

They returned to the studio. "What a wonderful place to throw an opening-night party!" said Claire. She saw herself moving easily among her celebrated guests and, fortified by a few lessons in Egyptian history and art, making amusing and informative little remarks about the decor.

"That's one thing he never went in for—openin'-night parties," said Harry. "He never stayed around for an openin'. As soon as the last dress rehearsal was over, he'd light out, all by himself, for Atlantic City or Hot Springs, and two or three days later he'd call up to find out about the notices and how the show was goin'."

"Amazing!" said Claire. "And how unlike Leroy Thompson."

"Who wants to be alone in Atlantic City?" said Thompson, careful to let no tinge of resentment color his voice.

"Didn't the Old Man ever marry?" asked Claire. As Oscar Farow's prospective heir, she felt that she had a right to use the familiar appellation.

"No, ma'am. He lived alone and he died alone."

"Why buy a cow when milk is so cheap?" said Thompson.

"What else is there to see?" asked Claire, apparently not hearing what he said. But the angry flicker of her eyelids gave him the pleasant sensation of having evened the score.

"Well, there's the offices and the dressin'-rooms," said Harry. "Oh, and the rehearsal room. That's somethin' you won't find in many theayters." A door from the studio led to a large, bare, oblong room. "You can rehearse a whole show in here, like if the boys are workin' on the stage, or even durin' a performance. It's absolutely soundproof."

"Oh, this is wonderful, Tommy!" said Claire.

"Yes, I've rehearsed here." He turned to Harry. "Isn't there some kind of a peephole in here, where you can see the stage?"

"Right over here." He opened a small sliding panel in one of the walls. "Come and take a look." Through the aperture, which was just a little above the last row of second-balcony seats, they could look squarely at the lighted stage.

"Did he actually watch the shows from here?" asked Claire excitedly.

13

Harry nodded. "Best seat in the house. You can hear every whisper, and what's more, you can tell how the gallery's takin' the show. There'd be hardly a night when he didn't ketch a scene or two. That's how he kept the performances up to scratch. The actors never knew when he was watchin', or from where, and so they had to keep on their toes all the time."

"I've always wanted to get a look through that knothole," said Thompson, "because it cost me a lot of hungry weeks. I was assistant stage manager on a production starring Florence Fulham—"

"With or without the chiffon veil?" said Claire.

He ignored the interruption. "Well, one day, during rehearsals, Phil Caglin, the stage manager, was home with a cold, and the Old Man said he had some business downtown and asked me to run the company through. It was the first time I'd ever been in charge and I guess I was feeling my oats a little. Anyhow, I started to do an imitation of the Old Man directing Fulham in the big love scene. She could take a joke and played right along with me, and the rest of the company nearly split a gut laughing, and I went home feeling like Henry Irving on his way to be knighted. Well, about three days later the Old Man called Fulham over and said, 'Miss Fulham'—he never called any actor by his first name—'Miss Fulham, could we just run that little love scene?' So what does he do but give a word-for-word imitation of my imitation of him!"

"No!" exclaimed Claire. "What did you do?"

"I sat there. What the hell else could I do? Everybody else was exploding inside but completely deadpan. And Fulham went right through it, without batting an eye. Then when he was finished he turned to me and said, 'Any suggestions, Mr. Thompson?'"

Harry grinned happily. "I was up there in the fly-loft, workin' on some lines, when it happened."

"Why didn't you tip me off about the peephole? I didn't find out about it until years later."

"He made me swear never to tell nobody."

"Did he give you your notice?" asked Claire.

"Of course not! He wouldn't give anybody the satisfaction of knowing that he cared that much. I stayed right on until the show closed, and we had a good long run too."

"Meet Miss Murphy," said Harry.

"That was the show. Only he never offered me another job, and I never asked him for one. But when I directed my first show,

Indian Summer, he came to a matinee and sent me a wire that just said: 'No suggestions, Mr. Thompson.' Kind of sweet, wasn't it?"

"Oh, and how!" said Claire, her eyes moist.

Harry shook his head sadly. "There'll never be nobody like him." At the far end of the rehearsal room another door led to a corridor, on which four or five rather gloomy offices opened. "Lots of good office space too."

"Well, I should say so! Why, you could take care of a whole staff here," said Claire, delighted to find that the building had economic potentialities as well as romantic associations.

"They'd have to wear those miners' lamps to find their way around," said Thompson, making up his mind that no matter what happened he would not give up his bright Radio City office.

"If you don't mind walkin' down the stairs," said Harry, "we can take in the dressin'-rooms on the way down."

"I'd rather walk down the Empire State Building than face that elevator again," said Claire.

They started down the five flights of iron-railed stone steps. On the floor below the offices Harry showed them a large room, with a table-high shelf surmounted by a strip of mirror running along the walls. In one corner were two wash basins, and a dozen rickety cane-bottomed chairs were scattered around. "Here's a fine big room for extras or a chorus. We once dressed twenty girls in here."

"That's something I've always wanted to do," said Thompson.

The next two floors had several rooms, each capable of accommodating four to six actors, and on the first floor above the stage level were five or six rooms designed for either single or double occupancy.

"Well," said Thompson as they went down the last flight, "with a cast of four, you'd have no problems at all."

"Forty—and then some!" said Harry.

"When you say that, smile, Harry. If costs keep on going up we'll soon be putting on nothing but monologues."

They followed Harry back past the doorman's cubicle to the star dressing-room, which opened upon the stage. Harry unlocked the door, in which had been set a five-pointed star made of rhinestones, some of which were missing. "Now you know what became of the Hope Diamond," said Thompson to Claire.

Harry opened the door almost reverently. There was a little reception room, a good-sized dressing-room, a bath, and a kitchenette.

Little was left of the former elegance, and the dust was thick everywhere.

"It would take a year ever to get this whole building clean," said Claire.

"Oh, no, ma'am! You'd be surprised what you can do in a week, with soap and water and a little elbow grease. Just give us the word, and we'll shine it up for you in no time."

Thompson, oblivious to the grime and disrepair, recalled the names of the great stars who had tenanted this room over a period of nearly forty years. Some he had known personally, some through their performances, some only by reputation, but they all figured in his hagiology. Their collective presence hallowed this dingy apartment, and, like Harry, he approached it almost as though it were a shrine.

"Some pretty good actors have looked at themselves in that mirror," he said.

"Some of the best," said Harry in a hushed voice. "It'd take me an hour to remember the names of all of them. Arnold Daly, Mrs. Fiske, Joe Jefferson, the Barrymores, Sarah Burnheart, that Eyetalian lady—what was her name again?—oh yeah, Deuce!"

"Oh, I wish I'd seen her!" said Claire.

"They tell me she really could act," said Thompson, his eyes glistening with excitement.

"Well, if you ask me, she was the greatest of them all. To look at her you'd think she was a wardrobe woman, but once she got out there, boy, could she troupe! Why, I'd stand there in the wings night after night, not understandin' a word that she was jabberin' about, just watchin' and watchin', and damn near forgettin' the curtain cues." He sighed deeply. "Well, I guess I've showed you about all there is to see." He locked the door of the dressing-room, and they walked silently back to the stage.

"Oh, there's Tony now!" cried Claire.

Her rather thin voice, which always grated a little upon Thompson's sensitive ear, dispelled his reverential mood and he made an involuntary grimace as Anthony Weir, who had been strolling around on the stage, came over to greet them.

"Sorry to be so late," he said, "but I got involved in an examination before trial and I just couldn't get away any sooner."

He kissed his sister-in-law's cheek and shook hands with Thompson and Harry.

16

"It doesn't matter," said Claire. "We've had a wonderful guide in Mr.—er—"

"Just Harry," said the carpenter. "Nobody ever remembers the Baumrucker." He detained Thompson as the others walked to the stage door. "I guess it's none of my business," he said in a low voice, "but do you think maybe there's a chance that—?" He broke off.

"I don't know yet, Harry."

"Well, I sure hope so! Some of the shows we've had in here and some of the people—well, it's like spittin' on the Old Man's tombstone. With you takin' over, it would be sort of like old times."

"Well, thanks, Harry," said Thompson, flattered and touched by the man's sincerity. He fumbled in his pocket, and as he shook Harry's hand slipped a ten-dollar bill into it.

"No, no!" protested Harry.

"Buy yourself a bottle of Scotch. I'd have brought one along for you if I'd thought of it."

"Well, God bless you! And here's hopin'!"

Thompson joined the others. As they emerged into the alley the solid impact of the heat struck them.

"Oh, let's get out of this, pronto!" exclaimed Claire.

"Shall we go to my office and talk things over?" asked Weir.

"I could use a drink," said Thompson. "Let's find an air-conditioned bar."

"Let's go to my apartment," said Claire.

"It'll be hot as hell there." He was afraid he would not be able to get away and he did not want to be alone with her.

"It's not so bad with the blinds down and the fan on," she said, "and this girdle is driving me crazy."

Claire lived in the country but maintained a Park Avenue apartment consisting of a big, comfortable living-room, two bedrooms, and a combination dining-room and kitchenette. A visiting maid kept the place in order, and an excellent restaurant in the building sent up meals. It was a little stuffy when they entered, but the drawn Venetian blinds had kept out the sun, and the huge electric fan soon set the air in motion.

"Rustle up some drinks, Tommy," she said. "I'll have a bourbon and soda, and don't make it too weak, please."

She went into the bedroom. Thompson removed his coat and pulled his wet shirt away from his body. Weir sat erect in a straight-backed chair, apparently cool and comfortable. He seemed never to perspire, and his neat, well-cut double-breasted jacket and starched wing collar were a reproach to Thompson's unpressed linen suit and crumpled sport shirt.

"Ginger ale for you, Tony?" asked Thompson with the courteous solicitude in which he invariably veiled his malice.

Weir moistened his lips. "Ginger ale or anything soft."

By the time Thompson had prepared the drinks Claire returned. "Sorry, boys," she said as the eyes of both men involuntarily followed her. "But I'll park it where it won't wobble." She settled into a big armchair, drink in hand. "Well, cheers!"

Weir moistened his lips again as the others took a long pull at their highballs, then sipped a little of his ginger ale. "Well, what do you think?" he said.

"I think yes," said Claire. "It's a wonderful theater with a wonderful tradition, and I think we can go places with it. I only wish we could move Give Them in there; then we'd really clean up." She was referring to a play called Give Them All My Love, currently a great success, which she and Thompson had produced.

"Well, that's out of the question," said Weir. "You've got a contract with the Stuyvesant people, and they're not going to let you out as long as you stay over your stop clause."

"Which won't be for two years, I hope, I hope," said Claire, rapping the wooden coffee table.

"I hope so too. No, it's the long-range proposition that I had in mind when I suggested this. You'll be producing lots of other plays, and if you get a hit you'll be sitting pretty, having it right there in your own house. How do you feel about it, Tommy?"

"Well, I don't know. For one thing, I think the location is lousy—"

Claire interrupted sharply, "Everybody can't be on Forty-fifth Street! If you've got the show, they'll go to Canarsie to see it."

"Pardon me, I thought I was being asked for my opinion." He knew that Claire had made up her mind to buy the theater and he thought that he would be in a better position if he made them talk him into it.

"Well, I'm not so much worried about the location," said Weir. "After all, it's right in the district. If it's a good, workable theater—and, of course, it always was—I'd take a chance on the location. But that's just a lawyer's point of view. The technical end is up to you."

"I think it has just about everything," said Claire before Thompson could reply. "Good acoustics, good seating capacity, a wonderful stage, a rehearsal room, even a magnificent Egyptian harem that Tommy could move into."

"Thanks, chum," said Thompson.

"No, really, I think there's everything in its favor—unless the setup is going to make it too tough to swing."

"Well, I'd better give you the whole picture so that you'll know exactly what you're in for," said Weir.

"Excuse me, but I could use a refill, please."

Thompson mixed another drink for her and one for himself. "You all right, Tony?" he asked needlessly, for Weir had hardly touched his glass.

"Fine, thank you," said Weir, running his tongue over his lips.

"Go ahead, Tony. Sorry," said Claire.

"Well, I represented the Old Man for nearly twenty-five years and I probably got to know him as well as anybody did—though that's not saying much. Anyhow, like so many poor boys that come up in the world, he was always haunted by the fear that he'd have to end his days in the poorhouse. Every time he produced another hit I used to ride him a little about it, but he never really lost that feeling. Well, he never married, you know, and there wasn't a soul of his own blood in the world, not even a second cousin. So when it came to making his will, he left everything, except for a few personal bequests, to the Beth-Israel Home for the Aged, up in the Bronx. 'If I don't end up in the poorhouse,' he said, 'I want to do a little something for the less lucky ones. It's the only way I can show my thanks to God.' That was his way of putting it."

"What a wonderful man he must have been!" said Claire with a rush of vicarious filial affection.

"Yes, he was. Well, when he died the trustees of the Home thought they had come into a fortune. Like everybody else—except me and his accountants—they expected the estate to run to millions. But by the time we paid all the debts and got through adding and subtracting, about all that was left was the Farow Theater, and even that had a bank mortgage of a quarter of a million on it."

"But I don't understand it," said Claire. "All those years of success—what became of it all?"

Weir shrugged. "He gave it away, squandered it, spent it foolishly. He liked to live well and to make expensive gifts to ladies; and he never could say no to an old friend who was up against it.

Then he put a fortune into that art collection of his—Egyptian antiques and oil paintings and God knows what—a million dollars, some say. He thought he knew all about those things, but I guess he didn't, and the dealers played him for a sucker. When we came to auctioning it off, it didn't bring ten cents on the dollar. Even at that, most of the stuff went to people who wanted to own something that had belonged to Oscar Farow."

"What a tragedy!" said Claire.

"Well, you know the old saying, that I learned at my mother's knee—'Shoemaker, stick to your last.' I've never known it to fail. A fellow can be as smart as a whip in his own line. But then he'll start fooling around with something else, and before you know it, he's on his uppers. Anyhow, that's the way it worked out, and the old folks' home, instead of inheriting a fortune, found that all they had on their hands was a liability. Do you know what it costs a year just to keep that theater dark? Forty thousand dollars. And that's just for taxes, interest, and insurance, without even a stage-doorman's wages."

"That's a lot of dough," said Thompson.

"Yes, it is. And they're worried. They've tried leasing it and booking it, but they haven't had a hit in there since the Old Man passed away and they're way behind on their interest payments to the bank. The property is assessed for three-quarters of a million, but if they could find somebody who wanted to put up a hotel or an office building, they'd gladly unload for a half-million."

"And let that lovely old theater be torn down!" exclaimed Claire.

"Well, that's what's happened to all the old favorites, one by one. The Casino, the Knickerbocker, the Criterion, Daly's, Wallack's, the Madison Square—I've watched them all go. You can't stop the march of progress. But to get back to the Farow. A buyer would have to spend another quarter of a million to tear it down and excavate for a big building, and the way construction costs are today, they just haven't been able to find anybody with that kind of money. So they've decided that the best thing to do is to turn it over to somebody who may make a go of it and help them to salvage a little something. And that's where we come in."

"How is it that the bank hasn't taken it over?" asked Thompson.

"What would they do with it? They're no more equipped to operate a theater than the Home is. Banks aren't allowed to play gambling games, and we all know that's what show business is. But they have a right to protect their equity by sitting on it and letting you gamble; and that's what their proposition is. The whole point is that this looks to them like a good gamble. They're counting on the personal element, and when you get right down to it, what else can you count on in this business? They know your record in picking out the right plays to back and Tommy's record in producing them successfully. And, of course, though maybe I shouldn't say it, they've got a little confidence in me too. After all, there aren't many angles of this business that I haven't been mixed up with." He chuckled. "I even tried writing a play once. But I soon gave that up. I could get the characters on all right, but, somehow or other, I couldn't get them off," he concluded with a hearty laugh.

Claire giggled obligingly, but Thompson did not even trouble to smile at this venerable cliché.

"How much money would it take?" asked Claire.

"Well, this is the offer, made with the bank's approval. The purchase price would be four hundred thousand. You'd assume the bank's first mortgage of two hundred and fifty thousand, and they might even reduce the interest rate from five to four per cent. That leaves a hundred and fifty thousand, for which the Home would accept a purchase-money mortgage for a hundred and twenty-five, plus twenty-five in cash."

"What's a purchase-money mortgage?" asked Thompson. "Not that it really matters."

"Well, in effect, it's a second mortgage."

"You mean, all it would cost me is twenty-five thousand?" asked Claire.

"You'd have to figure another twenty-five or so for repairs and other contingencies—maybe another fifty. Say seventy-five altogether, at the very outside."

"Well, I'll make that much out of Give Them, won't I?"

"I should certainly think so."

"But what if we run into the red? Won't I get in deeper and deeper?"

"No. We'll provide for that by setting up a corporation, so that you won't be personally liable. They'll agree to that. After all, if it didn't work out and you had to give up the theater, they'd be no worse off than they are now."

"Then you think I should take the risk?"

"Taking everything into consideration, yes. After all, my dear,

I'm only concerned in looking out for your interests. I consider that my duty. The last thing poor Charlie said to me was, 'Tony, promise me that you'll take care of things for Claire.' And it's on that basis that I always advise you."

Claire suspected that this death-bed injunction of her late husband's had been invented by her brother-in-law, and she wondered what percentage of the potential profits he would expect for engineering the deal. But she had great respect for his business judgment. Besides, she was thrilled by the prospect of stepping into the shoes of Oscar Farow. She glanced at Thompson, who was ostentatiously twirling his glass, indicating that all this was a matter that did not concern him. "Shall we do it, Tommy?"

"Well, don't look at me. I wouldn't know a purchase-money mortgage from a fright-wig. But if you want to bring sunshine into the lives of a lot of old folks in the Bronx, it's all right with me. Only let's not put too many of them on our first-night list."

"Freely translated, that means yes," said Claire to Weir. "All right, let's shoot!"

"Good! Then I'll go ahead." He looked at his watch. "I've got to get a train to Long Island."

Thompson rose and reached for his coat. "I've got to run too."

"No, don't go," said Claire. "I want to talk to you about that play."

"Well, all right." It was obviously useless to try to escape.

"I think I'll take a quick shower," said Claire when Weir had gone. "Pour yourself another drink."

Thompson called the box-office of the Stuyvesant Theater and then, lighting a cigarette, sat brooding over his submissiveness. The telephone rang, and he answered. "Oh, just a minute, I'll call her." He pounded on the bathroom door. "It's Hilda. She wants to know what you're up to."

"I'll be right there!"

Thompson went back to his drink. A moment later Claire came into the living-room, wearing nothing but mules and a bathing cap. "I'm sorry there's no staircase," she said.

"Anything for a change," said Thompson. It would, of course, have been much simpler for her to pick up the extension telephone in the bedroom.

"Are you free for dinner?" she asked him.

"Well, I—"

22

"Hello, Hilda," she said. "No, I think I'll have dinner in town and drive home afterwards. Don't wait up for me, but you might leave a snack in the refrigerator."

Pleasantly caressed by the alcohol, Thompson looked at her appraisingly. She was at least forty, but did not even look her admitted thirty-seven. Her skin, of which she took excellent care, was deliciously fair and clear; and the fleshiness against which she waged a losing battle had not yet blurred the strong curves of her well-proportioned body.

She hung up, pulled off her bathing cap, shook her blond hair loose, and came over to sit on his lap. "Why don't you take off that hot necktie?" she said, fumbling at the knot.

"I think I'll take a shower too." He ran a swift forefinger down her spine.

She squirmed and slid off his lap. "You have such wonderful ideas," she said, pulling him to his feet.

"I'd like a cigarette, please," said Claire when they lay relaxed on the wide bed. Thompson took two cigarettes from the bedside table, put them in his mouth, lighted them, and handed her one. "Thanks. Are you really serious about doing that play?"

"Yes. It's the best script I've read in two years."

"Oh, it's beautifully written, no doubt about that. Only—"

"Only what? It's a damned good play."

"Do you really like all that incest and all that?"

"Well, I'll tell you about me and incest: I can take it and I can let it alone. But what's good enough for Sophocles is good enough for me. Anyhow, there's no incest in it. They just talk about it."

"Yes, but that's really what the play's about. It's all so sort of grim and gloomy."

"That's frequently true of tragedies. And that's what this is."

"I just wonder if there's an audience for it."

"There's an audience for anything if it's good enough. What are we doing, dreaming up candy bars or trying to produce scripts we like?"

"Well, I think we have to be practical. A flop, these days, costs you plenty."

"Can I quote you on that?" he said, his anger beginning to rise. "I guess you must be way in the red."

"I don't mean it that way. But this is going to be a big production, with all those sets. Were you thinking of it for the Farow?"

"Well, one of the best things you can do with a theater is put a play in it. Unless you're planning to turn it into a penny arcade."

"It's just that I'd sort of like to open it with a splash."

"Well, if you can think up something better than a well-written play by a new author—!"

"Who is the author? Do you know him?"

"Never heard of him before. Irina Lanski brought the script in."

"Has he written anything else?"

"All I know about him is that he's young and he lives somewhere in Connecticut. But he's got something. I know that."

"Don't you think the script needs a lot of work?"

"Every script needs a lot of work. Plenty of work was done on Give Them, even after we opened in Philadelphia."

"Yes, but with an experienced author like Freddie—"

"Even Freddie must have written a first play at some time—probably in collaboration with Richard Harding Davis. But look," he said, "don't let me talk you into this. I like the play and I'm going to do it, but if you'd rather not—"

"Of course I do! God, but you're touchy. All I'm doing is expressing an opinion." She wanted to add, "After all, I'm the one who supplies the money," but she checked herself in time. She knew how sensitive he was about his financial dependence on her and that he was capable of sacrificing his business interests to his pride. Besides, though she never would have admitted it, even to herself, she was none too sure of her own judgment of plays, and she was largely guided by his.

"Who were you thinking of for that girl's part?" she asked in token of surrender.

"I thought maybe Emily Crandall," said Thompson, somewhat appeased.

"Oh, she'd be wonderful! But you'll never be able to fish her out of that Beverly Hills swimming pool. And she'd want a million dollars a week."

"Don't worry, I'll cast it."

"I'm not worrying," she said, tweaking his nose. "Why don't you get Carlo on the phone and order us some dinner?"

He reached for the telephone and called the restaurant. "What do you want?"

"Not much; it's too hot. And there's that little matter of the bathroom scales. What are you going to have?"

24

"Hello, Carlo," said Thompson to the headwaiter. "This is Leroy Thompson. Mrs. Weir and I would like some dinner sent up. Well, I'd like some vichyssoise, a mixed green salad, and some strawberries. No, no cream, but you might pour a little kirsch over them."

"That sounds wonderful," said Claire. "Only I don't know about the vichyssoise. Maybe a clear soup."

"Well, make up your mind. Carlo's time is worth money."

"Oh, well, one little cup of vichyssoise isn't going to hurt me. I'll have the same."

"Make it two of everything," said Thompson. "Anything else?" he asked Claire.

"I guess not. Wait, don't hang up yet. I think maybe, if I'm going to drive to the country, I'd better have a little sandwich too. Turkey on whole wheat, please."

"And a turkey sandwich on whole wheat. Mayonnaise?" he relayed to Claire.

"No mayonnaise."

"No mayonnaise," said Thompson.

"Well, just a drop maybe," she said.

"Yes, mayonnaise," said Thompson.

"And instead of the strawberries I think I'll have a coffee parfait. It's nice and refreshing in this weather."

"Make it one strawberries and one coffee parfait," he said. "Yes, I think that's all—for the moment anyhow." He hung up. "He says they've got some lovely mashed potatoes and baked macaroni. And how's about a yummy rice pudding?"

Claire laughed ruefully. "Tomorrow I'm swearing off, cross my heart. Say, do you think the heat will hurt us at the Stuyvesant tonight?"

"I just called Joe. He says they're practically out now."

"Really!" exclaimed Claire elatedly. "Oh, darling, isn't it wonderful to have a hit?" She threw her arms around him. "Why don't you kiss me?"

She awoke with a start, sat up abruptly, and looked at her bedside clock. Thompson was lying on his back, breathing heavily. "Hey, wake up," she said, nudging him in the ribs. "That waiter will be here any minute."

He yawned, stretched, and got slowly off the bed. "There are too goddam many waiters in the world."

"Oh, I feel divine," said Claire, stretching her arms and legs.

The buzzer sounded just as Thompson finished dressing.

"Nice timing," said Claire. "I won't be five minutes. Oh, and tell them to send the car around in an hour. With the top down," she shouted after him.

While the waiter set the table Thompson called the doorman and gave him the instructions about Claire's car. Then he occupied himself with a highball until she joined him, looking very fresh and gay in a bright print. They dined pleasantly. Thompson, completely relaxed, radiated charm and affability, and Claire, basking happily in this gracious effluence, industriously cleared her plate. She got him onto the subject of Oscar Farow, and he obligingly poured out a stream of anecdotes about the Old Man, to which she listened attentively. After all, if she was going to occupy a haunted house it was fitting that she should be properly briefed on its ghostly tenant. It was a most successful little dinner, and when her car was announced she said, "Why don't you drive out to the country with me? It'll be hot as hell sleeping in town tonight."

"Not in my place."

"Oh, you and your old air-conditioning! You'd get a good night's sleep, and Felix could drive you in in the morning."

But Thompson was firm, knowing that if he accepted, his sense of well-being would soon wear off and he would begin to find her irritating.

She drove him to the Stuyvesant Theater but, much to his relief, did not get out. The box-office treasurer was just about to pull down his shutter when Thompson entered the lobby.

"Hello, Joe," said Thompson. "How are we?"

"Clean. And eight standees."

"In this weather? Christ, what dopes!"

"I guess you must have something they want to buy," said the treasurer.

"Advance sale go off today?"

"A little, but not enough to hurt. We're practically clean for this week. Just side stuff and singles, but they'll go easy. I figure we may drop a little around the Fourth, but we'll bounce right back in August. All you got to think about with this one is your New Year's Eve price scale."

"And keeping Handsome Hugh on the wagon."

The treasurer whistled. "You got a point there!"

26

The audience was roaring with laughter as Thompson quietly opened the entrance door and tiptoed into the theater. The ticket-taker held out his hand, then dropped it and greeted Thompson in a whisper. The head usher, seeing the door open, switched on her flashlight and welcomed him smilingly. He patted her cheek and moved over to the head of the side aisle, quickly counting the standees, who slouched uncomfortably behind the last row of seats—there were indeed eight. Then he slithered halfway down the side aisle and leaned against the wall, where he could look either at the stage or into the faces of the spectators. Hugh Mollison, the play's star, was on; in spite of the attention and the laughter of the audience, Thompson's practiced eye told him at once that the heat was having its effect—on both sides of the proscenium. Mollison and his fellow-actors, sweltering beneath the cruel lights, were merely giving "technical" performances, going through their accustomed routines mechanically, carefully conserving their energy. The response of the audience was largely mechanical too. The play had been running for more than six months; those who came now had their opinions already formed and began laughing almost as soon as the curtain went up. The theater, equipped with an air-cooling system, was perceptibly cooler than the streets, but in another hour the heat that rose from the bodies of twelve hundred closely packed human animals would make the place unbearable. The laughter would become more and more forced; handkerchiefs would flutter, programs rhythmically beat the thick air. By the end of the play actors and audience would be in a state of exhaustion.

Thompson looked on for ten minutes or so, noting little lapses in the performances, exaggerated gestures, mistakes in timing, false readings, wrong emphases—small things, imperceptible to anyone but a sensitive and highly trained specialist in the art of acting. When the heat abated he would watch the show through, make detailed notes on the performances, and then call a corrective rehearsal. But in this weather, all one could do was let the actors strictly alone and pray they did not collapse.

He glided softly down the aisle to the iron pass-door. Some heads turned as he clanked the door open and went quickly through. The gray-haired, shirt-sleeved stage manager, who stood just outside the proscenium, looked up from his prompt book. "Hello, boss," he said. "Any standees?"

"There *were* eight," said Thompson. "But I guess some of them have melted away by now."

The stage manager grinned and sweepingly wiped his brow. Thompson stood beside him for a moment, looking at the actors on the lighted scene and smiling involuntarily as each new wave of laughter rolled across the footlights. Then he moved quietly upstage, exchanging a word or two with the operator of the portable switchboard and with the actors who stood around or sat whispering together on a wooden bench, waiting for their entrance cues. He was king here and all his subjects adored him. He walked around behind the backdrop, which was painted to create the illusion of a garden seen through the French windows of the country-house stage setting. At the other side of the set Hugh Mollison's dresser stood waiting with a Turkish towel, a comb, and a large powderpuff. Thompson nodded and moved downstage. A stout middle-aged woman in lavender slacks and a flowered blouse leaned against a stage brace, fanning herself with a garden hat.

"Hello, Fatso," said Thompson, coming up behind her and patting her rump.

"Ow, Sir 'Enry," she said, in exaggerated Cockney, "and me a myden lydy."

Then she straightened up and clapped the hat on her head as Hugh Mollison strode across the scene, flung open a door, and made his exit, to the accompaniment of laughter and applause. He waved a greeting to Thompson and hurried over toward his dresser. The stout woman waited until the applause subsided, then, speaking directly onto the stage so that she could be distinctly heard, but presumably addressing Mollison, she said in a clipped voice, "Oliver, you *did* forget to water the geraniums!" A roar of laughter greeted her as she flounced upon the stage. Thompson smiled in apppreciation and strolled over to Mollison. The star was drying his sweating hands, while the dresser dabbed his face with the powderpuff.

"Jee-sus!" he said. "It's murder out there tonight. And, boy, are they tough!"

"Well, how would *you* like to be in a theater on a night like this?" said Thompson.

"Why, you small-time shill—!" said the actor. Then, hearing his cue, he handed the towel to the dresser, took a large bunch of roses from a property man, and strode on stage again. After listening to a few more lines of dialogue Thompson left the theater by the stage

28

door. On the way out, he handed a cigar to the doorman, who sniffed it appreciatively.

Since his divorce, four years before, Thompson had lived in a Fifth Avenue hotel. The large, bright, air-conditioned suite on the sixteenth floor was very expensive, but he was willing to pay for comfort, convenience, and freedom from housekeeping problems. He tipped liberally, and the whole staff of clerks, bellboys, valets, waiters, elevator operators, and telephonists was at his command. He could get room service at any hour of the night, his telephone messages received careful attention, and he was protected from unwelcome visitors. And if a late guest lingered until morning, the management ignored the irregularity.

When he reached his apartment it was not yet ten, and he made preparations for a long, pleasant, solitary evening. From his large collection of albums he selected his evening's program: the Eroica, Sacre du Printemps, Pictures at an Exhibition, Schumann's Carnival, and some Chopin waltzes. He loaded the record-player, got into his pajamas, and settled down in an armchair with a box of cigars and a bottle of brandy beside him.

Enveloped in a haze compounded of tobacco smoke, alcohol fumes, and the rolling reverberations of Beethoven's strong chords, he ruminated with satisfaction upon his estate in life. He had reason to be pleased with himself. Not only was he the producer and director of the season's most solid hit—standees on a torrid June night—but he was generally recognized as one of the three or four most important figures in his field. The critics respected him, the dramatists eagerly sought his directorial services, the actors idolized him and considered it a privilege to appear in his productions—and, as though that were not enough, money was pouring in too, faster than he could spend it. At thirty-eight he was at the top of his profession, the major part of his career still ahead of him. (Oscar Farow had been producing hits at seventy!) Though he cursed the handicap that had made it impossible for him to be a great actor, he no longer brooded over his frustration. In fact, the brilliance of his success had almost reconciled him to his lesser destiny. And the memory of the tragedy that had nearly destroyed him, four years before, no longer racked him, except in moments of depression or during the long hours of occasional sleepless nights. He had overcome everything, fought through everything, achieved a position of eminence entirely—well, almost entirely—through his own talents and determination.

Now, another step forward: his own theater, a theater identified with the most spectacular American showman of the century. Of course, it would not actually be his. Claire's money was buying it, and she would be the nominal owner—he wondered what share of it she was prepared to give him—but she was buying it only because of her association with him and her confidence in his ability to put on plays that would make money, not only for the producer, but for the theater that housed them. Without him as a partner and a source of supply, she would be as dependent as the bank or the old people's home upon the gambling game of picking a winner. As long as he was free to choose the plays and produce them as he liked—and that afternoon he had demonstrated to himself that he could control Claire's occasional attempts at rebellion—he was quite willing to let her and Anthony Weir occupy themselves with the tedious details of theater operation. The busier she was with payrolls and box-office statements, the less time she would have to meddle with his productions.

All in all, from a professional point of view, his situation could hardly be happier. It was only his personal relationship to Claire that did not altogether satisfy him. Not that he disliked her or had grown tired of her charms. He still found her physically attractive—at times, very strongly so—and though he had little respect for her intelligence or her taste, she supplied him with a pleasant companionship when he felt the need of it. She was vivacious, warm, and a good listener. If there were no bond other than mutual attraction, they could go on agreeably as lovers until the attraction began to wane and they drifted quietly apart, without melodrama or heartache, perhaps still good friends.

As it was, his personal life was bound up almost inextricably with his business life. It was impossible to keep them on different planes. Often—as on that very afternoon, for example—when he had no particular desire to see her, business matters brought them together; and on such occasions she never allowed him to forget that he was her lover as well as her partner. If he was unresponsive he provoked a resentment in her that colored their discussion of practical affairs; so, for the sake of getting things done, he was often compelled to act a role he did not feel. Slight though this emotional bondage was, it chafed him. His quick pride recoiled from the suggestion that his position was that of a kept man. He knew that any such notion was nonsensical. Claire benefited as much from their partnership as he did, perhaps more. He reminded himself, pleased with what he regarded as his honesty, that he had never pretended to be in love with her; on that score she certainly had no excuse for illusions. But women were not governed by logic, and he was irritated by the suspicion that she felt him indebted to her for her emotional as well as her financial expenditures. Sometimes he had the uneasy feeling that she was in love with him; once or twice, all his defenses had been aroused by what had sounded like an oblique suggestion of marriage. He had pretended not to notice the hints, but if it ever became a real issue, he was quite prepared to face it, as brutally as might be necessary. He wanted less of Claire rather than more. Besides, the memory of Louise Henry made the very thought of marriage repugnant to him. Fearful of surrendering himself to that memory, he picked up the new play that he was planning to do: reading aloud certain scenes to get the sound of them, marking passages he thought needed cutting or rewriting, visualizing the settings and the arrangement of the props, working out little pieces of stage business, pondering the suitability of this or that actor. It was past three when he finished. He heated some milk on his electric stove, took two sleeping tablets and fell asleep just as the sky was beginning to pale.

II.

When Eric Kenwood came home from work the radio in the dining-room was going full blast.

"Hello, Pop," he said, shouting to make himself heard. "Isn't the game over yet?"

His father moved his head jerkily and, with an awkward gesture, motioned Eric to silence.

"Runners on second and third," said the radio announcer, his voice rising stridently over the shouts of the crowd in the ball park. "A full count on Blumberg. O'Donnoll steps on the rubber, checks the runners, goes into his wind-up and delivers the three-two pitch. Blumberg swings—and he misses! And that's all for the Red Sox in the last half of the eleventh!"

"The Jew bastard!" said Luke Kenwood, spitting disgustedly into the big brass cuspidor beside his wheel chair.

Eric went out to the summer kitchen at the back of the house, where his mother was preparing supper. She looked up and smiled as she heard him enter. "Hello, son."

"Hello, Ma," he said, kissing her.

"Somebody from New York was trying to get you on the phone."

"From New York? Did they say who it was?"

"No, I told them you'd be home about now, and they said for you to call some operator when you came in." She fished a scrap of paper out of her apron pocket. "Operator forty-two."

"I wonder who it could be." He took the memorandum and went back to the dining-room. "Pop," he said, leaning over the back of Kenwood's chair, "can you turn that off for a minute? I want to make a phone call." The telephone was on a shaky old writing desk between the front windows.

"It can wait till the game's over," said his father. He bawled into the radio, "Come on, you mugg, get it in over there!"

Eric checked a protest. Better to let the call wait than to get involved in a long, senseless argument. Swallowing his annoyance, he went upstairs, stripped to the waist, hung his damp shirt over the back of a chair to dry, and soused his face, neck, and chest with cold water. Even with the faucet on he could hear the blare of the radio. There was nothing wrong with his father's hearing, and he sat within reach of the controls, but he always insisted upon turning up the radio to its full volume. Eric put on a T-shirt, lit a cigarette, and went down to the summer kitchen again.

"Did you get them?" asked his mother.

"No. I can't use the phone with that radio going."

"Well, I guess it'll soon be over. I don't know why it's taking so long today."

"It's an extra-inning game."

"Oh, is *that* it?" she said, without the faintest notion of what he meant. He began setting the trestle table. In warm weather they almost always ate in the summer kitchen. The radio was switched off, and the silence was like a soothing caress. Amelia Kenwood breathed an involuntary sigh of relief. "You better go make your call now. I'll finish laying the table."

It took Eric a long time to get the New York operator. The call had to be routed through Hartford, and there was a great hubbub of buzzing and clicking, punctuated by feminine voices murmuring apologies and exhorting patience.

"Who's calling you from New York?" asked his father.

"I haven't any idea."

"Some dame, I guess."

"I don't know any dames in New York." Or practically anywhere else, except right here in Coltertown, he reflected. Now he had New York and once more gave his name and number. Another long silence, and then the operator intoned, "I'm sorry, Mr. Kenwood, but the party has just gone out and is expected back in an hour. Shall I try it then?"

"Yes, please." The nagging delay and the inability to complete the call made him tense and anxious. Before he had merely been curious about it; now it seemed a matter of great importance. He was angry at his father and was tempted to say, "If you'd let me make the call earlier I probably would have caught whoever it was before they went out." But to protect his mother he avoided a quarrel for which Kenwood would have made her pay in the end.

He went out to the summer kitchen, sliced the bread, filled the glasses with cider, and then, while his mother filled the plates, returned to the dining-room to wheel his father to the table. Kenwood, perversely, insisted upon walking. Eric helped him out of the wheel chair, handed him his two canes, and kept close behind him as he made his way slowly and erratically to the summer kitchen. Two or three times he would have fallen had not Eric been there to steady him. Mumbling angrily, Kenwood shook him off and continued on his painful course. Amelia watched him with anxious eyes but said nothing, taking the canes as Eric helped him into his chair.

Usually Eric tried to enliven the supper hour with news of the factory or bits of gossip about his fellow-workers, most of whom were known to his parents. But tonight he was silent, preoccupied by the inexplicable telephone call and worried about the problems his father's deterioration presented.

Kenwood, exasperated by the failure of the Red Sox to win the

33

game, and even more by his dependence upon Eric, was silent too. He had made up his mind to walk in order to show Eric that he did not need his help, and had succeeded only in showing that he did. Worst of all, he chafed under the knowledge that Eric was, more and more, treating him like an invalid who had to be humored. He told himself that he was being patronized, condescended to. Well, nobody was going to baby him, particularly not his own son.

Amelia did her best to keep the conversation going. She rambled on about the high price of meat, Cousin Elizabeth's rose fever, a new muffin recipe she intended to try as soon as the blueberries were ripe. She really wanted to tell Eric about Dorothy's visit to the doctor and the confirmation of her suspicion that she was pregnant; but her husband had forbidden her to mention their daughter's name in his presence. She hoped that when the grandchild was born Kenwood would relent; but she was far from confident that he would. Meanwhile she would be careful to say nothing about it.

In the middle of supper the telephone rang and Eric ran to answer. It was only Sylvia Jethrow. She had a headache and thought she had better not go to the movies after all. He was relieved, for if he went out he might miss the call from New York. He advised Sylvia to take an aspirin, go straight to bed, and sleep off her headache. But she did not want to go to bed. It was just that she did not feel up to going to the movies. And since they had a date, she kept urging him to come around to keep her company. He was not clever at thinking up excuses, so in desperation he told her about the New York call. Her curiosity aroused, she brightened immediately and plied him with questions, none of which he could answer. It was fifteen minutes before he could get her to hang up, and then only by assuring her that he loved her and that if the New York message was anything exciting he would call her back at once.

When he went back to finish his supper his father wanted to know who had called. Eric, resisting the impulse to tell him that it was none of his business, gave an abbreviated account of his conversation. Kenwood made some sarcastic remarks about women; but Amelia said that the poor girl must be lonesome and she thought that Eric should go around. If the call came through it could be transferred to Sylvia's house.

"I don't want to go to Sylvia's," said Eric testily.

"All right, son. You do whatever you want to do."

Eric got the wheel chair and helped Kenwood into it. His father,

34

who still felt the effects of that long walk, did not protest, even when Eric began to wheel him. In spite of his spirit of defiance he was succumbing more and more to his helplessness. Eric pushed him out to the front porch, where he liked to sit evenings, watching the cars whirl by, critically comparing the models and trying to identify the occupants. Sometimes an acquaintance would wave as he sped past, or slow down to exchange a few words with him. Sitting and watching were a miserable substitute for the active life he had always led, and there were not enough sports events and quiz programs on the air to keep him occupied. His failing vision made reading increasingly difficult, and the uncoordinated movements of his hands precluded even the simplest manual skills. The number of visitors was decreasing too. Like a clergyman who berates the faithful for the backsliders, he vented his bitterness against the absentees upon those who still came, so that they in turn were inclined to stay away.

Luke Kenwood had grown up on a small farm in the Adirondacks, near the Canadian border. His hard-working people were harsh and narrow, and led a cheerless, meager existence. At fifteen, when he finally finished grade school, he got a job as kitchen helper in one of the large Lake Placid hotels, and stayed on for several years, devoting his spare time to developing his talent for baseball. Before long he was paid to pitch Sunday games for a semi-professional team. For several seasons he worked his way up through the minor leagues. Just before the entry of the United States into the First World War the Boston Red Sox bought his contract, and his ambition to become a major-league player was achieved. But he had few opportunities to play, and at the end of the season he was drafted and inducted into military service.

By the time he was sent overseas he was already a corporal, and when his unit reached the front line he was a top sergeant. He saw plenty of action but, except for a light wound from a shell splinter in the bloody battle of Belleau Wood, came through the war unharmed. Upon demobilization, his commanding officer, Captain Eliot Ainsworth, whose respect Kenwood had won by his coolness under fire and his authority over his men, offered him a job in his factory at Coltertown, Connecticut. Kenwood gladly accepted, realizing that as a ballplayer about the best he could hope for was five or six years. A good, steady, lifetime job was much more appealing.

35

Coltertown was a pleasant little community in the Connecticut River valley, about fifteen miles from Hartford, and Kenwood soon found himself at home there. Eliot Ainsworth, who took a paternalistic interest in all his employees, suggested that Kenwood apply to the Norris family for board and lodging. The household consisted of Amelia Norris, her invalid mother, and Elizabeth Keene, a distant relative, known to everyone as Cousin Elizabeth. Amelia was a teacher in the local grade school. Her father, who had also been a teacher, had left almost nothing except the house, and Amelia's small salary was hardly enough to keep things going. She had asked Cousin Elizabeth to move in and help with the housework in return for her keep, and the middle-aged, rootless woman had jumped at the offer. A boarder meant more work, but Amelia liked to keep busy, and the additional income was very welcome.

Luke Kenwood was an almost ideal boarder. Except for the unpleasant habit of chewing tobacco that survived from his baseball days, there was little to complain about. He was neat and orderly, made few demands, and minded his own business. He confined his drinking to Sundays and holidays, when he would drive off, sometimes as far as Hartford, or even beyond, in search of alcohol and female society.

A year after Kenwood moved in, Amelia's mother died. Since there seemed to be no good reason for keeping the big rambling house, she put it up for sale. Kenwood was very much disturbed. He had been in Coltertown long enough to know that he could not hope to find comparable living quarters, and after thinking it over for a while he asked Amelia to marry him. She was several years his senior and no beauty. However, it was not romance he was looking for. Having lived under the same roof with Amelia for so long, Kenwood knew that she had rare qualifications for wifehood. She was even-tempered, considerate and self-reliant, and a superb housekeeper. He had a good job with an assured future and had decided to stay in Coltertown. So why not settle down in a comfortable house with a comfortable homemaker?

Amelia's first impulse was to say no, but the more she thought about it, the more acceptable the proposal seemed. She was certainly not in love with Kenwood, but then she was not looking for romance either. She had just about dismissed marriage from her thoughts and saw herself dragging out her days as an old maid schoolteacher, living with strangers, and perhaps ending up in the poorhouse. To that bleak prospect marriage to Kenwood offered an attractive alternative. It promised companionship, security, the maintenance of her own household in her own old home, and, best of all, the gratification of her longing for children. As for Kenwood, he was vigorous, manly, steady, industrious, sober. What more could she hope for? So she ended by saying yes.

Since Kenwood's wages as shop foreman were quite adequate for their needs she gave up her teaching, which she had never enjoyed and for which she had no vocation.

While they were driving back from a week's honeymoon in Boston, Kenwood told Amelia that Cousin Elizabeth would have to find another place to live, pointing out that if Amelia had sold the house Cousin Elizabeth would have had to go anyhow. Though there was no disputing the logic of this, Amelia could not bear the thought of turning the pathetic creature out. But Kenwood was firm. When the time came to tell Cousin Elizabeth, it gave Amelia an added pang to find that she was quite prepared for the news. All her life she had been shunted about, never finding an anchorage anywhere. She had nothing but the small pension to which her father's service in the Civil War entitled her. Fortunately she was able, with Amelia's help, to get a minor job on the housekeeping staff of the Coltertown Hospital, where she could live.

By this act of authority Kenwood established a mastery he never relinquished. Less than a year after her marriage Amelia gave birth to Eric; seventeen months later Dorothy was born. Kenwood accepted the responsibilities of parenthood as a matter of course, but made it clear, from the very beginning, that he expected unquestioning obedience. The children soon learned submission, for any show of rebellion met with crushing severity. In his own way he loved them and for the most part was not unkind to them: he was simply incapable of warmth or tenderness. Happily for them, their mother lavished love and understanding upon them, and they turned to her for the satisfaction of their emotional needs. As for Amelia, her children and her household more than made up for what was lacking in her marriage. Nor was Kenwood's iron rule either unfamiliar or wholly distasteful to her. She had grown up in the patriarchal tradition; her stern father conditioned her in childhood to masculine authority. Modern ideas of female independence seemed to her unfeminine, if not downright immoral. She had her own way in everything that did not affect Kenwood's comfort or violate his narrow and arbitrary standards of conduct; and that was quite enough for her.

Several years after their marriage Kenwood resumed his solitary excursions in search of liquor and women. Amelia, who looked upon these lapses as one of the unpleasant aspects of normal masculine behavior, never complained or even alluded to the subject. Though she did not quite admit it to herself, she was not displeased by Kenwood's extramarital love-making. He was not a subtle lover, and she was always repelled by his animality and by the foul odor of stale chewing tobacco. The diminution of his demands gave her only relief.

When Eric was about ten Kenwood went to an American Legion convention in Philadelphia. He had been prospering in the boom years of the late twenties, had put away a few thousand dollars, and was now assistant general foreman of the Ainsworth factory. He had a wonderful time in Philadelphia, but not long after his return his physical condition began to alarm him. Suspecting what was wrong and afraid that if it became known he might jeopardize his position in the rather puritanical community, he avoided consulting any of the Coltertown doctors and went instead to a quack in Hartford, who confirmed his fear that he had contracted syphilis. He put himself in the man's care and after some months was discharged as cured.

It was not until seven or eight years later that his health began to fail. Shooting pains and minor functional disturbances, which he attributed to advancing age, became more frequent and more acute. He had always boasted that he had never had a sick day in his life and bitterly resented the impairment of his robust constitution. At last, when the perfect physical coordination, of which he had always been so proud, began to fail him, and his vision too became affected, Amelia insisted that he consult Dr. Oxman, the most respected of the Coltertown doctors. The doctor, after a long series of tests and a relentless cross-examination, told him bluntly that he was in the first stage of locomotor ataxia, that his condition was incurable, and that he had better face the fact that he would gradually decline into a state of general paralysis.

Kenwood was staggered. Still in his middle forties, he had had every expectation of working for another twenty-five years, perhaps becoming general manager of the factory, and putting by enough to end his days in comfortable retirement. Now it was a

38

question of how soon he would have to give up his job. He had nothing. All his savings had been invested in a building-loan society that had gone under in the 1929 financial disaster. During the depression years he had been glad to hang on to his job at reduced wages. Now that things were picking up again he was just beginning to get back on his feet. Even worse than the economic outlook was the prospect of physical incapacity. He had no aptitudes and no resources that were not bodily. To him, invalidism was both terrifying and shameful.

He could not long conceal the truth from Amelia or from his employers. His symptoms became increasingly evident, his temper worsened, his efficiency declined. He stumbled and fell, dropped things, ran into people. Some days he was not able to go to work at all. His employers put up with him as long as they could, but the inevitable day of dismissal came at last. He got his paycheck, was driven home by a fellow-worker—he no longer could manage a car —and his active life was at an end.

That had been eight years ago, and Dr. Oxman's prognostications were being relentlessly fulfilled. His sight was failing, he could no longer control the movements of his limbs, he was imprisoned in his wheel chair. Next year would be worse, and the year after that worse yet. He sat staring at the passing cars, chewing his unsavory cud and reflecting upon the bitterness of his lot. He cursed his helplessness, cursed the ill luck that had brought it upon him, cursed those whom it had alienated and those who ministered to it. When Amelia, who with Eric's help had put the kitchen in order, came out on the porch and offered to read the Coltertown Evening Standard to him, he told her irritably that if he wanted to know what was in the paper he was quite able to find out for himself— though they both knew it was not true.

Eric took the garbage out to the incinerator and burned it. Then he started for his room, glad to be able to spend the evening with a book. When he was halfway upstairs the telephone rang again. He was fearful that Sylvia had changed her mind about going to the movies; but this time it was the New York operator. Presently a voice with a strong Continental accent said, "Hello, Mr. Kenwood. This is Irina Lanski."

"Who?" said Eric.

"Irina Lanski. You sound as if you had never heard of me. Perhaps I should remind you that I am your agent."

"Oh yes, of course! How do you do, Miss Lanski." He had never met her or even talked to her, and it had not occurred to him that the call might be from her.

"Well, I'm rather exhausted from trying to get you on the phone," she said.

"I called you back as soon as I got home but—"

"Oh, don't apologize. It's as hot as hell here in New York, and my nerves are drenched in sweat. I'm calling you about your play."

"You mean The Clouded Mirror?" asked Eric, still confused by her unexpected call.

"Why? Have I some other play of yours?"

"No, I don't mean that. Only you wrote me that you like it and that you thought you might be able to—"

"Exactly! Well, if we were a little better acquainted, you would know that I am a woman of my word."

"You mean that somebody—?" said Eric, unable to finish the sentence.

"Yes. And not just somebody. I suppose you have heard of Leroy Thompson?"

"Yes, of course!"

"He wants to talk to you about it."

"You mean he might want to produce it?"

"Well, I don't think he just wants to engage in a literary discussion. It's a little hot for that." Her voice had an edge on it. "Can you be at my office tomorrow at two? He wants to see us at three, and I think we'd better have a little talk first, especially since neither of us knows what the other looks like."

"You mean you want me to be in New York tomorrow?"

"Yes. Are you having trouble in hearing me? Or is it just this horrible accent of mine?"

"No, no," said Eric. "But you see I have a job here. I'd have to ask for permission to take a day off. And that wouldn't give me time to get to New York tomorrow."

"Well, how about Thursday then?"

"Could it wait until Saturday? I only work a half-day, and it would be a little easier."

"Not for me, unfortunately. I'm going away for the weekend, and I'm sure Mr. Thompson will be too. Anyhow, if you keep him waiting his enthusiasm may begin to cool. Theatrical managers are very unstable creatures."

40

"All right then. I'll do my best to get there Thursday."

"You don't sound very interested in getting your play produced, Mr. Kenwood," she said.

"Why, of course I am! Only—do you think he really means to produce it?"

"Well, I can't guarantee that until the contract is signed—and perhaps not even then. I think he has certain reservations about the play; he may suggest certain changes, but if I did not feel he were definitely interested, I assure you that I would not be running up my telephone bill like this."

"Oh, I'm sorry! I didn't mean to—" exclaimed Eric, feeling guilty about the telephone bill.

"It's perfectly all right. I was just indulging in a figure of speech. You know my address, don't you?"

"Yes, I have all your letters."

"Are you an autograph collector too?"

"What's that?"

"Nothing at all. I'll expect you then on Thursday at two."

"Yes, I'll be there, unless—"

"Unless what?" she asked, exasperated. "Isn't it settled?"

"Yes, yes! I'll definitely be there," said Eric hastily.

"Good! Until Thursday then!" She hung up quickly before he could even say good night.

Eric, his mind in a state of confusion, walked out to the front porch.

"Who was it, son?" asked his mother.

"Irina Lanski."

"Who is that?"

"She's that dramatic agent in New York, that I sent my play to."

"Sounds like a kike," said Kenwood, spitting over the rail of the porch.

Eric ignored the interruption. "She says that Leroy Thompson is interested in the play."

"Is he a man who puts plays on?" asked Amelia.

"Yes, he's a well-known New York manager. I saw one of his productions in Hartford once. I have to go to New York Thursday to see him."

"Is the factory shut Thursday?" asked Kenwood.

"No, I'll have to take the day off. Mr. Thompson wanted to see me tomorrow, but I put it off until Thursday."

"Did you figure out what it's going to set you back, between the fare to New York and maybe being docked a day's pay?"

"I'll save it on something else."

"Yes, of course you will," said Amelia. "Anyhow, if he puts your play on he'll pay you something for it, won't he?"

"Oh, sure! If a play is a success the author makes a lot of money out of it. But Miss Lanski isn't certain that he's going to do it."

"Then what are you going to see him about?" asked his father.

"To talk it over with him. It's the first time I've ever had a chance even to meet a New York producer."

"Throwing away a lot of good time and money just to let some New York squirt give you the razzle-dazzle! I used to know one of them guys, ran a burleycue house in Beantown. They finally sent him up for a ten-year stretch in Atlanta for peddling dope."

"Leroy Thompson isn't a burlesque manager," said Eric. "He's one of the most important people in the American theater."

"Aw, nuts! They're all alike, them theayter people—a lot of tramps and hopheads. Why don't you forget about all that theayter crap and spend your nights studying some good trade? There's always a future for a good mechanic."

"Maybe there is, but I'm not interested in a trade."

"Oh, that's not good enough for you, I guess!"

"That has nothing—!"

"Well, I think it's wonderful to be a writer," Amelia interposed, anxious to avert a quarrel. "Father always used to say that he wished he had gone in for something like that instead of just teaching school to the end of his days."

"You'd have all ended up on the poor farm if he had," said Kenwood.

Amelia's interruption had served its purpose. Eric saw a chance to get away. "Well, I've got some reading I want to do. Good night, Ma. Good night, Pop."

"Good night, son," said Amelia, kissing him. "We'll pray for the best."

As he entered the house he heard his father resume the attack. The argument would go on for hours, and he felt guilty about deserting his mother; but if he stayed he would lose his self-control, making matters worse. Besides, he was still so bewildered by Irina Lanski's call that he wanted to be alone and examine its implications.

He stripped to his shorts, took off his glasses, and stretched out on the bed, his eyes closed, his hands clasped under his head.

Anger at his father and at his own ineptitude blurred his brain and obstructed his thoughts. He had fumbled and stuttered, on the telephone, like a schoolboy. The dramatic unexpectedness of Irina Lanski's call and her manner of expressing herself had made it hard for him to grasp immediately the full import of her news. He had asked a lot of inane questions, had failed to get the point of her joke about autograph collecting, and in general had behaved like an idiot. He writhed unhappily as he heard the echoes of her cool sarcasm.

Of course she could not understand his hesitation! As a play agent, it must have seemed strange to her that a young author should be reluctant to leave his job for a day in order to see a manager who was interested in his play. She could not know that Eric had no reason to think seriously of himself as an author and that his job was a very practical reality. With the Christmas orders piling up at the factory, he was afraid permission to take a day off might be refused. He would go anyhow, and would not lose his job if he did; but it would create a bad impression and damage his reputation for dependability. He could pretend to be ill, but he dismissed that subterfuge almost immediately—not because he was afraid of being found out, but because he did not like to do anything that savored of dishonesty. He had inherited his father's conscientiousness and his mother's sense of moral obligation. Much as he disliked his job, he felt bound, while he held it, to do what was expected of him. Of course, he could not possibly have made all that clear in a telephone conversation with a woman whom he had never met and who lived in the remote world of the theater. With the memory of that slow, cultivated voice still jabbing at his self-esteem, it seemed more important to him to convince Irina Lanski that he was not a callow fool than to discuss his play with Thompson. He had exchanged letters with her and had heard her voice, while Thompson was only a name and a speck of light in the theatrical firmament, as glittering and as remote as Sirius. He could not believe that the manager had any intention of producing his play.

It was almost by accident that he had established contact with Irina Lanski. Several years before, when he was in an Army hospital, he had begun writing his first play. When he got his discharge it was only half-finished. Nearly a year elapsed before he resumed work and completed it. He had only an old broken-down typewriter and was a poor typist besides, so Sylvia had volunteered to make a neat transcript for him. Eric had mailed it, in turn, to four or five New York managers (including Leroy Thompson) with whose names he happened to be familiar. They all sent it back either without comment or with a brief letter of rejection. He had heard somewhere that managers seldom read plays submitted by unknown authors, and he hit upon what seemed to him a very shrewd device for putting them to the test. He lightly gummed together the twenty-fifth and twenty-sixth pages of the typescript, not aware that this is a common practice among beginning writers. Almost every time the play came back the pages were still stuck together. He did not know, either, that most playreaders, unless their interest is quickly aroused, merely read the first ten or fifteen pages, skipping through the rest, scanning a scene here or there, and reading the final pages. Convinced that no one had even looked at the play, he decided that further submissions would be useless. He consulted his friend James Duncan, of the staff of the Coltertown Evening Standard, who assured him that it was impossible for a new author to get any attention unless he submitted his work through an agent. He referred Eric to a theatrical periodical, in which dramatists' agents customarily advertised. Acting upon the suggestion, Eric began to send his play around to the agents. Several of them offered to read and criticize it, upon payment of a fee, which, of course, he could not afford. (He could not afford the fifteen dollars he had already spent on postage.) The others merely wrote they were not interested. As a last hope, he sent the typescript—its pages now crumpled and spotted with tobacco and coffee stains—to Irina Lanski, the one remaining name on his list. She too sent it back, but to his amazement she enclosed a long, critical letter. She told him that she did not feel it advisable to submit the play for production, not only because of its subject matter—it dealt with the tragic life of Anne Hutchinson—but because of its static presentation and lack of dramatic focus. Nevertheless, she felt that he had a distinct talent and urged him to go on writing, suggesting that he choose a theme nearer to his own experience.

It was the first word of encouragement he had ever received. Greatly elated, he set to work at once on a play about life in an Army training camp, finishing it in a month and sending it off to

44

Irina Lanski, full of hope. She sent it back in a few days with a sharp letter rebuking him for careless writing and clumsy craftsmanship, telling him that if he ever expected to get anywhere as a playwright, he would have to think through his ideas, construct his plays solidly, and write with conviction.

Thoroughly depressed, Eric resolved to write no more. But as the shock of disappointment wore off he began to see the justice of the agent's criticism and the soundness of her advice. He had really done a sloppy job: a hodgepodge of unrelated incidents and hastily sketched characters, without form or direction. He wrote her a long, overfervid letter, full of self-castigation and abject apology. Her reply was detached and satiric: if bad writing were a crime, the jails would be overflowing, she said, and advised him to put his passion into his plays. Though the letter filled him with a sense of his own immaturity—he blushed with shame when he read it—it also had the effect of goading him on, and he soon began to write again, brooding over his material until he was able to shape it with a firm hand.

Again the typescript had gone off to Irina Lanski. This time the verdict was favorable. She liked the play very much, and though she thought it needed more work she was prepared to submit it in its present form. She warned him, however, against over-optimism. The tragic nature of the play would make it unacceptable to most managers, since they would see little hope of its financial success. In any case, it would take time to interest anyone in it. He wrote her a letter of thanks—taking great pains not to be too effusive—in which he assured her that he was not counting on anything. He had received her letter only ten days before and had not expected to hear from her again for months. In order to cushion himself against disappointment, he had persuaded himself that when he did hear from her the news would be bad. That was why he had been so wholly unprepared for what she had to tell him.

For hours he lay on the bed, wondering what Irina Lanski and Leroy Thompson looked like, and engaging them in long, imaginary conversations, unperturbed by their sophistication, impressing them with his self-possession and quick, incisive responses, and, finally, bidding them farewell with smiling good grace, his rejected play under his arm.

45

III.

On Thursday Eric got up at six, made himself a hearty breakfast, and put the kitchen in order. Carrying the lunch package his mother had put up for him, he went out the back door, to avoid waking his parents. Since Kenwood was no longer able to get upstairs, they had moved their bedroom furniture down to the front parlor, which they had seldom used anyhow.

He waited in front of the house for the Hartford bus. It would have been much cheaper to drive to New York, but the twelve-year-old car was in very bad condition; besides, his mother needed it for marketing, since she did most of her buying at a self-service market, where the prices were lower than in the stores that made deliveries. The through bus from Hartford to New York would also have cost less than the train, but it would have made him hours late for his appointment. He thought of calling up Irina Lanski and asking her to put off the meeting until late afternoon, but he was afraid that she might lose patience with him altogether.

He had hardly slept the night before. He was too excited about the trip to New York and too disturbed about the difficulty he had had in getting the day's leave. He had not been able to get in to see Warren Ainsworth until almost closing time. Warren, the son of Eliot Ainsworth, and about Eric's age, was in process of working his way up through the factory toward an eventual succession to the presidency. That was part of the family tradition. The sons began at the very bottom and learned every phase of the business. Warren's career had been interrupted by his Army service, and he was now in charge of personnel—several years behind schedule. He was not well suited to the job and was not popular among the

46

workers. He lacked his father's personal touch and was inclined to run the factory on the principles of military discipline.

At first he met Eric's request with a flat refusal, even rebuking him for making it. The factory was hardly able to keep up with its orders, and Warren considered it most unreasonable of him to ask for a day off at such a time. Eric pleaded the importance of the occasion, but to Warren it did not seem important. It was inconceivable to him that Eric was capable of writing a play that anyone could take seriously. Unconsciously he resented the very fact that Eric had written a play at all. Loyalty to the job was what the Ainsworths expected from their "big family" of employees, and if a man was thinking about the plays he was writing he could not be giving full attention to his work. Eric pointed out that he was up to date in his work and would work overtime to make up for the lost day. Warren was inclined to persist in his refusal, but he guessed that Eric would absent himself anyhow, and then he would either have to ignore the infraction of discipline and lose prestige or discharge Eric. He was not prepared to go that far, so he gave his consent, very grudgingly and with the warning that, thereafter, any such request would be denied, without discussion. Eric thanked him, but he was deeply offended. He rebelled at his subservience to a man for whom he had no respect. However, he and his family were dependent upon his job and, like most wage-earners, he had to put bread-winning before everything else.

He got to Hartford more than an hour before train time and wandered aimlessly around the railroad station, too keyed up to concentrate on the volume of plays he had slipped into his pocket. He wanted to buy a New York paper, but a whole day's pay had gone into his bus and railroad tickets, and even the expenditure of a nickel seemed an extravagance. Seeing himself in the full-length mirror of a weighing-machine, he was suddenly filled with misgivings about his appearance. His "Sunday" suit—the better of the two he owned—was wrinkled and baggy at the knees and his shoes were dusty. He should have shined them and put his trousers under the mattress the night before, but he had had too much on his mind. He had shaved hastily too, and there was a half-inch scratch on his chin. And he needed a haircut. He had intended to get one on the preceding Saturday afternoon, but instead he had gone off with a book to the abandoned apple orchard behind the house. There was undoubtedly a barbershop near the station, but he was afraid of missing the train, and reluctant to spend another dollar or so. He did have time to get his shoes shined, but even that would cost fifteen cents.

He glanced furtively around the waiting-room at the Hartford businessmen in their freshly pressed Palm Beach suits and gay ties and the women in their bright summer dresses and gaudy, barefoot sandals. How shabby and untidy he must seem to them—if they noticed him at all! New York would be worse yet; he could already see the eyes of Irina Lanski and Leroy Thompson meeting in unspoken comment upon this seedy country lout. In a sudden access of panic he decided to turn in his ticket and go back home, but dismissed the notion immediately and even managed to smile at his trepidation. After all, it was his play they were interested in, not his looks. He assured himself that the personal impression he made was a matter of no importance. Nevertheless, he went into the men's room and scrubbed his shoes.

On the way to the train he bought a New York paper after all, feeling that the approach to the city would be a little easier if he knew what was going on there. He had not been in New York since he had stopped over after his discharge from the Army; and then he had had only a day there, long enough to see an excellent performance of Macbeth. It had been an exciting experience: the only play he had ever seen in New York and the only professional production of Shakespeare he had seen anywhere. In fact, he had not attended more than perhaps twenty professional performances in his whole life, and these had been mostly touring companies in New Haven or Hartford. The various Army camps in which he had been trained had occasionally been visited by U.S.O. units, and he had seen—and sometimes participated in—productions by local amateur groups.

Although he knew very little about the theater, he knew a great deal about the drama. Amelia's father—whom Eric had never known —had been a keen drama lover and had left a shelf of plays that included the Greek, the Elizabethan, and the Restoration dramatists as well as Molière, Sheridan, Ibsen, Strindberg, Rostand, Synge, Shaw, and a few of the newer writers. In the course of his omnivorous reading Eric had gone through them all—some of them again and again. When he had read all the plays that the Coltertown Library had to offer too, Miss Bailey, the librarian, had arranged special loans for him from the larger collection in Hartford. As a result

48

of reading hundreds of plays, which he had never seen performed, he had a wide knowledge of how plays were constructed, but knew almost nothing of how they were projected in terms of the stage.

The only seat Eric could find in the crowded train was next to a stout, sprawling woman, who was sound asleep, a large suitcase in front of her. She stirred slightly as he squeezed into the narrow space beside her and tucked his feet under the seat. Hot and uncomfortable, he had a hard time manipulating the pages of the bulky metropolitan newspaper. He read column after column, fascinated and rather bewildered by the complexity of the city's life.

The train was past New Haven before he got to the pages devoted to amusements. The motion-picture page with its huge blaring advertisements, each confidently stating that the film it touted was a creation of historic importance, and each displaying a handsome couple clasped in an embrace that seemed to confuse love with contortionism, did not detain him long. But he read the theatrical news with great attention. Two items interested him particularly. The first was an announcement that Leroy Thompson's production of Give Them All My Love, the play by Frederic Haig, starring Hugh Mollison, would that night reach its two-hundredth performance. Eric read this announcement with mixed satisfaction and envy. The imminence of his meeting with Thompson gave him a vicarious proprietary interest in Haig's play, though he had never heard of it until that moment. At the same time he was depressed by the magnitude of the author's success. He had once read a magazine article on Haig's notable career, illustrated with photographs of the playwright taken at his country place in Bucks County, Pennsylvania. The only play of Haig's that he knew was an early one, which had been performed by a summer theater at a lake resort near Coltertown. It had seemed to Eric an empty and rather silly piece, dealing with people, situations, and emotions wholly alien and distasteful to him; but he recognized craftsmanship and saw how much he had yet to learn. However, if Haig's slick silken fabric was what the theatergoing public was looking for, what hope was there for his rough, homespun stuff?

The other item that interested him read: "Anthony Weir, well-known theatrical attorney, yesterday confirmed a rumor that his sister-in-law, Mrs. Claire Weir, is negotiating for the purchase of the Farow Theater. Since the death of Oscar Farow, the famous old playhouse has been tenanted by an almost unbroken string of flops, and is regarded as a big white elephant by the Beth-Israel Home for the Aged, which inherited it under the terms of the late impresario's will. Mrs. Weir has for the past few years controlled the purse strings of Leroy Thompson's productions, and her attorney did not deny that the Farow might become a Thompson showcase, though so far the producer of Give Them All My Love has announced no plans for the coming season. The amount involved in the deal was not disclosed, but it is understood to be in the neighborhood of $500,000."

Eric had never heard of Claire Weir and understood nothing about the intricacies of theater management or the financing of plays, but he had read a great deal about the spectacular career of Oscar Farow, and the association of Farow's name with Thompson's, together with the casual reference to the inconceivable sum of half a million dollars, made his own prospects seem dimmer than ever. He could not see how he and his play could possibly have a place in the Farow-Thompson scheme of things and reflected gloomily that he had indeed embarked upon a fool's errand.

It was a long time since breakfast, but he was too depressed to eat, and his sweaty, wheezing neighbor took away his appetite. When the train pulled into the 125th Street Station she awoke with a snort and a start. She looked at Eric in surprise. "Is this Grand Central Station?" she asked hoarsely.

"No, I don't think so," said Eric.

He got up and went out to the vestibule to stretch his cramped legs. Lack of sleep, the long, uncomfortable trip, and a general sense of futility made him dull and depressed. The dreary Harlem slum, seen through the grime-encrusted window, lowered his spirits even further. At last the train plunged into the long tunnel and crept through the maze of tracks to a halt. The platform was cluttered with baggage and jammed with passengers and porters. Caught in the densely packed crowd that inched its way up the enclosed ramp, he felt trapped and stifled and had to clench his fists and half shut his eyes to fight back a panicky sensation of claustrophobia.

The crowded waiting-room was as bad as the train, so he decided to eat his lunch outdoors, remembering a little park behind the Public Library. On his last visit to the city he had made a tour of the Library, spending nearly an hour in the drama section, marveling over the richness of its shelves and wishing he had constant access to them. The Library and the theaters were all that attracted him to New York. The city itself frightened and repelled him, and when he emerged into the swarming, noonday street he felt lonely and strange. A traffic officer directed him to the Library—he had forgotten that it was so near the station—and in a few minutes he was in Bryant Park. He put his parcel down on a broad bench, thankful for this little island of refuge, taking comfort in the grass, the flowering shrubs, and the strutting pigeons. For a good fifteen minutes he just sat there and let his taut nerves relax. Then his healthy appetite asserted itself. He smiled when he saw the provision his mother had made for him: thick sandwiches, hard-boiled eggs, pickles, two great slices of cake, an apple, and a banana. Hungry though he was, he could not eat half of it. He would have liked to keep the remainder for his return journey, but obviously he could not go to Irina Lanski's office carrying a package of lunch. He peered around in search of someone to whom he might offer it, but the crimson-lipped stenographers and neat clerks did not look as though they would welcome a handout; so he left it on the bench, regretful of the waste.

He took a long swig at a drinking fountain, stopped at the corner to ask directions, and set out for the Manhattan Theater, where Irina Lanski had her office. The theater, a survival of the nineteenth century, was closed for the summer, but an automatic elevator in the lobby gave access to the offices on the top floor.

The building had half a dozen tenants: a minor producer or two, a firm of press agents, a typing bureau. In the small, dark reception room of Irina Lanski's office a scrawny, untidy spinster sat between a typewriter and a small switchboard, her attention constantly shifting from one to the other.

"Yes?" she said in a grating voice, glancing up at Eric, without interrupting her rapid touch-typing.

"I have an appointment with Miss Lanski," said Eric.

The woman stopped typing to look him over. "Oh, are you Mr. Kenwood?"

"Yes, I am," said Eric, glad to be recognized.

"She's on the phone now. You're a little early."

"Yes, I know. My train—"

"Well, just sit down. She'll be through in a minute." She turned back to her typewriter, precluding further conversation.

Eric was rather surprised by the general mustiness and disorder of the dingy room, cluttered with filing cabinets, stacks of scrapbooks, paper-bound plays, and bundles of typescripts. He had not expected to find Irina Lanski in a setting that reminded him of Dickens. After a few moments the switchboard buzzed, and the angular woman, with a final quick dab at the typewriter, swung around in her swivel chair. "Mr. Kenwood is here." Then, without looking at Eric, she said, "Go right in," and swung back to her typewriter again.

The agent, seated at a large flat-topped desk, said in her rich, throaty voice, "How do you do, Mr. Kenwood. Do sit down, won't you?" As Eric took the plump but well-shaped hand he noticed that the fingers were stained yellow, and he was a little startled to see that she was smoking a small cigar, in an ivory holder. She was a handsome, stout woman of sixty, with clear blue eyes and a full sensuous mouth set in a broad Slavic face. Her white hair, cut quite short, was parted sharply in the middle and hung straight down. In spite of the weather she wore a dress of bottle-green velvet. Antique amethyst earrings dangled from her elongated, pierced earlobes, and around her neck was a heavy chain of dull gold from which hung a large cross set with amethysts. Though she was even more exotic than he had expected, she was less frightening, now that he was actually in her presence, than she had seemed in her letters and on the telephone.

She, in turn, quickly surveyed the gauche, unkempt, bespectacled youth, his cheap baggy suit and bulging pockets, and took an instant liking to him. She noted the sweep of his brow, the strong yet delicate structure of his face, and the honesty in his myopic gray eyes.

"Well, we meet at last," she said.

"Yes," replied Eric, wishing that he could think of something light to say.

"Do you ever indulge in these filthy things?" she asked, picking up a carton of cigars.

"No, thanks."

"Well, I'm glad that your habits are better than mine." She removed the stub from the ivory holder and lighted a fresh cigar.

"I read somewhere that George Sand used to smoke cigars."

"She was a little before my time, ancient though I am. But I used to know Amy Lowell, and I must say that I liked her cigars better than her poems."

Before Eric had a chance to say that he admired Amy Lowell's poetry the telephone rang. While Irina Lanski engaged in a brief, monosyllabic conversation, Eric glanced around the room. Like the outer office, it was cluttered and frowsy. The cracked, discolored walls were covered with framed photographs of authors, actors, and musicians, most of them autographed. There were several large old-fashioned bookcases, crammed to overflowing. On top of one was a Degas bronze statuette of a ballet dancer, in a faded, ragged cloth skirt, and on another a dusty plaster cast of Houdon's head of Voltaire. The desk was a wilderness of letters, books, and typescripts. In a large leather frame was a photograph of a gaunt man with burning eyes seated at a piano. Eric tried to read the inscription, but it was in an unfamiliar language.

"Yes," said Irina Lanski, hanging up and seeing his attention fixed on the photograph, "that is my dearest possession. Do you recognize him?"

"No, I don't."

"It's Ignace Paderewski."

"Who is he?" asked Eric.

She looked at him quickly and saw that his question was not facetious. She leaned forward and put her hand on his. "Do you mind my saying," she said, "that I envy you your youth?"

Eric flushed. "I suppose I should know—" But her warm, impulsive gesture made him feel less insecure.

"He was the greatest pianist of them all," she said. One hand shot upward in a dramatic gesture. "Up there!" The other hand pointed down. "All the others, by comparison, are down here. And a great patriot! A man who could sacrifice his art to become the leader of the Polish Republic. I should say the late Polish Republic," she added bitterly.

"Oh yes, of course I've heard of him. For the minute I—"

She was not listening to him. "He used to come many times to visit in Warsaw when I was a girl. In fact, my father claimed that he was a distant cousin, but I think he was just bragging. He used to sit and play for us by the hour, sometimes until daybreak."

"That must have been wonderful," said Eric with sincerity. He tried to picture Irina Lanski as a young girl, sitting in a house in Warsaw, listening raptly to the famous Paderewski. As so often happened, when he read a great novel or a great play, the horizons of his world were pushed back and his heart beat with excitement.

Irina Lanski nodded solemnly. "Yes, wonderful!" She exhaled

53

slowly. "Well, now let's talk about your play. I suppose you don't know Leroy Thompson?"

"I don't know anybody," said Eric with a touch of self-pity.

"You are lucky. I know everybody, and I assure you it's very depressing. When I read your play I thought immediately of Thompson. You understand, of course, that it is not the sort of play that the Broadway managers are itching to get their fingers on."

"No, I know that."

"No, strong meat is not their dish. They are tripe-dealers, pastry-cooks who coax the delicate appetites of their clientele with soufflés, creampuffs, gingerbread, lollipops. And everything well spiced so that you do not discover how rancid it is until after you have eaten it."

"But there are some good things—"

"Oh yes, many good things. Actors whose popularity overcomes the handicap of a serious play. Good authors whose previous success guarantees them a production. Chain-store heirs who can afford to take a deep plunge and who sometimes come up swimming. Eager groups of young idealists who blaze a trail that usually ends in bankruptcy or in Hollywood. And occasionally a Leroy Thompson, who combines taste with shrewdness, who finds a gold mine in Give Them All My Love and squares his account with God by producing The Clouded Mirror."

"Does he really want to produce it?" asked Eric, still unable to envisage that possibility.

"I can only tell you that he is greatly interested. But whether he will take the risk, I can't say. If it turned out badly, it might mean a loss of a hundred thousand dollars."

"A hundred thousand dollars!" exclaimed Eric incredulously. "You mean just to put on a play?"

"Yes, a play today costs almost as much as a bombing plane. It is something for a manager to think about. And, of course, he must consult his financial advisers. That means he must consult a certain Mrs. Claire Weir, who—"

"Oh yes. I read her name in the paper this morning. Who is she?"

"She is a Westchester commuter who believes in the self-propagation of money and who bets on plays instead of on horses. And, like so many lovers of horseflesh, she is less interested in the nobility of the contestants than in their chances of carrying off the purse. She will not understand your play, but she will understand its

54

commercial deficiencies. She will see that it is an expensive production, that its theme is not likely to be a popular one, and that there is little possibility of a motion-picture sale."

"It doesn't sound very hopeful," said Eric glumly.

"I simply don't know. I am just trying to make you understand what must be considered. Thompson is a young man, with very decided opinions of his own, and—for reasons that I need not go into—he has a strong influence over this bosomy country-club Maecenas who buys a theater as though it were a car or a washing machine."

"Yes, that's what I read," said Eric. "The Farow Theater."

"Poor Oscar Farow! He was a lecherous old charlatan, but he loved his theater, and it would have made him weep to see it fall into the clutches of a cosmetic-manufacturer's widow. Well, to get back to your play. It is just a question, I think, of how strongly Thompson feels about doing it. I must tell you, frankly, that I believe that will depend, to a large extent, upon your willingness to make changes."

Immediately Eric was on the defensive. "What changes?"

"Well, I prefer to let him tell you that. But I do want to—"

"I won't give the play a happy ending if that's what he wants. I'd rather not have it produced."

She looked at him and shook her head slowly. "You're a strong-minded youth, aren't you? But who said anything about a happy ending? Thompson is not an idiot. If he wants happy endings he doesn't have to send for them to—to whatever the name of that town of yours is."

"Coltertown."

"Yes, thank you."

"Then what does he want me to do?"

"He will tell you. And perhaps he will tell you some things of value. After all, it is quite possible that you have not yet completely mastered the art of writing plays." Her voice took on that satiric note which had flustered him so on the telephone.

"Yes, I know I have a lot to learn," he said a little angrily. "And, of course, I'll listen to his suggestions. Only—"

"Good! That is all I ask you to do—listen! And if you disagree with him, don't tell him so. Just listen and then think it over afterwards. You can always say no. But if you resist him, he is likely to drop the whole thing. I know him, and I assure you I am giving you good advice."

"Well, I'll do whatever you say," said Eric, greatly agitated. He realized now that his skepticism concerning Thompson's intentions had been mere insulation against the shock of disappointment. He had really been counting on a production, and now the doubts that Irina Lanski raised deflated his secret hope and made him choke with the fear of frustration. In spite of everything she had said, Thompson was a Broadway manager, governed by commercial considerations. What if the suggested changes were destructive of Eric's play? Was he willing to compromise the integrity of his work for the sake of getting a foothold in the theater? He told himself unhappily that he was not.

The door opened and the secretary came in. "It's time for you to leave, Miss Lanski," she rasped.

"Thank you, Myra. Oh, Mr. Kenwood, have you met Miss Leech?"

"Yes, we met outside," said Eric.

"Of course you did! You could not have got in otherwise. She is my guardian, my chauffeur, my accountant, my nurse, my confessor. In fact, she runs me and my life, and I am completely at her mercy."

Myra smiled frostily. "You wanted Mr. Kenwood to sign that letter agreement."

"Oh yes!" said Irina Lanski. She fumbled helplessly among the litter on her desk. "Where is the loathsome thing?"

"Right here," said Myra, like a governess finding a toy for her troublesome little charge.

"Right under my nose!" said the agent as Myra left the room. "The last place in the world I would have looked for it." She handed the typed sheets to Eric. "This is a form making me your exclusive agent for the sale of plays. It provides that I get ten per cent of whatever you earn from your plays. If you make a million dollars, I make a hundred thousand. If you make nothing, I get ten per cent of whatever that comes to."

Eric did not know what to do. He understood, in a general way, that agents receive a commission for their services, but he had often heard it said that nobody should sign an agreement without carefully reading every word of it, or, better yet, without consulting a lawyer. Confronted with this document, however, he was afraid that Irina Lanski might interpret his hesitation as a reflection upon her integrity.

She saw his embarrassment and came to his rescue. "If you want to look it over or show it to someone, it's quite all right. You can mail it to me when you get home."

"No, no," said Eric hastily. "I'm sure it's all right."

She smiled at the awkwardness of his remark. "Yes, I think you are quite safe in signing it. It is a form that all my clients sign and that the Dramatists' Guild has approved. I am a blasphemous, bad-tempered old hag, but I am not a crook. If I eventually get to heaven, it will certainly be by way of a pauper's grave."

"I didn't mean—" stuttered Eric, fearful that he had insulted her. And then, not knowing how to finish the sentence, he broke off and said quickly, "Is this where I sign?"

"Yes, all three copies, please. Now I sign." She scrawled illegibly and handed one of the copies to him. "This is for you to keep. And now you are bound to me by a tie stronger than love. I doubt if either of us will get rich, but I hope we shall be happy. Did you have a hat?"

"No, I never wear one," said Eric, folding the contract and putting it in his pocket. He should have said something gracious to her, but the moment had passed.

"Neither do I," she said. "Except when I go to mass. I wonder who first made the discovery that God prefers men to be uncovered and women covered. It seems to me that permanents must look much more attractive from above than all those shiny bald heads."

As they were about to leave the office Myra called to Eric, "Oh, Mr. Kenwood, did you have your play copyrighted?"

"Why, no, I didn't. I guess I should, shouldn't I?"

"Yes, of course," said Irina Lanski.

"What do I have to do?"

"We'll have some scripts typed up and take care of it for you if you like," said Myra.

"Well, if it isn't too much trouble—"

"No trouble. It's part of our business." She swiveled around and attacked her typewriter.

Leroy Thompson's office was in one of the buildings that make up the vast complex of Radio City. Eric, on his previous visits to New York, had strolled about Rockefeller Plaza and stared up at the skyscrapers but had never entered any of them. He gaped at the imposing interior with all the curiosity and amazement of the small-town visitor. The elevator that shot them up to the thirty-second floor gave him a thrill of childish excitement. He marveled at the impassive faces of his fellow-passengers. Thompson's bright, neat, air-conditioned reception room was in striking contrast to Irina Lanski's. Eric had never seen anything like it except in the movies.

"Oh, hello, Miss Lanski," said the pretty, young receptionist at the switchboard behind a little window. "I'll tell Mr. Thompson you're here." She announced them and told them to go right in, pressing a button that buzzed open the door to the inner offices. Eric, suddenly as frightened as though he were entering an operating-room, swallowed hard and moistened his lips.

Thompson sat at his desk of chromium and bleached mahogany waiting for them to enter. As always when he was expecting a stranger, he tried to avoid looking toward the door in order not to see the visitor's expression of shocked surprise. However, as the door opened and Irina Lanski entered, followed by Eric, he involuntarily turned his eyes in their direction and saw Eric gazing in amazement at the hideous capillary naevus that covered his left cheek. He felt a flash of hatred against Eric for that undisguised stare; and he was furious at himself for still caring about these inevitable reactions to his disfigurement.

This blotchy birthmark, this "port-wine stain," had profoundly affected Thompson's character and career. Sensitive by nature, he had been agonized all through his childhood and youth by the jeers and insults of his playmates and companions. Not robust enough to punish them physically, he had to satisfy himself with subjecting them to imaginary tortures. He had tried to protect himself by withdrawing within himself, trusting no one, giving himself to no one, and developing an attitude of detached cynicism, which, depending upon the nature of his relationships, had an impact that ranged from satiric humor to sadistic cruelty. As he grew older and the need for crude responses to crude gibes diminished, he sought to counterbalance his physical handicap by the effective use of his wit, his talents, and his personal magnetism. In his self-isolation he had staged so many dramas and enacted so many heroic roles that his theatric imaginings had more reality for him than the actualities of his life, and he had turned instinctively to the world of make-believe, both for refuge and for self-expression. Yet his burning ambition to become a great actor was impossible of realization. He had all the qualifications: voice, physique, temperament, grace, sensitivity; but that repulsive blemish negated everything else. Unless he confined himself to playing full-bearded characters there was no way of hiding it. No make-up, no disguise, could conceal it. For some years he had gone from doctor to doctor, spending every penny he earned, in vain attempts to have it removed. Neither electrolysis, radium treatments, nor any other therapy had resulted in anything more than a slight reduction of the dilatation of the swollen veins; finally he was forced to accept the verdict of incurability and to abandon his hopes of a great acting career. It was a cruel disappointment he had never fully got over. Luckily, though, in his years as a stage manager and player of small parts, he had acquired a sound knowledge of stagecraft and had revealed his potentialities as a director. To be a great director and producer was the next best thing to being a great actor, and, having reconciled himself as best he could to second choice, he made rapid strides toward his goal. His disfigurement made no difference now; all that mattered was his ability and the force of his personality. His position in the theater was an important one; he was successful, influential, and highly respected. Still, he could not look into a mirror without bitterness or meet a stranger's glance without a twinge of anger.

He rose, smiling. Eric, in his nervous self-absorption was unaware of the tactlessness of his gaze and its effect upon Thompson. Irina Lanski, however, had seen the quick contraction of Thompson's pupils and regretted that she had not thought to warn Eric.

"Hello, Irina. Hello, Mr. Kenwood." He shook hands and pointed to chairs.

As Eric was about to sit down he glanced toward the window and gasped. "I'd like to look at the view a minute."

"Help yourself," said Thompson. "There's no charge for authors."

Eric, moving to the window, looked unbelievingly at the stone forest of lower Manhattan, framed in the silver band of the converging rivers, and beyond, the murky stretches of Long Island and New Jersey receding to a dim horizon. "It's staggering," he said.

"I find it saddening," said Irina Lanski. "If men can do all this to glorify gasoline and canned soup, think what they could do if they glorified God!"

"Gasoline pays better dividends," said Thompson.

She leaned forward and put her hand solemnly on his arm. "That is where you are wrong, my friend. Mr. Kenwood, do you agree with me?"

"Yes, if we mean the same thing by God."

"This is going to be fun," said Thompson. "I haven't been to Bible class in years."

"Someday, Tommy," said Irina Lanski, "we will get very drunk together and I will explain God to you."

"There's nobody I'd rather have do it than you. But since we're all cold sober, let's talk about Mr. Kenwood's play instead. What have you been telling him?"

"Only that you have read the play and like it. Anything else I thought you had better tell him yourself."

"Well, I can go a little beyond that. It's a play that I'd like to produce if we can get together on certain things." He turned to Eric. "That is, of course, if you feel you'd like me to produce it."

"Of course I would. Only I'd like to know what you mean by 'certain things.'"

Thompson tapped a cigarette on the desk and lit it with great deliberation. "Is this your first play?"

"No, I've written two others."

"If Mr. Kenwood will forgive my saying so," interposed Irina Lanski, "the other two were what I would call exercises in playwriting. This, I think, is the first real one."

Thompson nodded. "Well, in my opinion—and that's a pretty damned good opinion—it needs a lot of work. You've got a good theatrical story and two or three good actable characters, and I like the writing. But to get right down to cases, I wouldn't want to produce it as it stands now."

Though Eric had made up his mind to listen patiently, Thompson's cocksureness made him bristle and he felt impelled to make a show of self-assertion. But before he could say anything Irina Lanski interposed again.

"I'm sure Mr. Kenwood would be happy to hear what you think should be done," she said.

"If he would, I'll be glad to sound off." He stared at Eric, waiting for an answer.

"Yes, certainly I would," Eric managed to say.

"In the first place," said Thompson, "it's very much overwritten. I'm not just talking about length, though it *is* too long by a good forty minutes. But I can cut the hell out of any script, so that doesn't bother me. What I mean by overwriting is a lot of unnecessary stuff that gets us nowhere—talk that clogs up the action and

60

throws the story off the track. In fact, the whole script is too much all over the place. It wants pointing up and pulling together." He picked up Eric's typescript from the desk and flipped the pages. "Take that courtroom scene. It's just a lot of deadwood. I'd throw the whole scene right out of the window."

"But that's impossible!" protested Eric.

Thompson put down the script. "Well, let's not waste our time talking about something that's impossible."

"No, what I mean is, that you have to see to what lengths Rhoda goes in order to save her father."

"You can put all that over in a couple of good dramatic speeches in her scene with the lawyer. You don't need a twenty-minute scene, fifteen actors, and a big set that's going to add five thousand dollars to the production cost. I wouldn't mind that if I thought it helped the play. But all you've got is just another routine courtroom scene, with a lot of dummies jumping up and down and yelling, 'I object, you object, he, she or it objects!' Personally, I object to the whole thing. Every time the curtain goes up and I see some decrepit member of the Lambs Club, in a white wig and a black gown, pounding a gavel and screaming, 'If you bastards don't come to order, I'll have you thrown out on your cans!' I want to get up and emit a loud Bronx cheer. I've heard people say that a courtroom scene can't miss, but whenever I see one I want to puke in the aisle."

"I still don't see how—" began Eric.

Thompson cut him off. "I've told you how. The lawyer—O'Toole, McNulty, Finklestein, whatever his name is—tells the girl what she has to do. She won't hear of it at first, but he talks her into it. A two-minute scene. Then, in the next scene, we learn that the old man has been acquitted. You haven't lost a thing. In fact, you've tightened up the play and strengthened it. It's the girl's willingness to do it that's important, not a lot of sustaining and denying and 'Answer the question, please, Miss Hildegarde,' and 'Your witness, Mr. Zanuck.'" He turned to Irina Lanski. "Do you see what I'm getting at, Irina?"

"Yes, I do. I once had to serve on a jury and I was constantly tempted to get up and say, 'Your honor'—though I must say he didn't look very honorable—'couldn't we just cut about ten minutes here?'"

Thompson laughed. "Why, you missed a great chance to become a national hero."

Eric did not even smile. He was too agitated by Thompson's sweeping condemnation of a scene over which he had slaved for days. Irina's facetiousness seemed out of keeping with the seriousness of the moment, and he looked upon her agreement with Thompson as disloyalty. But seeing that there was no use arguing the point further, he sat in silence as Thompson continued his criticism.

"All right, that takes care of the courtroom scene. Now, the next big thing that has to be fixed is the character of the father."

"In what way?" asked Eric.

Thompson stared at him coldly. "In every way. He's just a setup the way he is now—a sitting duck. Give him a black mustache and a horsewhip and you've got a reasonable facsimile of Simon Legree. By the time he makes his second entrance the audience will be hissing and tossing up vegetables."

"I didn't mean him to be a sympathetic character," said Eric.

"Sympathetic!" echoed Thompson. "Why, he make Judas Iscariot look like a department-store Santa Claus. Nobody is going to believe that a girl in her right mind would go through what she does for a zombie like that."

"She does it mostly for her mother's sake. Besides, people aren't always rational in their love relationships." He felt that he was not expressing himself forcefully, but Thompson's verbal gyrations confused him. He was like an awkward slugger trying to ward off the dancing attack of a light-footed boxer.

Thompson shook his head. "You've got to make the audience see what she sees in him. He's not even a human character, the way you've written him. Just a cardboard figure—and as empty as a small-town barbershop."

This allusion to his rusticity and his ragged hair was not lost upon Eric. And the boxer, seeing that the well-planned punch had landed, felt the satisfaction of having got even for that overlong stare.

"Those are the two main points," said Thompson. "But there are a lot of other things that need fixing." He leafed through the script again, picking out this flaw and that: clumsy exposition, faulty motivation, awkward manipulation of the characters, turgid writing. Eric, after a few feeble attempts at defense, sat stunned and speechless under the barrage.

At last Thompson flung the script on the desk. "That about covers it, I think."

For a long minute no one spoke. Then Eric, feeling that they were

62

waiting on him, said haltingly, "Why, to do all that—it would mean practically rewriting the whole play."

"What's wrong with that?" asked Thompson.

"Well, it's just that—what I mean is—" He broke off, not knowing what he meant. Thompson had mercilessly torn his creation to shreds, rudely demolishing his pride in his work and his high hopes for it.

Irina Lanski came to his rescue. "I honestly don't think it's as drastic as all that. The structure of the play is there, the story, the characters, in essence at least, if not fully realized; and certainly two-thirds of the dialogue. Mr. Thompson is not asking you to build a new house; only to repair the plumbing, so to speak, and perhaps make a few substantial alterations. That is how I see it."

"I'm not sure that the alterations should be made."

"That's entirely up to you," said Thompson curtly. "It's your cow." He rose and extended his hand. "Thanks for coming in. And if you ever have another play, I'd be glad to have a look at it."

Eric took the extended hand, with the dismal feeling that he was being dismissed and that the meeting had ended in utter failure. "Well, yes, of course. I'll be glad to," he stammered.

"Why don't you give Mr. Kenwood a few days to think the whole thing over, Tommy?" asked Irina Lanski. "After all, you've given him quite a lot to absorb, and I'm sure a few days more or less won't affect your plans."

"Oh, sure, whatever you say. I certainly would never want to keep an author from thinking."

She put her hand on Eric's arm. "Mr. Kenwood, I wonder if you would mind waiting a moment for me in the reception room. I have a business matter I must discuss with Mr. Thompson."

"Yes, of course," said Eric. He said good-by to Thompson and left the office.

"That was damned sweet of you, Irina," said Thompson, "to give me that opportunity to deliver an hour's lecture on the art of play-writing."

"What the hell is the matter with you, Tommy? Are you suffering from the heat or what? What do you expect of a boy when you take his first play and tear it up in front of his eyes? Do you think he is going to get down on his knees and kiss your hand in gratitude?"

"Everything I told him was for his own good."

She smiled quizzically at him. "When the dentist drills your teeth for your own good, do you look up at him with adoration in your eyes? Anybody would think you had never met a young author before."

"I never met one that smelled quite as strongly of the barnyard."

"If you want authors who know how to wear a dinner jacket I can bring in a dozen tomorrow. This boy can write. How many first scripts have you read that have the quality of this one?"

"If I didn't think he could write I wouldn't have had him in here. But if I'm going to take a chance on that play, it's got to be put into some shape where I think we've at least got a credible and actable script, for Christ's sake! If he doesn't want to do the work that I think has to be done, then he knows where he can put it!"

"I think you should give him a contract."

"Oh, is that what you think? Well, listen, darling, I'm not signing any contract until I see a revised script."

"No," she said. "You should give it to him now."

"Why the hell should I?" he asked irritably.

"Because if you do he will make the changes." She checked his attempted interruption. "Believe me, I know what I am talking about. I understand these young writers. This boy is insecure and needs encouragement. He does not believe that you are seriously interested in his play. But if you give him a production contract and an advance royalty, he will believe it and he will work."

"I don't see it. I'm running a theatrical business here, not a psychiatric clinic."

"What have you got to lose—two or three hundred dollars? You've taken bigger risks on less promising scripts."

Thompson recognized the truth of what she was saying and he had great respect for her judgment of plays and people. However, he did not want to give in too easily.

"Well, since you're so sure of him," he said, "will you pay me back the advance if he doesn't come through?"

"Certainly not. If I could afford to do that I'd give him a contract myself. Suppose I tell him that if he will agree to rewrite, you will give him a contract?"

Thompson ground out his cigarette. "You and your goddam Continental charm!"

She gave him a slow smile. "You won't regret it. But let me have a few days."

64

Eric sat disconsolately in the outer office. He felt like a child whose elders had sent him from the room while they discussed his problems. He had an impulse to go to the station; but that would make him look really childish; so he waited. He looked up quickly as Irina Lanski came out of Thompson's office. Her broad, impassive face told him nothing.

"Why don't we go and have a drink somewhere?" she said.

At a bar in the building, they found a table in a quiet corner. Irina Lanski ordered a double brandy and soda, and Eric, unaccustomed to daytime drinking and afraid of ordering the wrong thing, took the same. He sat silent, certain that she was going to reproach him for his resistance to Thompson and determined to defend himself resolutely.

She merely smiled at him and said, "I must say you don't look very gay."

"I don't feel very gay. I don't understand why he went to all the trouble of seeing me."

"I can tell you why. Because he likes your play."

"Likes it! He practically tore it up and threw it in my face."

"Cheerio!" She raised her glass and took a long swallow. "Well, I am a childless old maid, but I can understand how a mother feels when someone says to her, 'My dear, what a charming, adorable infant you have, but in heaven's name, why don't you clean its filthy little nose?' "

"He wants me to amputate its legs and cut out its heart."

"No. It is only your mother instinct that makes it seem so."

"No, it isn't. Take that courtroom scene." And he launched into a vehement justification of the scene. She made no attempt to check his volubility, but sat with her eyes fixed upon him, slowly sipping her drink.

When at last he paused, his face flushed and tense with emotion, she said, "Let me give you some advice. Are you going back home?"

"Yes, I have to be at work in the morning." He looked at his watch. "I guess I should be leaving for the station right now."

"It's only five minutes from here," she said, motioning to the waiter for the check. "What I want to suggest is that you don't think about the play at all for a few days. Go to your job and forget the play. Then take another look at it. Perhaps you'll decide that a little cleaning up might not be so bad for it—or, who knows, maybe even a little surgery."

Eric shook his head. "I don't see the use of it. I don't see how I could ever do all the things he thinks should be done."

"Suppose I could get you a contract?"

He looked at her, puzzled. "What kind of contract?"

"A contract from Leroy Thompson to produce the play. And, of course, an advance royalty."

"But he said he wouldn't consider producing the play unless—!" expostulated Eric.

"Unless you rewrite. But if you agree to do it, perhaps I can get you a contract immediately."

"Do you think he'd do that?"

"I can't promise, but I'll do my best to persuade him."

"I don't see how I could—"

"Don't decide now. Think it over for a few days." She took the check from the waiter and paid it before Eric could protest. "Don't miss your train."

"Yes, I haven't much time. Is there a bus or something I can get to the station?"

"I'll drop you. It's on my way."

By the time they found a taxi, and Eric had said good-by to Irina Lanski, the train had gone. There was another in an hour, but it would not get him to Hartford in time to connect with the last bus for Coltertown. He slumped down on a bench in the waiting-room, wrestling with his transportation problem, which, for the moment, drove everything else out of his mind. A taxi from Hartford to Coltertown would cost at least ten dollars, an expenditure he could not even consider. Unless he was lucky enough to get a lift, he would have to walk. He was a good walker, but it was over fourteen miles; in this heat, he could not hope to do it in less than four hours. He groaned inwardly at the prospect. He had been on the go for twelve hours. He was hot, dirty, and weary, and the strong drink had made his head swim. His aching body could not endure the discomfort of the wooden bench, and he made his way foggily to the washroom. Having found that he could get a private lavatory equipped with a shower, he spent a half-hour there, emerging clean and somewhat refreshed. It was well worth the seventy-five cents, particularly since he had not had to pay the bar-check.

As soon as the gate opened he boarded the train and found a seat in an air-conditioned car. His heavy eyelids closed and he dozed off. But, in a few moments, he was wide awake again. The thronging

66

sensations and emotions of the crowded day made sleep impossible. The unfamiliar bustle and turmoil of the city, the impersonal, swarming streets and buildings, the dizzy panorama that Thompson's lofty window had revealed and, most of all, the trying, painful meeting, inflamed his brain and rasped his nerves. He had sharp retinal images of Thompson's blotched, sneering face and of Irina Lanski's slow, detached smile. He went over every word that had been spoken, thought of all the things he might have said and should have said, and was furious at himself for his fumbling inarticulateness. He tried to account for his clumsy performance. In school, in the Army, in the factory, he had always managed to hold his own. In fact, he had more often than not felt distinctly superior not only to his mates, but to his teachers, officers, and employers. But this theatrical agent and this theatrical producer had been beyond his scope. They lived in a world with which he was wholly unfamiliar. Their self-assurance, their mannerisms, their sophisticated talk, crammed with extravagant metaphors and oblique allusions, unsettled and bewildered him. He could not accommodate himself to the tempo and the rhythm of their thoughts and their conversation. The belief that they considered him a crude country boy, and treated him accordingly, wounded and frightened him; and, being afraid, he felt a surge of hatred for them both. He told himself that he never wanted to see either of them again. As for his play, or any play he might conceivably write, the sooner he forgot about all that, the better. Irina Lanski had advised him to forget it, and he intended to do just that—not for a few days though, but for all time. Her hint of the possibility of a contract had renewed his hope only momentarily. She was just leading him on, playing upon his guileless credulity. Though for what purpose he could not imagine, unless it was that these artificial, insincere people could never come straight out with anything, and this was just her method of letting him down easily. His judgment reasserted itself for an instant to assure him that Irina Lanski was a person of character and integrity and Leroy Thompson an artist who respected his art, and that neither of them would have wasted all that time and trouble on a stranger unless they had serious intentions. But his bruised sensibilities rejected the solace of logic and common sense.

A thunderstorm broke as the train neared Hartford. Through the station windows Eric could see the sweeping sheets of rain. To go outdoors was unthinkable. Besides, he was famished. He had been tempted to go to the dining-car, but he knew that the prices were prohibitive. He went to the station lunch counter and ravenously consumed a hamburger, a slice of pie, and two cups of coffee. When the rain abated he ran to board a local bus that took him two miles on his way. At the end of the line he tried to pick up a ride, but car after car slithered by, so he turned up his coat collar and trudged along the dark road through the steaming rain. After walking a mile, he got a lift from a driver who had stopped for a red light. When the car turned off, three miles short of his destination, he had to tramp on for another hour in the continuing rain. It was past midnight when he let himself in the back door, drenched, bedraggled, and dog-tired.

On his way upstairs, he heard his mother calling him. She had lain awake, listening for him, and stood, in her nightgown, at the foot of the stairs.

"Hello, Ma," he said.

"I just wanted to be sure that you're all right, son," said Amelia.

"Yes, sure, I'm fine."

His weary, dispirited voice was not reassuring, but she was never one to ask questions. "Don't you want something to eat?"

"No, I ate in Hartford. You go to bed, Ma; it's late. I'll see you in the morning. Good night."

"Well, good night, son." Worried about him, she watched him go up to his room.

Eric flung off his clothes, threw himself naked on the bed, and fell immediately into a dead sleep.

IV.

Eric was too busy next day to think about his trip to New York. To catch up with his work he cut down his lunch period to twenty minutes and stayed an hour after closing time. He wished he could get out of going to Sylvia's for supper and avoid the long cross-examination to which he was sure to be subjected. But he had no plausible excuse and hated lying. If he failed to appear on Friday night, when her parents always went out to play cards and she and Eric were sure of being alone for several hours, she would not easily forgive him. He was a little late in arriving. Mrs. Jethrow readily accepted his explanation, but Sylvia, who attached great importance to the minutiae of social behavior, made no attempt to conceal her annoyance. She had looked forward to a half-hour with Eric before supper, and spent the time at the window, looking at her wristwatch every few minutes with increasing petulance. When Eric finally did arrive, they sat down immediately to supper. For once, he was grateful for Mrs. Jethrow's garrulity. Oblivious to Sylvia's sulkiness, she overwhelmed them with a twittering monologue that neither sought nor admitted response.

Sylvia's parents, like Eric's mother, came of old Coltertown stock. Samuel Jethrow was the proprietor of the town's only furniture store, which he had inherited from his father. He had entered the business upon leaving grade school, and for forty years had had no other occupation and few other interests. He was a large, heavy, taciturn man, slow of body and of mind, as devoid of malice as he was of temperament and ambition. The business was not a flourishing one, but, year in and year out, he managed to meet his modest living expenses and he was quite content to let things go at that.

Lydia Jethrow was almost the exact counterpart of her husband. She was a member of a lesser branch of the Graham family—one of the four or five clans that ruled Coltertown—and when she married Samuel Jethrow there was a general feeling (which she shared) that she had stooped a little. However, she had the shrewdness to realize she was no great matrimonial prize; a solid and respected merchant was about the best she could hope for.

She was a quick, birdlike creature, forever chattering and fluttering about, minding everybody's business and darting aimlessly from one interest to another. She had just enough education and just enough intelligence to make her aware that the world was not bounded by dining-room suites, penny ante, and Sunday-night suppers in the Congregational parish house; but she had no taste and no power of application. A great reader of magazines devoted to interior decoration, she occasionally attempted to modernize her husband's business by introducing "functional" furniture and fabrics in abstract designs. Jethrow, knowing that his wife's interest would soon be diverted, went on catering to his customers' preferences for red maple, cheap shiny veneers, and overstuffed velours.

Eric had known the Jethrows intimately since boyhood. Sylvia's brother George, who had been his schoolmate and close friend, had been drafted early in the war and trained as a bombardier. While Eric was still in training camp he received the news that George's plane had been shot down in a mission over the Ruhr. It was a heavy blow for the Jethrows. Jethrow became more reticent than ever. His wife plunged frenziedly into new, purposeless activities. Sylvia mourned her brother too, though they had had little in common. However, in her adolescent self-absorption—she was just finishing high school—her grief was outweighed by the effect of George's death upon her own career. Her plan to go on to a Midwestern state university had to be abandoned. Not only did she feel that it would not be right to leave her parents, but the loss of George's potential earning capacity altered the family's economic outlook. Accordingly, with a sense of martyrdom, she entered a business school in Hartford. By the time Eric was demobilized she was employed in the office of a Coltertown real-estate agent. Eric had never paid much attention to her: she had never been anything more than his friend's "kid sister." But when he came back he had suddenly seen her as a distinct personality, a ripening, vivacious young woman, dignified by economic independence and ennobled by the aura of sorrow. Impressed by the discovery and touched by the pathetic eagerness with which Samuel Jethrow and his wife welcomed his return, he felt a sudden rush of affection for them all; without being wholly aware of what he was doing, he attached himself to the household, as a sort of substitute for his dead friend. As he sat there at the supper table, hardly listening to Mrs. Jethrow's rambling discourse, it was disturbingly evident that they all regarded him as a member of the family.

While Sylvia and her mother cleared the table the two men went to the living-room, Jethrow with a cigar, Eric filling his pipe. They had few common interests, and neither had a talent for small talk, so the conversation went haltingly. They were both relieved when the others joined them.

"Are you young folks going to the movies?" asked Mrs. Jethrow.

"It's too hot," said Sylvia. "I think I'd rather just listen to some music. How about you, Eric?"

70

"Well, you know how I feel about movies."

"Yes, don't get started on that. Maybe if it cools off later, we'll walk down and get a soda."

"I certainly envy you," said her mother. "If it were up to me I'd rather stay quietly at home than sit and play cards on a night like this."

By means of this conversational formula, which varied only slightly from week to week, she not only scored off her husband but persuaded herself of the propriety of leaving Sylvia and Eric alone in the house.

As soon as her parents had left Sylvia removed Eric's pipe from his mouth, sat on his lap, and gave him a long kiss.

"Well," she said. "Are you glad to see me?"

"Of course I am!" He put his arm around her waist and kissed her again. Hearing footsteps on the sidewalk, she quickly slipped off his lap onto the sofa. It was still daylight, and passers-by could look in through the open windows. When the days were short she could pull down the shades; now such an action would be an invitation to public attention.

"You certainly don't act like it," she said poutingly. "You seem a million miles away."

"No, I'm not. It's just that I've been so darn busy these last few days."

"You haven't told me a thing about New York. Not that anybody can get a word in edgewise when Mother gets started." She linked her arm through his and snuggled against his shoulder. "Tell baby all about everything," she cooed.

There was a touch of coyness in Sylvia's tenderness that always embarrassed Eric a little. But the pressure of her body and the caress of her dark, silky hair upon his cheek were welcome.

"There's not much to tell," he said. "I went in to see my agent—"

"Oh yes!" exclaimed Sylvia. "Miss Lanski. What's she like?"

"Well, she's really quite a fascinating woman." He described Irina Lanski to her, unconsciously expressing an admiration that he did not even know he felt. His enthusiasm was not lost upon Sylvia. The elderly Polish woman was clearly no threat to her, but Sylvia was instantly hostile to anyone who occupied Eric's attention to the exclusion of herself.

"She sounds wonderful," said Sylvia. "I only hope she's somebody you can trust."

71

"I don't see why not. She's a well-known agent. And, anyhow, what could she do that could hurt me?"

"Oh, nothing at all, I guess. It's just that I know how you always trust everybody, and I think you have to be careful about people like that."

Eric did not know exactly what she meant by "people like that," but Sylvia's innuendo revived his own misgivings.

Sylvia nestled closer. "Got any of those nice kisses left?" she said in a little girl's voice.

"Maybe." He tilted up her chin and pressed his mouth hard against hers. She touched his lips quickly with the tip of her tongue and then drew away from him.

"I want to hear all about New York," she said.

Eric gave her an abbreviated account of the meeting with Thompson, making the whole thing sound very vague and casual. It was painful to him to admit defeat either to her or to himself.

"What a shame!" she murmured sympathetically. "All that long trip, just for nothing."

"Well, at least it gave me a chance to get acquainted with some people in the theater."

"Yes, that's true. In case you should ever write another play."

Though she had never quite dared to admit it to Eric, she thoroughly disliked his play and did not believe there was the slightest probability that anyone would ever produce it. She was pleased to have her judgment confirmed, and even more pleased that Eric, who had neglected her all week, was now back, licking his wounds and seeking refuge in her arms.

"Baby loves you just the same," she said, looking up at him and stroking his face. He held her close to him, but they drew apart again as they heard voices in the street.

"Let's go where we can have a little privacy," she said, almost in desperation. She was a little angry because she had been forced to make the suggestion. She preferred to create the illusion that she was yielding to his overpowering desire; yet it seldom happened that way. Inwardly resentful, she led the way up the stairs to her room.

Eric's reluctance sprang neither from lack of desire nor from prudery, but from an inner conflict he could never quite resolve. Having a strong sense of responsibility, he was perpetually troubled by his rather ambiguous relationship to Sylvia. They had drifted into it unintentionally, almost by accident. The affectionate sympathy that had drawn him to his friend's sister had developed into a stronger feeling. They were constantly together, sometimes in the company of other young people; then more and more alone. They took long hikes or drives, went dancing or swimming or boating at the neighboring lake resort, or picnicked in the rambling acres of neglected pasture and woodland that fringed the town.

One summer evening, when they had been all day together, the longing that obsessed them both swept away all inhibitions. That first experience, however, had been neither happy nor satisfying. Sylvia was a virgin, Eric a far from practiced lover, and the feeling of guilt, which neither of them could entirely shake off, made joyous surrender impossible. As their intimacy grew they found more pleasure in it, but it never attained complete spontaneity and unrestrained rapture. They always had to be on their guard against discovery, and the ever-present fear of pregnancy made Eric overcautious and Sylvia tense and fretful.

This unsatisfactory relationship had held them both half-captive for more than two years. From the beginning, it was tacitly understood that they would marry one day; but that day was of such uncertain date that they seldom alluded to it. The circumstances of their lives precluded an immediate marriage. Coltertown, like most other American communities, had an acute housing problem. There was not an available dwelling in or near the town. Sylvia's parents would have been glad to take her husband in, but the desire to get away from her mother was one of her strongest incentives to marriage. Nor could Eric ask her to live under the same roof with Luke Kenwood; to say nothing of leading a life of drudgery in a penny-pinching household. For it was the economic factor that made their marriage really impossible. Eric's parents were almost entirely dependent upon him, and there was no telling how long Kenwood would live or what additional expenses would be incurred as his disabilities increased.

In view of this uncertain outlook they had, by unspoken consent, never formalized their engagement. Sylvia had no ring, and they had never told anyone that they intended to marry. Yet, in a sense, they were bound. Both Eric's parents and Sylvia's took for granted the eventual marriage. And, in the eyes of the community, they were unofficially engaged; so that Sylvia almost never went out with another young man and Eric avoided going out with other girls. By

Coltertown standards they were very young, and so no immediate solution was demanded. Nevertheless, their situation was an anomalous one and they were both keenly aware of it. If they had been deeply in love with each other, irresistibly drawn together by their emotional and spiritual needs, they would undoubtedly have found a way to overcome all the obstacles to their marriage. As it was, a deep instinct of self-preservation made them acquiesce in an equivocal relationship that left open a door of escape. They had gone along like this, from month to month, from year to year, seeing each other almost daily, making furtive love whenever they could, and letting the future take care of itself.

V.

Fortunately for Eric, Sylvia was spending the weekend with some friends who had a summer cottage at the lake. He was tired and overwrought and glad to be alone. He had promised Irina Lanski he would telephone her on Monday, and he wanted to think about what to say to her.

Saturday was a half-day. With lunch and the household chores out of the way, he had the afternoon to himself. He wanted to get away from the house, if only to escape the deafening roar of his father's eternal ball game. He went to his room to get an anthology of modern plays, which he had borrowed from the library, and then impulsively picked up his own play too. He slipped out by the back door, clambered over a stone fence, and wandered off through the fields.

The Kenwoods lived on the edge of the town, where the houses were strung sparsely along the highway. Beyond and behind the house, the land undulated gently upward to some low hills, a mile or more away. It was a variegated landscape, without grandeur or notable topographical features, but quietly and intimately charming, and subtly overlaid with the rich patina of three centuries of human habitation. For six or seven generations the rugged settlers and their descendants had tried to wrest a living from the stony and unrewarding Connecticut soil, but the opening of the West and the ever-growing trend toward urbanization and industrialism had gradually drained off the farming population. Great stumps of once magnificent chestnut trees, destroyed by irremediable blight, dotted the rough meadows, where all through the spring and summer field flowers sprang bright and sweet. Tumble-down fences of rude fieldstone, reminders of long-forgotten boundaries, crisscrossed the land, here and there all but obliterated by wild tangles of blackberry and raspberry and grape. Blueberry patches straggled over sunny slopes, and hoary, untended apple trees still blossomed fitfully, yielding a crop of wizened, wormy fruit. A few brooks, foaming and rushing in the rainy season and dwindling down to a thin trickle when it was dry, twistingly traced the contours of the terrain. An overgrown cellar or blackened stone chimney was all that remained of once busy households.

For Eric, this gentle wilderness was an earthly paradise. From the time he could first be trusted to wander off by himself, he had explored its delights and its mysteries. He knew every tree and hillock, where the dogtooth violets and hickory nuts were to be found, where the moss was greenest and smoothest, where to drink in the sun and where to escape the wind. Always a daydreamer and a solitary, he had spent his happiest hours here, lying under a tree, lost in a book or in his fancies, identifying hidden birds by their calls or watching with delight the flamboyant tanagers, orioles, grosbeaks, and finches that fluttered and darted about. All through his schooldays he had continued to seek refuge and spiritual sustenance in this beloved haven. Then work, responsibilities, the Army, had shut it off from him. On his return he had introduced Sylvia to his Eden, and they had spent many pleasant and tender hours there together; but it could never mean to her what it did to him. She was neither fanciful nor particularly beguiled by the charms of nature, and she protested constantly against the minor discomforts of brambles, mud, and flitting insects.

Now he headed straight for a favorite white oak that dominated a little knoll and settled under it, sheltered by the spreading branches from the hot sun and refreshed by the light summer breeze. He leaned back against the huge, crinkled trunk, stretched his legs and arms, and felt his body relax. For a long time he sat there, with the book of plays lying unopened on his lap. Then suddenly he put aside the book and took up The Clouded Mirror.

His play had had its genesis in a minor local incident. In an obscure little valley, five or six miles from Coltertown, there was a cluster of half a dozen wretched shacks, inhabited by a few miserable families, the last feeble descendants of some of the early settlers. How they managed to exist no one knew or cared. They were left undisturbed in their squalor, except when some infraction of law or public decency brought them to the attention of the authorities. Shortly after Eric's return to Coltertown one of these episodes occurred. A resident of the town had found one of the inhabitants of the verminous colony, a ragged, half-witted girl of fifteen, screaming and writhing by the roadside, in the agony of labor. He had rushed her to the hospital, where she gave birth. Questioned as to the paternity of the child, she named her own father. The town was scandalized; punitive action was demanded. But the father denied the charge, and the baby died a few days after birth. So beyond the commitment of the girl to an institution for the feeble-minded, nothing was done and the public clamor soon subsided.

However, the incident made an impression upon Eric, and when his play about Army life was sent back to him by Irina Lanski, he found a new theme in this sordid occurrence. As so often happens, the development of the story carried it farther and farther from its origin, and when the play was done it contained almost no trace of the episode from which it sprang.

The play, as Eric wrote it, dealt with a solid middle-class household in a small town. The daughter of the family, an intense, passionate girl, falls madly in love with a married neighbor and forces herself upon him. The girl's father learns of the relationship and kills the man. He is indicted for murder and there is danger of his conviction. His lawyer, an old family friend, makes the girl understand that the only hope for her father's acquittal lies in her testifying that her dead lover seduced her under a promise of marriage. Still wild with grief, she at first refuses. But her strong attachment to her father and her alarm for her invalid mother finally overcome her resistance. At the trial she tells the manufactured story, and the father is acquitted. A few years later the mother dies, and the girl, crushed and chastened, devotes herself increasingly to her father. Then she

76

meets a newcomer to the town, a young man who is strongly attracted to her. Her hopes revive, and she soon finds herself deeply in love again. The young man has heard of the tragedy but he accepts the story of her betrayal at its face value and asks her to marry him. Her father, learning of her intention, tries, by one argument and another, to dissuade her. She persists, and he goes to the young man, tells him the true story of her earlier relationship, and warns him against marrying a girl without moral scruples, whom he can never trust, and who will, as likely as not, deceive him with the first man who strikes her fancy. Revolted, the young man leaves the town. She is stumped at first, but, suspecting her father's complicity, worms the truth out of him. He offers as his justification his belief that the young man is unworthy of her and that he would bring her only unhappiness. This new blow almost deranges her. She turns upon her father and in a frenzy of denunciation accuses him of a guilty love for her and tells him that his murder of her first lover and his dismissal of her second were motivated not by regard for her well-being but by sexual jealousy. She threatens to leave his house and to revenge herself upon him by making it appear that she had to leave in order to escape his advances. As she prepares to go, the father, overcome by fear of this new scandal and by a sense of guilt, shoots her and then turns the gun upon himself.

It was a grim, dark, stormy tale, one that might easily have been unbearably sordid and unpleasant. But Eric had written it with fervor and with poetic insight. The people of the play were all analogues or syntheses of Coltertown figures whom he had known all his life. He had a good ear, and he had endowed them with the characteristic savor of New England speech; yet the dialogue was not flat or literal, but artistically distilled into a kind of tragic nobility of expression. The psychological motivation was credible if not profound, and the steady and relentless progression of the story gave evidence of an authentic, though untutored, dramatic gift. It was these qualities, rare in any writer and exceptional in a young one, that had aroused the interest of both Irina Lanski and Leroy Thompson.

Eric had worked long and carefully on the play. He had sent it off with the conviction that it was a finished piece of work. Now, as he reread it in the light of Thompson's criticism, he saw many flaws and shortcomings. He had to admit that almost all the producer's objections were sound. The courtroom scene was indeed not only cumbersome and superfluous but prosy, wooden, and lifeless. It was apparent to him, now, that the reason he had had to slave over it was that he had never really felt it and had put it in only because it had seemed technically indispensable. With chagrin, he recalled his obstinate resistance to Thompson's strictures and to Irina Lanski's counsel to listen in silence. They must both have thought him dense, contentious, and intractable.

Thompson's criticism of the characterization of the father in the play now seemed valid to Eric too. The man was so harsh and brutal, so utterly lacking in any engaging quality, that it was hard to understand the daughter's attachment to him, an element of implausibility that weakened the effect of the whole play. As Eric pondered this he was startled and shocked by a sudden flash of self-revelation. He saw, all at once, that he had made this savage characterization the means of expressing his bitterness toward his own father. All the resentment that had been aroused in him by his mother's bondage, his sister's ostracism, and his own enforced submissiveness had been poured into the creation of this ogre. In castigating and destroying his heroine's father he had unconsciously paid off Luke Kenwood, and he was amazed and a little frightened as he remembered the savage joy that had gone into the hideous depiction. It troubled him to learn that he was capable of such vindictiveness; at the same time, though he was still a long way from self-understanding and self-integration, he was dimly aware of his good fortune in being able to find a vicarious outlet for his destructiveness.

He was so absorbed by his re-examination of his play and by his new insight into his own psychological processes that the afternoon slipped by swiftly. By the time he got back to the house his parents had long since finished supper. Kenwood scolded him for his tardiness, but Eric, in his elated preoccupation, took the rebuke good humoredly. He even felt a rush of sympathy for the unhappy invalid, and after he had eaten spent two hours playing checkers with him, something he had not done in months.

On Sunday, when Amelia returned from church, Eric drove over to his sister's for midday dinner. He preferred to spend the afternoon alone again, but he was fond of Dorothy and he knew, too, that he would please his mother by going. She could not go herself without arousing Kenwood's anger, and the next best thing was to get Eric's report of Dorothy's household. A secret report it had to be, for Kenwood had forbidden mention of his daughter's name in his presence.

Though this complete estrangement dated only from Dorothy's marriage, it was really the culmination of a life-long hostility. Kenwood and his daughter had never hit it off. He had always had an eye for feminine beauty, and he never forgave the girl for inheriting her mother's plainness. Like Eric, Dorothy was congenitally nearsighted and had worn glasses ever since she was five. She had been a rather sickly child too, sallow and anemic, and Kenwood had had no patience with her perpetual whining and lassitude. Her health improved as she grew older, and she developed into a robust young woman; but by that time their mutual antipathy was too deeply rooted to be eradicated. When Dorothy was old enough to understand the cause of her father's illness, she lost altogether any remaining vestige of respect. She had Amelia's innate purity without her sweetness, and Eric's intensity without his objectiveness, and she looked upon her father as a moral leper.

Upon her graduation from high school she went to work in the Ainsworth factory, where Eric was already employed. She and her father quarreled more and more—she had inherited some of his bad temper—and when Eric was discharged from the Army she made up her mind to leave home. With the return of the soldiers, jobs for women were no longer so plentiful, and while she was looking for something she met Leon La Pointe.

La Pointe, a widower of forty with three young children, ran a small but profitable dairy farm near Coltertown. He took a liking to Dorothy, squired her to a dance or two, and after several months' acquaintanceship asked her to marry him. She was well aware that she was being invited to become an unsalaried replacement for the middle-aged woman who looked after La Pointe's household. But she liked the prospect of presiding over the neat farmhouse and helping in the management of the prospering little business. Besides, unlike her father, La Pointe was good-humored and easygoing. All in all, she had hardly hoped for more.

Familiar with her father's opinion of French-Canadians and of Catholics, she expected opposition, but she was not prepared for the violence with which Kenwood received the news. He was convinced that she was marrying La Pointe only to shame and humiliate him. Since he could not prevent the marriage, he revenged himself

79

by cutting Dorothy off entirely and forbidding either her presence or the mention of her name in his house.

Dorothy, of course, continued to see Eric, who paid frequent visits to the farm. Amelia managed to meet her on marketing trips, and, almost every day, when Kenwood took his afternoon nap, they talked on the telephone. Though Dorothy cared little about her father's animosity, Amelia could not reconcile herself to her daughter's banishment. Her one solace was that the marriage had turned out well. La Pointe, who was a little in awe of Dorothy's superior education and Yankee practicality, let her do things in her own way. She managed her young stepchildren with authority tempered by kindness, and now, after a year of marriage, she was expecting a child of her own.

In anticipation of the arrival of the baby, the La Pointes had felt it advisable to have a household helper and had taken in Cousin Elizabeth. The poor old woman, nearing eighty, had long since been dismissed from her minor position at the hospital and had been eking out her small pension with odd jobs of sewing and baby-tending. The La Pointes could not afford the wages of an able-bodied worker; she was better than nobody, and was so abjectly grateful for being saved from the poor farm that they felt the satisfaction of doing a magnanimous deed.

"I hear you been to New York," said La Pointe to Eric when they were all gathered around the dinner table. "Did you go up that there Empire State Building?"

"No. I didn't have time."

La Pointe shook his head. "Boy, you'd never get me to go up there." Hartford was the largest city he had ever seen, and he was a little disappointed that his brother-in-law had brought back no report of the one feature of metropolitan life that fascinated him.

Dorothy questioned Eric eagerly about his trip. She had not read his play and would certainly not have liked it if she had, but she had great respect for his intellectual attainments and for his ambition to become a writer. The squirming of the three active, hungry youngsters and the clatter of Cousin Elizabeth's cutlery made conversation difficult. La Pointe did not understand a word of what Eric was talking about, never having seen a play and having no conception of what the functions of a writer were. So while Eric and Dorothy talked he joked with the children, heaped the emptied plates, and ate noisily. Some neighbors dropped in after dinner, and

80

Eric soon excused himself and went home to read his play again and make notes for revisions.

On Monday he could hardly keep his mind on his work. When the lunch bell rang he hurried from the factory, obsessed by a new anxiety. Now that he had decided to revise his play, he was afraid that Thompson might have lost interest in it and would decline to go ahead. Over and over he bemoaned the tactless behavior that had perhaps destroyed his chances of a production. He could not wait to talk to Irina Lanski, yet he dreaded to hear what she might say. The nearest pay-station was a good half-mile away, and he ran most of the way. Breathless and nervous, he had to repeat the number twice before he could make the operator understand him. It took a long time to put through the call, and he shifted around uneasily in the booth, his throat contracted and his palms sweaty. At last the connection was made, and he fumblingly deposited the required coins.

"Hello, Miss Lanski. This is Eric Kenwood."

"Oh, hello there!" said the agent with a tinge of mockery. "I can hardly hear you. Have you got laryngitis?"

"No. Is that better? Can you hear me now?" The sound of her voice reassured him a little. He could visualize her now; she no longer seemed remote and strange, but almost an old friend.

"Yes, much better," she said. "Well, what have you been doing with yourself since I saw you?"

"I've been doing a lot of thinking."

"That's sometimes good. And?"

"Well, I've gone over the play a few times and I think I'd like to go ahead and make those changes."

"I'm glad to hear it. I was hoping that you would."

Eric hesitated a moment, half afraid to introduce the subject of Thompson. "I thought you might want to tell Mr. Thompson."

"Yes, of course. I'll tell him at once if he's in town. If not, as soon as I can reach him."

"And do you think—?" He broke off, not daring to ask the direct question.

"Well, I don't know. I'm afraid he rather got the impression the other day that you didn't want to—"

"Yes, I know, and I'm awfully sorry. But it was all so sudden and unexpected that—"

"He's a man who requires a certain approach," she said. "But I

81

assure you I'll do my very best to persuade him. How long do you think it will take you to do the work?"

"Well, I have to do it in my spare time, you know—evenings and weekends."

"Can you give me any idea—two weeks, four weeks?"

"I think about a month should be enough."

"Good. Well, I'll let you know about Thompson as soon as possible."

"And you think that—?" he asked again, craving some definite assurance.

"My dear Mr. Kenwood," she said with a trace of impatience, "I have told you I would do the very best I can. If you want me to make promises that I may not be able to keep—"

"No, no, certainly not!" said Eric hastily.

"In the meanwhile I suggest that you go ahead with the revisions. Even if we fail with Thompson, it is a good idea to improve the script as much as possible."

"You mean there might be some other manager—?"

"It's not inconceivable."

The operator interposed to ask for more money. Since there seemed to be nothing more to say, Eric bade Irina Lanski good-by and hung up.

Though he ran back to the factory he was five minutes late and had to forego his lunch. His talk with Irina Lanski had not allayed his uneasiness. She had not given him the encouragement he had hoped for. He reflected morosely that he could have told her his intentions by letter and saved the dollar and a quarter that the call had cost. Wondering how long he would be kept in suspense, he despondently turned to the dull duties that robbed him of so many precious writing hours.

VI.

Leroy Thompson had spent a long weekend at Claire's country place in Westchester County. On Tuesday morning her butler-chauffeur drove them both into town. They were meeting Anthony Weir at lunch, to discuss the details of the acquisition of the Farow Theater. Claire, who had some shopping to do first, dropped Thompson at his hotel. Stretching himself out on a sofa, he looked listlessly through his mail and telephone messages. He did not feel refreshed and told himself that he would not care if he never saw Claire's bar or bed again.

There was nothing in the mail to interest him. The telephone slips served only to infuriate him, for, besides messages from Irina Lanski and several other business acquaintances, there were a half-dozen notations of calls from his former wife. That could mean only one thing: she wanted money. What it would be for, this time, he could not guess, but he was determined to refuse, no matter what the nature of the demand. He picked up the telephone to call Irina Lanski, assuming that she wanted to talk to him about Eric's play, but before the switchboard operator could answer he said, "Oh, to hell with it!" and hung up. He felt no interest in Eric's play or any play. He poured himself a large glass of tomato juice, spiked it liberally with Worcestershire sauce, and went back to the sofa.

The telephone rang. Sure that it was Isabel, he was inclined not to answer. But, once on his trail, she would never desist, and he concluded that he might as well talk to her now as later.

"Hello, Tommy," said the familiar high-pitched voice. "This is Isabel."

"Why, what a surprise," he said.

"I've been trying to get you all weekend."

"If I'd known that, I wouldn't have gone away."

Her voice took on the whining tone that had always driven him frantic. "You don't have to be so sarcastic about it. I know you don't want to talk to me. And I wouldn't dream of calling you if it weren't on account of Doris."

In spite of himself Thompson was a little worried. "What's the matter with her now?" he asked.

"Well, she looks so pale and thin, and she's got this cough that just hangs on and on and—"

"Why don't you take her to a doctor?" he interrupted.

"What do you think I've been doing but taking her to the doctor's, two or three times a week? I just wish you could see the bills."

"I appreciate that."

"Oh, don't worry, I'm not asking you to pay them."

"Why not?"

"Because I'd rather deprive myself than go through the humiliation of asking you for anything. But Dr. Wolfe says that she'll never shake off this cough unless I can get her out of the city for the summer. She needs sun and sea air, he says."

"Good idea."

"I've thought that myself all along. And now that the doctor says so I feel it's the only thing to do. So I've been asking around and I've just heard about a nice quiet cottage on the Cape that I can get from now until Labor Day. Only they must have an answer by Thursday."

"It sounds like just the thing," he said, knowing very well what would come next.

"Yes, it's ideal. But, of course, I couldn't possibly swing a thing like that alone. They're asking fifteen hundred dollars for it."

"Fifteen hundred dollars! Why, I can get you Buckingham Palace for seven-fifty."

"Well, I know it's a lot. But that's the way summer rentals are these days, and there's nothing you can do about it."

"Why pick out the Cape, where they play strictly to the sucker trade? There are lots of places along the Jersey coast—"

"Yes, that's typical of you," she complained. "Westchester and Long Island—that's for you. But I'm supposed to bury myself alive in some little hovel in Jersey."

"Maybe you could find a big hovel, with a ballroom and a wine cellar."

84

"If I'm going to have the care and responsibility of nursing Doris, I'm not going off to some God-forsaken place where I don't know a soul. Besides, I have a chance of getting some summer stock work on the Cape."

"Christ, are they that hard up for actors?"

"That's right! Go ahead and insult me. I could think of a few things to say too, but, thank God, I'm not built that way. Only I'd just like to know what you do with all the money you're making."

"That's easy. I give it to you."

"Ha, ha!" said Isabel bitterly. "You seem to have plenty of money to go around buying theaters with, but when it comes to the health of your own child that's another matter. What do you care if she grows up and has weak lungs all her life? Well, since that's your attitude I'll meet you halfway. If you'll pay a thousand toward the rent, I'll pay the other five hundred. God knows where I'm going to dig it up, but I'll sacrifice anything to get that poor baby into the sun."

Her exaggerations and distortions infuriated Thompson. He longed to do her physical violence. Experience had taught him the uselessness of argument. Once she had launched upon one of these campaigns, peace could be bought only at the price of capitulation. So, after a few more recriminations on both sides, he ended the conversation by saying he would think it over and let her know later in the day. But he knew, now, and so did she, that he would give her what she asked.

He could have refused, for he was under no legal obligation to pay her anything but her alimony, and he did not believe that she needed the money or that Doris's health was nearly as bad as she had made it out to be. Yet, though he seldom saw the child now, and got little satisfaction when he did, he could not altogether shake off his sense of responsibility.

In the taxi on his way to his luncheon appointment, he cursed Isabel, for the ten thousandth time, and himself, for ever having got involved with her. He had met her during the rehearsal of a play in which he was stage manager and she a minor member of the cast. At that time he had been about twenty-five and Isabel Saunders twenty. A diminutive creature, not much more than five feet tall, she had a ripe, womanly body, large liquid eyes, and a plaintive, appealing voice. Thompson, attracted to her, began at once to employ the whirlwind tactics at which he was already expert. But this time he did not win his usual easy victory. Isabel, though flattered by his attentions, was too shrewd to surrender for anything less than marriage. She was one of that multitude of untalented, stage-struck girls who by sheer persistence manage to worm their way into the theater; she knew that she would never get very far by her own efforts. On the other hand, no one could doubt that Thompson had great gifts and the prospect of a bright future. So, for Isabel, he represented not only economic security but a means of rapid self-advancement. Hence she held her ground until he, his appetite whetted by the unaccustomed resistance, recklessly agreed to marry her.

He regretted the step almost as soon as he had taken it. She was humorless, dull, whining, and demanding. He found her charms to be no more enduring than those of any of his previous infatuations. Only this time he was bound by the ties of marriage, and before long by those of paternity. The birth of Doris drew him and Isabel together again for a time; but nothing could hold them, and after four or five years they were living in a state of almost open enmity. Their quarrels grew more frequent and more violent. Thompson paraded his infidelities, in the hope of goading her into divorcing him. But she felt that she had nothing to gain by divorce. He was well on the road to success, and though he no longer did anything to advance her career as an actress, her position as the wife of a prominent figure in the theater gave her a certain importance she would not have had as a divorcee. As for him, his married status had its advantages too; it made it possible for him to pursue his amorous inclinations without fear of complications.

Then, on a visit to Hollywood, he met Louise Henry and, for the first time in his life, had fallen in love. She was a vivid, spirited, beautiful young actress, who, after a brief stage career, was making a great success in films. He felt that at last he had met a woman with whom he wanted to spend the rest of his life, and she reciprocated his feelings. He flew back to New York to ask, plead, beg for a divorce. Though by this time the marriage had become intolerable even to Isabel, she once again made skillful use of her bargaining power. By prolonged refusal of his agonized importunities, she drove him to the point of agreeing to give her anything she demanded. What she finally wrung from him was complete custody of Doris (now seven), alimony in the amount of one thousand dollars monthly, and a cash settlement of fifty thousand dollars. Successful

86

though he was, Thompson had no such resources available. He had to make most of the settlement in the form of promissory notes, secured by a lien on his future earnings. But he would have willingly mortgaged himself for life in order to remove the obstacle to his marriage to Louise.

When the financial terms had been agreed upon a new difficulty arose: Isabel was reluctant to spend six weeks in Reno. Thompson, who was preparing a new production, in which Louise Henry was to star, could not afford to be away from New York for so long. After much persuasion Isabel agreed to accept the additional bribe of a winter's expenses for herself and Doris at a fashionable Santa Barbara hotel. She set off for Reno, and Thompson, frantic with joy, telephoned the good news to Louise, who was engaged in the filming of a motion picture. She expected to finish just about the time that the divorce decree would be granted, and it was arranged that they would meet in New York the moment she could get away, get married, fly to Bermuda for a ten-day honeymoon, and then go into rehearsal.

At the end of six weeks that had seemed endless to Thompson, he received word from Reno that he was free. There were the usual delays at the studio; another ten days dragged on before Louise could get away. By now Thompson was in a frenzy of impatience. Then came the long-awaited call from California. Louise was taking an afternoon plane and would be in New York at noon next day. Thompson did not know what to do with the intervening hours. He tried to work but found it impossible. His brother Andrew, a doctor in White Plains, happened to be in town and dined with him. Then he went to see a play, but he could not focus his attention on the stage and left at the end of the first act. Remembering that a picture Louise had made several years earlier was being shown at a neighborhood theater in Washington Heights, he taxied there, and feasted his eyes upon the few scenes in which she appeared. When he got back to his hotel he could not stay in bed and sat up reading until he dozed off. At eight he was awakened by the telephone. It was Louise, joyfully saying good morning from the Chicago airport.

He picked up his car at the garage and got to La Guardia Airport an hour before the plane was due. It had left Chicago on schedule and was expected to arrive on time. But it did not arrive on time. Repeated questions brought only the same response: the plane had

87

left Chicago on schedule and there had been no report since. At last an airline official appeared and reluctantly told the little group of anxious friends and relatives that the plane had developed engine trouble in the mountains near Stroudsburg, Pennsylvania, and had presumably crashed.

Thompson never clearly knew how he got out of the airport. Nor did he have much memory of his breakneck drive to Stroudsburg. When he arrived there it was late afternoon. The wreck had been located and a searching party had gone out to bring back the bodies. No one had survived. He waited leadenly, for six hours more, until the hearses arrived. The bodies were laid out in an undertaking establishment, for identification. Thompson was drawn there by an insane impulse. No recognition of those charred and mutilated lumps of flesh was possible, but on what had been a hand there gleamed the emerald ring with which he had pledged himself to his beloved. He uttered an animal scream and fainted.

He was taken to the Stroudsburg Hospital, and as soon as it was safe to remove him his brother took him to his home in White Plains. He remained there for months, under constant supervision, for he had several times attempted suicide. At last he was able to return to normal life, but not to his normal activities. The play had been abandoned, his office was closed, and he drifted about aimlessly, drinking hard, sleeping little, and struggling against the gnawing consciousness of his inner emptiness. He came out of it slowly though, and when he did find the courage to undertake the production of another play it turned out well. It was now four years since Louise's death, and he had gone on from one success to another. He took satisfaction in the knowledge that he had not gone to pieces as many another man might have. He had survived the crucifixion of his emotions as he had overcome the handicap of his blemished face. He was successful in his profession and successful with women. But the inner emptiness was still there, and the sleepless nights when he could not exorcise the image of Louise; and the days, like today, when the hateful, wheedling voice of Isabel brought back all those memories.

He was lunching at the Arlington Hotel, which was much frequented by theatrical people. Anthony Weir and Claire had not yet come in. Always annoyed at being kept waiting, he moved restlessly from table to table, greeting acquaintances, aware of the many actors who were focusing their attention upon him in hope of a nod of recognition. When Weir entered the dining-room Thompson pretended not to see him. The lawyer, waving and smiling right and left, came over briskly and took his arm. "Hello, Tommy," he said.

"Oh, there you are!" said Thompson with feigned surprise.

"Sorry to be late. But Claire phoned just as I was leaving the office. She's been held up somewhere and says she'll join us later. So we may as well get started."

As they seated themselves at the table reserved for them Thompson's glazed eyes took in the tall, dapper figure of the lawyer, so neat in his double-breasted jacket and wing collar, and he disliked him more than ever.

"Will you have a little drink?" asked Weir, unconsciously wetting his lips.

A drink was the last thing Thompson wanted, after his alcoholic weekend, but unwilling to pass up the opportunity to torture his companion he ordered a Scotch old-fashioned.

"And for you, Mr. Weir?" asked the waiter.

"Bring me a little dry sherry. No. I think I'll just have tomato juice."

They gave their lunch order too; then, after a few commonplaces, Weir plunged into the business that had brought them together.

"Well," he said, "we've got the details of the Farow Theater deal pretty well worked out. We're taking title through a corporation, of course, so that there'll be no personal liability on Claire's part. The bank and the Home understand that, so they're not selling under any false assumption. We're incorporating in Delaware because the tax situation is more favorable there. Oh, and in case you're interested, we're calling it the Auclaire Theater Corporation."

"Why not Eclair?" asked Thompson, bored with all these legal details.

Weir laughed loudly but mirthlessly. "Well, we never thought of that. Of course, it's just an ordinary business corporation, but I've made the powers broad enough to permit almost any kind of theatrical activity. There'll be no preferred stock and just the one class of common. Claire will hold eighty-five per cent of it, and she's insisted that I take the other fifteen."

"That makes practically a hundred per cent," said Thompson, almost speechless with anger.

The lawyer pretended to be completely oblivious to the rage that vibrated in Thompson's voice. "She wanted me to have twenty, and

I said ten, so finally we split the difference. Of course, that's in compensation for legal services, for which I'm making no charge, and for general business advice, which, in view of my experience in this game, will be a little helpful." He laughed again. "At least I hope so. I'm quite willing to take the gamble, and if it doesn't pan out you'll never hear a kick out of me. As a matter of fact, if this were ten years ago, I'd be glad to do it for nothing, just to help things along. But the way things have gone up, I tell you a feller is lucky if he comes out even on December thirty-first. And, of course, I'm not getting any younger either. Not that I know so many who are," he added with another hearty laugh.

Thompson did not join in the laugh. He had not even been listening, for it took all his self-control to keep from lashing out at the cold-blooded man of business. As always when he held himself back, the wine-colored blotch took on a purplish hue. At last he managed to bring out a variant of a well-worn dramatic cliché. "I can't imagine why you're telling me all this," he said.

The parody was lost on Weir. "Well, I just wanted to give you the complete picture. After all, you're in this thing too."

"Am I?" asked Thompson with mock innocence.

"Yes, I'm coming to that. The actual management of the corporation will be in the hands of the directors and officers. There'll be three directors: Claire, you, and I. And we'll be the officers too. Claire will be president; you'll be vice-president; and the feller who does all the dirty work, the secretary and treasurer—well, that's where I come in."

Thompson whistled. "Jiminy, vice-president! The goal of every red-blooded American boy. That calls for another drink." He beckoned to the waiter. "Sure you won't join me in this one?"

"No, thank you. I know it all sounds pretty formal," Weir went on. "Especially to a layman, who isn't used to thinking in legal terms. From a business point of view it's very desirable to keep the producing end and the theater end completely separate. Under this setup, Leroy Thompson and Company will not be obligated to put its productions into the Farow Theater, and the Auclaire Corporation will not be obligated to book the Thompson productions. But when we get past the legal technicalities and right down to brass tacks, you and Claire are in on both ends and you'll work it out to your mutual advantage. In other words, it's a case of one hand washing the other."

"I get it," said Thompson.

Weir felt that it was time to make an attempt at appeasement. "Of course," he said, "if we should happen to get a couple of hits in there, the theater might pay off very handsomely. In that case, there's no reason why the officers shouldn't be paid substantial salaries, especially since they'd be tax deductible as business expenses. So, if things go well, we might be able as officers to persuade ourselves as directors to cut a nice little melon." He laughed loud and long. "Like that feller in Gilbert and Sullivan's Mikado. You know the one I mean."

"Bill Sikes?" said Thompson.

"No, that's Dickens, isn't it? Well, I can't think of it now. But what I'm getting at is that if we play our cards right, we may all make a dollar out of this thing."

Thompson was not mollified by this belated sop. He was raging inwardly, not only against Weir but against Claire. He understood now her delayed appearance. She did not want to be there when Weir broke the news to him that he was to have no financial or other effective interest in the management of the Farow Theater. Indeed, it came as a complete shock to him. He had expected that she would give him at least a quarter, perhaps a third, of the stock in the theater corporation; or, at any rate, let him buy it at a nominal price. There was really no reason why she should, since the financial risk was entirely hers; but their business and personal relationships were so intimate that he had taken it as a matter of course that she would. He felt sure that she had intended to and that Weir had talked her out of it; but her willingness to be influenced by the lawyer merely aggravated his resentment. Nor did the fact that he was to be one of the three directors of the corporation lessen his disappointment and anger. That seemed to him an empty formality, for Claire and Weir would have the power to outvote him if any real issue arose. If he had followed his impulse, he would have thumbed his nose at them both and refused to have anything to do with the theater corporation. However, his judgment and his sense of humor restrained him from doing anything so childish. He had no right to demand anything, and a membership on the theater directorate was better than nothing; he was confident that in everything that did not concern money he could outmaneuver them both.

"So now," said Weir with a mechanical smile that attempted to be genial, "it's up to you to produce the hits."

"Why mention anything as simple as that?"

"Never heard it called simple before," Weir guffawed. "But I must say you make it look that way, my boy. Oh, that reminds me. Claire gave me that play to read over the weekend—The Cloudy Mirror, is that it?"

"She did?" said Thompson, not thinking it worth while to correct him.

"Of course, your judgment of scripts is better than mine—"

"Oh, I wouldn't go that far!"

"Well, I would. Just as I'm probably a better judge of a brief than you'd be."

"I wouldn't know a brief if I found myself in bed with one."

"No reason why you should. Every man to his trade. But I've been fooling around with the theater a good many years now, and while I can see where the script has got a lot of points, I'm wondering whether the feller who puts down his money at the ticket window won't find it a little strong."

"Well, of course," said Thompson, "I've got a lot of weak scripts on my desk."

"No, I don't mean it that way. And don't think I'm trying to tell you how to run your business. As far as I'm concerned personally, give me Shakespeare and you can have all that song-and-dance stuff. But we've got to recognize the fact that what the average theatergoer wants today is entertainment."

"You've certainly got something there." Thompson rose abruptly as Claire came bustling into the dining-room. "Sorry, but I've got an appointment at the office."

Claire hurried over to the table with simulated breathlessness. "Excuse it, please! Goodness, you're not leaving already, are you, Tommy?"

"I've got someone waiting for me at the office," he said with deliberate implausibility.

"I just couldn't make it any sooner. Gabrielle was supposed to give me a fitting at twelve, but when I got there—"

"Yes, so Tony told me," said Thompson, cutting her off coldly. "Well, see you all soon."

"Are you free for dinner?"

"I thought you were going back to the country."

"I was, but I could phone and—"

"Sorry, but I've got a date."

92

She watched him go and then sat down at the table. "Stormy weather!"

"He's a tough customer," said Weir. "I tried my best to—"

"I knew he'd be furious. I really think, Tony, that I should let him have a piece of the theater."

He leaned forward and put his hand paternally over hers. "My dear, I've known a lot of women in my time, and I think I understand them. They're all inclined to let their emotions run away with them—even the finest and the brainiest. What you do with your private life is nobody's business but your own. But, if you'll excuse my saying so, I think that when it comes to business matters you need a little guidance. And if you'll take the advice of a feller who's only interested in what's best for you, you'll keep the two things strictly separate. Just bear that in mind and, take my word for it, you'll save yourself a lot of headaches."

Claire sighed. "I suppose you're right. All the same—" She broke off as the waiter came over to take her order.

When Thompson got back to his office he made out a check for a thousand dollars to Isabel's order, enclosed it in an envelope with a sarcastic note, and sent it, by messenger, to her apartment. He could not bear the thought of talking to her again. Then he asked his general manager, Murray Fineman, to come in. Fineman was a bald, paunchy man of sixty, who had spent all his life in the theater. He had an incurable ambition to be a producer and again and again had scraped together enough money to make a "shoestring" production. Every one of these ventures had been a complete disaster; after each failure he had had to seek salaried employment either as a company manager, in New York or on the road, or, as at present, in some more important capacity. He had been in general charge of Thompson's business affairs for several years, and the producer relied completely upon him. He was honest and methodical, he knew everything there was to know about theatrical management—and nothing else whatever. Though he had a secure and well-paying job with Thompson, he was still constantly in search of a play to produce and of the means of producing it.

"Hi, Murray," said Thompson, "how's show business?"

"No complaints at the Stuyvesant," said Fineman complacently, as though he were solely responsible for the success of Give Them All My Love. "We damn near went clean last night, all but a few of those lousy side seats that are practically out in the alley. And the rest of the week looks okay. They keep nibbling away, and there's always somebody at the window. Not big, but steady."

"How are the brokers holding up?"

"Pretty good, Tommy. Some of the little fellers send back a few—singles mostly. But the hotels go out on their regulars and come through with quite a nice bunch of orders. Like six pair from the Carlton last night. You haven't got a thing in the world to worry about."

"How's that great man, Slobby Mollison?" asked Thompson.

"He's all right. He's always got some beef or other, but what the hell, I guess he wouldn't figure he was a star if he didn't beef."

"What's griping him now?"

"Oh, his dressing-room. I get that every performance. We've got those big fans in there, but according to him it's ten degrees hotter than hell."

"Boy, how he gets around!"

"You know, I was thinking, Tommy, might not be a bad idea to put a little air-conditioning unit in there. I been looking around, and I can get one on a twenty-five-buck-a-week rental basis. It'll make him happy till he thinks up something else to squawk about, and anyhow, it's a handy thing to have around. What do you say?"

"Sure. Anything to keep the son-of-a-bitch quiet." He knew the discomfort of a stifling dressing-room and its debilitating effect upon a performer. "By the way, how's his breath these days?"

"Well, I got a whiff last night, and to tell you the truth, I think maybe he was hoisting a few over the weekend, if you know what I mean."

"I've got a general idea," said Thompson, running his tongue over the roof of his mouth. "Well, as long as it's just weekends."

"Brother, you said it. It's the last thing I think of, every night before I close my eyes. Say, Tommy, how's the Farow Theater deal coming along?"

Thompson frowned involuntarily. "All right, I guess. I just saw old Tony Blackstone and he seems to have things well in hand."

"Well, I hope you're getting a nice piece of it for yourself."

"How do I rate a piece of it?" asked Thompson, looking at him coldly. "I'm not putting in any dough."

"What of it? Where are they going to get with it if you don't give them the shows?"

"I'll bite," said Thompson curtly.

94

Fineman saw that he did not want to discuss the subject. "You coming around to the Stuyvesant tonight?"

"I may drop in."

"Okay, see you later."

Thompson picked up the telephone. "Get me Irina Lanski." Anthony Weir's objections to Eric's play had dispelled his last doubts about producing it.

VII.

Eric waited anxiously for news of Thompson's intentions. Since he had to leave for work before the arrival of the morning mail, he telephoned his mother each day during lunch hour to ask if there was a letter from Irina Lanski. After work he rushed straight home to see if the afternoon mail had brought the expected letter. Every time the telephone rang he leaped to answer it. He was moody and tense, and, as the days went by, he became more and more silent and abstracted. He could not eat, his fitful sleep was troubled by disturbing dreams. His father's querulous comments provoked him to sharp rejoinders; to avoid an open quarrel he kept out of Kenwood's way as much as possible. Amelia concealed her anxiety and refrained from questioning him. Sylvia, however, was less reticent, reproaching him for his aloofness and taciturnity. When scoldings had no effect, she resorted to tears. Their relationship was growing strained, but Eric did nothing to ease the situation. He made several attempts to begin work on the revisions, but he could not concentrate; as his conviction that Thompson's answer would be unfavorable grew, he lost incentive.

When more than a week had passed he found the suspense unbearable. He decided to call Irina Lanski, preferring an outright negative answer to this harrowing uncertainty. Returning from work with the intention of putting through a call to her, he found a bulky envelope awaiting him. His heart sank, for he assumed that she had sent back his play. He went to his room to avoid his mother's questioning eyes. When he tore open the envelope he found that it contained a number of printed documents and a long letter from the agent. He raced through the letter, but in his excitement all that he could take in was that Thompson wanted to go ahead with the production. Letter in hand, he rushed downstairs and out to the summer kitchen.

"Good news, Ma!" he shouted, waving the letter. "I've got a contract for the production of my play."

"Well, that's wonderful, son!" said Amelia, overjoyed by the change in him and only vaguely understanding the cause of his elation. "I've been so anxious about you lately, I hardly knew what to do. Now I hope you'll be yourself again and eat your food and all."

"Yes, of course I will," said Eric, hardly having heard what she had said. He threw his arms around her and kissed her, then went upstairs again, completely forgetting his usual kitchen duties.

He carefully reread Irina Lanski's letter. She began by saying that, relying on her assurance that Eric would make the required revisions, Thompson had agreed to give him a production contract. She explained that this merely meant that the producer was taking an option on the play; the actual production was contingent upon the changes being made to his satisfaction and upon his being able to find the right actors. She was enclosing a contract which, she said, was the standard form prescribed by a collective agreement between the Dramatists' Guild of the Authors' League of America and the producing managers, for use in all professional New York productions. Upon the signing of the contract by Thompson and Eric and its approval by the Dramatists' Guild, Eric was to receive a payment of one hundred dollars and further monthly payments in the same amount until the play was actually performed in public. These payments were in advance of royalties and were to be deducted from the first royalties earned; but they were not returnable in the event that the play was not produced. He would be required to join the Dramatists' Guild, as an associate member, since the managers were under agreement to produce plays only by Guild members, and she enclosed the necessary application blanks. She pointed out that the contract specified February first as the play's production date, but that this was merely to allow ample time for rewriting, casting, and unforeseeable delays. Actually Thompson wanted to begin rehearsals in mid-September and, after a few weeks' tryout, open in New York early in November. It was therefore, she said in conclusion, of the utmost importance that Eric make the agreed changes quickly, for Thompson would not proceed with his plans until he had a satisfactory script in his hands.

All these conditions and regulations were unfamiliar to Eric. He had to read the letter three times before he fully grasped them. At supper he volubly retailed the contents of the letter to his parents. They understood little of the import of what he was saying, but Amelia was quite content to share his joy without giving too much thought to its cause. Kenwood, who had always been hostile to Eric's literary activities and still clung doggedly to his conviction that all theater people were thieves and scoundrels, was impressed by the fact that someone in New York was willing to pay Eric for something he had written.

After he had helped his mother in the kitchen Eric called Sylvia to tell her the good news. If he had been more tactful and mature he would have prefaced his announcement with an apology for his moody behavior or with some expression of affection. If she had been less possessive and self-absorbed, she would have received it with enthusiasm. All she could think of was that he was more interested in his play than in her; and her grudging and chilly congratulations deflated him and made him feel that she cared nothing about his career. The conversation had only the effect of widening the breach.

Eric read Irina Lanski's letter again, then studied the enclosures. The production contract, besides specifying the dates, advance payments, and royalty terms, also provided for the manager's participation in the play's earnings in England and other foreign countries, and in the revenue from motion picture, radio, amateur, and a dozen other rights (even including grand opera), to which Eric had never given a thought. Also, there were numerous inexplicable references to various articles, sections, and subdivisions of a "minimum basic agreement." Eric found a copy of this among the papers and began to read it, but soon gave up the attempt. It was a closely printed document of fifty pages, and he could barely understand the nature of the subject matter, much less its meaning or its relation to his play. His writing had been prompted solely by a creative impulse,

97

a need for self-expression. He had vaguely hoped that someday he would be able to make a living as a writer; but it had never occurred to him that the sale of a play involved more than a simple monetary transaction, that it was governed by an intricate set of regulations dealing meticulously with the most minute details of production and exploitation and attempting to make provision for every conceivable contingency. The typed playscript that had been merely the overt manifestation of his emotions and imagination took on the aspect of a substantial commercial commodity over which managers and authors bargained, motion-picture companies waged competition, and arbitration boards knitted their brows. He suddenly saw himself as an important figure whose pen had set in motion an imposing industrial and financial machinery.

Perhaps what impressed him even more was the invitation to join the Dramatists' Guild. He had heard of this organization but had always assumed it to be a select body, composed of the elite—successful writers, like Frederic Haig and a dozen others whose names and plays were known to him. Even if Irina Lanski had thought it necessary to explain to him that "associate" membership in the Guild was open to anyone who cared to apply for it, but that full membership was limited to those dramatists who had actually had plays produced, Eric would still have felt the pride that every craftsman takes in even remote association with the masters of his craft, the emotional satisfaction and sense of security that is derived from a fellowship based upon a common language and common ideals. With this new and exhilarating feeling of "belonging" and with his head spinning from an excess of emotional expenditure, he tumbled into bed and slept soundly for the first time in two weeks.

Thanks to Irina Lanski's insight and experience, he now had the necessary incentive to work on his play. His actual working conditions were excellent, for he had the whole second floor of the house to himself and could shut himself up alone, undisturbed by the telephone or Kenwood's unquenchable radio. His job, however, made sustained writing difficult. He did manage to get in some solid work during the long Fourth of July weekend, but when that was over the factory workday was prolonged until seven and the Saturday half-holiday suspended. He came home tired and had to ply himself with coffee to keep awake. Then, when he did get to bed, his overstimulated brain would not let him relax, and he got up insufficiently rested and faced with another wearisome day at the factory. Sylvia, too, made demands upon his time. She refused to understand why he had to seclude himself and attributed his neglect solely to indifference. To appease her and to satisfy his own sense of responsibility, he had to give up many precious working hours.

The work itself went well enough when he was able to concentrate on it. The numerous cuts and modifications that Thompson had suggested presented no problem. In fact, he discovered other passages that could be improved too. The excision of the courtroom scene proved a simple operation after all. What gave him trouble was the alteration of the character of the girl's father. This involved a modulation of almost every scene; and though he had discovered the psychological block that had prevented him from creating a credible character, he had not altogether succeeded in removing it. So, seizing every available hour, he rewrote and rewrote, and the weeks slipped by.

He was working away one night at the end of July when his mother knocked on his door. Irina Lanski was on the telephone. He hurried downstairs, fearful of bad news. But she was merely calling to inquire how he was getting along.

"Thompson is holding up all his plans," she said, "and he is getting a little impatient."

"Well, I hope to get it all finished this weekend."

"Good. Then I can promise him the script for next week?"

"Oh no, not next week. The whole thing will have to be retyped."

"How long will that take—two or three days?"

"More than that. About two weeks I should think."

"Good God!" she exploded. "Two weeks to type a script! Are you writing it in Chinese?"

"Well, we're working overtime at the factory now," said Eric apologetically. "So I can only work at it evenings and Sundays."

"Can't you get someone else to do it for you?"

"No, I don't think so." Sylvia had always typed his scripts for him, but, in view of the strained relationship he did not feel that he could ask her to spend the hot summer nights at the typewriter. He typed slowly and badly, and a session at his decrepit machine always left him with strained eyes and an aching back. All this he could not explain to Irina Lanski.

"Well, then you'd better send the script to me," she said. "I can have it typed here in forty-eight hours. Two weeks is simply impossible."

"All right, I will," said Eric reluctantly. He had not counted on this additional expense. When his first advance payment had finally arrived, the deductions for typing, for Irina Lanski's commission, the copyright registration fee, and a year's dues in the Dramatists' Guild had reduced the hundred dollars to a little more than forty, and against that had to be charged his trip to New York and other incidental expenses, so that almost nothing was left. This new typist's bill would take a substantial part of the next payment, and there was still no certainty that the play would be produced. In fact, if Thompson was not satisfied with the revisions he could drop the play without even making the second payment. Indeed, when Eric had finished the new version he had the sinking feeling that it would not come up to Thompson's expectations. Fearing the worst, he sent it off to Irina Lanski early the next week.

Another week of anxious waiting dragged by until late one night the Western Union agent called to read him a telegram from Irina Lanski: "Please meet me at Thompson's office tomorrow at four."

This noncommittal message threw Eric into a new turmoil. It gave no clue to Thompson's reaction to the play. Did it mean that he was now satisfied with it and was ready to go ahead, or merely that he wanted to discuss further changes? One thing seemed certain: he had not wholly rejected it; and to that extent the message was reassuring.

What was of more immediate concern to Eric was the problem of going to New York the next day. There was no doubt that he had to go. The peremptory tone of the message made it apparent that it would be inadvisable to seek a postponement. In any case, he did not know where to reach the agent at this hour of the night; as for absenting himself from work, one day was as bad as another. He had a fleeting impulse to call Warren Ainsworth at his home and explain the urgency of the situation, but he knew that he would be met not only with a flat refusal but with a sharp reprimand for his unwarranted intrusion upon the personnel manager's privacy. On the other hand, if he simply took the day off without permission he might very well lose his job, a disastrous prospect indeed. He paced his room, sucking at his pipe, in a torment of indecision. At last it occurred to him that if he could borrow Leon La Pointe's car he would be able to put in a morning's work and by driving fast still get to New York in time for the appointment. He could make up the lost afternoon by working nights. Even so, it was a risk; but he had to take it. He went down to the telephone, routed La Pointe out of bed, and arranged for the loan of the car.

Getting the car, however, was something of a problem, for he had to pick it up at the La Pointe farm before he went to work. He could have asked Amelia to drive him out, but it was not easy for her to get away from the house in the early morning hours. He also wanted to avoid the long explanations and the inevitable wrangle with his father. So he got up at daybreak and walked the six miles to the farm. At the noon-hour he took fifteen minutes to eat his lunch and then set off for New York, without asking permission. To leave, after a refusal, would be to magnify his offense. He preferred to take his chances on squaring himself with Warren Ainsworth next day. As he drove along his uneasiness kindled in him a sense of rebellion against the economic subservience that hampered and thwarted him at every turn. He had no strong political convictions, but his creative spirit cried out in protest against a social order that condemned most men to a monotonous routine of joyless labor and made them stifle their spiritual hungers in order that they might buy bread.

La Pointe's car was relatively new and in first-rate condition. Once out of New Haven, Eric was able to make good time on the express highways. But he had underestimated the delays of New York traffic. When he finally crawled through streets congested by trucks and buses to the vicinity of Thompson's office, he discovered that he could not leave his car at the curb. It took him another twenty minutes to find a parking lot that had room for him. A good half-hour late, he burst breathlessly into the producer's office, where Thompson and Irina Lanski were waiting for him.

"All right, I won't report you to the Dramatists' Guild this time," said Thompson, cutting short Eric's profuse apologies. "Well, I've read your little opera—in fact, I've read it three times—and I think we're getting somewhere."

"I worked hard on it," said Eric, his heart leaping.

"Hard work is the secret of my success too. It still needs a lot of work, I think." Eric managed to check a protest and Thompson went on. "The old man no longer is Dracula's twin, but he still has some speeches that are reminiscent of Hitler's lighter moments. But I've got them marked, as well as a few other sticky places that need fixing up."

Eric groaned inwardly at the prospect of more rewriting, but he listened in attentive silence as Thompson detailed the further changes he wanted made. "But that shouldn't involve more than a few days' work," said the producer in conclusion. "Whatever else has to be done in the way of cuts and this and that, I can handle in rehearsal. So, adding it all up, I think we're close enough to go ahead."

"You're really going to produce it?" said Eric, afraid to believe it.

"Well, I thought that's what we were shooting at. Unless you have some better idea."

"No—what I mean is—well, it's just that I'm glad to hear it," stammered Eric.

"That's my mission in life—to make everybody happy. Well, here's the setup. I'm figuring on starting rehearsals about September fourteenth. I've got three days in New Haven penciled in, beginning October twelfth, and then two weeks in Boston. That would bring us into the Farow here the week of the thirtieth. Of course, that's all subject to casting and acts of God and of the public enemy."

"Why, September fourteenth is only about six weeks off," said Eric, clutching his knees.

Thompson nodded. "That's right. So we'd better get down to a discussion of casting right away."

"Perhaps I should explain to Mr. Kenwood," interposed Irina Lanski, seeing Eric's bewildered look, "that the contract requires the author's approval of the cast."

"Oh, I see," said Eric.

"Before I go signing up a lot of actors I want to be sure that you have no objections to them," said Thompson. "So I'll give you my ideas and you can give me yours."

"Well," said Eric, not detecting the irony, "I haven't seen many plays and I really don't know much about actors."

"Then maybe I'd better tell you—"

"Oh," interrupted Eric. "I did see one actress who I think would be good as Rhoda." Rhoda was the name of the heroine of his play.

"Did you?" asked Thompson with elaborate patience. "Who was that?"

"Well, she was in a U.S.O. company that gave a performance at Camp Wendell when I was there. Her name was Miss Upton—Virginia I think it was."

Thompson laughed. "Ginny Upton! Well, that would certainly

be keeping it right in the family!" Then, seeing Eric's puzzled look, "But I guess you don't keep up with the boudoir chitchat."

"No, I don't."

"It just happens that she's Hugh Mollison's girl. He's packing them in in a little number called Give Them All My Love that I have a hand in."

"Yes, I know that—I mean about Hugh Mollison being in that play. But does that make any difference?"

"No. Makes it quite clubby, in fact. Only I don't see Ginny in that part. She's never played anything but comedy for one thing."

"Yes, I saw her in a comedy," said Eric. "But she seemed to have a—well, I don't know how to describe it—a kind of inner something—"

"I know what he means," said Irina Lanski. "There's a quality there, an esprit. I've felt it myself."

"Well, I think Ginny's a good actress," said Thompson. "But not for this part. Anyhow, I'm shooting higher than that. I'm making a play for Emily Crandall." He turned to Eric. "I suppose you know her work?"

"I've seen her a few times in the movies. And I just wonder—well, I don't know much about acting, of course—but she seems to be shallow and rather cold."

"That's that Hollywood deadpan technique. If anybody moves a muscle the cameramen go on strike. But once I get her face out of that plaster cast and have her moving around the stage, believe you me, I'll get a performance out of her."

"Excuse me for butting in, Tommy," said Irina Lanski. "But don't you think she's a little old for it? It seems to me that much of the pathos of the play comes from the fact that the girl is young, eager, impulsive. And I don't think that's Emily."

"Well, she's past the age of puberty, there's no maybe about that. Between you and me and the gossip columns, she'll never see thirty-five again. But I ran into her at an opening about six months ago, and she looked marvelous. I'm not worried about her being able to look it if we dress her and light her shrewdly. I don't say that she's ideal casting for the part. But we've got a problem with this play." He turned to Eric again. "I suppose you know that this isn't the kind of opus that the big outboard motor and diaper tycoons of Winnetka and Moline are breaking down the doors to see."

"Yes, I do."

"As a matter of fact, I doubt if you'd find another top producer who would take a chance on it, especially the way costs are today."

"I've already told Mr. Kenwood that," said Irina Lanski.

"Well, I like the play and I'm willing to take the gamble. But I feel that we've got to give it everything we can. And to me Emily Crandall spells box-office insurance in a big way. She'd be a ten-week sell-out in Sam Slick of Punkin Crick, and I figure that if we can start off with a bang we may really get this thing rolling."

"Yes, I think perhaps you are right," said the agent.

"I know I'm right." He looked at Eric.

"I don't think my opinion is worth much," said Eric.

"The next thing is to get her signed up. I talked to her last night. She's just finished a picture and doesn't have to do another until next summer if she doesn't want to. And she's interested in doing a play. So I'm flying to the Coast tomorrow with the script and a line of conversation that would sell Lenin's tomb to the Pope. If you'll pardon the expression," he said to Irina Lanski.

"I'm only sorry that I'll be deprived of the pleasure of your company in the next world."

Thompson laughed. "If I can wrap this up I think we're in, and I'm betting that I will. Now, about the other parts. I think I've got them pretty well lined up—the principals anyhow." He read a list of actors whom he had in mind for the various roles. It was merely a formality, since Eric had never heard of any of them and had no suggestions of his own. In fact, he was so dazzled by the imminence of the production he only half heard what Thompson was saying.

"Well, that about covers it," said Thompson, rising. "Get busy on those changes, and I'll let you know when we're ready to shoot."

Eric and Irina Lanski left the office together. "Well," said the agent with a quizzical smile as they stood waiting for the elevator, "I hope you don't think I've made too bad a botch of things."

"Oh no, of course not. I never expected I'd get this far with it," said Eric. "Thank you very much." The occasion called for a far more adequate expression of appreciation, but he could not voice the gratitude he felt. He did ask her to have a drink with him, but she had another engagement and hurried off, promising to keep him informed of developments.

After a hearty supper at a lunch counter Eric started back to Coltertown. He was an experienced driver and handled a car automatically; otherwise he might not have made the return journey in safety, for his thoughts were certainly not on the road. He kept telling himself, over and over, that in three months the play he had written would be performed by a world-famous motion-picture star, under the direction of a brilliant producer, in a historic theater. He tried to visualize himself meeting Emily Crandall and the other actors, watching the rehearsals, going to New Haven and Boston for the tryout, attending the opening performance in New York. He wondered what he would be required to say and do, how he would behave in the unfamiliar surroundings and with unfamiliar people. He was so unprepared for it all that he could not make it assume any semblance of reality. To cushion himself against crushing disappointment, he kept telling himself that a dozen things might yet happen—Thompson might die or change his mind, the right actress might not be obtainable, the play might be abandoned in rehearsal—he had better not count on anything. In this fashion the four hours passed unnoticed, and he was home almost without knowing how he got there.

Next morning he was summoned to Warren Ainsworth's office. The young executive received him with a hostile frown and did not even ask him to sit down. "I understand you didn't show up after lunch yesterday. What was the idea?"

Eric began to explain the urgency of his errand, but Ainsworth cut him off. "Why didn't you ask my permission? I was right here all morning."

"I didn't want to bother you," said Eric lamely.

"You mean you were afraid to, because you damned well knew I'd say no."

It was true, but he did not have to put it so harshly. Eric was an efficient worker; in all his years at the factory he had seldom been absent. He could easily make up the lost time and the output of the factory would in no way be affected. Young Ainsworth knew this, but he was under a compulsion to assert his authority. Ill suited for his post and disliked by the workers, he compensated for his sense of insecurity by an arbitrary display of power and an inflexible enforcement of discipline.

"I'm very sorry," said Eric. "I wouldn't have gone, if it hadn't been absolutely necessary. This play that I've written means a great deal to me and—"

Ainsworth cut him short again. "Look here, Eric, you'd better get this straight. What you do in your spare time is up to you. If you want to write plays or sit on a flagpole, that's your business. But as long as you're working here we expect you to be on the job during business hours. Is that clear?"

"I'm practically up to date," said Eric. "And I'll be all caught up by the end of the week."

It was not easy to stand like a culprit before this arrogant young man of his own age, whose power to control the conditions of other men's lives was vested in him through no effort or talent of his own, but merely through the accident of being his father's son.

"That's not the point," said Ainsworth. "We're carrying a peak load right now, and I'm not going to have people taking time off when they happen to feel like it. It sets a bad example and it's bad for discipline. As a matter of fact, I've a damned good mind to fire you."

Eric felt like saying, "All right, goddam you, I'll be happy if you do." But instead he said, "If you'll just let me—"

"Let me finish, will you?" said Ainsworth sharply. "I'm not going to fire you, because we take a personal interest in our people here, and we don't like to let anybody go." (He was parroting his father.) "Besides, your father was with us a hell of a long time and I know that your folks depend on you. But I just want to warn you that if this happens again I may have to do what I think is best for the morale of the plant. All right, that's all I've got to say." He picked up some papers from his desk and pretended to be absorbed in them.

Thus peremptorily dismissed, Eric left the office smarting under the chastisement. He had wanted to tell Warren Ainsworth what he thought of him, but he could not afford the luxury of self-assertion. Never until now had he been so painfully conscious of his economic bondage. His writing, which had been a means of emotional release for him, now appeared as a means of liberation from his servitude.

VIII.

The day after his talk with Eric, Thompson left for California to see Emily Crandall. The decision to go had important psychological implications for him. Like many successful dramatists, stage directors, and actors, he regarded motion pictures as a childish and inferior form of theatrical entertainment. Though he recognized the potentialities of the medium, he did not believe that they could be realized under the industrialized conditions that prevailed in the Hollywood studios. An independent artisan, accustomed to following his own tastes and judgment, without hindrance or interference, he was repelled by the synthetic assembly-line production methods, the studio politics, the craven concessions to religious, racial, and economic pressure groups, the crass catering to the lowest instincts of a mass audience. On the personal side, he rebelled against submission to the whims and prejudices of the studio executives, most of whom he regarded as ignoramuses. He had directed two or three films that had been quite successful commercially, but he had derived no satisfaction from his work, and for years had brusquely declined all offers.

Hollywood, with its vulgar pretentiousness, its attitudinizing, its hysterical self-satisfaction, and its cultural isolation, he had always disliked. Since Louise Henry's death he had regarded it with utter detestation and had altogether shunned it. It was in Hollywood that he had spent his last happy hours with her—the last happy hours he had known—and it was from Hollywood that she had taken off on her fatal journey; so, with complete irrationality, he associated Hollywood with his tragedy and blamed it for robbing him of the one woman he had loved. He knew that this was nonsense; yet it took all the resolution he could summon to bring himself to the point of returning to the hated place—for the purpose of engaging another actress to star in another production of his. Once he had made the decision, he felt that he had accomplished something important. By winning this victory over his morbid obsession, he had, to some extent, loosened the death grip of the lost girl.

He had never been professionally associated with Emily Crandall but had known her since the days when she had been a rising young actress, well on the way to becoming a stage star. However, the Hollywood offers had been too tempting to resist. For the past ten years she had been a great success on the screen. She had always expressed a desire to appear in a play again, and Thompson himself had tried two or three times to induce her, but her contractual obligations and the incomparably greater financial rewards of Hollywood had kept her from accepting. Now, however, she was in a somewhat precarious situation. Her last two pictures had succeeded only on the strength of her great popularity. The professional gossips, always ready to tear down the idols they had elevated, whispered the suspicion that she might be on the decline. A few more such dubious successes, they hinted, and she would be "through." For swift and dazzling as the ascent to Hollywood stardom may be, it is often matched by a catastrophic descent into the abyss of obscurity. Thompson, sure that the actress was fully aware of this, intended to make use of the argument that by scoring a brilliant success on the stage she would be seen in a new light by the movie moguls and would make a triumphal return to Hollywood. The soundness of this reasoning did not concern him as long as he could convince her; and his telephone conversation with her had made him feel she was ready to be convinced. He boarded the plane, pleased at having outfaced his phobia and confident of the success of his mission.

Meanwhile Eric had to go through another period of waiting, during which he continued to toil away at his script. Writing was an effort now, for he was continually tired and was beginning to feel the strain. Only the nearness of the scheduled production kept him plodding away. The receipt of the second advance payment spurred him on too. Deductions for typing and commissions reduced the payment to sixty-odd dollars, and, on balance, he was not very far ahead financially. However, the mere fact that someone thought well enough of his work to be willing to pay him for it gave him a tremendous psychological boost.

On Friday he went around to Sylvia's for supper, the first time in weeks he had kept his standing engagement. His reception was decidedly chilly. Sylvia was sulky and aloof; her mother scolded him archly for neglecting them; Jethrow, as usual, said little, but his manner lacked its customary friendliness. However, the women thawed perceptibly when Eric mentioned the possibility of Emily Crandall's appearance in his play. The mere prospect threw Lydia into a twitter of ecstasy, already enjoying, in anticipation, the en-hancement of her own social prestige as the mother of the girl in whose boy friend's play the dazzling Emily Crandall might appear. Sylvia was impressed too, suddenly seeing Eric as a dashing young author whose talents enabled him to hobnob with the great. That meant she would be hobnobbing too, and she imagined herself chat-ting intimately with the film star, over a cup of tea or perhaps a cocktail (for undoubtedly a celebrated artist like Emily Crandall would be a little too sophisticated for tea). She did not express her elation, however, partly because Lydia gave no one a chance to express anything, mainly because she was determined to make Eric woo himself back into her good graces.

Eric was not averse to doing so. He felt he owed her an apology for his neglect. He explained the circumstances, assured her that his feelings had not changed, and asked her forgiveness. This she finally granted, but not until she had made him listen to a long recital of harrowed days and tear-stained pillows. She saw every-thing in terms of melodrama, and when at last she threw herself weeping into his arms, it was with a fine cinematic flourish of which Emily Crandall might have been proud. The evening ended as their Friday evenings usually did.

Eric had been moved by her emotionalism, touched, as any man is likely to be, by a woman's unhappy tears. He had let himself be carried away by his desire to soothe and reassure her. Yet, on re-flection, her lamentations seemed excessive. She knew, or should have known, how much his work meant to him; but nothing less than his constant and undivided attention seemed to satisfy her.

It disturbed him too that their reconciliation, if it could be called that, had expressed itself in almost wholly physical terms. Her avidity had always seemed somewhat indelicate to him. His few sexual adventures before the beginning of his intimacy with Sylvia had been prompted by adolescent curiosity or by propinquity and had given him little satisfaction. In fact, he had a distinct feeling of guilt about them. Not only did his devotion to his mother make him idealize all women, but he had a strong puritanical streak in him, and these casual encounters had seemed to him degrading to himself and to womanhood. He had justified his relationship to Sylvia on the ground that it was in effect a marriage, the formalization of which had been merely delayed. He was not conventional, and the form seemed unimportant; it was only the content that mattered. But lately he had begun to have his doubts. If theirs was really a marriage of true minds, why did it not give him the emotional and spiritual satisfaction that should spring from such a marriage? He was too divided, too confused, too immature, to see all this clearly and objectively, yet he knew that he had more hungers than one and that his union with Sylvia did not bring him completion. Still he felt morally bound to her and had no thought of avoiding his obligation. Suddenly it occurred to him that if his play should be a success there would no longer be a reason for putting off their wedding. For a moment he was filled with unaccountable panic. But, he quickly told himself, that was still a very remote contingency indeed, and there was no immediate need for facing its full implications.

A few nights later Irina Lanski called him to say that Thompson had returned from Hollywood with Emily Crandall's signed contract in his pocket. Eric was so overjoyed that he could hardly talk coherently. "Why, that's wonderful," he managed to say at last. "Just wonderful. Then rehearsals will really begin next month?"

"Yes, the fourteenth. It's announced in this morning's papers. I've sent you some clippings. How are you getting along with the revisions?"

"I'm just about finished. I've made most of them right in the script and inserted a few pages here and there. Will that be all right?" Even in his happiness he dreaded another typist's bill.

"Yes, send it right along, so that Thompson can have his rehearsal scripts and parts made. I don't know if he'll want to see you again about the script, but in any case I think you'd better plan to be here a few days before rehearsals begin, to meet the cast and for conferences if he wants them."

"Am I supposed to be in New York for rehearsals?" asked Eric hesitantly.

"Well, my dear, good, young Mr. Eric Kenwood," she exploded. "Don't you want to be here?"

"Why, yes, I guess I do."

"I should rather think so! A young author not to be at the rehearsals of his first play! Have you got something more important to do?"

Eric felt that he was making a fool of himself. "Of course not. Only, you see, I have to arrange to get away."

"Well, in heaven's name, arrange it then! And for the tryout and at least a week after the opening too. Sometimes changes are necessary even then. So you had better plan on a good two months. Hello! Are you there?" she asked irritably.

"Yes, yes, I'm listening!"

"All right, I'll see you in about four weeks then. And be sure to put that script in the mail tomorrow. Perhaps you had better send it special delivery."

"I will. And I want to thank you for everything, Miss Lanski."

"I'll pray for you. And if my influence in those quarters is what I believe it to be, you'll have a hit. A rivederci."

Amelia came out of her bedroom in her faded wrapper. "Is it good news, son?"

"Wonderful, Ma!" He threw his arms around her and kissed her. "Emily Crandall is going to be in my play, and it's going into rehearsal in four weeks."

"I'm very, very happy for you, son," she said, her eyes filling with tears. She seldom went to the movies, but Emily Crandall's fame was known to her. She recognized this as an event of importance.

Since he had learned Thompson's plans Eric had wondered how he could manage to get to New York for rehearsals. Now, with the beginning date only a month off, he had to take decisive action. He wanted to be there, and Irina Lanski's peremptoriness left no doubt in his mind that he must be there. Yet, though it was simple for her to sweep aside all obstacles, it was not so simple for him to ignore the hard economic facts that governed his existence.

The solution that suggested itself most readily was to ask for a two months' leave of absence. It was the very worst time of year to make such a request, and his recent encounters with Warren Ainsworth gave him little hope of a favorable response. After much self-debate he decided to go over the younger man's head and appeal directly to Eliot Ainsworth. It was an irregular procedure, but it seemed to offer the better hope of success. Accordingly, he applied next morning for an appointment. The factory owner had no free time that day, but his secretary told Eric she could arrange it for eleven the following morning.

During his lunch hour he was amazed to receive a visit from his friend James Duncan, who was in general charge of editing the news of the Coltertown Evening Standard. Duncan, having seen the announcement of Eric's play in the New York newspapers, came around to the factory, accompanied by a photographer, to get a picture and a news story for the next day's edition. Surrounded by a knot of fascinated fellow-workers, Eric self-consciously answered Duncan's questions and posed for the photographer. The news spread quickly through the factory. In the course of the afternoon dozens of people found occasion to pass his desk and ply him with questions about Emily Crandall. Since he had never met the film star and knew far less about her than most of his questioners did, his answers were necessarily brief and disappointing.

A letter from Irina Lanski, enclosing newspaper clippings, awaited him at home. It was evident that the news of his play—or, rather, of Emily Crandall's engagement—was of considerable importance; the theatrical columns carried such headlines as "Emily Crandall to Return to Stage in New Thompson Production," "Emily Crandall Signed for Young Author's First Play." The items, which were accompanied by the star's photograph, recited the essential facts and gave the dates of the tryout and the New York opening. Even though the names of thousands of persons appear in every day's newspapers, there is something about seeing one's own name in print that impresses even the most celebrated; and for Eric, of course, this prominent reference to himself in the great metropolitan journals was a dazzling experience. He read the clippings three times before showing them to his parents. Amelia read them slowly aloud, her eyes shining with pride, and Kenwood, to assure himself that she was not making it up, focused his failing vision upon the paragraphs, his cud rotating in his jaws.

Promptly at eleven next morning Eric was admitted to Eliot Ainsworth's office. The factory owner was busy, but it was a point of pride with him always to find time to attend to the personal problems of his employees.

"Sit down, Eric," he said affably. "How's your father these days?"

"He's in pretty bad shape. And Doctor Oxman says there's no

hope that he'll ever get any better. In fact, he thinks it's only a question of time before he'll be completely paralyzed."

Ainsworth shook his head gravely. "Too bad. It's really a very tragic case. He was one of the most dependable men we've ever had here, and I'd have sworn he was good for another twenty years. Now he's just a burden to everyone, and to himself too, I'm afraid."

"Yes, it's pretty hard for an active man like him to find himself getting more and more helpless."

Though Ainsworth felt a certain amount of sympathy for the cripple, he had the moral conviction that Kenwood was wholly to blame for his misfortunes and that what had been visited upon him was no more than the just punishment for his own misdeeds. At the time it had become apparent that Kenwood would have to give up his job, Ainsworth had been confronted with the problem of making some financial provision for him. Kenwood was far below the age at which the Ainsworth employees were eligible for retirement upon a pension, but his long years of faithful service entitled him to special consideration. If his incapacitation had been due to a paralytic stroke or an automobile accident, Ainsworth would have provided him with a liberal allowance. Since, however, it had been the result of what his employer regarded as a highly reprehensible moral lapse, he had granted him only fifty dollars a month. That the burden resulting from this act of moral justice had to be borne by Amelia and her children did not influence Ainsworth, a devout man, brought up in the belief that the sins of the fathers shall be visited upon the children and that the suffering of the innocent is a regrettable but inevitable concomitant of the punishment of the guilty.

"And how's that fine good mother of yours?" he asked.

"She's very well. Only it's quite a strain, being tied down to my father, the way she is."

"It must be indeed," said Ainsworth sympathetically. "She's a remarkable woman. And her father before her was a great old fellow too. I don't know whether you know it, but he was a teacher of mine in grade school."

"Yes, so Ma told me. Well, Mr. Ainsworth, I know how busy you are and I don't want to take up too much of your time."

"Well, you know how it is, with the Christmas rush on."

"Yes, sir, I do, and I'm sorry to bother you, but I have something very important to ask of you—important to me, that is."

"Go right ahead, and if it's within reason, we'll do what we can." He assumed that Eric wanted an increase in wages and decided to make a noncommittal response, so that the raise would be more impressive if he did finally give it.

Eric braced himself for the unusual request. "I'd like to have two months' leave of absence, sir." He hurried on, before Ainsworth could protest. "I've written a play that's going to be produced soon and it's absolutely necessary for me to be in New York during rehearsals. You might be interested in these." He fished in his pocket for the clippings.

Ainsworth put on his glasses to read the items. "Well, that's very interesting—very interesting indeed! I had no idea we had a literary genius right here in our midst."

Actually he had heard talk of Eric's play and the possibility of its production. Since Eric had mentioned Emily Crandall to the Jethrows, Lydia had been busily spreading the news around. Though the Ainsworths were hardly in her social circle, news traveled quickly in Coltertown.

"I don't think I'm exactly a genius," said Eric. "But this play means a great deal to me, and if you could give me the leave I'd greatly appreciate it. I know it's a lot to ask, but I don't think it will upset things here. Steve Cruger, who's been working with me for over a year, understands the job and I could go over the whole thing with him before I'd have to leave."

"What about your family? Isn't your help needed at home?"

"Financially, yes. I'd have to go on with that. But if you could just continue my pay, I'd make it up, of course. If I happen to make any money out of the play I could pay it back pretty quickly. Otherwise, you could deduct five or ten dollars a week from my paycheck."

"Yes, I see." Ainsworth ran his hand reflectively over his chin. "It's a bad time of year to let anybody off. But, of course, the circumstances are unusual and I see what this means to you."

"Thank you, sir," said Eric hopefully.

The next moment his heart sank as Ainsworth said, "Have you discussed this with Warren?" His personal interest in Eric's family and his understanding of how important the production was to Eric inclined him to grant the request, particularly since he knew that Eric's job in the stockroom could be done by any fairly intelligent, reliable clerk. But he was a disciplined man and a great believer in conformity to established routines. Properly, Eric's request should have been addressed to the personnel manager, and Ainsworth felt that he should not sanction this departure from procedure. Also, there was a delicate question of family relationship involved. He knew Warren was insecure in his job, very much on the defensive, and quick to resent an infringement upon his authority.

"No, I haven't," said Eric.

"Well, this is really in his department, you know."

"Yes, I know it is," said Eric. "But frankly, Mr. Ainsworth, I thought I'd find you more sympathetic. I'm afraid Warren doesn't like me very much."

"Oh, I'm sure you're just imagining that! It's just his manner, that's all." He laughed. "Hasn't quite got over the Army yet. I was the same at his age. Men are a lot like whisky—takes time to mellow them. So you go talk it over with Warren and I'm sure he'll do whatever is within reason."

Though pleased by Eric's recognition of his own superior humaneness, he could not acquiesce in an employee's criticism of his own son. He often remonstrated with Warren for his tactless treatment of the workers and was reasonably sure that Eric was right in fearing that his request would be denied. But, here again, the moral considerations outweighed the human ones. It was more important that an employee should be kept in his place and Warren's prestige maintained than that he should follow his impulse and grant a favor that would cost him nothing and yet was of vital concern to the petitioner.

Eric rose. "Well, I'm sorry I took so much of your time."

"Not a bit, Eric, not a bit. You're one of our big family here. Whenever there's anything you want to talk over, why, just come right in. Good luck to your play. And maybe someday you'll introduce me to that lovely Miss Crandall. She's one of Mrs. Ainsworth's favorites."

Eric knew that he had lost, but he felt he had to go through with the formality of making his request to Warren Ainsworth. He stopped at Warren's office and was given an appointment for three o'clock. When he went to lunch he found himself the center of a flurry of excitement. The Evening Standard appeared at noon, and copies of it were passing from hand to hand. On the front page were photographs of Emily Crandall and of himself and a three-column headline: "Emily Crandall to Star on Broadway in Play by Eric Kenwood." The news story was largely a rewrite of what had appeared in the New York papers, together with brief accounts of Emily Crandall's scintillating career and Eric's inconspicuous one. All through the lunch hour Eric was surrounded by hand-shakers and backslappers, who congratulated him, wished him luck, or hinted facetiously at his intrigues with famous movie stars.

At three o'clock he went to see Warren Ainsworth and renewed the request for a leave of absence. Warren had seen the Evening Standard and had been irked by the prominent display of Eric's name and likeness. He would have been delighted to become ac-quainted with Emily Crandall; yet a privilege that was denied him was freely accorded to this underling. Moreover, he was furious at Eric for having gone over his head. At lunch his father had men-tioned Eric's request with a recommendation that it be granted—enough in itself to make Warren refuse. So he met Eric with an abrupt no, not even giving him an opportunity to present his case.

Prepared though Eric was for this refusal, it was not easy for him to take the only remaining course of action. The surrender of his job might well have disastrous consequences for himself and his family. He had had to face that fact ever since it became apparent that Luke Kenwood's active years were over. All through high school Eric had planned to work his way through Yale, hoping at the end of two years of undergraduate work to enter the uni-versity's School of the Theater. It was heartbreaking to give that up, but his sense of family obligation outweighed all other considerations.

He had had no trouble in getting a job at the Ainsworth factory. When he was called up on the first draft he was rejected as physi-cally unfit for military service because of his defective vision. Eliot Ainsworth, who was chairman of the draft board, was well ac-quainted with the economics of the Kenwood household, and since there was a colorable excuse for Eric's deferment he availed himself of it. Eric was able to continue to work for another two years.

Then he was called before the board again. The need for men being greater now, Eric was certified for limited service. For nearly two years he was shifted from unit to unit and from camp to camp. Twice, accident prevented his being sent overseas. The first time he was hospitalized with pneumonia just as his division was about to leave for an embarkation port. The second time he fell off a high ladder and severely fractured his leg. He was in a plaster cast for three months, and when the cast was removed he still needed care.

By the time he was fit for service again Germany had surrendered and he was given a medical discharge and sent home.

He had been immediately re-employed at the Ainsworth factory. As long as he did his work satisfactorily his job was secure and he was sure of slow but steady advancement. To give up that job was to cut his moorings and set himself adrift upon an uncharted sea. If he walked out of the Ainsworth factory he would effectually be closing every door in Coltertown behind him.

For this pleasant, bustling little New England community, with its wide elm-shaded streets, its town meeting, its old steepled churches, its modern high school, its small but well-stocked library, had many of the aspects of a feudal society. Almost the whole economic life of the town centered in half a dozen small factories that produced cheap toys: tin dancing men and boxers, tiny automobiles made of bright plastics, rattles, rubber balls with bells inside, skipping ropes, yo-yos, miniature china dolls.

Several of these factories had been in operation for a century or more and all were owned and controlled by four old Coltertown families: the Ainsworths, the Grahams, the McBanes, and the Manchesters. These clans, multiply and intricately interrelated, constituted an oligarchy that effectively dominated the economic, social, and political life of the community. Not only were the factories in their hands, but one or another of the families owned the town's one modern hotel, its only bank, its only newspaper, its small department store, and two of its three automobile agencies. They packed the school board, the hospital board, and the library board; they administered the Community Chest and had majorities in the vestries of the Congregational, Presbyterian, and Unitarian churches. They had sent many legislators and one lieutenant-governor to the state capital and had had several representatives in Congress; and their private domain, the country club, was the unofficial seat of local government.

So numerous and comprehensive were their enterprises that there was hardly a household in Coltertown that did not depend upon them for its subsistence. Aware of the power they wielded and of the responsibilities that it imposed, they looked upon themselves as the ordained—perhaps divinely ordained—guardians and mentors of their dependents. They constantly referred to the community as "one big family" (sometimes "happy" was thrown in, for good measure), and they vigorously discharged what they conceived to be

117

their parental duties and obligations, meting out rewards and punishments with even-handed firmness. Though they demanded no formal oath of fealty, they made it clear that they expected unswerving "loyalty" from those for whom they provided. They prided themselves on their ability and determination to "take care" of their "people" without "outside interference." In effect, this meant that labor unions were taboo. The few attempts that had been made to organize the factory workers had been unsuccessful, partly because of the strength of the employers' opposition, mainly because so many of the employees were women, who filled the years between school and marriage with a job and had no interest in the organization of labor. The owners had set up sick benefits and retirement pensions, making it clear that they were actuated by benevolence, not by obligation. In short, the employers ran their businesses as they saw fit. Those who did not like it were free to find employment elsewhere—or, at any rate, to look for it.

That was Eric's dilemma. Warren Ainsworth's enmity precluded the possibility of re-employment at the Ainsworth factory, if his play should fail. Further, a few words dropped here and there about his infractions of discipline, his unreasonable requests, his "quitting" at the busiest season of the year, above all, his "disloyalty" to the Ainsworths, after all they had "done for him and his family," would make it almost impossible for him to find other employment in Coltertown. True, Coltertown was not the only place in the world, but the chances of his finding a job elsewhere that would pay him enough to enable him to live away from home and still provide for his parents were slim indeed. Besides, how would his mother manage without him?

In giving up his job he was staking everything on the chance of his play being enough of a success to relieve him from immediate economic pressure. This was a crisis, a turning point in his life. The circumstances were more favorable than they might ever be again. If he did not avail himself of this opportunity, another might never present itself. He could not have taken the gamble if he had not had some slender resources: a painfully accumulated savings account amounting to about seven hundred dollars. He counted on this to see him through at least until his play opened. He intended to go on giving his mother the accustomed forty dollars a week and, by the exercise of the strictest economy, to live in New York on another thirty-five or forty. The further advance payments from Thompson would help a little too. At best, it was a slender margin, and it was far from improbable that at the end of two months he would find himself penniless, jobless, and with no prospects.

When he got home he found his mother in a state of elation. She had read the Evening Standard story with pride and joy. All afternoon people had been calling up to offer congratulations and ask questions. Even Kenwood shared the excitement. The newspaper had mentioned his name and had referred to him as "an old Coltertown resident." It was the first time in years that any public notice had been taken of him, and he swelled with vicarious importance.

After supper Eric had a long, intimate talk with his mother. He explained the necessity of his attending the rehearsals and the tryout, described his fruitless interviews with the two Ainsworths, and told her of his intention to give up his job. Though she tried to conceal it, Eric could see how much this news disquieted her.

"I hope you don't think I'm making a mistake, Ma," he said.

"Not if it's what you think is the right thing for you to do, son. You're the only one who has any right to decide that. Goodness!" she exclaimed, "I wonder what makes that Warren Ainsworth so mean. He's had just everything, that boy—money, a good home, a good education. Sometimes it just seems to me that the more people have themselves, the less they want others to have. I can't understand it."

"I guess he was sore at me for going to his father. Maybe I made a mistake, but I thought I'd have a better chance with the old man."

"Well, I'd have thought so too. I don't understand what's got into Eliot either. He was always one to pride himself on doing things for people. Do you think maybe if I went to see him? After all, we've known each other since we were children. And your father worked faithfully for the Ainsworths for a good twenty years, until things went wrong."

"No, Ma, I don't want you to go asking favors of the Ainsworths."

"Oh, don't worry about that part of it. If there's one thing I haven't got in me, it's one little smitch of false pride. Anyhow, I don't see where it's any favor. It's no more than what's right and fair, and I wouldn't mind telling him so."

"It wouldn't do a bit of good," said Eric. "He would have said yes in the first place if he'd wanted to. And now he wouldn't want it to be known around the factory that he'd overruled Warren."

"Well, I think that's mighty small, and I don't respect him for it. But I guess maybe you're right."

"I just hope you don't think I'm being selfish about this whole thing."

"Selfish!" echoed Amelia. "Why, my heavens, you haven't got a selfish bone in your whole body. I'd like to know where you'd find any other boy that's given up all you have, just to take care of his father and mother. And don't think there hasn't been many a night when I've laid awake thinking and worrying about it."

"I really haven't given up anything much."

"Oh, don't tell me, son! I know it all too well. I know what it meant to you, giving up going to college. And all the years you've been working away at the factory. You weren't cut out for factory work, and I know how miserable you've been there, just hanging on to your job because we needed the help."

"That's nothing to what you've had to give up. You've had to sacrifice your whole life."

"No, I haven't. I don't call that sacrifice, for a wife to do her duty to her husband. You get married for better or worse, and if you're any kind of a person you've got to be prepared to take what comes. I know it's hard for you to realize it, son, but he was a good husband, and a kind one too, until this sickness took him." Her eyes filled with tears. "He's a changed man, Eric, and it's all because of his affliction. It's a terrible thing for a strong, active man to sit day after day in a wheel chair, with his eyesight failing him and hardly able to help himself. I often wonder how I or anybody would take it if they were in his shoes. That's what we must try not to forget when he has his bad days. It's not him, it's the sickness in him."

"Yes, I try not to forget it."

She put her hand on his. "I know you do, son. Don't think I don't know how patient you've been, even though I'm not much for talking about it. It's different with man and wife; and I'm sure he'd do as much for me if things were the other way around. Maybe that's not the modern idea of marriage, but it's the way I was raised. But it shouldn't have to be that way with children. Young people should go their own way in life and not be tied down to the old. That's why I want you should always do what's best for yourself."

"If things work out the way I hope, this will be best for all of us," said Eric.

"Of course it will. So let's just hope and pray. And if it doesn't, why, I guess we'll all get along somehow. We always have. I guess if I had to I could still go back to schoolteaching."

"You certainly could not!" said Eric indignantly. "You know very well I wouldn't let you do any such thing. I can always find some kind of a job if I have to." He was not convinced of that and said it merely to reassure her.

"Certainly you can. So don't you worry about anything, except just doing what's best for yourself." She put her arms around him and kissed him. "And God bless you in everything you do. You're the finest son any mother could hope for, and you deserve only what's good."

"Thanks, Ma," said Eric. Always inarticulate, he could not find the words to express the love that filled his heart.

To avoid another unpleasant encounter with Warren Ainsworth, Eric wrote him a note, telling him he intended to give up his job at the end of the month. By that time, he pointed out, his assistant would be sufficiently trained to take over without impairment of the factory's operation. He left the note with Warren's secretary and went on to his work, a little frightened now that he had taken this bold step, but nevertheless elated at having set foot firmly upon the adventurous path he had chosen to follow.

Later in the morning he was a little startled to see Warren Ainsworth stride into the stockroom and come bearing down upon him, his face red with anger. In his hand he held Eric's note.

"What's the idea of all this letter-writing?" he said without preamble. "If you've got something to say, why don't you have the guts to come in and say it?"

"I didn't want to bother you again," said Eric, struggling to keep his temper.

"You mean you're not man enough to tell me to my face that you're quitting, isn't that it?"

"No, it isn't. And I don't think you have any right to say I'm quitting. I asked you for a leave and you wouldn't give it to me. So there was nothing left for me to do but resign."

"Oh, so that's how it is," said Warren. "Well, let me give you this straight: I'm not accepting any resignations, understand?" He tore up the note and threw the pieces on Eric's desk. "You're fired. And that means you're through at the end of this week."

This was an unexpected blow, for it meant the loss of an additional two weeks' pay, which Eric could ill afford. "Do you think that's quite fair?" he said. "It seems to me I'm entitled to some notice. I could have waited until the last week to tell you, but I wanted to give you plenty of time to make a replacement."

Warren knew there was justice in what Eric said, but the knowledge that he was in the wrong merely added to his wrath. "You mean you were doing me a favor?" he asked sarcastically. "Well, thanks a million, but I don't want any favors. I'll tell you what's the matter with you. You're getting a little too big for your britches. And we've got no room for that kind around here." He started to go, then turned back and said, "And another thing—we've got no use around here for quitters. So don't bother about ever asking to be taken back on again."

"Don't worry, I won't!" said Eric to Warren's departing back. Fuming with rage, he wished that he had had the quickness to think of some fittingly insolent retort. But even in the midst of his anger he welcomed the abrupt termination of his employment, and found pleasure in the prospect of so soon leaving the factory, forever.

When he called for Sylvia that night he found her suffering from one of her cyclic headaches, accompanied as usual by a fit of depression. In these slight indispositions she saw herself as the victim of a special malignity and expected everyone to be impressed by the tragic spectacle. She greeted Eric with a wan smile and an air of patient resignation, and they said little on their way to the motion-picture theater. Nor, once there, did it improve her mood to see that Eric was the center of attention. Several people in the lobby came up to congratulate him, the ticket-seller and the ticket-taker had a smile for him, and as he and Sylvia followed the usher's flashlight down the aisle there was a little ripple of excited interest.

On the way back to Sylvia's home he told her of his plans. Not wanting to go into the details of his quarrel with Warren Ainsworth, he simply said that, failing to get a leave, he was giving up his job at the end of the week. Sylvia heard the news in amazement, almost in consternation.

"My goodness!" she said. "Quitting your job like that! I didn't know you were so rich."

Eric laughed. "I'm hardly what you'd call rich. All I've got in the world is that money in the savings bank, but I'm hoping it will see me through until I make something out of the play."

"Yes, and what if you don't? Where will you be then? It seems to me you ought to have a little more sense of responsibility."

"Maybe I ought. But this is a chance that may never come again, and it means too much to me to pass up. Anyhow," he went on, "I've talked the whole thing over with Ma and she agrees with me."

"Well, of course. She always agrees with everything you say or do. The least you could have done would have been to talk it over with me, before just giving up your job like that."

"Well, I naturally thought you'd want me to do what's best for myself," he said, a little frightened by this evidence of her possessiveness.

"I must say I think you're being very selfish about the whole thing. In the first place I don't see why you have to go there at all. I'm sure that Emily Crandall and Mr. Thompson know how to put on a play without your being there."

"Yes, of course they do. But I have to be there, in case more changes are necessary. Besides, it's a wonderful chance for me to learn something about the practical side of the theater. It will be a big help to me when I write my next play." He might have added that, above all, he was prompted by the healthy vanity of the artist, who desires, above all things, to see his creation take form.

Sylvia blinked and two large tears rolled slowly down her cheeks. "Yes, that's all very nice for you. But what am I supposed to do—sit here all by myself while you have a good time in New York, running around with a lot of actresses?"

Eric brought the car to a stop in front of the Jethrow house. "I'm not going for a good time. And even if I knew any actresses, I guess they wouldn't want to go running around with me. And it's only for a few weeks, dear."

"I don't call two months a few weeks." The tears were flowing freely now. As always, Eric was deeply distressed by them.

"Well," he said desperately, "I'll write often and call you up once in a while. Maybe I'll even be able to get away for a few days and come home." Then, suddenly brightening, "And, of course, you could come to New Haven for the tryout."

Sylvia wiped her eyes and blew her nose. "Well, we'll see." She opened the door of the car and got out. "Good night."

"Wait a minute," said Eric, sliding out from under the wheel. "Don't you want me to come in with you?" He invariably did.

"No, not tonight. My head is just splitting. All I want to do is just get right to bed and try to sleep it off."

"I certainly hope you do." He tried to kiss her, but she turned away and his lips brushed her cheek.

"Good night," she said. Holding her handkerchief to her mouth, she hurried into the house.

IX.

The announcement that Leroy Thompson had succeeded in signing Emily Crandall for his first production of the new season had caused a great stir in the world of the theater. It was generally regarded as another proof of his managerial shrewdness, and he was well pleased with himself. Claire was pleased too. She had had grave doubts about Eric's play, but with Emily Crandall in it she felt hopeful not only of its success, but of a handsome return on her investment in the Farow Theater. Though, instinctively, she saw in the film star a potential rival, she told herself that, as a business woman, she could not allow such personal considerations to impair her judgment. Besides, there was no telling where Thompson's roving fancy might light; the risk was no greater from Emily than from any girl who happened to be in one of his productions, or, for that matter, happened to walk into his office or meet him at a cocktail party. She could never be sure that he was faithful to her, but in the absence of positive proof to the contrary she preferred to believe he was. What to do, if she found out otherwise, could be decided when it happened.

Anthony Weir, too, was impressed by Thompson's coup. He had even less faith in The Clouded Mirror than Claire had; but he concurred in the Broadway opinion that Emily Crandall was "wonderful box-office" and that a play in which she appeared "couldn't miss." Public reaction to her engagement seemed to confirm that opinion. From the moment the announcement appeared, Thompson's office was kept busy with requests for opening-night tickets, and soon the mail orders began pouring in, though the opening was nearly three months off. By the end of the first week, the accumulation of orders—some of them for as far off as the Christmas holidays—was so great that an extra clerk had to be employed to handle them.

Ticket orders accounted for only part of the hustle in Thompson's office, which for many months had been almost inactive. Tentative budgets, covering every detail of production and operating costs, were prepared and discussed; a publicity campaign for New Haven and Boston, as well as for New York, was mapped out; Thompson spent long hours with Arthur Eckstein, the scenic designer, debating the best method of projecting and changing the play's numerous scenes; a famous couturier was induced to fly to Hollywood to consult Emily Crandall about her costumes (since she was not due in New York until the beginning of rehearsals); "theater-party" agents tried to book entire performances for resale by charitable organizations; advertising men offered "tie-ins" that would publicize the play in return for Emily Crandall's endorsement of some mercantile product.

What really swamped the facilities of the office, however, was the flood of actors in search of employment. Though it was the quietest time of the theatrical year, when presumably most of the performers were vacationing, visiting their distant homes, or playing summer theaters, the mere announcement of Thompson's plans was, as always, the signal for a mass assault upon his office. He had never succeeded in developing a wholly successful defense against this recurring invasion. He did manage, by means of a private entrance, to avoid the clamorous aspirants who crammed the reception room to the point of suffocation and overflowed into the public corridor. A notice, conspicuously posted, informing the applicants that appointments would be made only upon written request, received scant attention; most kept their places in the densely packed throng until they pushed themselves or were pushed to the receptionist's window. Each was armed with what he (or, more often, she) regarded as a valid excuse for being granted the exceptional privilege of seeing Mr. Thompson. Some had, or claimed to have, letters of introduction from the producer's friends or from persons prominent in the social, business, or professional worlds. Others said that they were sent by agents or had been asked to come in. They pleaded, cajoled, threatened, demanded, but without success. In a patient monotone the harassed receptionist reminded them that it was necessary to make written application. Though this mechanical performance of her duty often subjected her to sarcasm and even downright abuse, she never replied in kind. For Thompson, who in his early days in the theater had known the trials of job-hunting, insisted that everyone be received with courtesy. He had, several times, dismissed receptionists who had allowed themselves to be provoked to rudeness. There were too many offices where actors met with insults or thinly veiled contempt, and he prided himself upon his reputation for considerate treatment.

He gave a great deal of thought to the handling of this casting problem. Actually, for a director of his experience, interviewing actors was largely a waste of time. In the eighteen or nineteen years he had been in the theater, he had employed or worked with hundreds of actors and had met or watched the performances of hundreds more. He kept a file of the actors whose work he knew but seldom had to refer to it, for his memory was excellent. With occasional assistance from agents, he could cast almost any play without seeing an unfamiliar applicant. But remembering his own youthful difficulties and aware of the heartbreaking disappointments that await newcomers in the theater, he always tried to offer a little encouragement and even a few opportunities to those who were trying so desperately to break in. Whenever he did a play, he made it a point to employ at least one person who was new to Broadway; and he always spent a few days in interviewing strangers, so that some among the hundreds who stormed the seemingly impenetrable barrier had the satisfaction of passing it and of being able to boast that they had come face to face with the great director.

Once or twice, in his first years as a director, he had tried to see everyone who came to his office. He soon gave that up. For the news spread like a forest fire, and the more he saw, the more came pouring in. By evening when his head was throbbing, the crowd was greater than when the day began. So he hit upon the plan of requiring written applications. That had several advantages. It eliminated a certain number of the lazy, the cynical, and the easily discouraged; it gave him a chance to exercise some selectivity; and it enabled him to space his appointments and relieve the degrading scramble and congestion of his outer office.

The applications poured in. By the scores and the hundreds they came; hand-delivered letters, posted letters, registered letters, special delivery letters, telegrams. They ranged from penciled semi-literate scrawls on grimy postal cards to carefully typed business communications on engraved stationery. They were written in red, green, purple, and white ink on monogrammed and scented paper in pastel shades, on letterheads of hotels, clubs, and the Y.W.C.A., in the bold script of finishing schools and the shaky scratches of old age. They were jaunty, whimsical, pathetic, truculent. Some were embellished by little drawings or jingles; many were supplemented by press notices from obscure newspapers, mimeographed biographies, or the printed cards used by radio registries. Certain phrases occurred over and over: "I am an actor, not a type," "I can play anything that I can look," "An interview will be to our mutual advantage," "I am attractive—or so my friends tell me," "Of course, I haven't done anything on Broadway, but—"

As far as Thompson was concerned, all the thought and effort that had gone into the composition of these letters were wasted. He paid no attention to their form or to their content, for he did not engage actors on the basis of their epistolary skill or their self-estimation. Bad actors often wrote very good letters; but good actors sometimes did too. And modesty was a rare characteristic in actors of any quality. He ignored the letters entirely until the final stage of casting, when only the minor parts were unfilled. The principal and secondary parts were assigned to actors who were known to him, personally or by reputation, or who were recommended by the two or three casting agents in whom he had confidence. Whenever possible, he employed actors who had worked for him in previous productions. By the time he got around to the letters, he selected, more or less at random, a few hundred from among the thousand or fifteen hundred that had come in. Experience had taught him that any two hundred would offer a fair cross-section of the applicants and that not one in ten would have any real qualification for the professional stage.

Actually, actors fell into three fairly well-defined categories. First, there were the stars and the leading players, known to every manager, director, playwright, and critic and to a large part of the theatergoing public. They were the cream, the elite of the profession, who, through sheer talent or sheer personality—often a combination of the two—had risen to the top. Numbering a hundred or a hundred and fifty, at most, they were in constant demand and could not only command high salaries but accept or reject parts, as they chose.

Below them were the hundreds whose names were hardly known outside professional circles but who constituted the solid, expert, dependable body of the acting craft. Year after year they were seen in the important secondary and supporting roles, sometimes understudying and eventually replacing the leading players, or else themselves playing leads in touring companies. Since there were always far more of them than there were parts available, they had to engage in a continuous competitive struggle for employment. Their livelihood depended more upon the unpredictable destinies of the plays they did manage to get into than upon their own efforts, for a fine performance counted for little in a play that ran only a week, whereas the acceptance of a stupid part might mean a two years' engagement. Some were youngsters who were on their way to the top, and some were oldsters who had passed the peak of their popularity; but, for the most part, this group consisted of actors who had never aspired to great eminence or who had given up hope of ever attaining it and were reconciled to a life of relative obscurity and absolute insecurity. For their careers had neither plan nor continuity, and they were constantly beset by uncertainty, frustration, and disappointment. Their comparatively high salaries were delusory, since long periods of unemployment reduced them to an average level that barely ensured decent subsistence; often they had to seek temporary work in other fields. What future they had depended upon the capricious favors of the theatrical producers; and fading beauty, failing memory, or any one of a hundred disabilities could put an end to those favors. Yet, with few exceptions, they clung to their precarious careers, partly because they had not fitted themselves for any other, mostly because they loved the theater with an ardent, inextinguishable passion and no other life had any meaning for them.

At the lowest level were the thousands of desperate aspirants who took part in the fierce, disorderly struggle to "break into the theater"—an aptly graphic phrase, for that was exactly what they tried to do. From every town and hamlet they converged upon New York, determined at any cost to get a foot in the stage door.

They clamored for the attention of influential agents, elbowed their way into managers' reception rooms, and wrote interminable letters in variegated inks upon assorted notepaper. Some brought with them a carefully hoarded little store of money, enough to keep them going for a few months or a year; others had allowances from indulgent families; mostly they had to provide for themselves, until the gates swung open. They worked as models, telephone operators, sales clerks, laboratory assistants, stenographers, truck drivers, bell-boys, doctors' receptionists, ushers, tea-room hostesses, keeping body and soul together, until the lightning struck. Few of them doubted that it would strike, eventually, for each believed himself to be the favored possessor of a special talent or the object of a special providence. Many had taken steps to equip themselves for their chosen career, ranging from attendance at courses in "dramatics" offered by freshwater colleges to disciplined training in some good professional school; and some had had a certain amount of practical experience with amateur companies or summer theaters. But even of these only a few possessed those natural attributes, those intangible qualities of body and mind, without which even the most thorough training is of no avail. And there were many, many others who were without preparation of any sort. Footloose, vain, and undisciplined (or perhaps, if the inner truth could be known, unconsciously seeking compensation for some deep-seated sense of frustration or inferiority) they daydreamed of a brilliant stage career, without troubling to acquire even the rudiments of the exacting craft they hoped to practice. Eventually many of them became discouraged, but there was never a lack of newcomers to fill up the ranks, to clog the wheels of theatrical production, and to increase the difficulties of the true professionals who struggled for a living on the fringes of the theater's labor market.

Yet among all the misguided, the unqualified, and the incompetent, there was always a handful made of the genuine metal. Thompson and the few directors like him, who took their responsibilities to their craft seriously, were always willing to sift through a mountain of slag in the hope of discovering one of these unrefined nuggets. Now and then he did make such discoveries, and many established actors were grateful to him for having been the first to recognize their abilities.

So postal cards went out to two hundred letter-writers, and he prepared himself to spend several days in tedious and preponderantly fruitless interviews. Only six or seven small parts remained open, and some of these were combined with understudies and assistant stage managerships. The chances of any of the favored two hundred was about one in thirty—even less for the female applicants, who always outnumbered the male by at least two to one.

Thompson approached these interviews with mixed feelings of pleasure and distaste. Seated behind his large, flat-topped desk, with the imposing skyline at his back, he was a towering and awesome figure to the trembling novices. He enjoyed his power to impress them and, if he chose, to give a nod that might alter the course of some young person's life. On the other hand, he could never wholly overcome his dread of meeting strangers. Most of the visitors knew him by sight or had heard descriptions of his appearance, yet there were few who could check that quick, involuntary look at his blotched face. Each time it happened, he had to make an effort to maintain his impassivity and repress his hatred. The applicants never noticed his agitation; they were too conscious of the importance of the occasion, too intent upon making the most of the few precious moments.

He concealed, too, the satiric delight that he took in observing each successive "entrance." The pattern repeated itself endlessly. The door opened briskly to admit another neophyte, who came striding or flouncing in, with a fixed, grim smile that belied the insouciance it was intended to denote. Yet, amused as he was by his visitors' ineptitude, he felt sorry for them too, and did his best to put them at ease. Everyone was given a friendly greeting, asked to sit down, and allowed a reasonable time for self-exposition. Usually a glance or a few words were sufficient basis for his appraisal. He placed great reliance upon first impressions, believing that an actor whose appearance, bodily grace, and voice did not immediately interest him, who did not "bring something on with him," would not be likely to interest an audience either. If a girl did not know how to walk from the door to his desk, there was no reason to believe that she would know how to walk across a stage; if a youth's voice sounded thin and unresonant in his office, it was not likely to be more effective in an auditorium. In a small part the actor had no time for slow ingratiation: his impact had to be instantaneous. The exceptional cases were too infrequent to affect the general rule, and, almost always, he judged by his first impression. But all were given an opportunity to say their say, and as they stumbled or

130

raced through their carefully rehearsed pieces Thompson fixed his eyes upon them in simulated attention, his thoughts elsewhere. If they happened to be pretty young girls, he sometimes relieved his boredom by imagining them in other situations: the careful coiffure lying in tumbled disorder upon a pillow; the intent eyes roving in wild excitement; the neatly painted mouth loose with passion; the glistening tinted fingernails clutching at his shoulderblades.

One day, in the midst of all this tiresome interviewing, he was surprised to receive a telephone call from Florence Fulham. There was something she wanted to see him about. He asked her to come in late in the afternoon when the day's deadly routine was over. He awaited her arrival with great interest and curiosity. It was more than ten years since he had seen her; he wondered what she looked like and what she wanted.

When the receptionist announced her he had her shown in at once and left his desk to greet her. He put his arms around her and kissed her warmly, quickly taking in her appearance. She looked wonderful. She had hardly changed since the days she had been the favorite of the public—and of Oscar Farow. It was evident that she had taken care of herself. Thompson guessed that she was past fifty, but she had kept her youthful figure, her skin looked young and fresh, and her graying hair was skillfully dyed. He offered her a cigarette, and they spent a few minutes exchanging friendly compliments. He said graceful things about her looks and she commented on his successful career, which she had followed with great interest.

"I thought you were living in Arizona," he said.

"I was, until a few weeks ago. You know, when the Old Man died, I decided to retire. I'd been with him for so many years that somehow I couldn't see myself working for anybody else. And then along came Jack Whaley, an old beau of mine from way, way back, and asked me to marry him, and before I knew it I said yes."

Thompson nodded. "I heard about that."

"Yes, I never thought I'd marry, but it turned out very well. Jack had to live in Arizona on account of his asthma, and I had a very happy seven years out there, just being a wife and playing contract and catching up on my reading. Then, last spring, Jack passed away, poor darling." Tears filled her eyes and she paused for a moment. "So, I was on my own again, and then—don't laugh—suddenly, the itch to put on grease paint got hold of me. So I asked

131

the nice man at the railroad station to sell me a ticket to New York, please, and—well, here I am!"

Thompson was genuinely amazed. "You're going back on the stage?"

"If anybody will have me."

"Why, that's the biggest piece of news I've heard since the Johnstown flood."

"I hope it won't be quite as disastrous as that," she said. "Anyhow, a little bird whispered that there's a part that might be right for me in a play that old pixie of a stage manager, Leroy Thompson, is producing. So I just took my courage in my two hands and dialed the number." The little bird was her old friend Irina Lanski, who had urged her, under a pledge of secrecy, to call Thompson.

He knitted his brows. "Well, Flossie darling, I don't need to tell you that I'd rather have you in the play than anybody I can think of. But there's nothing in this one—well, with the possible exception of one part."

"One part is all I was hoping for. I always hated doubling."

"But this is the part of a mother—in fact, Emily Crandall's mother."

"Well, I suppose I could be Emily Crandall's mother."

"Not north of the Mason and Dixon line."

She smiled. "That's sweet of you, Tommy. But mothers have changed since Whistler's day. Is it a good part?"

"Not bad. Except that she dies halfway through the play—and offstage, at that."

"Wonderful! That means I can get to bed early. I got out of the habit of late hours in Arizona."

"I'm stuck with a contract that gives Crandall sole star billing. And by the time I pay her, there's only peanuts left. I had to fight to hang on to my gold fillings."

"Goodness, do you make everybody beg so hard for a job?"

"Now, you know damned well I don't mean it that way!" he protested.

"I know you don't, Tommy," she said soothingly. "You're being very charming and considerate about the whole thing. But let's be sensible about it. I don't expect to walk in after all these years and be handed a star part. I know how quickly the public forgets and how little it matters what you did ten years ago."

"Now, wait a minute!"

"No, it's true, and you know it just as well as I do. Anyhow, I don't mind telling you I'm a little scared and not too sure that I can handle *any* part. So a little one will suit me very well for a beginning. And then working with you—that would really give me the confidence I need. I don't seem to know many of the people who are producing these days, and I'm sure that none of them ever heard of me. I understand that you're going into the Farow too."

"Yes. Remember the time I put on an imitation of the Old Man and he came right back with an imitation of me?"

She laughed, but her eyes were moist again. "Indeed I do! And very sweet of him it was not to fire you. You really were a bad boy! And here I am, putting my life into your hands. Oh, about the money part of it. I've asked Wilbur Reeper to represent me, and anything you two agree on is all right with me. Would it be possible to read the play or is that going too far?" She had already read a copy that Irina Lanski had lent her and had decided that she wanted to play the part, but she thought it wise to make at least a show of indecision.

Thompson picked up a script from the desk. "Can you read it overnight?"

"Certainly. What better would I have to do? It's a long, long time since I've read a part for anybody, but I'd do it for you if you asked me nicely."

"Don't be silly!" he said impulsively. "If you want the part it's yours."

"Thank you, kind Mr. Thompson," she said, hugging the script in both her arms. "I'll take very, very good care of this. And may I phone you in the morning?"

"If you could. I've got three women up for the part, and I was going to decide tomorrow. We go into rehearsal next week."

"Oh, dear," said Florence, distressed. "I never thought of that! I'll be taking a job away from somebody who's probably got her heart set on it. Maybe I shouldn't." She held the script out to him.

"Look, Flossie, I can put up with anything but Christianity."

"Oh, is that so? Well, don't think I haven't heard about all the nice things you're always doing for people." She blew him a kiss. "I'll phone you bright and early. Yes, I know, not too early!"

Thompson, who had been exhausted by his arduous day, felt revived and elated. Florence Fulham, charming and gracious as ever, had set in motion a warm flood of happy memories and associations.

And her parting reference to his reputation for kindness and generosity had made him swell with pride. Most of all, though, he was excited at the prospect of having her in the cast of The Clouded Mirror. The actresses he had been considering for the part were all as well qualified to play it as was Florence; she had never been a great actress, and her success had been due to Oscar Farow's skillful management of her career. That was undoubtedly why she wanted to make her reappearance under the guidance of a director who was not only brilliant in his own right but had had his training under the Old Man. Thompson was flattered by this tribute to his skill; and from his point of view the return of the former star, under his management, in a cast that already could boast of Emily Crandall —and at the Farow Theater besides!—was a piece of superb showmanship, redolent of that plushy sentiment that theater-worshipers adore.

When Florence called him next morning to say she wanted to play the part, he was overjoyed and sent at once for his business manager.

"Murray," he said casually, watching for the effect of his announcement, "I've engaged Florence Fulham for the part of the mother."

Fineman's astonishment came up to his employer's expectations. "Florence Fulham! Since when is she back in circulation?"

"I'm putting her back. How do you like the idea?"

"Well, Florence Fulham! That's still quite a name. And, say, come to think of it, in the Farow Theater too. Boy!"

Thompson nodded happily. "Is good, yes?"

"How does she look?" asked Fineman.

"She looks marvelous. Too good almost. That's the only thing that worries me. We'll have to iron all the wrinkles out of Emily or they'll never believe that Flossie is her mother."

"How come she's willing to play a bit like that?"

"Salesmanship, my boy, salesmanship."

"You've sure got it," said Fineman admiringly.

"Listen, Murray, call up Wilbur Reeper right away and get the terms settled. Try to get her for five hundred, but go to six, if you have to."

Fineman whistled. "Five hundred for that part! We've got it budgeted for two fifty."

134

"Listen, do you know what the Old Man paid her?"

"Yeah, but not with Emily Crandall in the same cast. Anyhow, he was sleeping with her."

"Well, give me time," said Thompson. "At that, you could do a damn sight worse. Look, Murray, save it on something else."

"Like what?"

"How the hell should I know? Use less paper clips or something. For Christ's sake, let me live, will you? This is the fancy lettering on the cake, that extra red satin bow on the Christmas package. What am I around here anyhow, a showman or a goddam certified public accountant?"

Fineman shrugged his shoulders. "You're the boss," he said calmly. "What about her billing? Olmsted's got it in his contract that nobody's name except Crandall's comes ahead of his."

Thompson looked worried for a minute. "I never thought of that. Well, you'll just have to work it out with Reeper. What the hell am I paying you for?"

"That's something I've never been able to figure out. You never listen to anything I say. Oh, has Tony Weir said anything to you about the booking contract?"

"No. What's the hurry about that? We're not opening for nearly two months."

"Well, I guess so. I'd just like to know what the terms are, so I can work out my operating budget," said Fineman.

"All right, I'll call Tony today. Get busy with Reeper right away, will you?"

"Okay. Only don't sign up any more stars till I show you a few figures."

Before Thompson got around to the distasteful task of calling Anthony Weir, the attorney called him. "Hello, my boy," he said. "How are things shaping up?"

"Everything seems to be under control," said Thompson. Though he had known Weir for years, the lawyer's unctuous familiarity always annoyed him.

"That's great. All set with your cast?"

"Practically."

"Well, there's a young lady sitting here in my office, Miss Suzanne Merchant. She's had quite a little stage experience, and I'm wondering if you could give her a minute of your time."

135

Thompson swore softly to himself before answering. "I'm pretty much set. And I've got a whole officeful of people waiting to see me."

"I'll bet you have! She's tried three or four times to see you, but she tells me it's like trying to break into the White House." His loud, mirthless laugh blasted Thompson's ear. "So she's appealed to me to use my influence. I told her I didn't know if I had any, but I'd spend a nickel to find out."

Much as Thompson would have liked to refuse this pointed request, he knew that to do so would be sheer rudeness. "All right, send her around," he said, "and I'll see what I can do."

"Well, I appreciate that, Tommy. She understands, of course, that it's all subject to her being right for something. Just a chance to get into the sanctum sanctorum and tell you about herself is all that she wants. Shall I give her a note or anything?"

"No, just have her come around," said Thompson, finding it hard to conceal his impatience.

"Her name is Merchant, Suzanne Merchant."

"Yes, I've got it. Oh, while you're on the phone, Murray Fineman asked me to talk to you about the booking contract."

"I haven't forgotten it. Only I've been pretty busy. I'm planning to go off on a little vacation, at the end of the week. I've got to get out of town to get away from the people who are after me for opening-night seats." His guffaw made Thompson wince.

"It's just that Murray wants to get together with you on the terms."

"Well, I guess Murray and I won't get into any fist fight about the terms." Thompson held the receiver away from his ear to escape the blast of laughter. "Tell him to come in tomorrow morning. But I may not have the actual contracts ready until I get back."

Thompson hung up and addressed a string of obscenities to the telephone instrument. Ten minutes later the receptionist announced the arrival of Suzanne Merchant. She had evidently come over straight from Weir's office. Thompson deliberately kept her sitting in the crowded outer office for over an hour. When she finally came in he was pleased to see how tense and jumpy she was. The moment he saw her, any remote doubt that he might have had about the nature of Weir's interest in her vanished. He remembered having seen them together several times in restaurants and at opening nights. He recalled, too, that he had seen her once or twice on the

136

stage. She was one of those bit players who had just enough stage presence to give a passable performance in a small part and who had no prospect of advancing beyond that. She was a dark, full-bosomed girl, pretty and vivid, but in a rather obvious way and without any real character in her face or personality. She dressed and made up with so much care that the effect was marred by the beholder's consciousness of the means by which it was achieved.

"It's awfully nice of you to see me, Mr. Thompson," she said with attempted nonchalance. "We did meet once at Pinelli's, but I'd hardly expect you to remember that."

"I remember it very well," lied Thompson.

"I hope you don't mind my asking Mr. Weir to call you. I've been trying to get in for two weeks, but so has every other actor in New York. And it just happens that I know Mr. Weir through going to high school with his secretary, so I thought—"

"Yes, Helen is a nice girl," said Thompson impassively.

"Isn't she a peach? And from the way he depends upon her, I guess he'd just be lost without her. Well, I don't want to take up your time. I was just hoping that there might be something—of course, it wouldn't have to be anything big."

Thompson repressed a satiric retort. "Well, there's nothing big left, I'm afraid."

"Yes, that's what I mean. Just anything to get a chance to work under your direction and show you what I can do. I've had quite a bit of experience, though nothing really important so far." She rattled off the usual trivial details. "If I could just read something for you. I always think that's better than talking about yourself."

"Well, I don't know," said Thompson. He was about to dismiss her with the customary noncommittal expression of interest, but it occurred to him that it would be more politic to refuse her on the basis of a reading than on a perfunctory interview. He picked up a script and leafed through it. "All right, take a crack at this scene," he said, handing her the script.

The girl gulped in fright. "Just cold like that?"

"If you want to take it outside and look it over for a few minutes—"

"No, I think I'll just plunge in, if that's all right with you."

"Whatever way you want to do it. I'll cue you."

It was a short scene and she read it competently enough. "That sounds fine," he said.

"I hope it's something like what you want. Maybe I *should* have looked it over first."

"No, it was all right. Just give me a few days, will you? I've had three or four girls read the part and a couple more are coming in. I'd like to just think about it."

"Oh, of course!" She rose and extended her hand, beaming upon him. "Thanks ever so. Shall I drop back in a day or two?"

"No, I'll let you know. Just leave your number with the girl outside."

"All rightee. I'll just say my prayers and keep my fingers crossed." She flashed another smile at him and walked with studied ease to the door. As she opened it she turned for another quick look at him, but he was already telling the receptionist to send the next applicant in.

Thompson did not like the girl and liked even less having her forced upon him by Weir. However, in view of his close business association with the lawyer, it seemed foolish to offend him needlessly by ignoring a request that could easily be granted. The part was small and unimportant; it did not matter much who played it. He had intended to give it to one of several young girls who had never played in New York but in whom he saw signs of talent. One in particular, Lily Prengle, seemed very promising. But Suzanne Merchant would do, and by engaging her he would be giving himself a trading point with Weir if he ever needed one. Fineman was always scolding him for his indifference to such practical considerations. Here, for once, he could easily subordinate his temperament to his business judgment. In fact, he might very well have done so if Claire had not introduced the subject at dinner.

"Oh, by the way, Tommy," she said, "there's some young actress that Tony talked to me about—some friend of Helen's, I believe— Suzanne something-or-other—"

"Yes, he sent her in to see me."

"Oh, did he? What's she like?"

"She's a dark dish, with floating udders."

"Can you use her for anything? Tony says she has quite a lot of talent."

"I'm sure she has," said Thompson. "But it's not the kind you're allowed to exhibit in public."

Claire was a little shocked. "You mean she's somebody Tony is going around with?"

"I've never heard it described that way before."

"So that's why he was so intent about it! Well, well, you never know, do you?"

"With Tony, I'd think you'd always know."

"Still, if you *could* use her. Some bit or something—that part of the little neighbor—Aggie, isn't it?"

"She read it for me."

"Not good?"

"Stinko!"

"Well, in that case, of course—! I just thought if you could do Tony a favor, without it hurting the play—"

"When I need a couch for casting, I'll have it in my own office, not in Tony's."

Weir's high-pressure methods infuriated him. He could have put up with the lawyer's direct appeal to him, but not with his use of Claire as an intermediary. No business consideration could make him tolerate such attempted dictation. He ruled out Suzanne Merchant, regardless of any possible consequence.

"Well, you know best," said Claire.

He leaned across the table and patted her cheek. "Spoken like a marine!"

X.

When Eric went to get his final paycheck the cashier told him he had been instructed to give him an extra week's wages, in lieu of notice. It was not the practice of the Ainsworths to discharge old employees without notice, and though Warren's anger had not cooled, he thought it best to conform to the established custom. Eric, who had been worried about losing two weeks' pay, was glad to get even half of it. He used the money to buy a cheap suit and a pair of shoes, for his wardrobe was lamentably scanty and he felt the need of making a decent appearance.

The two weeks that still remained were interminable. Except for the period of his hospitalization and for a few brief vacations, he had worked steadily since he was eighteen, either at the factory or in Army camps. Unaccustomed to idleness, he did not know what to do with himself. He puttered fitfully about the house, helping his mother and busying himself clumsily with long-neglected minor repairs.

He was under constant tension too, for the atmosphere at home was not pleasant. Kenwood had been outraged by Eric's resignation from the factory, or as he regarded it, his dismissal. For an able-bodied man to be content to be idle, with no other prospect than the hypothetical earnings of something he had written, seemed to him shocking evidence of shiftlessness and irresponsibility, and he persisted in telling Eric so. Eric took refuge in silence. Whenever he felt his temper going he left the house to avoid a quarrel. Amelia too, with her industrious nature and her traditional morality, was troubled to see a healthy young man hanging about the house during working hours, even though she sympathized wholeheartedly with his aspirations.

The La Pointes also strongly disapproved. A good hard day's work was Leon's measure of life. Dorothy, though she had a better understanding of Eric's aims, regarded his pursuit of them as sheer self-indulgence. So, after two strained and uncomfortable visits to the La Pointe farm, Eric stayed away. Nor did he enjoy the curious stares of the townsfolk. His brief fame had been erased by his almost incredible behavior at the factory. After all, Emily Crandall was only a shadow on a screen, the Ainsworths were the staff of life. Unhappily conscious of universal condemnation, he waited impatiently for the moment of his departure.

Most of the remaining evenings he spent with Sylvia. Her petulance had given way to sad-eyed wistfulness, and on the last night she clung to him tearfully, as though he were going off on some dark expedition from which he might never return.

"Good-by, lover," she said. "Your baby's going to be awfully, awfully lonesome." She burst into convulsive sobs. "Oh, God, I don't know how I'm going to stand it!"

Eric fondled her and tried to comfort her, promising to write often and to call up now and then. After a final long embrace he walked slowly home, much shaken, and telling himself that she was really a sweet, lovable girl.

Rehearsals were to begin on Thursday, but Thompson had suggested that he come in Monday to meet the members of the cast. To give himself time to find a place to live, he left home Sunday.

For several days he had hardly exchanged a word with Kenwood, but when it was time for him to leave, the sight of his father, sitting helpless in his wheel chair, impelled him to make the parting a friendly one. "Well, I've got to go along, Pop," he said, putting a hand on Kenwood's shoulder. "Wish me luck, will you?"

Touched by the unaccustomed gesture of affection, perhaps seeing himself, in a flash of recollection, setting out to seek a career, Kenwood put his hand over Eric's. "Well, sure I do, boy. And I hope that Jew-woman and that snowbird don't take you for a buggy ride."

Eric had long ago given up the attempt to convince his father that Irina Lanski was not a malignant Jewess nor Thompson a drug addict, so he merely said, "Don't worry about that! And take care of yourself."

He picked up his battered cowhide suitcase, into which he had crammed most of his belongings. Amelia went out to the road with him. "That was nice of you, son, to make it up with your father like that."

When the bus came along he took her in his arms and kissed her tenderly. "Don't worry about anything, Ma."

"I won't, son. And I just hope everything turns out the way you want it."

He swung the valise onto the bus and stood at the door, waving to her until she was out of sight.

He intended to find a hotel near Times Square, feeling it would be an advantage to be within easy walking distance of the Farow Theater and of the offices of his agent and his producer. With this in view, he carefully studied a street plan of the theatrical district. When he arrived at the midtown bus terminal, early in the afternoon, he had a sandwich and a cup of coffee, then, valise in hand, set out to find a lodging, wondering how many other eager young men were, at that very moment, following the same pattern.

However, his sense of adventure gave way to weariness and anxiety, as he trudged up and down, block after block, constantly shifting the heavy valise from hand to hand. There was no lack of hotels in the long, dingy streets east and west of Broadway, but some had no vacancies, others were prohibitively high, still others were so grimy and ill smelling that Eric, accustomed to cleanliness, could not stomach them.

After two hours of fruitless search, he found a place in a hotel near Madison Square Garden: a tiny, dark room, with a narrow window opening upon an inner court. The bed, chest of drawers, and sagging armchair filled it almost completely; the rug was worn threadbare, the wallpaper was faded and discolored. But it had a miniature bathroom and was moderately neat. It cost three dollars a day, which was more than he wanted to pay, for he had limited himself to a daily expenditure of five dollars, but he had seen nothing better and he was already a good half-mile from both the theater and Thompson's office. He unpacked and arranged his belongings, far from happy at the prospect of spending a month in this cheerless cubicle, so unlike his pleasant airy room at home.

He had supper in a crowded, untidy cafeteria on Broadway; then, feeling restless, set out to walk. But he did not enjoy shuffling along in the dense, jostling Sunday night crowds. Returning to his room, he spent several hours writing long, affectionate letters to his mother and to Sylvia: it was always easier for him to write what he felt than to say it. He covered page after page, until weariness drove him to bed. The stuffiness of the room, the uproar in the court, and his own state of excitement kept him awake until almost daybreak.

Used to early rising, he awoke at seven and went out to breakfast. Then, not knowing what to do with himself, he walked around to the Public Library. Finding it was not yet open, he bought a newspaper and sat on a bench in Bryant Park. At ten o'clock he went to Irina Lanski's office. He had nothing to see her about, but it gave him something to do. Myra Leech was typing away, busily, in the outer office.

"Oh, hello, Mr. Kenwood," she said, glancing up.

"Is Miss Lanski in?"

"No," said Myra, her fingers flying over the clattering keys. "She's gone to Baltimore for a tryout. I don't expect her back till Wednesday. Anything I can do for you?"

"No," said Eric. "I just wanted to say hello."

"She'll be in Wednesday." The telephone rang, and she swiveled in her chair to answer it.

"Well, I guess I'll run along," said Eric as she finished her telephone conversation and swiveled back to the typewriter. "Good-by."

"Good-by, Mr. Kenwood," said Myra, pulling the completed page out of the typewriter and inserting a fresh one.

Disconsolately he left the office. His appointment with Thompson was nearly five hours off. He wandered aimlessly up Broadway and spent a long time staring vacantly at the shiny new cars in the display windows of Automobile Row. At Columbus Circle the Park offered a welcome escape from the noisy, dirty streets. He strolled slowly along the leafy paths, among the strutting pigeons and the uniformed nursemaids, clustered in gossiping groups or scolding their high-strung small charges. Then, tired from dragging his feet for so long, he went to the zoo cafeteria and carried his tray to a small table on the terrace. It was pleasant, sitting there in the sun, watching the grunting seals as they darted through the sparkling waters or flapped about clumsily on the concrete. He was surprised at the snatches of German, French, and languages wholly unintelligible that reached him from the other tables. He did not know that this was a gathering place of European refugees, to whom New York offered little opportunity for a continuance of the agreeable Continental practice of outdoor eating.

After lunch he strolled down Fifth Avenue, staring at the sumptuous shop windows and at the passers-by, so smartly dressed, so brisk, so seemingly self-assured. He wondered if he could ever feel at ease in this glittering world; seeing no likelihood of it, he found consolation in telling himself that he would never want to.

Though he was still ahead of time, Thompson did not keep him waiting long.

"Hello, Eric," he said, shaking hands warmly. "Glad to see you. You look as though you were prepared for the worst."

"That's not the way I feel," said Eric, delighted by Thompson's friendliness. "This is the moment I've been waiting for."

"Well, we'll try not to let you down. Oh, I want you to meet Eugene McCarthy, who's stage-managing the show," said Thompson, introducing a thin, wiry man, with a lumpy nose, protruding ears, and bad teeth beneath a scraggly mustache. "Mack, this is the author of the opera, or so he claims."

McCarthy grinned, seizing Eric's hand in an iron grip. "Glad to know you, Mr. Kenwood," he said in a grating voice.

"Glad to know you, Mr. McCarthy."

"Just make it Mack."

"He has the manners of a baboon," said Thompson, "but beneath his unprepossessing exterior there beats a heart of gold."

McCarthy laughed. "Gold-plated anyhow."

"I'm having the cast come in to pick up their parts and I thought you'd like to look them over," said Thompson.

"Yes, I certainly would," said Eric.

"Did Irina tell you about my scoop in getting Florence Fulham for the mother?"

"No, she didn't. Is she a good actress?"

Thompson looked at him in amazement. "You never heard of Florence Fulham?"

"I don't know much about actors," said Eric apologetically.

"Well, Mack, I guess that dates us all right. Get out the crutches and the upper plates and let's hobble over to Sailors' Snug Harbor." Seeing Eric's embarrassment, he gave him a brief account of Florence Fulham's career. Then, picking up a portfolio, "Here are the sketches of the sets if you'd like to take a look at them."

Eric eagerly examined Arthur Eckstein's wash drawings of the settings. In his script he had described them only briefly, and he was delighted to see how well the designer had caught the mood and atmosphere of the play. "They look wonderful!"

"I threw out the first two lots of sketches. But Eckstein's a hell of a good designer once you get him cut down to size."

McCarthy laughed again. "Wait till he starts bringing the lights in. You'll be lucky if there's room on the stage for the actors."

"I've been to the mat with him on that already. I told him that anything over two carloads is out." He turned to Eric. "This is a goddam tricky production. I want those scene changes to go like that!" He snapped his fingers two or three times. "So I figured the best way to do it is with a jack-knife stage."

Not having any idea what a jack-knife stage was and not wanting to make another display of ignorance, Eric merely nodded.

The actors had now begun to arrive. One by one, they were shown into the office. Always considerate of his actors, Thompson had established the pleasant ceremony of having the members of his casts come in a few days before rehearsals to get their typed parts and to be told the starting hour. Knowing how important morale is in an acting company, he spared no pains to win the confidence and esteem of his players from the outset, greeting them with a friendly smile and facetious but good-humored remarks that made them feel they were being inducted into a select little circle—as indeed they were. In turn, he introduced them to Eric and to McCarthy. Many of them were known to the stage manager, who hailed them with such pleasantries as "Jesus, have I got *you* on my hands again?" "Are you still drawing to inside straights?" "Hello, beautiful. I saw part of your face on my television set Sunday night." Those he did not know he gave a crushing handshake and a crisp "Glad to know you!"

Eric's heart was pounding with excitement and his hands were clammy. Never having met a professional actor, he was so overawed he could do no more than mumble a few words. He envied them their easy manners and apparent self-possession. He was both disappointed and relieved that Emily Crandall, Florence Fulham, and Reginald Olmsted (who was to play his heroine's father) were not expected. The star was still in Hollywood; the two others, as befitted their importance, did not study from parts but from the complete scripts which they already had.

"Well," said Thompson to Eric when the parts had all been distributed, "what do you think of your cast?"

"I think they're all fine."

"Yes, it's a pretty damned good company, if you ask me."

"When did you have one that wasn't?" said McCarthy.

"Don't yes me, McCarthy," said Thompson. But he was pleased by the compliment. He turned to Eric. "And that concludes the afternoon performance. Unless you've got something on your mind."

"No, except that I just can't wait for rehearsals to begin."

"Thursday at twelve at the Farow is the time and place. Know where it is?"

"Yes, I do."

Thompson extended his hand. "Good luck. Oh, as long as you're here, you may as well have a session with my publicity man."

He conducted Eric to a small office occupied by a bald, tubby man, who wore thick-lensed rimless glasses. "This is Nathan Winternitz," said Thompson, "the most unprincipled bastard that ever manhandled a typewriter. Doc, meet Eric Kenwood, author of The Clouded Mirror, a play I intend to produce, as you may have heard."

"I only know what I put in the papers," said Winternitz, shaking hands with Eric. "As to my being a bastard, my mother says she doesn't think so."

Thompson laughed, clapped Eric on the shoulder, and left him with Winternitz. The press agent was a voluble, fidgety man, subject to periodic fits of melancholia. For three years he had been paying frequent visits to a psychoanalyst, so that, in spite of his large salary, he was perpetually in debt. The nickname "Doc," by which he was generally known, was attributable to a youthful study of medicine, with which he had not progressed very far: on his first visit to the dissecting-room he had fainted and had never had the courage to return. He had turned to journalism and then to publicity work, and now was one of the foremost theatrical press agents.

"All right," he said, offering Eric a cigarette. "Suppose we start from scratch." Then with anxious deference, "Unless you'd rather start somewhere else."

"No," said Eric, laughing. "I guess scratch is as good a place as any."

"Good! Then scratch it is." He questioned Eric in considerable detail about his parentage, education, and military career, making notes on a large yellow pad.

"Hm," he mused, looking at the notes. "What have we got to sell here? No years behind the plow. No garrets. No beachheads. You were never a newsboy?"

"No."

"No. And of course you're not President either. So that's out. I'm looking for an angle," he explained.

"I'm afraid it's not a very interesting biography," said Eric.

"Don't apologize. Authors are always difficult. They don't have jewels that are worth stealing, their legs are usually hairy and knobby, which is no good for the slicks, and their sex life is of such a complex and esoteric nature that it is comprehensible only to bearded brigands with Viennese accents." He looked up with bright eagerness. "You haven't been laying anybody who would rate an editorial in the New Republic?"

"No," said Eric, "but my father once pitched for the Boston Red Sox."

"Well, why the hell don't you say so? Now we're getting somewhere."

"He was only with them a year. And I think he only pitched two or three games."

Winternitz shook his head reproachfully. "Don't be a defeatist,

146

Eric. As I see this thing taking shape in my mind, he won the World Series practically singlehanded. Southpaw?"

"Yes."

"This is getting better and better. And, of course, you write your plays with your left hand."

Eric grinned. "And with a left-handed fountain pen."

"Facetiousness will never get you anywhere. And another thing, don't come around here with any slavish New England worship of veracity. I spit upon such narrow, Congregational bigotry. Factual accuracy is all very well for the small-souled and the earthbound—statisticians, physicists, and suchlike cattle. But we poets—and I include you in that category as well as myself—should eschew such mundane grubbing. If Shakespeare chooses to present Brutus with a grandfather clock and Keats prefers to have Cortez discover the Pacific, who are Cotton Mather and Einstein to say them nay?"

He called up a photographer and arranged a sitting for Eric. As Eric was leaving he said, "Since you haven't asked me, I don't mind telling you that I like your play. But, nevertheless, I think it may be a success."

Though everybody had been so free and easy, Eric sensed that Thompson, McCarthy, the actors, even Winternitz, were all, like himself, in a fever of expectancy. After dinner he walked briskly down Fifth Avenue to Washington Square, poked about in the mazes of Greenwich Village, and walked all the way back to his hotel again.

The next two days he busied himself with sightseeing. He visited the Metropolitan Museum of Art and the Museum of Natural History, went by subway to Wall Street and saw Trinity Church, the Sub-Treasury, the Stock Exchange, Washington Market, St. Paul's, and City Hall. He was beginning to get the feel of New York and to be a little less frightened of it. On Wednesday afternoon he went to be photographed. It was the first time he had posed for anything more than a snapshot, and he was impressed by the photographer's complicated equipment and slow, careful workmanship. When he got back to his hotel he found that McCarthy had left a message to the effect that Emily Crandall's departure from Hollywood had been postponed and that rehearsals would not begin until Monday.

Eric, who had been living in a state of mounting excitement, did not see how he could live through another four days of waiting.

For months he had suffered through one period of anxious suspense after another. The strain was becoming unbearable. His temples throbbing and his hands trembling, he threw himself on the bed and almost wept. He was tired of sightseeing, tired of walking the streets, too wrought up to think or to read. He lay there a long time, breathing heavily, suffused again with fear and hatred of the monstrous, swarming, impersonal metropolis, where he had not a single friend or even a casual acquaintance with whom he could while away a few hours. Unable to face another long evening in his dreary little room, he went to the Radio City Music Hall. He watched the inane Hollywood movie and the elaborate stage spectacle without interest, slightly disgusted by the wasteful expenditure of money and talent that had gone into the production of this vast, tasteless emptiness.

In the morning he went around to Irina Lanski's office in search of consolation. Busy with appointments, she took the production delay quite as a matter of course. He spent some time in the drama section of the Public Library, skipping through a volume of plays by Granville Barker and reading a few of Max Beerbohm's dramatic criticisms, then went back to the Metropolitan Museum to study the paintings of the French Impressionists and their successors. He had not had much opportunity to look at paintings, and Cézanne, Van Gogh, Manet, Degas, and Renoir were little more than names to him. After a little while he was pleased to find that he could distinguish the salient characteristics of each painter and that each spoke in his own strong and exhilarating idiom. It was a stirring revelation, opening up a whole new field of aesthetic experience. Next morning he went back to the Museum and spent most of the day there, discovering fresh meanings in the paintings and responding to them with deeper appreciation.

The nights were dreadful. He simply could not sleep; not only because he was lonely and tense, but because of the incessant, nerve-wracking noise. The hotel was inhabited mostly by minor actors, musicians, and night-club entertainers, who spent the hours before work rehearsing and the hours after work in conviviality. The weather was so warm that the windows were never closed, and from them poured a head-splitting cacophony of radios and phonographs, of telephone bells and alarm clocks, of vocalized scales and endlessly repeated songs, of violins, trumpets, saxophones, clarinets, harmonicas, and accordions, of snoring and whistling, of violent altercation and raucous, drunken laughter and loud, screaming demands for silence. It began at noon, reached its climax after midnight, and did not subside until after five in the morning. When, after sleepless hours, Eric's heavy eyelids drooped, he would be startled awake again by the crashing of a bottle on the pavement of the court or the sudden eruption of a lovers' quarrel.

On Saturday he went to the matinee of Give Them All My Love. His narrow budget made no provision for amusements, and he felt guilty about these extra expenditures. But it was years since he had seen a professional performance of a play, and, besides, he felt that he owed it to himself to see a Leroy Thompson production. The Stuyvesant Theater was filled to capacity, mostly with middle-aged women, who greeted Hugh Mollison's first entrance with enthusiastic applause. Throughout the performance his comic antics evoked a continuous murmuring and giggling, often swelling into gusts of delighted laughter. Eric hated the play. Like an earlier play of Frederic Haig's he had seen, it had a thin and conventional plot, tricked out with glib wit, contrived situations, and whimsical sentiment. To Eric it seemed utterly devoid of meaning or integrity, the very antithesis of the nobility, poetry, and spiritual revelation that he regarded as the essential qualities of the great art to which he sought to dedicate himself. Yet once again he had to recognize the author's deft and skillful craftsmanship, the shrewd economy, the sure hand that never allowed the interest to flag, the cunning employment of the tricks of the theater. He saw how far he himself was from such command of his material and wondered if he would ever attain such technical perfection.

He left the theater unsatisfied and full of misgivings. The applause at the end of the performance had been vociferous. On every side he heard the rapturous comments of the twittering women. If this was the sort of thing that the theatergoing public wanted, what hope was there for his own sprawling, brooding, somber play? When he wrote it, he had no thought other than to express himself as honestly and as forcefully as he could. The acting and production were incidental matters to which he had given no consideration, assuming that if the play were good enough it would be well received. Now he saw how heavily he had to depend upon the popularity of Emily Crandall and the directorial skill of Leroy Thompson (of which he had just seen a brilliant example). At any rate, he was lucky that his play had come into such good hands.

On Sunday the occupants of the court slept late, so Eric was able to sleep too. He had intended to take a trip to Coney Island, but it rained hard all day. He called up his mother and then Sylvia. Amelia was happy to hear from him, but she had written him all the trivial items of domestic news so there was not much to talk about. The conversation with Sylvia was brief too. She was in one of her weepy moods and talked about little but her pitiful loneliness, showing slight interest in his activities or state of mind. He dashed to the corner for lunch, returned with two bulky Sunday newspapers, and spent the rest of the day going methodically through the news sections, the drama sections, the book-review sections, the sports sections, the magazine sections, even the comic sections. Then, with time still on his hands, he toiled away at the crossword puzzles, the double-crostic, and the cryptograms. Since the postponement, he had looked fearfully for a message telling of further delay; and he often glanced at the telephone, expecting it to ring. But there was no message, the telephone did not ring, and he went to bed almost persuaded that tomorrow the long-awaited day would dawn at last.

XI.

For Eric the delay had meant only more anxious waiting; for Thompson it had created some serious problems. Under the strict rules of the Actors' Equity Association, the trade union to which every professional actor had to belong, rehearsals were limited to four weeks. During this period the actors received a small weekly sum as rehearsal pay; but on the twenty-ninth day they went on full salary regardless of whether public performances began or not. Every producer tried to keep the rehearsals down to four weeks to avoid the heavy expense of paying the actors when they were not playing to revenue-producing audiences. Since The Clouded Mirror was scheduled to open in New Haven on a Thursday, Thompson had set the beginning of rehearsals for exactly four weeks before the opening date.

Emily Crandall was due from California on Wednesday. Her expected arrival revived Thompson's memories of Louise Henry, and it was not easy for him to bring himself to meet Emily at the airport. However, his presence was a courtesy she would expect and he had to go. Besides, he was influenced by the same hope of exorcising Louise's ghost that had steeled him to make the trip to Hollywood.

On Tuesday night, however, his telephone rang and an unfamiliar voice said, "Hello, Mr. Thompson, this is Doctor Thwaite of Beverly Hills. I'm Miss Emily Crandall's physician and I'm calling you at her request."

"Is anything wrong?" asked Thompson, fearing the worst.

"Well, Miss Crandall is suffering from a severe migraine headache. She's subject to them, especially when she's under nervous tension. It's not serious, but she's in considerable pain and in no condition to fly to New York."

"I'm sorry to hear it," said Thompson. "How soon do you think she'll be able to get here?"

"We're doing everything possible for her, but sometimes these things are a little stubborn. I should think we could get her off by the end of the week."

"Not before then? I've got a pretty rigid rehearsal schedule here. In fact, we're supposed to start on Thursday."

"Yes," said the doctor, "Miss Crandall is well aware of that and asked me to tell you how disturbed she is. She wanted to talk to you herself, but the more quiet we can keep her, the sooner she'll get over this. If you don't mind my suggesting it, I think a reassuring telegram from you would have a good effect. She's very worried about upsetting your plans."

"You don't think she'll get away before about Friday, is that it?" persisted Thompson.

"Friday or Saturday, I should say. An extra day's rest here may make all the difference in the world when she gets to New York. If you want to call me tomorrow, I may be able to be more definite, but I'd count on Friday at the earliest if I were you."

Thompson took his telephone number, asked him to tell Emily

not to worry, and hung up. He was angry and alarmed. Everything had gone along so smoothly, and now, on the eve of rehearsals, this had to happen. Was Emily really ill or was this just a device to make him feel how dependent he was upon her? The doctor sounded convincing enough, but then he might be a friend of hers (or a lover, thought Thompson sardonically) and in league with her; or else, actress that she was, she might be shamming the symptoms of an ailment. Suppose her arrival was delayed further, or suppose she changed her mind and did not show up at all? He had a binding contract and Equity was firm about disciplining its refractory members no matter what their eminence, but an actress's physical fitness to play a part was something about which doctors often disagreed; even if Equity did suspend her, it would not matter much to her, since it would mean only that she was barred from appearing on the stage and would in no way interfere with her screen career.

He threshed about the room, lighting cigarettes and putting them out after a puff or two, helping himself liberally from the brandy bottle. There were three choices to be considered. He could begin on schedule with the other members of the company, working in Emily when she arrived; he could cancel the New Haven performances and spend the time rehearsing, thus giving himself four full weeks before opening in Boston on Monday night; or he could stick to his plans and rehearse only three and a half weeks instead of four.

Each had its disadvantages. Emily appeared in almost every scene, so that he would gain little by beginning without her; besides, his resultant restiveness would communicate itself to the actors, who were always sensitive to a director's moods. The cancellation of the New Haven booking would give him the full rehearsal time but would disrupt his production program. Because the cost of hauling scenery into a New York theater, setting it up, hanging the lights, and then taking everything down and hauling it out again, was prohibitive, it was customary to have the dress rehearsal in the place where the first public performance was given—in this case New Haven. Also, the half-week there would enable him to straighten out any mechanical difficulties—an important consideration with a complicated scenic production—and would give the actors a chance to feel easy in their parts by the time the play opened in Boston. A rough opening in New Haven was not a very serious matter; in Boston it might mean the difference between a bad two weeks' engagement and a very profitable one. So he decided reluctantly to adhere to his booking schedule and to get the play on in three and a half weeks. Emily Crandall, after her long absence from the stage, really needed the full four weeks, but he hoped that by working on Sundays and calling a few extra night rehearsals he could make up the lost time.

On Wednesday he told Winternitz to inform the newspaper drama editors of the postponement of rehearsals (preferring an official explanation to the garbled versions that were bound to appear when the news leaked out) and instructed McCarthy to notify the cast and Eric. He called Claire in the country and spent a half-hour trying to get her to view the situation with a calmness that he himself did not feel. Then he spoke to the dress designer, Louis-Jean Amiel, and told him that he would have to rearrange his schedule of costume fittings. Amiel (always referred to as Louis-Jean) was the internationally known couturier, who, over Murray Fineman's agonized protests, had been sent to Hollywood, at great expense, to confer with Emily, so that the work on her costumes could be begun before her arrival in New York. Thompson was quite prepared for the hysterics with which Amiel received the news. On the verge of tears, the designer insisted that it would be absolutely impossible for him to have the dresses ready in time. Thompson, accustomed to dealing with feminine natures, succeeded, by flattery and cajolery, in getting him to accept the revised schedule.

That evening, after calling Dr. Thwaite and learning that Emily was much better, he watched the performance of Give Them All My Love and went backstage at its conclusion to give the assembled actors notes on their shortcomings. Even Hugh Mollison was not spared the facetiously exaggerated commentary on the errors that had crept into the performance. The actors were grateful for this discipline, for it was impossible for them to maintain their perspective, and they relied upon the producer's vigilance to keep them up to the mark. Mollison accepted Thompson's invitation to go to a bar, but after one drink asked to be excused in order to catch a train to New Canaan, where he lived. Thompson guessed that Virginia Upton was waiting for him somewhere and did not try to detain him. He joined some acquaintances at a neighboring table and sat drinking with them until two o'clock.

Next day Emily Crandall telephoned. She was profuse in her apologies and begged him to forgive her. She was feeling much,

much better and had moved from her house in Mandeville Canyon to her bungalow at Malibu Beach in order to be thoroughly rested for her journey. She was definitely leaving on Saturday, was looking forward eagerly to rehearsals, and was tremendously excited about the whole thing. Thompson, in turn, showered her with compliments and expressed tender solicitude for her well-being. All the while he was talking to her he kept wishing that he were working with someone less dull and wondering if he could succeed in concealing from her how much she bored him.

Claire had come into town and was somewhat reassured by his report, but she could not feel wholly at ease until Emily was safely in New York. Counting upon a success, she had authorized alterations and repairs in the Farow Theater that far exceeded her original plans, and she was getting anxious about her heavy investment. Thompson was outwardly sympathetic, but since she had not seen fit to give him an interest in the theater, he saw no reason why he should worry about her financial problems. He accepted her invitation to stay overnight in her apartment. Like Eric, he was beginning to find the days and nights unbearably long and preferred not to be alone.

The Friday morning papers carried the news that Emily Crandall's husband, Count Pedro Portagas—he was her third—had arrived in Las Vegas and filed a suit for divorce on the ground of mental cruelty. Thompson was highly pleased. This marital disagreement not only explained Emily's nervous tension but assured him that she would be glad to put three thousand miles between herself and the buzz of Hollywood gossip. He was delighted, too, to escape the annoyance of having the Count, whom he regarded as a complete imbecile, hanging about during rehearsals. Evidently, he told himself, mental cruelty had nothing to do with the mind—or, at least, not in Nevada.

In the afternoon he went to Claire's country place, returning to New York Saturday night in order to get to the airport on time Sunday morning. He drove out with Nathan Winternitz, in a rented limousine, intending to take Emily to her Park Avenue hotel. But as they walked across the parking lot to the arrival gate Winternitz pointed out a long cream-colored car with California license plates, bearing only the letters EC. "Little Em'ly's houseboat," he said.

"Sure enough!" said Thompson. "She drove me around in it when I was out there. It cost nine thousand bucks."

"Well, EC come, EC go," said Winternitz.

"I'll murder you!" said Thompson, kicking his shin.

Clustered about the arrival gate was a large group of photographers, newspaper reporters, friends of arriving passengers, and a sprinkling of the idly curious. Prominent among them was Emily's chauffeur, dressed in a maroon livery that matched the upholstery of the car. He recognized Thompson and nodded condescendingly to him.

"How do you always manage to get in with the big brass?" asked Winternitz. He greeted several of the newspapermen and then sought out the photographer he had engaged.

"Hi, Tommy," said a dapper little man in a plaid sports jacket, putting an arm around Thompson's shoulder.

"Hello, Paul," said Thompson not too cordially. Paul Kipner was one of the numerous New York representatives of Emily Crandall's Hollywood agents, Screen Celebrities, Incorporated. The agency had almost succeeded in talking Emily out of signing with Thompson. They got ten per cent of all her earnings; since her stage income could not possibly come up to her screen salary, they considered it bad business for her to forsake Hollywood for Broadway. It had taken all of Thompson's verbal ingenuity and personal charm to induce Emily to disregard the advice of the agency.

"Well, I'm glad we were able to wrangle it so that Emily could do this show for you," said Kipner.

"That's what I like about your outfit," said Thompson. "You're in there pitching every minute."

Kipner, who was not too nimble-witted, glanced quickly at Thompson, suspecting sarcasm, but the producer's face radiated earnestness and sincerity.

The plane was on time, to the minute. As it taxied to a stop and the ground crew wheeled the movable staircase into place, the waiting crowd swarmed out through the gate. The alighting passengers greeted their friends and then, impressed by the battery of cameras, stood waiting for Emily to appear. She delayed her exit from the plane until all the other passengers were out, and emerged, followed by her maid, Nellie Duff, an angular, middle-aged Scotchwoman. As Emily came slowly down the steps Thompson went to greet her, but he was swept aside in the rush of reporters and photographers. The chauffeur relieved the maid of the small overnight bags, while Emily, carrying a great bunch of long-stemmed roses

155

and an alligator jewel-case with gold mountings, submitted graciously to the questioning of the reporters. They were particularly interested in getting the details of her marital difficulties and asked her, pointedly, whether either she or her husband had formed a new romantic attachment.

"Oh no!" she protested. "There's nothing like that at all. Bo-Bo and I are still the best of friends, and we expect to see a lot of each other. We just agreed to disagree, that's all," she added, rather pleased with herself for having hit upon this happy phrase.

When the reporters had finished, the photographers went to work. First they had her inhale the scent of the flowers, with an expression of simulated ecstasy; then the bouquet was handed over to the maid, and Emily was photographed warmly grasping the hand of the pilot, a war hero, who had been detained on the field for this purpose. Then she was directed to ascend the steps and pose in the doorway of the plane, waving and laughing. She submitted patiently to all this maneuvering, well aware of the importance of having herself brought constantly to the attention of the public. Thompson knew, too, that all this publicity was helpful to his production; but it wounded his ego to be in the background while all eyes were focused on this actress, who accepted the universal homage as a matter of right. He had a childish desire to do something that would make her look ridiculous.

In the middle of her posing and posturing, Emily caught sight of him. "Hello, there, Tommy!" she called. He smiled back and blew her a kiss.

"Well, I finally made it, didn't I?" said Emily, as she and Thompson hugged each other.

"And looking like somebody's little sister." He really was delighted to see how fresh and youthful she looked.

She laughed with pleasure, and they posed together. Winternitz hovered about to make sure that Thompson's unblemished cheek was presented to the camera. As soon as the photographer had finished, Emily was surrounded by a group that included Paul Kipner, a representative of World-Wide Films, the motion-picture company that employed her, an assistant manager of the hotel to which she was going, an airport official who wanted to assure himself that she had had a comfortable trip, and several autograph seekers. In the midst of this entourage she moved slowly toward the gate. The

156

chauffeur had brought her car around and helped her into it. Her maid and Kipner followed.

"Can I give you a lift back to town, Tommy?" called Emily. "There's plenty of room."

"Thanks, I've got a car," said Thompson. He had no wish to be part of her retinue.

"I'll see you in the morning then. And I can hardly wait!"

"The Farow, at twelve," said Thompson.

"Don't worry! I'll be right on the dot." She waved to him, the chauffeur tapped his horn lightly, the gaping spectators drew back, and the long, gleaming car rolled slowly away.

"You're slipping, Doc," said Thompson. "Where's the motor-cycle escort?"

"I had it all fixed," said Winternitz, "and then the Police Commissioner and I agreed to disagree. Confidentially, we're both in love with the same patrolman. However, I have arranged for a twenty-one-gun salute from the Staten Island ferryboats, and tonight every inmate of the Death House gets a turkey dinner."

"Well, she got here, goddam her. And you've got to admit she looks marvelous."

Winternitz licked his lips. "She fills me with desire. In fact, I can think of nothing in the world that I want more, except some scrambled eggs and a good hot cup of coffee."

"All right, let's go eat," said Thompson.

XII.

On Monday Eric arrived at the Farow Theater a half-hour before noon. He was surprised to see a crowd of untidy adolescents obstructing the front of the theater. He had to push through them to enter the lobby, where three or four painters were at work.

"Where do you think you're goin', Charlie?" asked one of the men as Eric picked his way among the scaffolds, ladders, and paint pots.

"I want to get in to the rehearsal."

"Well, you can't get in this way. Around by the stage door."

Eric went out on the sidewalk again and asked one of the waiting crowd where the stage door was. A dozen voices obligingly directed him. He entered the iron gate and went down the littered alley to the wooden entrance door. In the little doorman's lodge sat Patrick Gurney, the day man. He was a superannuated stagehand, whom everybody called Pop. Employed by Oscar Farow for many years, he had been rewarded with this sinecure when he became too old for active service. When Claire had organized the staff of the theater she had wanted to discharge not only him, but Harry Baumrucker, the master carpenter, Charles Ankrim, the master electrician, and Ira Whitestone, the master property man. Pop was nearly eighty, the others all past sixty, and she wanted to employ younger men. Under the regulations of the stagehands' union (known as Local Number One) the "house crew," once engaged, could not be dismissed until the end of the season, and she felt that it was too risky to be tied down for a whole year to these elderly men. Thompson had protested not only for sentimental reasons—all of them had been employed at the Farow from the day it opened—but because the three "heads" were first-rate mechanics, skilled artisans who could deal with any backstage technical problem. He knew how important a dependable and resourceful stage crew is to the smooth functioning of a production. For once, Anthony Weir, who had a much better grasp of the organizational side of production than did Claire, sided with him. So Claire yielded and re-engaged the veterans. They knew that they owed their jobs to Thompson, and he knew that he had won their unswerving loyalty and devotion.

"Who you lookin' for, sonny?" said Pop in a thin voice as Eric stood uncertainly in the doorway.

"I'm looking for the rehearsal." He had to repeat it twice before the old man understood him.

"Twelve o'clock," he said. Then, suspiciously, "You in the cast?"

"No, I'm the author of the play."

"Oh, the author," said Pop, not impressed. "Well, go right ahead in. There's some of them there."

Eric followed the direction of the gnarled forefinger and found his way onto the stage. It was the first time he had ever set foot on the stage of a professional theater and he trod carefully and with a certain awe. Except for the faint illumination from the skylights, the stage was lighted only by a large, glaring, naked electric lamp, suspended in a wire cage, just inside the curtain. The rest of the house was in darkness. On the stage were twenty-five or thirty plain wooden chairs, several long, backless benches, and a few battered tables. The stage manager and his two assistants were arranging some fifteen of the chairs in a semi-ellipse facing the auditorium.

"Oh, hello, Mr. Kenwood," said McCarthy. "I guess you met Glad and Pete in the office the other day."

Eric shook hands with the two young assistants, Gladys Kaye, a dark, intense girl who wore a green eyeshade and had a bright yellow pencil stuck in her hair, and Peter Quirt, a tall, thin, pimply, inarticulate youth, whose technical experience in a Texas community theater had impressed Thompson. Quirt disappeared for a moment and returned with a large galvanized pail half-filled with sand, which he placed in front of the row of chairs to serve as a communal receiver for cigarette butts.

Eric hovered in the background, not wanting to be in the way. The actors began to arrive, exchanged smiles and greetings with him, but paid no further attention to him. Their manner was quite different from what it had been in Thompson's office. There they had been vivacious and self-assured; here they moved about softly, with a hushed air of expectancy. When Thompson came in they all focused on him, hoping for a nod or a word. He, too, was tense and preoccupied. With him were Winternitz, Fineman, and his secretary, Katherine Swayne, a robust, deep-voiced, businesslike girl.

Thompson greeted Eric curtly, then frowned involuntarily as Irina Lanski came in. She shook hands with them and said to Thompson, "I hope you don't mind my being here."

"No, of course not," he lied. He did not like to have anyone, except his immediate associates, present at rehearsals and had not invited her. However, as the author's agent, she had a certain right to be there; in any case, he did not want to insult her.

"Shall we go and sit out front?" she said to Eric, wanting to be as inconspicuous as possible. He followed her to a little wooden staircase with a hand rail that bridged the orchestra pit and gave easy access from the stage to the auditorium. They seated themselves a few rows back, near another sand-filled pail. She took out one of her little cigars. Eric lit a cigarette.

159

Claire came down the steps and up the aisle. "Hello, Irina," she said with a quick, curious glance at Eric.

"Hello, Claire darling. I don't think you've met the author. This is Mrs. Weir."

"How do you do, Mr. Kenwood?"

"How do you do?" said Eric shyly. He remained seated, not from impoliteness but merely because he was too excited to think of these niceties. Claire thought him rude and sullen and took an instant dislike to him.

"We'll take good care of your carpet," said Irina Lanski, noticing Claire's anxious look at her cigar.

"It isn't that," said Claire. "It's just that fire is one thing I'm really terrified of."

The agent patted her hand. "Don't worry, darling. I promise you we won't burn down your theater."

Claire forced a laugh and took a seat several rows behind them. Suddenly Eric saw Thompson stride quickly across the stage. The producer had seen Florence Fulham come in and he hurried over to where she stood, trying to summon the courage to walk out upon the stage. She had not entered the theater since Oscar Farow's death; this was truly an ordeal for her. It suddenly occurred to Thompson, too, how hard it must have been for her to elbow her way through the crowd on the sidewalk waiting for a newer star, of whose supporting cast she was a member. In fact, she had edged her way from the taxi to the gate, unknown and unnoticed, and she felt lonely and forgotten as she walked down the familiar alley and through the door from which she had so often emerged in triumph.

Thompson kissed her warmly and, taking her by the hand, led her across the stage and introduced her to the other actors. Their deference and the affectionate greeting of Reginald Olmsted, with whom she had played years before, dissipated her sadness. She began to feel at home now, and among her own people, and she was deeply thankful to Thompson for his tact and graciousness.

"Is that Florence Fulham?" asked Eric.

"Yes," said Irina Lanski, blowing her nose. "I feel that I would like to kneel and kiss Leroy Thompson's hand. He understands that it is not easy to enter, for the first time, the graveyard where one's youth is buried."

Thompson left Florence Fulham chatting easily with Olmsted and walked across the stage, looking at his watch. It was five minutes

160

to twelve. Everyone kept glancing in the direction of the stage door, watching for Emily Crandall's arrival. Thompson beckoned to Fineman. "Murray," he said, "maybe you'd better wait outside for Emily and get her through that pack of hyenas. If necessary, kill a couple of the little bastards. That's an order."

"This'll go on every day," said Fineman. "I'll see what I can do about having a cop around mornings and when we break."

As the minutes passed, Thompson grew increasingly impatient. He was a stickler for punctuality and his actors knew it. Was Emily deliberately delaying her arrival in order to show her importance and to make a star's "entrance," or had some illness or accident detained her? To conceal his restlessness and uneasiness he lit a cigarette and gave his secretary some perfunctory instructions. It was twenty minutes after twelve, and twenty-five. The actors' conversations were becoming more and more desultory. Many of them glanced furtively at their watches. Claire got up, walked around the back of the auditorium, and took a seat on the other aisle. Nathan Winternitz went over to her. "It's all my fault. I should have explained to her that there's three hours' difference between California and New York time. Artists don't think of such things."

"She might at least have telephoned," said Claire.

"Well, there's one thing I must say for Miss Crandall," said Irina Lanski to Eric, "she knows how to build up suspense. I hope she can do it as effectively when there's an audience in the theater."

At twelve-thirty Thompson walked over to the table at the side of the stage where McCarthy was aimlessly shuffling scripts and parts. "You'd better call her hotel, Mack."

"Okay, but I'll take a look outside first to see if she's on the way."

Everybody watched him as he walked briskly across the stage. Five minutes later he came back. All eyes followed him again as he walked toward Thompson.

"Well?" said Thompson.

"She's out there. Making with the autographs. Murray says she'll be another couple minutes."

The import of what he was saying communicated itself to the actors. There was a general buzz, and they all concentrated their gaze toward the stage door.

Another seven or eight minutes passed before Emily entered, accompanied by Fineman, Paul Kipner, and her maid, who carried two small bags. Emily was dressed in a pale pink slack suit and open sandals through which gleamed scarlet toenails. Her eyes were bright, and she seemed to be bursting with energy. One of the novices began to applaud; several of the younger actors automatically joined in, but the more seasoned ones merely glanced at each other with raised eyebrows.

"Tommy," said Emily, rushing toward Thompson with outstretched hand. "I'm terribly sorry! Do forgive me, won't you? Just as I was leaving, California got me on the wire and I simply couldn't get off. And then all those fans outside, of course. I can't tell you how awful I feel."

The truth was that, unable to get to sleep the night before, she had taken two powerful sleeping tablets. Her maid had been an hour getting her out of bed. Once up she was so sluggish she had to drink four cups of strong coffee before she was in condition to go to the theater. Then, just as she left the hotel she took a Benzedrine tablet, which was now just beginning to arouse her to a false vivacity.

"It's all right," said Thompson, patting her hand with affected good humor. "Do you want to freshen up or anything before we start?"

"Oh no, I'm fine! Let's start as soon as you're ready."

"All right, let's go then," said Thompson, with a malevolent look toward Paul Kipner, who was going down the steps to the auditorium. He had not been invited either, and had offered no apology for turning up. It would have relieved Thompson's feelings to have asked him to leave or at least to have made some sarcastic reference to his presence, but he restrained himself.

He placed Emily in the middle of the row of chairs and asked Florence Fulham and Reginald Olmsted to sit on either side of her, introducing them briefly. Emily acknowledged the introductions with bright-eyed animation. The other actors were quickly assigned to places consonant with their importance. Thompson stood facing them, waiting for everybody to settle down.

"All right, quiet please, everybody!" barked McCarthy.

"All we're going to do today is read the play," said Thompson, "so that everybody can get acquainted with who's who and what's what. We're doing this just for your information and mine, so don't let me see any acting. In fact, anyone caught attempting to act will have to spend an hour listening to soap operas." Everyone laughed. Thompson having accomplished his purpose of putting them a little more at ease, came down to the auditorium and took a seat that was not near any of the other listeners.

"All ready, boss?" asked McCarthy, peering out into the darkness.

"Yes," said Thompson, taking a pull from a pint bottle of brandy he carried in his coat pocket.

"Okay. Heads up, everybody," said McCarthy. "Act One. Scene One. Greg enters, goes to phone, dials."

"Hello, is Mrs. Collins there?" said the actor who was playing Greg, reading the first line of the play in a voice trembling with nervousness.

And so the reading of the play began at last. Emily, Florence Fulham, and Olmsted read from complete scripts and had familiarized themselves with the play. Most of the other actors had not read it, and their parts, or "sides," contained only the lines they had to speak and the "cues," which consisted of the four or five final words of the speeches immediately preceding. Since these tags of speeches were often wholly unintelligible without the context, the actors had merely a general idea of the purport of their scenes and an even vaguer notion of the play as a whole. Hence this first reading was of great importance to them; it acquainted them not only with the play, but with their relationship to it and to the other characters. They listened attentively, moving their heads from side to side, like spectators at a tennis match, as the dialogue shifted back and forth, watching at the same time for their cues.

The reading proceeded haltingly. The actors were all nervous and self-conscious, sitting up there on display under the glaring light, knowing that the eyes and ears of Thompson and his invisible associates out front were focused on them. They fumbled and stumbled over their lines, misreading and mispronouncing words, putting emphases in the wrong places, often missing cues. McCarthy and his assistants sat at a table to one side, following the text line by line. When there was a "business cue"—the ringing of a telephone or doorbell or the firing of a shot—he would say, "Ding-a-ling-a-ling!" or "Brrrr!" or "Bang! Bang!" If an actor missed a cue he would call him sharply by name. There were many typing errors and omissions in the parts, and each time one of these occurred there was great confusion. The reading stopped entirely while McCarthy located the trouble and the actors made the necessary corrections. Whenever this happened, Thompson would rise and walk impatiently up and down the aisle, pausing to light a fresh cigarette or take another drink.

Emily, overstimulated by the Benzedrine and aware that everyone on the stage and in the auditorium was waiting to hear her read, sat rigidly in her chair, trying to control the trembling of her hands and lips. When her first cue came she plunged into her opening speech with far too much vehemence; then, conscious of her own loudness, went to the other extreme, so that at times she was almost inaudible and the other actors had to strain to hear their cues.

When the reading began Eric listened with great eagerness; but as it proceeded he grew more and more depressed. He had expected the actors to illuminate his text and bring it vividly to life, but as they limped and struggled it sounded dull, flat, and devoid of meaning. He leaned far forward, trying to hear, squirming at every verbal mistake or false reading, and tearing at his cuticles until his fingers bled.

When the first of the two acts came to a flat conclusion McCarthy said, "Curtain! End of Act One!"

Thompson got up quickly. "All right, take five minutes."

"Five minutes!" rasped McCarthy. The actors all rose to stretch their cramped limbs and get a quick smoke. Emily's maid hurried up to her with a glass of water and a small toilet case and helped her freshen her make-up. Thompson saw Claire coming toward him; not wanting to hear what she had to say, he pretended not to see her and hurried to the lavatory.

"Well," said Irina Lanski to Eric, "how do you like your play?"

"It certainly doesn't sound very good," said Eric gloomily.

"You are not opening tonight, you know. So don't begin to worry just yet."

"Didn't you think it sounded bad?"

"Oh, an average first reading, I should say. I do think Tommy is going to have a little work with dear Miss Crandall. But after all, when you consider that she's been shut up in those sound stages for ten years—!"

"But the other actors!" said Eric. "That man who plays the father. I could hardly hear him."

"You probably won't until the opening night. If Reggie Olmsted's performance were all we had to think about, we could already congratulate ourselves on a resounding success." She rose as Claire came up the aisle. "Excuse me."

164

As the two women went to the lounge Eric wandered over to the other aisle, where Winternitz, Fineman, and Kipner were talking together. They paid no attention to him, and he went back to his seat and lit another cigarette. The actors had begun to drift back. Presently Thompson came down the aisle, calling, "Whenever you're ready, Mack!"

"Second act!" shouted McCarthy. "And don't let me see anybody drop a cigarette butt on the stage, either now or as long as we're in this theater. There's a bucket there, so please make use of it."

The actors slipped back into their places, and the reading of the second act began. Like the first, it dragged along confusedly, with long, irritating interruptions for corrections. Eric slumped unhappily in his seat. It was torture to listen, and he was glad when it was over.

"We'll take a half-hour," said Thompson the moment the reading ended, "and then we'll read it again."

"Everybody back in half an hour," bellowed McCarthy.

The actors dispersed, most of them leaving the theater for coffee and something to eat. Emily sat motionless. The effect of the Benzedrine was wearing off and she was beginning to wilt. Seeing that she needed reassurance, Thompson started for the stage. As he went down the aisle Kipner hurried after him and seized him by the arm. "That Crandall is going to turn in a great performance, Tommy," he said in an intense whisper.

"You don't have to sell her to me," said Thompson. "You've got my signature to a binding contract."

Kipner looked offended, then laughed. "You're always there with the old razzamadazz," he said, slapping Thompson on the back.

Emily looked up as Thompson came over to her. "Well, how do you feel?" he said, smiling.

"Not so good. I sounded awful, didn't I?"

"If you'd been any better, I'd be worried. All we were doing it for was to get everybody acquainted and straighten out the bugs in the script."

Kipner came up and put an arm around Emily. "You were terrific! You're going to be a knockout in this part!"

"Well, I wish I thought so," said Emily.

"What are you talking about? *You* tell her, Tommy."

"Don't you want something to eat?" asked Thompson, ignoring Kipner.

165

"I'd love a cup of coffee. Could somebody—"

"I'll send my secretary. Kate!" he called.

"Right here," said Katherine Swayne, bustling up. "Just coffee, Miss Crandall?"

"Yes. Just black coffee. And very hot, please."

"Right!" said the secretary, already on her way.

"Is there some place I could relax for just a minute?" said Emily in a small, pathetic voice.

"Yes, sure," said Thompson. "We're got the dressing-room all fixed up for you. Didn't they tell you? Pete!"

"Yes, sir!" said Peter Quirt, hurrying over.

"Show Miss Crandall where the dressing-room is."

"Right this way, Miss Crandall," said Peter.

"Thank you very much," said Emily with a wan smile. She and her maid followed Peter to the star dressing-room, which had been especially redecorated and refurnished for her. Claire had balked a little at the expense, but Thompson had seen Emily's luxurious accommodations in the Hollywood studio and wanted to make her relatively modest theater quarters as attractive as possible. As Emily went to the dressing-room she passed Florence Fulham, who was making a call from the coin-box in the corridor. The two women smiled at each other. Florence watched Emily enter the celebrated suite that the older woman had occupied so often and so long. The use of a dressing-room during rehearsals was a privilege accorded only to stars. Now, like the other actors, Florence would be sitting out the long hours on the uncomfortable wooden chairs, the sole furniture of the stage.

Eric invited Irina Lanski to have a drink with him, and they walked up the alley together. The unruly crowd of youngsters still clustered about the gate and made egress almost impossible.

"Hey, mister!" said a raucous, unkempt girl, "when is Emily coming out?"

"Not for a few hours," said Eric, shoving his way through the crowd, followed by Irina Lanski. Everyone who had come out had given the same answer, but Emily's admirers regarded it as a ruse to get rid of them, and they stolidly stood their ground.

"Filthy little beasts!" said the agent as she and Eric crossed the street to O'Leary's bar-restaurant. "If these are the new generation and the parents of the one to follow, then God help American civilization!"

166

"Maybe it's not their fault," said Eric. "Maybe they're just products of an educational system that fixes our attention on success rather than on what goes on inside of us."

Several of the booths in the bar were occupied by members of the cast, who waved and smiled at Eric. He and Irina Lanski found an empty booth; she ordered a double brandy and soda and he a sandwich and a glass of beer.

"This American system of play production always makes me want to shriek and tear my hair," she said. "I have been nearly thirty years in America and have heard nothing but talk about efficiency and what is called, I believe, know-how, but I have never got used to the miracles of inefficiency and don't-know-how that I see performed in the American theater. In Europe a brilliant director like Leroy Thompson would be the régisseur of an established state or municipal theater. He would have at his command a permanent company of trained actors and a permanent staff of technicians, all accustomed to working together in the closest cooperation. Your play would have been read and discussed for many weeks, perhaps many months, and the actors would come to the first rehearsal thoroughly familiar with every line of the text and already saturated with the parts they are to play. The theater would be equipped with a complete and flexible machinery for staging and lighting a play, including cycloramas, revolving stages, projection machines, and I don't know what all. And it would have a storehouse filled with scenery, properties, and costumes, suitable for almost any conceivable play, whether classical or modern. But what happens here? On the stage, at the first rehearsal, sits a group of actors, assembled God knows how and from where, who have never seen each other before and who have not even read the play in which they are to perform. And in exactly four weeks, to the very day, they must be prepared to give a finished performance before a critical audience. If you want to know just how finished, go and see nine-tenths of the exhibitions in our Broadway theaters. And so with the productions. Everything is started from the beginning—scenery, costumes, lighting equipment—as though no one had ever done a play before; and with an appalling waste of time, energy, and money. And when the play closes, whether it runs a day or a year, everything finishes with it. The actors are disbanded, the scenery is burned, the costumes are sold to the ragman. And with the next play the whole process is repeated all over again. Nothing is learned, nothing is saved, there is no permanence, no continuity, no program, no pattern, no objective, no ideal. It is all waste, waste, waste—like cutting down the forests, like exhausting the rich soil, like allowing the great flood waters to go unrestrained and the garbage pails to overflow with the sustenance of a starving world. Grown-up children in a gigantic nursery, smashing their shiny toys with a hammer, for papa is rich, and tomorrow the man from the United Parcel Service will bring a new and shinier lot. But not of such children as these, my dear young friend, is the kingdom of heaven."

Eric listened with rapt attention, forgetting for the moment his concern about his play. His knowledge of the theater was almost entirely literary. Everything she said about the apparatus of play production was new and revealing to him. But what interested him more was that she shared his belief in the importance of spiritual values. His mother had that belief too, and he tried to emulate her example of expressing it in terms of daily living. His creative nature, however, demanded a philosophical and artistic expression as well, and Irina Lanski was almost the first person he had ever known who seemed to feel the same deep need. As he listened to her he had a warm and comforting feeling of kinship.

"Well," she said as the actors began to file out, "I think you had better get back to the rehearsal. I hope you will forgive me for my soap-box oration. It is a lucky thing that the pulpit of my church is not open to women, for I would have bored the devout to the point of heresy."

"I wish I could tell you how much it's meant to me," said Eric. "I haven't met many people who have your point of view. Will you talk to me again sometime?"

She smiled. "If you can put up with a garrulous old maiden aunt—!"

She did not go back to the theater with him. He pushed his way alone through the still-vigilant crowd. Fineman, Winternitz, and Kipner did not come back either, and Claire was the sole occupant of the auditorium. Eric wanted to sit beside her and become better acquainted, but her cold nod discouraged him, and he sat by himself, several rows away.

When all the actors except Emily had assembled, Thompson sent McCarthy to ask if she was ready. She was, and a moment later she appeared. During the interval she had removed her perspiration-drenched underwear and her maid had given her an alcohol rub-down and had massaged the muscles of her neck. She put on fresh clothing that Nellie had brought along, drank a pint of coffee, took another Benzedrine tablet. Thus artificially stimulated, she was able to return to the stage, looking fresh and alert.

To Eric's relief the second reading sounded very different. The actors had got over their initial strangeness and nervousness. Their parts were in order, they understood their relationship to one another and to the play, and they began to put some meaning into their lines. Even Emily was far more at ease and read with clarity and good phrasing.

"All right, children," said Thompson when the reading came to a close, "and thank you." Then by way of encouragement, "That wasn't too bad, and I think we'll go on for another day or two anyhow." He waited for the inevitable laugh. "Tomorrow at twelve, and we'll start breaking it in, right from the beginning."

"Everybody at twelve tomorrow," echoed McCarthy.

Thompson climbed up on the stage, said a few complimentary words to the principal actors, and went over to Emily. "Darling, that sounded like a little bit of all right."

"I only hope I'll be able to do it," she said.

"I'm not worried about that, so why should you be?"

Eric approached rather shyly. He had asked McCarthy to introduce him to Reginald Olmsted and Florence Fulham, and they had been most friendly. Now he wanted to meet Emily.

"Excuse me, Mr. Thompson," he said, "but I haven't met Miss Crandall."

"Oh, I'm sorry! You certainly are two people who should get together. Emily, meet Mr. Kenwood, the author of this horse opera."

"How do you do, Mr. Kenwood?" said Emily with a mechanical smile, barely touching his outstretched hand. In the Hollywood hierarchy a young unknown author ranked far below a director, cameraman, or costume designer, and only slightly above an expert make-up artist.

"I've just been telling Emily how good she's going to be in this part," said Thompson in an effort to prod Eric into the required compliments.

"Yes," said Eric, "I was disappointed in the first reading, but I thought the second one was much better."

This hardly came up to what was expected of him. Emily turned to Thompson as though she had not heard. "Do you think someone could see if my car is here, Tommy?"

Thompson dispatched Peter Quirt on this errand and went on engaging Emily in flattering small talk. Eric, feeling completely out of it, said, "Well, I think I'll go along. Good night."

"Good night," said Emily with a frigid little smile.

Thompson was more cordial. "See you tomorrow, Eric. And don't get too drunk tonight. We may find we need a new second act."

Eric laughed and left the theater. Only two or three eager adolescents were at the gate, but when he reached the sidewalk he discovered the reason. The waiting throng, together with a large number of adult passers-by, had gathered about Emily's limousine. The chauffeur, accustomed to such attention, sat erect at the wheel, impassive except for an occasional frown and turn of the head when some exploratory finger ventured to touch the car. Impressed by this magnificent chariot, the like of which he had never seen, Eric crossed the street and joined a staring group that preferred a full view of the car's unobstructed side. He listened with interest to the comments, which ranged from the reverential to the ribald. Suddenly one of the lookouts, posted at the gate, shouted, "Here she comes!" Instantly the car was abandoned and the mob swarmed to the gate to greet its owner. Emily appeared, flanked by McCarthy and Peter, and followed by her maid. From the waiting crowd arose a deafening chorus of shrill, screaming voices, and a hundred upraised arms flourished autograph albums and fountain pens.

Eric looked on for a few moments, in utter amazement, then walked back to his hotel, tired but happy. His talk with Irina Lanski, his first real contact with the world of the theater, and the encouraging second reading of the play combined to give him a feeling of exhilaration and eager anticipation. After a quick supper, he wrote long descriptions of the day's events to his mother and to Sylvia.

Thompson did not share Eric's optimism, and at dinner he expressed his misgivings to Claire. "I'm really worried about that gal."

"I thought she read quite well the second time," said Claire.

He shook his head dubiously. "She's hopped up and jittery. I don't know if she'll be able to make the grade or not."

"You're just tired."

"Maybe that's it. Well," he said, beckoning to the waiter, "let's see what another old-fashioned will do for me."

XIII.

The next day things went better. Murray Fineman had visited the local precinct. At his request, reinforced by the persuasiveness of a twenty-dollar bill, a patrolman had been assigned to special duty at the Farow Theater. When Eric arrived shortly before noon the officer was keeping loiterers on the move.

On the stage the chairs had been pushed back, and Eric was puzzled to see the floor crisscrossed with heavy lines in varicolored chalks. Peter Quirt explained that each color indicated the outlines of one of the settings, with the gaps denoting doors and windows. The stage managers were placing chairs, tables, and benches to represent the furnishings of the first scene, for one of the absurdities of the production system was that none of the actual scenery or properties could be used during rehearsals without payment of full salaries to carpenters, property men, and electricians. Since no producer was willing to incur this expense, the actors had to put up with kitchen chairs, rickety tables, and imaginary or incongruous substitute props all during rehearsals. For illumination they had only the blinding work light from whose harassing glare they tried to protect themselves by means of dark glasses, eyeshades or turned down hat brims. If the play called for music or sound effects, these had to be simulated by the stage managers or merely imagined, and the delicate task of coordinating them with the action of the play had to be deferred, too, until the dress rehearsal. This insufficiency of preparation often resulted in a stumbling first-night performance that could well jeopardize the play's chances of success. The audience and the critics judged the performance only by what they saw and could not be expected to take into account the obstacles that the actors had to overcome.

171

Accompanied by her maid, Emily arrived a few minutes before twelve. Thompson was relieved to see her on time and bade her a smiling good morning, at the same time appraising her physical and mental state. She seemed vivacious and self-possessed, but he could see that it was all artificial. She spoke graciously to the principal actors and nodded with the proper degree of reserve to the lesser ones and to Eric.

"Is everybody here now?" Thompson asked Gladys Kaye, one of whose duties it was to keep the attendance record.

"Yes, sir, all here."

"Let's get started then."

"Stand by for Act One, Scene One," barked McCarthy.

As Thompson turned he almost collided with Eric, who was teetering uncertainly, not knowing quite where to go.

"I think you'll be more comfortable out front," said Thompson a little sharply. He accepted an author's right to attend rehearsals but preferred not to be constantly aware of his presence.

Script in hand, Eric descended to the auditorium and took a seat in the second row, but his weak eyes could not endure the glare of the work light, and he soon moved back out of its range.

Thompson, also holding a script, took the center of the stage. His hat was pulled down over his eyes and the brandy bottle protruded from his coat pocket. He briefly described the setting of the first scene, pointing out the location of doors and windows, and explaining which of the chairs and tables represented a sofa, an armchair, a desk, a bookcase, a fireplace fender.

Eric listened attentively. In his text he had described the settings only in the sketchiest and most general terms; he had not even visualized them very clearly. He was interested primarily in his characters, his ideas, and the quality of his writing. He had little feeling for decoration and little understanding of the practical requirements of stage production. To a director and, above all, to actors these were matters of paramount importance. An actor's movements were necessarily determined by the shape and dimensions of the settings, the situation of the means of ingress and egress, and the nature, size, and position of the furniture. The imperfect "sight lines" and acoustics of the average theater and the narrowly limited playing area (particularly in a multi-scened play like Eric's, where the settings had to be small) required the planning of every move and gesture in order to ensure visibility and audibility and to heighten the plastic and dra-

172

matic effectiveness of the performance by creating the illusion of unstudied grace and ease.

Thompson's understanding of these problems and his ability to solve them sensitively, subtly, and at times brilliantly, made actors eager to work under his direction, for they knew that he helped them get the most out of their parts and make the best use of their talents. Good directors were as rare as good playwrights and good actors. Many a play and many a performance were ruined by directorial ineptitude.

Unlike lesser directors, who approached rehearsals with no clearly conceived over-all pattern and groped their way along by a process of improvisation and trial and error, which often produced a weak and fumbling result, Thompson spent weeks in preparatory work, studying and analyzing every scene and every speech and evolving a firm and comprehensive design, so that he came in knowing exactly what effect he wanted to create and the precise and detailed means of achieving it. During the first days of rehearsal he seldom left the stage. Pacing in front of the actors, he gave his exact and authoritative instructions, moving them about—sometimes by actual physical manipulation—like men on a chessboard, each move a step forward in a carefully planned campaign that led to a predetermined end.

As the rehearsal of the first scene progressed line by line, Eric, who was watching closely, was puzzled and a little worried. He was unable to grasp the significance of Thompson's preoccupation with minute details of physical movement. His interest was in the meaning of his play and the dramatic conflict of his characters. He could not see what difference it made whether an actor turned this way or that, whether he rose or sat on this line or another, and at what particular moment he lighted a cigarette or put it out. A dozen times he was impelled to come forward and call Thompson's attention to a misreading or a mistake, but he could not summon the courage to make himself so conspicuous. Knowing nothing about acting, he did not understand the necessity of coordinating words and action —he had studied Hamlet's speech to the players, as literature, not as an essay on the art of acting—and he did not realize that it was hard for an actor to read a line effectively unless he knew what his body was doing when he read it.

Occasionally, when it was necessary for the effectuation of his scheme of movement, Thompson would transpose a line, delete an impeding word or phrase, give one actor an interjection to break or punctuate another's overlong speech. Each time he would turn his head and say to the invisible Eric, "If the author doesn't mind," or "If that's okay with you, Eric," for Eric had the contractual right to disapprove any textual change. Though Eric saw no reason for these minor alterations, he saw no reason either for objecting, so he gave his monosyllabic assent, for which Thompson hardly waited. At one point, when Thompson said to one of the younger actors, "No, don't sit on that speech!" and the actor replied, "Oh, I'm sorry, sir; it says he sits," Thompson said, "One of the first rules of acting is never to pay any attention to an author's stage directions." To appease Eric he added, "I hope the author isn't in the theater." The actors laughed, and Eric, who cared nothing about his stage directions, said, "No, he's not."

After spending over two hours in laying out the stage business of the first scene, Thompson called a half-hour recess. The actors dispersed as usual for some refreshment; Emily retired to her dressing-room. She had conducted herself very well. Not yet called upon for any interpretation of her part, she had carried out Thompson's mechanical instructions in a workmanlike manner, for she used her body well and moved freely and easily.

Eric hurried up to Thompson just as the latter was leaving the stage. "Oh, Tommy," he said, finding the courage to address the director by his familiar name, "I just wanted to tell you that there are three or four places where I don't think Miss Crandall is reading the lines the way—"

Thompson interrupted sharply. "She's not wearing the right shoes either. She'll read the lines when the curtain goes up." With that he strode off. Rebuffed and wishing he had kept quiet, Eric walked across the street to the bar. Peter Quirt, Gladys Kaye, and Lily Prengle, a pale, slender girl, who was playing the part for which Suzanne Merchant had unsuccessfully applied, were sitting in one of the booths. They invited Eric to join them. He accepted gladly, and their warmth and friendliness made him forget the sting of Thompson's rebuke. He had been in New York for ten days now, and this was almost his first social contact. These were young people like himself, eager, ambitious, and taking their first uncertain steps in a professional world that fascinated and frightened them. When it was time to go he offered to pay the check, but was relieved when the others insisted upon paying their own share. Gladys, who took pride in her brief professional experience, explained that it was the custom among ac-

174

tors, who frequently dined together in the course of production, to go Dutch. "And that goes for authors too," she added.

Eric returned to his seat in the theater as Thompson began to break in the second scene. Presently Claire, with a curt nod, took a seat across the aisle. Feeling that they should become better acquainted, Eric went over to her. "Good afternoon, Mrs. Weir," he said.

"How do you do," said Claire with a disapproving glance at his cigarette.

"Well, I'm glad we're really getting started," said Eric, not knowing quite what to say.

"I think we're disturbing Tommy," she said as Thompson glanced over his shoulder.

"Yes, I guess we are," said Eric, moving back to his seat.

"Do be careful with that cigarette, won't you?"

"Yes, I will." He wondered what he could do to ingratiate himself with this chic woman of the world, who obviously found him gauche and uninteresting.

The rehearsal progressed smoothly. By the end of the afternoon almost half of the first act had been blocked out. Thompson complimented Emily upon her aptitude, and she told him what a pleasure it was to be working again in the theater after so many years' absence. He went to Claire's apartment, aching with weariness after his six hours' concentrated work but pleased with the way things were going and considerably reassured about Emily. Claire waited on him in a self-effacing and companionable way, and he felt comfortable and even a little tender.

"I don't think much of that author of yours," she said. "He looks and acts like a hillbilly."

"He's a little wet behind the ears, but he'll be all right once he gets the cornsilk out of his hair."

"Do you think he really wrote the play? He doesn't look to me like anybody who could write anything."

"He certainly didn't write the letters of Lord Chesterfield, if that's what you mean. But he's got something, don't kid yourself."

"Nothing that would be of any interest to me. I definitely don't like him."

"Well, that gives me one less rival to worry about," said Thompson, kissing her.

On Wednesday morning everybody at the theater was talking about the weather. It was the season of equinoctial storms, and the newspapers carried alarming stories of a Caribbean hurricane that had caused great damage in Florida and was sweeping up the Atlantic coast. The Weather Bureau experts were uncertain whether it would spend its velocity at sea or twist its way through the North Atlantic states. The day was sultry and oppressive, and everyone was uncomfortable and rather ill at ease.

At twelve-fifteen, Emily had not appeared. Thompson decided to do what he could without her. He knew that she had an early appointment for a fitting at Louis-Jean's and assumed that the exacting and temperamental designer had detained her beyond the agreed time. So he worked, as best he could, with the other actors, reviewing what he had done the day before and making a minor adjustment here or there.

At one o'clock he instructed McCarthy to telephone Louis-Jean's. The stage manager returned with the information that Emily was on her way to the theater. A few minutes later she arrived, looking pale and tired. "I'm awfully sorry, Tommy," she said petulantly, "but that damned little swish wouldn't let me get away."

"It's all right, darling," said Thompson soothingly. "Are you ready to begin?"

"Well, I'd like a few minutes to freshen up," she said crossly. "I've been on my feet since nine-thirty and I'm just about pooped."

Without waiting for his assent she walked off to her dressing-room. The other actors exchanged glances at this not unexpected display of temperament. Thompson, annoyed, said sharply, "All right, let's go right on."

A full half-hour passed before Emily came back. "Okay, I'm ready now," she said curtly, without apology for the further delay.

Thompson now took up the play at the point he had left off the day before. Though he knew exactly what he wanted to do, it was hard to get it done. Emily was sullen and uncooperative, had to be told everything three times, and quibbled endlessly about every little point. Thompson, fuming inwardly, managed remarkably well to keep his patience; seeing, at the end of an hour, that he was making little progress, he called the customary recess somewhat earlier than usual. The break was welcome; the tension was beginning to get on everybody's nerves.

During the interval Thompson debated with himself the advisability of putting on a temperamental act of his own but decided against it. Emily could make things very hard for him if she wanted to, and a show of authority at this point might provoke her to unmanageable insubordination. If he gave her her head for a day or so, without letting her get completely out of control, her ego would probably be sufficiently gratified and she would be more amenable. For his own emotional satisfaction he would have liked to slap her face or humiliate her in some way before the whole company, but he was far too shrewd and self-disciplined to indulge in any such act of folly. Later on, a carefully calculated outburst might be useful; for the time being it would be better to maintain an unruffled exterior and behave as though nothing were wrong. So, having fortified himself by liberal recourse to the brandy bottle, he went back to the auditorium.

Feeling that not much was to be gained by breaking new ground, he decided to spend the rest of the afternoon in going over what had already been worked out. It was not time wasted, for only by constant repetition could the actors acquire the necessary smoothness. He told the company to begin with the opening of the play and sat out in the first row in order to see the action in perspective.

For a time the rehearsal proceeded methodically. The actors were beginning to know what they were expected to do, and if they did make a slip McCarthy, who had written every minute detail of stage business into his script, corrected them. Occasionally Thompson would stop them to refine a point or make some slight change. All this was in accordance with the ordinary rehearsal routine.

Suddenly, however, while Florence Fulham was in the middle of a long speech, Emily sprang to her feet. "I'm sorry," she said to Florence; then, turning toward Thompson, "Tommy, I just don't feel comfortable in this scene."

Thompson took his feet off the rail of the orchestra pit and leaned forward. "What bothers you about it?"

He knew very well what bothered her and was not unprepared for this moment, but he wanted a little time to figure out how to handle it. The scene was an intimate one in which the heroine's mother pleads with her to give up her married lover. She had several long, emotional speeches, while the daughter, touched, listens almost in silence. It was one of the few scenes that Florence had and almost the only one that gave her a chance to show her ability. In order to display Florence to the fullest advantage and enable her to make the most of the scene, Thompson had placed her on a sofa, in the center

177

of the stage, with Emily on a low stool, nearer the footlights, so that Florence, in speaking to her, would also be speaking directly to the audience, her whole face visible from every seat in the house.

What irked Emily was this high-lighting of Florence. If Emily were playing a similar scene in a motion picture, the camera focus would be almost entirely on her, with only enough reference to the mother to keep her in the scene. During most of the long speeches the mother would merely be heard on the sound track, while the audience was confronted with mammoth close-ups of Emily's face, stained with great glycerine tears. Yet here she was, huddled in a corner of the stage, with only her profile showing and almost no lines to speak, while a member of her supporting company monopolized the attention of the audience.

"Well," she said in answer to Thompson's question, "it's just that I don't feel right, playing it this way. It seems very unnatural for her just to sit and sit like this."

The other actors, seated at the back of the stage, had been studying their parts or talking in whispers, paying little attention to the routine repetition of scenes; now they were all eyes and ears, for they fully understood the significance of what was going on and awaited the outcome with deep interest. For Florence Fulham it was a tense moment and a vital one, but she gave no indication of it. She put her script on her knees and sat with folded hands as though she were merely waiting politely for the director and the star to finish their discussion. Only Eric was uninterested and impatient. The implications of Emily's objection were entirely lost upon him, and he wished that they would all stop worrying about these mechanical details and get on with the interpretation of the play.

"It doesn't hit me that way," said Thompson, feeling his way carefully. "She respects her mother and is moved by what she says. At the same time she's got this crazy infatuation for Wes, and she doesn't want to give him up. So she sits there, tense, nervy, taking it all in and trying to make up her mind."

"Yes, trying to make up her mind. That's just it! When I've got a problem and am trying to make up my mind, I have to get up and move around. I don't huddle up on a footstool and just sit still."

"Well, it's easy enough to get you moving around. But I deliberately didn't, because for my dough it's twice as effective this way. That's why I've got you on a low stool, where you look cramped and hunched up. It creates just the feeling of tension and strain that

178

you're talking about—and economically, without a lot of strutting and stamping around. It looks fine from out here."

"It doesn't feel fine," retorted Emily sharply. "Of course, I can do it that way technically if that's how you want it. But I think there should be some emotion in this scene. And I can't get any emotion into it if I don't feel right in it. My God, she's a sexy girl who's being asked to give up the man she's crazy about. If you want me to play it like a department-store dummy, why, that's up to you. But don't expect me to make it look like anything."

The actors listened in shocked amazement. None of them would have dared to speak to Thompson in such a manner and they wondered what he would do. But he remained impassive, giving no sign that anything out of the ordinary had happened.

"Well, of course, I don't want you to do anything you don't feel," he said. "Let's run the scene from the beginning, and you play it the way you feel it and let me see how it looks. All right, Flossie, if you don't mind."

"Certainly not," said Florence, rising. "Shall I take it from my entrance?"

"No, no, just from your first long speech. Give her the cue, Emily, will you?"

"Oh, just a moment, please." Emily turned and called to her maid. "Nellie, bring me my cigarettes and lighter."

Thompson swore inaudibly as the maid hurriedly complied. This was going to be even worse than he had expected.

"All ready?" said Emily to Florence.

"Whenever you are, Miss Crandall," said Florence serenely.

Emily gave the required cue, and Florence launched into the first of her long speeches. Suddenly Emily sprang to her feet and began pacing back and forth across the stage directly in front of Florence. Thompson could hardly believe what he saw. If the scene were played that way, not only would Florence be obscured from the audience during half of her speech, but attention would be entirely upon Emily, since the eyes of a spectator always follow a moving object. In the middle of her speech Florence stopped and put down her script.

Emily turned and looked at her. "I'm sorry," she said, with badly simulated innocence, "is that my cue?"

"No," said McCarthy. "Your cue is 'as they were in the past.'"

"That's what I thought!"

"Am I to go on?" said Florence to Thompson.

He gave her an appealing look. "Please. This is just to see how it looks. Or wait, maybe we'd better start it again. Back where you're seated, Emily, please."

"Why, of course!" said Emily sweetly.

"And this time try walking upstage, will you, instead of stage right? I'm afraid you'll mask Miss Fulham if you cross her like that."

"Oh, is that what the trouble was?" She turned to Florence with an apologetic laugh. "I'm terribly sorry, dear. I wasn't even thinking of where I was going. I just had the impulse to go and I followed it. But if walking upstage makes it easier for you, why I don't mind a bit."

Florence did not move a muscle. "However the director wants it."

"Try it upstage, Emily," said Thompson.

As Emily walked toward the stool there was an audible buzz from the actors who were seated at the back of the stage. Suddenly Emily swung around sharply. "Christ!" she said, stamping her foot, "does there have to be all that talk?" She turned to Thompson. "Gab, gab, gab! Chatter, chatter, chatter! How the hell is anybody supposed to concentrate?"

"Watch that talking offstage!" shouted McCarthy.

"They can say what they like about Hollywood," said Emily, resuming her seat, "but at least people have the decency to keep quiet when there's a rehearsal going on. Are you ready?" she said to Florence.

"Whenever you are, Miss Crandall."

They began again. This time Emily paced upstage and down again. It was not quite as bad as before, but it still had the effect of diverting attention from Florence to her. When her turn to speak came, Emily moved over, almost directly behind Florence, so that Florence, in order to address her, would have to turn her face almost entirely away from the audience. Florence glanced out at Thompson. He gave no sign, and she went stolidly on with her speech. In the middle of it Emily walked away from her and, facing front, flashed her lighter and lit a cigarette. Thompson had been waiting for this from the moment Emily asked for the cigarettes. He knew, as did everyone else present except Eric and a few of the novices, that a flash of fire on the stage will blot out the noblest words that were ever written.

"Excuse me, Flossie," he said. Florence stopped, instantly, and he addressed Emily. "Are you just having a smoke, darling, or are you planning to do it that way?"

"Well, I thought I would. I always smoke when I'm nervous and worried and I thought she might too. And with another long speech coming up, it gives me something to do. Anything wrong with it?"

"Well, if you're going to use the cigarette, I'd rather you lighted it on one of your own speeches."

Emily gave another apologetic laugh. "Why, of course! Goodness, I can light it anywhere you say. I'm just trying to give you the general effect of how I feel the scene. If there's anything that doesn't look right, why, just tell me. Shall we go back?"

"No, it's getting late and I want to do Scene Three before we break. Let me think about this scene and see what I can work out."

There was a brief pause while McCarthy, blueprint in hand, instructed his assistants to arrange the chairs and tables for the next scene. Then Thompson took over, and the rehearsal period proceeded without further incident. Emily tried to behave as though nothing had happened and obediently followed Thompson's directions. She was painfully conscious of the silent hostility of her fellow-players, and when the company was dismissed she went swiftly to her dressing-room without a word to anyone.

As Thompson went over to talk to McCarthy he saw Florence Fulham, seated on a bench, obviously waiting to talk to him. He knew there was trouble ahead, and as he gave McCarthy his instructions he tried to think of the best way to smooth things over. When he had finished with the stage manager Florence came toward him. "Could I talk to you for a minute, Tommy?"

"Sure. Let's sit down."

McCarthy, fully understanding the situation, quickly gathered up his belongings and bade them a brisk good night.

Thompson patted Florence's hand. "I'm sorry for what happened, Flossie."

"Tommy, I hope you won't think I'm being difficult—" She was on the verge of tears and had trouble keeping her voice under control.

"I never met anyone less difficult in my life," he said.

"It's sweet of you to say so. But I'm going to ask a great favor of you. I want you to let me turn in my part, please. It's only the third day of rehearsals and you told me yourself that you had several other people in mind. I know I have a run-of-the-play contract, but I'm hoping you won't hold me to it."

"To hell with the contract! But I want you in that part. I'd never be satisfied with anybody else, now that I've heard you read it. Listen, darling—"

"No, Tommy, please!" Her tears were beginning to flow. "I'm terribly sorry to have to do this. I like the part. You told me it was small, and I said I didn't mind and I don't. And I love working with you. But it's eight years since I've been on the stage and this is important to me. What's the good of my doing it if I can't even play the one good scene I have? Oh, damn it! I wasn't going to cry!"

"You'll play the scene and they'll rave about you. Don't let yourself be thrown by little Missy's shenanigans. You don't think for one minute I'm going to let her get away with it, do you? I just thought I'd give her a chance to get that Hollywood stuff out of her system. That's why I didn't crack down on her."

She shook her head. "No, I don't want to be the cause of any trouble. She's a big star and a big name and big box-office and you've got to think of that. The success of your play depends on her, not on me. So let me go, and let her have the scene and everybody will be happy."

"I won't be happy," he said. "Don't forget that I'm a big shot too in my own small way. And when I ope my mouth, let no dog bark —and no little bitch either. When we get to doing this rodeo, it's going to be done the way I want it, and any little sweetheart of the silver screen who doesn't like it can go back to wherever the hell she came from." He put his arm around her. "Look, darling, I'm going to ask you to do something for me—"

"No, don't try to persuade me."

"Wait till you hear what I've got to say. All I'm going to ask you to do is give me a week. No, listen! If you come to me one week from today and still want to be released, I promise you I won't even argue about it."

"It will never work out," she said. He pleaded and begged and at last she reluctantly gave in. He thanked her and kissed her, and she left the theater, feeling considerably reassured. Thompson thought he should say a few words to Emily, but the door of the dressing-room was closed; it was obvious that she was simply waiting for everybody to leave, so he decided not to go in.

"Everything going along all right, Mr. Thompson?" said Pop as he passed the doorman's lodge.

He smiled and waved his hand. "Couldn't be worse, Pop!" he said, secure in his knowledge of the old man's deafness.

182

He said nothing to Claire about his difficulties, knowing she would only get upset without contributing anything to their solution. After dinner they went to the opening of a new play, a bungling piece, atrociously acted and certain to be a failure. But its very ineptitudes amused him and kept his mind off his troubles. After the play they went to Pinelli's and had supper at a large table with half a dozen friends. It was very late when he got back to his hotel, but he could not sleep, for in spite of his bravado he was by no means sure of his ability to keep Emily in hand. If he were forced to make a choice between Emily and Florence, he would have to let Florence go. His recognition of that hard truth made him choke with rage, and he imagined himself subjecting Emily to obscene and degrading tortures.

On Thursday the weather was hot and humid and the suffocating air was surcharged with electricity. The Weather Bureau forecast thunderstorms, to be followed by a sharp drop in temperature and high winds as the hurricane rushed northward. The actors at the Farow were glum and silent. Their physical discomfort aggravated their uneasiness about Emily's behavior, and they awaited the day's developments with anxiety. Thompson arrived haggard from worry and lack of sleep. Emily appeared five minutes early. She entered, smiling, with an ingratiating "Good morning!" that included everybody.

Thompson, stroking the enormous satin-covered candy box she was carrying, said, "An apple for teacher?" Her pallor and the dark patches under her eyes were not reassuring. For the first time she looked her age.

"Don't be greedy, darling," she said with an artificial giggle. "These are for everybody." With all eyes upon her, she untied the big satin bow, took off the lid, and moved about from person to person. "Have some, won't you?"

The actors murmured their thanks as they helped themselves to the exquisite little Viennese chocolates, which had cost more than twenty dollars.

"Hey, save some for me!" said Thompson with exaggerated playfulness, reaching for a handful of chocolates and stuffing several into his mouth. He had to do something to cover the awkwardness of the situation and to relieve everyone's embarrassment at this obvious and pathetically childish attempt to make amends. He could only hope that it was indicative of something more than momentary contrition.

"I'll leave them right here," said Emily when she had finished making the rounds. "Please help yourselves, won't you? They're all for you."

"Don't you like chocolates, Miss Crandall?" asked Lily Prengle, trembling at her own boldness.

Emily beamed upon her. "Oh, I adore them. But I have to keep thinking of the old silhouette. Well, maybe just one!" With a giggle, she snatched a chocolate and popped it into her mouth, then turned to Thompson. "All right, boss-man, I'm rarin' to go!"

But he knew that it was not so. He tactfully avoided rehearsing her scene with Florence and went on to the final scenes of the first act. Emily was most tractable and followed his instructions unquestioningly, even with manufactured enthusiasm, but she had to strain as the Benzedrine lost effectiveness and she paused frequently to wipe the perspiration from her palms. Thompson, feeling sorry for her, several times turned his attention needlessly to other members of the cast merely to give her a brief respite. He saw her look of relief when the interval came at last. When it was over he began with a scene in which she did not appear in order to give her an additional half-hour's rest.

The sky had been darkening, and suddenly the expected storm broke with dramatic fury. Vivid flashes of lightning, visible through the skylight, were followed by the reverberating roll of thunder. The rain came in great sheets that beat upon the glass panes with the solid impact of steel. As the storm increased in violence, the actors grew more and more uneasy, glancing up at the rain-swept skylight and recoiling from the roar of the thunder. Soon it became almost impossible for them to make themselves heard. Thompson clapped his hands loudly to get their attention, so that he could call a halt. But before he could speak, there was a blinding flash, then a deafening peal of thunder.

Emily, who had grown paler and more hollow-eyed as the storm progressed, uttered an unearthly scream and threw herself upon the stage, burying her face in her arms.

"Oh, God! Oh, God! Oh, God!" she shrieked. "Oh, God save me! Oh, Jesus, save me! Mother! Mother! Mother!"

Thompson was the first to reach her. He bent over her and, in spite of her struggles, succeeded in picking her up in his arms. As he balanced himself, another bolt flared and cracked. "Oh, save me, save me!" Emily screamed again, clinging desperately to him. "I can't stand it! I'll go crazy if it doesn't stop! Oh, Christ, make it stop!"

"You're all right now. Everything's all right. It's all over now," said Thompson; then roughly to the anxious crowd that surrounded him,

184

"Get out of my way!" A lane was quickly opened for him. He carried Emily, still clutching him and moaning in terror, to the dressing-room. Her maid, McCarthy, and Florence Fulham followed.

Thompson put her down gently on the chaise longue, while Nellie quickly drew the window curtains to shut out the lightning flashes. The storm was moving off, and in the dressing-room the sound of the thunder was muffled. Thompson forced his brandy bottle between Emily's lips and made her take a long swallow. "That's a little better, isn't it?"

Emily sobbed chokingly. "Oh, God, I'm terrified. I always have been—always, ever since I was a baby." Thompson looked sharply at her. She was not acting: her fear was genuine and deep.

"I think if she could just lie here for a little while, Tommy," said Florence. "I'll stay here with Nellie, and we'll put some cold compresses on her head."

"All right; come on, Mack," said Thompson. He closed the dressing-room door. "See if you can raise her chauffeur and get him around here. She's through for today."

As he went back to the stage it occurred to him that this was the first time Florence had entered the star dressing-room since her last appearance under Oscar Farow, and he wondered irrelevantly what her thoughts were as she viewed its new decoration and its new occupant. The cast crowded around to inquire about Emily. "She'll be all right in a few minutes," he said curtly, glancing curiously at Peter Quirt, who was busily sweeping the stage. In the excitement, the chocolates had been spilled and trodden upon, and Peter was cleaning up the mess.

McCarthy came back and reported that he had located the chauffeur. The car would be around presently. "Do you want to go ahead with the rehearsal?"

Thompson looked up at the skylight and then at the faces of the actors. The rain was still coming down hard, and everybody looked tired and strained. "No, let's call it a day. I can't do anything with that goddam noise. Anyhow, there's not much I can do without Emily now. You'd better dismiss them."

"Attention, everybody!" shouted McCarthy. "That's all for today. Everybody tomorrow at twelve, and that don't mean five minutes after."

"Precise old bugger, ain't he?" said Reginald Olmsted. Everybody, including McCarthy, laughed.

"He used to announce the time on the air," said Thompson. "Oh, there's just one thing. I'm getting a little behind schedule, and we may have to start night rehearsals next week. So please arrange your love lives accordingly."

This brought another laugh, and then those who had come prepared for rain began to leave the theater. The others waited for the storm to abate. Before long Pop hobbled onto the stage to say that Emily's car had arrived.

"All right, tell her, will you? No, wait, I'll tell her myself."

He went to the dressing-room. Emily was sitting up on the chaise longue, a damp cloth on her head. Florence sat beside her, holding her hand.

"How's it going?" asked Thompson.

"Much better, thanks. I'm sorry to be such a nuisance."

"Forget it! I have an aunt who reacts the same way." He invented this female relative for want of something better to say. "Your car's here and I think you'll be better off if you go home and get into bed."

"Well, I think so too. Only what about the rehearsal?"

"I've dismissed the company. I've done about all I wanted to do today anyhow."

"Then I think I *will* go." She got up and, turning to Florence, kissed her impulsively. "Thank you for being so nice to me!"

"Why, it wasn't anything at all!" said Florence, blushing.

Assisted by Nellie and Thompson, Emily went to the stage door, where McCarthy was talking to the chauffeur, who had brought a large umbrella with him.

"Sure you're all right?" said Thompson as Emily stepped under the umbrella.

"Yes, thanks. And please forgive me."

"Think I should go with them?" asked McCarthy.

"I don't know. Well, yes, you may as well. She may want something done."

"Thanks, chief," said McCarthy. "I've had a yen to ride in that circus wagon ever since it first knocked me for a loop." He turned up his coat collar and hurried up the alley.

"Don't you want to share my umbrella?" said Florence, coming up behind Thompson as he stood in the doorway.

"I don't mind if I do. And while I'm up, I'd like to get in on a little of this kissing too." He kissed her cheek affectionately. "You're for me, kid. Could I talk you into having a little drink with me?"

186

"Yes, I think you could if you really tried."

They went to Pinelli's and sat in a quiet corner over a long drink. They had both had enough of Emily for the day and avoided referring to her. Instead they sought refuge from the dismal present in the roseate past, spending a happy hour romanticizing the good old days of Oscar Farow. He invited her to have dinner with him, but she had an engagement, so he stayed on and dined alone, thankful that Claire was in the country. Later in the evening he called Emily's maid. A doctor had been in and prescribed some medicines and treatments to relax her. Sleep was what she needed more than anything else, in Nellie's opinion. Thompson agreed and sent Emily his love. He needed sleep too, but he could never shut his eyes before midnight. He put the Beethoven Ninth and the Missa Solemnis on his record-player and let the sonorous waves roll over him.

Friday was a day of particular tension for the majority of the cast, for it was the last day of their "probationary" period. Emily, Olmsted, Florence, McCarthy, and two or three other actors had signed "run-of-the-play" contracts, under the terms of which the manager waived his right to dismiss them and guaranteed them employment for as long as the play ran. In return, the players agreed to remain in the cast, for the duration of the run, thus assuring the manager of their continuing services, a very important consideration where prominent actors were involved. The minor actors merely had "minimum" contracts, which gave the manager the right to dismiss them, without obligation, during the first five days of rehearsal. If they were called for rehearsal on the sixth day, the manager could dismiss them thereafter only upon payment of two weeks' full salary. Consequently the actors anxiously awaited the fifth day, when the manager usually made up his mind.

The tension was aggravated by everyone's awareness of Emily's instability and by the disturbing, unsettled weather. During the night the temperature had fallen sharply, as predicted. The city was lashed by a violent gale that whistled down the canyon-like streets, carrying away hats, tearing down shop signs, smashing plate glass, blinding pedestrians with whirling eddies of debris. People with upturned coat collars shouldered their way along in the lee of buildings, or, at the risk of perilous collisions, butted the cold wind with lowered heads.

The alley of the Farow Theater swirled with flying litter. On the drafty stage the actors huddled in their overcoats or walked up and down to keep their blood in circulation. Every time the stage door opened a chilling gust sent papers flying and set the pendant work light and the overhead rigging swaying and creaking. From the roof came the incessant rattle of the skylight panes.

Thompson usually spent a few minutes exchanging pleasantries with the actors, but today no one was in the mood for levity. He went over to McCarthy, who was standing with Harry Baumrucker, looking up at the skylight. "Anything we can do about that bloody racket, boys?"

The carpenter shook his head. "I came around early, thinkin' it might give you some trouble, and I been up there nearly an hour. There's nothin' loose up there, but with all that glass there's just nothin' you can do about it, with a wind like this."

"Yes, I remember playing here once when we had one of these things going. It was a heavy piece about a lot of trapped miners, and the wind would hang around up there until somebody had a speech about, oh, God, how much longer do we have to endure this awful silence, and then down it would zoom z-z-z-z-z! It's about the only time in the show we got a laugh."

A few of the actors tittered feebly; the rest listened in glum silence. Reginald Olmsted came forward, rubbing his hands. "I say, Tommy, couldn't we get a little heat in here? You'll have us all coming down with pneumonia."

"How about it, Harry? Any chance of heat?"

"Well, it's City Steam, you know," said the carpenter. "I called them and they said they don't start till October, unless they get orders from the Health Department."

"And the Health Department's in Bermuda, I suppose. Well, boys and girls, look's like we'll just have to make the best of it." He turned to McCarthy. "Is Emily here?" he asked, thinking she might be in the dressing-room.

"No, sir," said McCarthy reluctantly. "Her maid called me this morning. She had a bad night and she can't get here before one at the earliest."

"Oh, nuts!" said Thompson under his breath. "All right, let's do as much as we can without her. Start at the beginning."

"Stand by for Act One, Scene One," shouted McCarthy. "Pete, set the props."

"Yes, sir," said Peter, swiftly swinging the chairs and tables into place.

"Want me to stand in for Emily?" asked McCarthy.

"Let Gladys do it. She looks it a little more than you do."

Gladys curtsied. "Thanks, Mr. Thompson."

Lily Prengle came forward quickly. "Excuse me, Mr. Thompson," she said tremulously. "Could I do it?"

"Do what?" he asked irritably.

"Stand in for Miss Crandall. I know it."

"What do you mean you know it?"

"I know the part. Don't you remember, you told me to study it if I wanted to?"

"Well, you haven't let the grass grow under your feet, have you? Sure, go ahead if you know it."

Ordinarily there was an understudy for every part in the play, so that, in case of illness, someone was always ready to step in. But with a star of Emily's importance, it was impossible to offer the audience a substitute. If she was unable to go on, the performance would have to be canceled. So Thompson had engaged no understudy for her. However, when Lily had asked him for a script, in order to study the part on her own, he had readily acquiesced. He always did what he could to encourage ambitious young actors.

As Thompson came down the steps to the auditorium Eric walked down the aisle toward him. "I'm worried about Miss Crandall," he said.

"Boy, you're right on the ball," said Thompson with unconcealed sarcasm.

"Do you think she'll be able to go through with it?"

"If I could answer questions like that, I wouldn't be mucking around the theater. I'd be down at Belmont Park, picking the winners."

"What will happen if she can't?" Eric persisted.

"I'll jump off the Leaning Tower of Pisa. It's more chic than the Empire State Building, don't you think?" He moved down to the orchestra rail. "Whenever you're ready, Mack," he said, unscrewing the cap of his brandy bottle. Eric went back, angrily, to his accustomed seat.

The rehearsal began, and the actors went through their lines and business, mechanically, until the first entrance of Rhoda, the play's heroine. So far, the actors had made little attempt at characterization and had barely begun to memorize their lines. All that would come in due time. But for Lily Prengle this was the one chance to show Thompson what she could do. She came on, prepared to give a performance—and, to the surprise of everyone, she did give a performance. From the very first line she threw herself into the role, imbuing it with all the eloquence and passion she could command. The effect was electrifying. The other actors took fire from her, instinctively matching her emotion with theirs. For the first time, the values of the play became apparent. Eric leaned forward, thrilled, and the rest of the cast, forgetting their nervousness and discomfort, watched intently and approvingly. Whenever McCarthy attempted to correct some slight error Thompson motioned him to silence. Lily, aware of the impression she was making, went on with mounting fervor and brought the scene to a fine conclusion. At the end the other actors, always appreciative of excellence, burst into spontaneous applause.

Thompson rose in his seat. "Very pretty, Mrs. Siddons!"

"Thank you," said Lily almost inaudibly, her face flushed and streaming with tears.

"All right, boys, let's see what gives with Scene Two."

As Lily joined her congratulatory fellow-players and the stage managers came forward to rearrange the furniture, Emily strode onto the stage. Arriving unnoticed in the middle of Lily's scene, she had been standing just outside the entrance to the stage. There was a sudden embarrassed silence, for it was obvious that she had been listening. Her eyes were hard with anger and her mouth tightly set. Without greeting anyone she walked to the edge of the stage and said to Thompson, "I'm here, if you want to do the first scene."

"Hi!" said Thompson with a wave of his hand. "Yes, let's do the first scene."

While the stage managers rearranged the furniture again, Emily, still ignoring everyone, slipped her arms out of the sleeves of her mink coat, drew it about her shoulders, lit a cigarette, and sat, quite apart from the others, waiting for her entrance cue. When it came she deliberately ground out her cigarette on the floor and, script in hand, walked over to take her place, leaving her handbag on the chair she had vacated.

Her first scene was with Richard Ismay, who played the part of her married lover. In the middle of one of his speeches she said, without apology, "My God, it's freezing in this dump of a theater."

"Sorry, honey," said Thompson sympathetically. "I wish there were something I could do about the weather, but I haven't any pull —not with the life I've led."

"Shall I go back?" asked Ismay.

"Just to the beginning of your speech."

190

He began again, and again Emily interrupted. "Nellie!" she called. "Have you got any tea in the dressing-room?"

"Yes, Miss Crandall," said the maid.

"Go and make me a cup."

"Very good, Miss Crandall." She hurried off.

"Back to the beginning?" asked Ismay.

"If you please," said Thompson.

"I'm sorry to put you to so much trouble," said Emily sarcastically.

"No trouble at all, Miss Crandall," said Ismay politely.

"What am I supposed to do, freeze to death? My God, you'd think it was a command performance or something. Well, what are you waiting for?"

"Nothing."

"All right then, go ahead, go ahead!"

He began again. A few minutes later she interrupted once more, this time with a loud sniffle. "Jesus, I hope I'm not getting a cold," she said. "Wait till I get a handkerchief." She looked around. "Where in hell did I leave my handbag?"

"It's right here, Miss Crandall," said Lily Prengle, bringing it to her.

Snatching the handbag roughly from Lily, Emily let it slip. It fell to the stage, spilling out the usual clutter of cosmetics, keys, and cigarettes.

"You clumsy little bitch!" shouted Emily, stamping her foot.

"I'm terribly sorry, Miss Crandall," said Lily, terrified. She and Emily bent at the same instant to pick up the bag, their heads colliding painfully. "I'm so sorry," whimpered the girl. "I hope I didn't hurt you."

"Sorry! Sorry! In a pig's ass, you're sorry!" screamed Emily. "What the hell are you trying to do, you little tramp—kill me?" She rushed at Lily and slapped her face, right and left, before anyone could intervene. Then Ismay sprang forward and held her arms while Olmsted led the sobbing Lily away. Emily, with maniacal fury, threw Ismay off, picked up the script, and hurled it across the orchestra pit, barely missing Thompson, who stood at the rail, paralyzed with horror. "There's your goddam script!" she said. "And you know what you can do with it!" Shrieking obscenities, she flung chairs and tables around. It took the combined strength of Ismay and McCarthy to restrain her at last.

Thompson was on the stage by now. "Take her to the dressing-room, boys," he said sharply. As Emily, sobbing hoarsely, was half led, half carried off, he clapped Peter on the shoulder. "Hurry up and get a taxi!"

Thompson went to the dressing-room. Emily lay on the chaise longue, panting heavily. "Get her into her coat," he said. Nellie and McCarthy complied, not without difficulty. "Better carry her, Mack. She'll never be able to walk."

McCarthy picked her up in his arms; she slumped against his shoulder. "Go with her," said Thompson, "and don't leave until she's got a doctor and a nurse and whatever she needs. If you need me, phone me here or at the office."

He stood at the stage door while McCarthy carried Emily up the windswept alley. Then he walked back slowly to the stage. The actors were waiting gloomily, some of them clustered about Lily. When she saw Thompson she sprang to her feet and rushed to him.

"Oh, Mr. Thompson, please forgive me! I know it's all my fault and I feel so awful about it. But I didn't mean to do anything wrong, honestly I didn't!"

He took the sobbing girl in his arms and held her soft, slender body close to his. "Don't be silly. It's not your fault."

"I'll do anything to make up for it. Only please don't fire me, please don't! You've been so wonderful to me, giving me this chance. I'll die if you fire me now."

"I'm not going to fire you, you little dope. Go sit down and shut up." He kissed her forehead, swung her around, and gave her a shove. She went back to her chair and sat looking at him with frightened, swimming eyes.

Thompson addressed the assembled company. "Well, boys and girls, let's call it a day. Everybody here at twelve tomorrow, please. And that means everybody," he added by way of reassurance. Ordinarily the probationers would have been delighted by this guaranty of security, but now the whole future of the production was in jeopardy.

Florence rose. "May I say a word, Tommy?"

"The chair recognizes Miss Fulham."

"Well, it's just that I feel that we should all keep very, very quiet about what's happened. It's not going to do the play or anybody any good to have it talked around. So I think we should agree that we'll just keep it all right in the family."

There was a general murmur of assent. Thompson said, "Thanks for saying it for me, Flossie." But he knew that twenty actors could not be depended upon to keep secret so juicy a bit of scandal.

The actors gathered up their things and drifted out of the theater. Olmsted lingered. "You're not really expecting to go on with her, Tommy?" he said.

"You know as much about it as I do. What do you say we just let it ride and see what happens?"

"About all we can do, I expect. Charming place, the theater. My father was all for my going into the Army. Damn near broke his heart when I put on grease paint. I often wish I'd listened to the dear old chap."

"Never too late, Reggie. You've got the makings of a first-rate parachute jumper. I'm thinking of going into the embalming trade myself." He noticed Eric getting into his overcoat and went over to him, feeling that he should make some amends for his rudeness. "Having fun, Eric?"

"Not very much. What's going to happen now?" Though still resentful, he could not help admiring the self-possession with which Thompson handled the whole situation.

"You're always right there with the hard-to-answer questions. Maybe this breeze will blow the goddam town off the map, and that'll solve all our problems." He clapped Eric on the shoulder. "See you tomorrow!"

He went to his office and called Fineman and Winternitz into conference. They received his news glumly, aware of the gravity of the situation.

"What about the press," said Winternitz, "respecting whose freedom Congress shall make no laws? I suppose you know that this is going to push Stalin right off page one, and jeez, will he burn!"

Thompson smiled wryly. "The cast crossed their hearts they wouldn't tell."

"Pardon me, effendi," said Winternitz, "are you referring to dues-paying members of the Actors' Equity Association, sometimes referred to as Thespians, an appellation derived from Thespis, reputed founder of the drama of ancient Attica, cradle of our Western culture?" He looked at his watch. "In twenty minutes flat, I'll have the entire fourth estate on my neck, and I just washed it this morning too."

"See what you can do with the boys, Doc," said Thompson. He relied upon Winternitz, who was on excellent terms with the drama editors, to have the story handled as discreetly as possible.

Winternitz sprang to his feet and saluted. "Entendu, mon capitaine! You may depend upon Winternitz to carry the message to Garcia, but gosh you're not making it easy." As he ducked out of the office Thompson threw a desk calendar at him.

"What about the bookings?" asked Fineman.

"Well, you'll have to cancel New Haven."

Fineman whistled. "They're practically sold out for the engagement. Twelve thousand fish in the kitty. That's a lot of moola."

"All right, it's a lot of moola! And there's a lot of gold buried at Fort Knox. So what? I can't open this show in New Haven three weeks from last night. Do I make myself clear?"

"Well, we'll just have to refund, I guess," said Fineman ruefully. "What about Boston?"

"Hold on to Boston for a few days more. That doesn't look good either, but I don't want to let it go until I'm sure."

"They've got a big advance in Boston too."

"Listen, Murray, why don't you go out and rob a bank or something? But first go around to the booking office and explain the whole thing to them. Tell them we'll let them know definitely by the middle of next week." The telephone rang, and the receptionist announced McCarthy. "It's Mack. He may have some news, though I doubt it. Okay, Murray—or is there something else on your mind?"

"Tony Weir went off on his vacation without ever sending around those booking contracts for the Farow. I wanted to tell you sooner, but you've been so busy I didn't like to bother you."

"I'm never too busy to hear about your troubles, Murray. But the way things look now there's no great hurry about booking the Farow."

"Will they hold it for you if you have to postpone?" asked Fineman.

Thompson looked at him. This was something he had not thought of. "Why, certainly they'll hold it! I'll take it up with Claire. Of course, there's a good chance we may not open at all."

"I guess you know that you're already in for twenty grand—at least twenty!"

"Get the hell out of here, will you? Jesus, if I ever do Hamlet I'll know where to look for the first gravedigger—*and* the second!"

"I'm just trying to tell you what the score is," said Fineman, stalking out of the office in a huff.

Thompson sent for McCarthy. "Well?"

"Well, we got her home, all right, and put her to bed. She was carrying on like nobody's business, but we got the doctor there on the double—Corcoran, I think his name is—and he gave her a shot to quiet her. Then he phoned for a nurse and Nellie called up some doctor in Hollywood—some peculiar name that I can't remember—"

"Wait a minute!" said Thompson. "Was it Thwaite?"

"Yeah, that's it."

"He was taking care of her out there. Go ahead."

"Well, Nellie told him what was what, so he said he'd see what he could do about a plane. Then about fifteen minutes later he called back to say he was leaving pronto and was due in here first thing in the morning. By that time Emily was asleep and the nurse was there, so I thought I might as well pull out."

"Maybe we ought to get in touch with her family or somebody. Has she got any people, I wonder?"

"I talked to Nellie about that," said McCarthy, "and it seems not. She's an only child and her mother's been dead for years. She's got a father, but according to Nellie he's an old jerk that she set up in a gas station in Omaha and hasn't seen in God knows when. Then there's that husband of hers, Duke Something-or-other—"

"Count Pedro Partagas, otherwise known as Bo-Bo. He'd be worse than nobody. Anyhow, he's in Nevada, getting a divorce."

"That's what Nellie said. So I asked her, well, what about friends —some girl friend, or maybe a boy friend. But Nellie says there's nothing like that, right now—at least nobody she cares that much about. Of course, she knows a lot of people on the Coast, but Nellie's afraid of spreading it around out there, with the gossip columns and everything. She did call that agent here, but I don't think there's much he can do."

"Paul Kipner!" said Thompson, horrified. "Good God, imagine having nobody in the world to turn to except some Hollywood specialist and Paul Kipner! That's pretty tragic." In sudden panic he wondered how many he could turn to. At least he had Claire and his brother Andrew.

"Yeah, I was thinking the same thing myself," said McCarthy. "You know, I feel kind of sorry for her in a way. I think half the time she doesn't know what the hell she's saying or doing." He rose. "Anything I can do for you?"

"Not a thing, Mack. Thanks a lot. You've been a big help."

"Well, this has been kind of a headache for you. I'll be in my room, if you do want me. Oh, Dick Ismay is out there. I told him I'd let you know. Do you want to see him?"

"Is he quitting?"

"He didn't say," said McCarthy tactfully. "Shall I send him in?"

"Yes, may as well. Oh, and if I'm a little late tomorrow, just take them through without me. Let Lily read the part."

"Say, wasn't that kid good, though?"

Thompson passed his hand over his forehead. "Too damn good, if you ask me."

"Yeah, you've got something there. Well, so long, chief, see you tomorrow."

He left, and a moment later Richard Ismay entered, obviously ill at ease.

"Sit down, Dick. What's on your mind?" said Thompson, knowing the answer.

"Well, I hate to bother you, Mr. Thompson, when I know all you're up against," said the actor, wetting his lips, "but I just had to see you and—"

Thompson stretched out his hand. "You're turning in your part?"

"Well, yes, sir, I'm afraid I am." He took the part from his pocket. "I've been offered another job and I feel that I have to take it."

"You didn't waste much time, did you?" said Thompson, taking the creased pages from him.

"They've been talking to me about it for a long time, and I had to give an answer today, because rehearsals start Monday. It's the new Jack Homburg production and—"

Thompson laughed. "Jack Homburg!"

"Yes, I know. But it's a fat part and he's giving me a good salary. I've got a wife and baby and another one in the oven, and I can't afford to turn it down. Naturally, I'd rather work for you, but the way things look now—"

"You don't have to explain to me how things look now," said Thompson sharply.

"All I mean is—"

"I know what you mean." He held up the part. "Of course, you know that I don't have to accept this."

"How do you mean?" said Ismay nervously. "It's only the fifth day."

"Technically the fifth day ended when I dismissed the company this afternoon. Technically you owe me two weeks' salary." He

196

laughed aloud at the look of horror on Ismay's face. "Don't worry. I wouldn't want to come between an actor and Jack Homburg." He threw the part on the desk and rose. "I've got a few things to do, so if—"

The actor rose hastily. "Well, thank you very much, sir," he said profusely. "And I hope you won't hold this against me."

"What the hell do you think I am, a Sicilian vendettist?"

Ismay leaned over the desk and grasped Thompson's hand. "I can't tell you how sorry I am. And I do hope everything turns out for the best for you."

"That is as God wills," said Thompson, withdrawing his hand from the clammy grip.

Ismay left, and Thompson, with a grimace of disgust, wiped his hand on his trousers. In spite of what he had said, he resented the actor's defection and resolved not to employ him again. He believed that actors should consider it a privilege to be engaged by him—in fact, most of them did—and he could not forgive a player who left his employ for that of a notoriously incompetent producer, no matter what the circumstances.

He put off calling Poundridge, afraid that Claire would feel it her duty to come to town immediately. Not wishing to spend the evening listening to her lamentations, he dined with Winternitz, and after dinner went around to the Stuyvesant Theater. The howling winds had no effect on business there. As usual, the house was packed —a state of affairs that went a long way in compensating for the disasters at the Farow. He spent an hour in the box-office, watched the performance for a while, and then, feeling that it was sufficiently late to telephone Claire, went up to the house manager's little office, where he could talk in privacy. As he had expected, even his very subdued version of the day's occurrences threw her into a state of consternation.

"If you'd only called me earlier," she said, "I'd have come right in to keep you company."

"That would have been nice, but this is the first moment I've had. It's been a pretty hectic day, when you add it all up."

"Yes, I can imagine, you poor darling! That wretched little—"

"Well, she's a pretty sick girl," said Thompson.

"Oh yes! A spoiled, conceited, self-centered little good-for-nothing, you mean. If she's so sick, why did she take the part in the first place?"

"There's not much use going into that now. I think maybe we'd better get together in the morning, though, and talk things over. Can you be at the office at eleven?"

"Yes, of course! I could even drive in now, except that the weather's so awful."

"Don't do that," he said. "It's much too late and I'm dead on my feet."

"Oh, you poor dear, you must be! Where are you now?"

"Just on my way to dinner."

"Goodness, haven't you eaten yet? You'll get sick if you don't take better care of yourself."

"No, I'm all right, darling—that is, unless I get hit by a falling skyscraper. You have a little wind up there?"

"A little wind! It's the worst thing I've ever seen in my life. We've had some trees down, but not near the house, and none of the copper beeches, thank goodness. Well, love and kisses to you, honey. Do get a good rest and I'll see you at eleven."

"Good night. Love to you."

He went backstage, for what remained of the performance, talked to the actors and stagehands, and watched bits and snatches of the play from the wings. He invited Rose Lowden, who played the feminine lead, to have a drink with him after the show, and sat in her dressing-room while she removed her make-up and changed her clothes. She was not embarrassed by his presence. At one point, when she asked him to turn his head away, he complied instantly. They had known each other for a long time, and she was used to having him about. Like most actresses who worked in his productions—and many who did not—she was a little bit in love with him. She was happily married and the mother of two children, and, though she liked him to kiss and fondle her, she had made it clear that he must not go too far. So they kept up a sort of running flirtation, showering each other with loving epithets and expressions of violent passion, a game that amused and titillated them both. Thompson believed that any woman's resistance could be overcome, but since he was only mildly attracted to Rose Lowden he did not want to risk wounding his ego by putting her to the test.

They went around to Pinelli's and sat drinking and gossiping for an hour. When he dropped her at her apartment he gave her a hearty good-night kiss, to which she responded with equal heartiness. It was an agreeable ending to what had been a very bad day indeed.

XIV.

Eric left the theater in a state of agitation. It was evident that there was small likelihood of Emily's continuance and that the production might have to be indefinitely postponed or possibly abandoned. He went across the street to O'Leary's and telephoned Irina Lanski. She had someone with her and suggested that he come around to her office, in an hour, when they could talk freely. He sat down at a table and ordered a sandwich and a glass of beer. The radio was on, tuned to a program of jazz records, which was interrupted presently for the hourly news broadcast. The news was mostly of the hurricane. Eric, who was only half listening, sat up in alarm as the announcer described the progress of the storm in central Connecticut. Several communities had been badly hit, with property damage and some loss of life. Among the towns affected was Coltertown. Terrified, Eric hurried to the telephone booth and put in a call to his mother. After a long wait a Hartford operator informed him that service to Coltertown had been interrupted and there was no telling when it would be resumed. He leaned back against the wall of the booth, trembling, his heart in his throat. Then, feeling that he must get home at once, he called Grand Central Terminal. There was an express to Hartford in twenty minutes. He hurried to the station, ignoring the traffic signals and dodging among the trucks and taxis, something he would not have dared to do two weeks earlier. He made the train, with five minutes to spare. Not until he sank, panting, into a seat did it occur to him that he should have telephoned Irina Lanski, who would be waiting for him.

But Irina Lanski, Emily, Thompson, his play, all seemed unimportant now. His one thought was for the safety of his parents, the

La Pointes, Sylvia and her family. He tried not to think of what he would do if anything serious had happened to any of them, his mother in particular. He remembered that he had a letter from Sylvia in his pocket. Preoccupied with his worries about Emily, he had merely glanced at it; now he read it more carefully. It contained the usual complaints about his absence and her resultant loneliness; the only real news was that she was planning to leave that very evening on her annual two weeks vacation—deferred until the end of September, at her employer's request. Knowing that Eric would be in New York, she had accepted the invitation of a married schoolmate, who lived in the Berkshires, to spend the holiday with her.

Eric had been irritated by Sylvia's constant harping on his neglect of her. He had expected her to be more sensible of his obligation to be in New York and more interested in what he was doing. Now, as he visualized her lying dead or maimed, he reviewed their relationship from its very beginnings and convinced himself that he had been guilty not only of neglect, but of bad faith: he should have married her long ago, obstacles or no obstacles. His common sense reminded him that the obstacles were as much of her making as of his, but in his emotional state he brushed aside these reasonable arguments and stigmatized himself as callous and selfish. By the time the train reached Hartford he was overwhelmed by anxiety and remorse.

There was still no telephone service to Coltertown. Sick with worry, he hired a taxi to drive him over, unmindful of the cost. The erratic storm had hardly touched Hartford, but along the highway to Coltertown, uprooted trees, overturned cars, and, here and there, a collapsed barn testified to the hurricane's havoc. Repair crews were at work on the fallen power lines. At several places, where road obstructions channeled the traffic to one lane, swearing, gesticulating state troopers tried vainly to relieve the congestion. As the taxi crept along, Eric's dread of what awaited him grew and grew. He reproached himself for having gone to New York instead of fulfilling his duty at home, shutting his eyes to the fact that his presence in Coltertown would not have lessened the wind's velocity.

The fourteen-mile trip took over two hours, and it was quite dark when he reached home. The street lights were out, but the car's headlights revealed the great branches that had been torn from the fine old elms lining the road. Eric rushed into the house, which was feebly illuminated by long-unused kerosene lamps and stubby candles set in saucers. In the dining-room his father sat in his wheel chair beside the silent radio, chewing his quid and aimlessly moving his hands.

"Hello, Pop!" Eric shouted, throwing his arms around Kenwood. "Are you all right?"

Kenwood blinked. "Eric! Where the hell did you come from?" He was genuinely glad to see his son.

"How's Ma? Is she all right?"

Before Kenwood could answer Amelia came running in from the kitchen. "Eric! Eric!"

He kissed her, holding her close. "Thank God you're all right. I heard the news on the radio and then I tried to get you on the phone—"

"Yes, I wanted to call you too. But, of course, I couldn't. Oh, son, I'm so glad you're here!"

"What about Dorothy and Leon?"

"They're all right. And the Jethrows too. Sam Jethrow came around this morning to see about us. Their place wasn't even touched. My, it's good to see you!"

Eric threw off his coat and sat down, weak with relief. "I thought I'd never get here. Is there any damage?"

"Well, it's not as bad as it might have been."

"What happened?" asked Eric anxiously.

"Let's not talk about it now. Get yourself rested first. You must be just about worn out."

"No, tell me!"

She told him briefly. The wind had increased in violence, all night. Just before dawn the whole house trembled on its foundation, as an uprooted black oak in the back yard crashed onto the roof, tearing a large hole in it. "It's an act of providence that nobody was sleeping upstairs. When I saw what happened, I got down on my knees and thanked God that you weren't home."

Eric rose. "I think I'll go up and take a look."

"I'll go with you. Just wait till I get a lamp."

"Well, Pop," said Eric, "that was a lucky escape. You might have all been killed."

"Might have been better for me if I had."

"Now, Pop, what's the idea of talking like that?" said Eric as Amelia entered with a lighted lamp. But he knew that what his father said was true, and his heart went out to him.

He followed his mother upstairs to his room. A great jagged branch had ripped the window sash away and rested on his bed. If he had been home he could hardly have escaped serious injury—perhaps death. In the adjoining room a large section of the ceiling had fallen directly on the spot where his parents' bed had once stood. Eric was suddenly nauseated as he contemplated what might have happened.

The attic was even worse. The roof, long in need of repair, had crumbled under the impact of the tree's massive upper branches. To Eric's surprise, the gaping hole had been hastily patched with some old planks, so that it was partly rainproof.

"Who did that?" he asked.

"Leon. He's been working here all day. I don't know how I'd have managed without him. Only I didn't want to talk about it in front of your father."

Dorothy had driven over at daybreak. After seeing the damage, she returned home and asked Leon to go over and help. He had willingly complied—for once his mechanical talents counted for more than the superior mental attainments of the Kenwoods. Amelia had managed to keep her husband in the front rooms. If Kenwood knew of Leon's presence, he had enough good sense left to keep quiet about it.

Leon had done what he could to relieve the dangerous pressure on the rear wall of the house and had roughly repaired the roof. Expert in all technical skills, he had done, singlehanded, what ordinarily would have taken two men twice as long. Eric felt less guilty about his absence, for he would have been of little practical help.

While he ate his supper he gave Amelia a softened version of the events at the Farow, not wanting to add to her worries. She was too tired and too glad to have him home to ask many questions or to listen very attentively. He felt that, perhaps, he should go around to the Jethrows, on the chance that Sylvia had not yet left, but the garage door was blocked by debris and he did not relish taking the long walk to the Jethrows in the cold wind.

He went to bed in Dorothy's old room and, away from the harrowing din of the hotel court, slept long and hard. When he awoke he sat up in bed and looked around in perplexity, not remembering, for the moment, where he was. Leon was already busy in the yard. He had induced two of his neighbors to help him take down the tree and cart it away, in return for the valuable oak wood. Eric offered to help, but Leon told him bluntly that if he really wanted to be useful, he should go around to the farm and give Dorothy a hand. Eric put on some old work clothes of his father's, cleared the garage door, and set off for the farm.

Coltertown was buzzing with activity. The factories had shut down, partly because of the power failure, partly so that the employees could repair the damage to their homes or lend their neighbors a helping hand. As usual, reflected Eric, it took a catastrophe to bring out the best in everybody. Week in and week out the pulpit, the press, the public platform, and the citizenry in general paid lip-service to "neighborliness" and "community spirit," but it was only in a time of trouble, such as this, that people forgot their selfish interests and animosities, their religious prejudices and class distinctions, and pitched in to do what needed to be done. Everywhere the townsfolk were busy, cleaning up the streets and the yards, making repairs, providing for the homeless, removing furniture from houses that threatened to collapse. Truck owners were hauling away the debris; war veterans were helping direct traffic; everyone was animated by an uncommon spirit of friendliness and concern for the common good.

On his way to the farm Eric went by Sylvia's house. Lydia answered the doorbell. "Oh, hello, Eric. What a surprise!" she said rather coolly, looking at his patched, baggy clothes and his unshaven face. She did not ask him to come in.

He apologized for his appearance, explaining that he had left his own clothes in New York.

"Yes, I see," said Lydia. "When did you get here?"

"Last evening. I wanted to come around but I couldn't get the car out."

"And it's such a long walk. Well, Sylvia will be terribly disappointed, I know. The poor child has been so lonesome. It would have meant a lot to her to see you."

"I didn't think she'd be home. She wrote me that she was planning to leave right after work yesterday." He was painfully aware of how lame his excuses sounded.

"Well, we were worried about her leaving in that storm. So she waited until this morning. If you'd come an hour sooner, you'd have caught her. And I'm sure if she'd known you were here, she would have put off going."

"Oh, I wouldn't have wanted her to do that," said Eric. "She sounds pretty run-down and she needs the vacation."

"Yes, she hasn't been feeling any too well. And her state of mind isn't too good either. I suppose you'll be going right back to New York."

"I don't know just how soon. There's been a little delay in the production of my play."

"Oh, is that so? Well, that's too bad. Will you excuse me now? I've got some milk heating and I'm afraid it may boil over."

"Yes, of course. I've got to get over to the farm anyhow."

He drove off, feeling very contrite. It was clear that the Jethrows were offended by what they regarded as his neglect. He could not continue to allow his relationship to Sylvia to drag on, in this indeterminate fashion.

Dorothy was pleased to see him and to have someone to help her. Eric was hardly a substitute for Leon, but he did relieve her of some of the heavier chores. She had begun to fill out, and her approaching maternity was now quite evident. It was a long, long time since the brother and sister had spent a whole day together and both enjoyed it. When Leon returned just before dark, he was amused by Eric's sweat-streaked face and sagging body. "How's the new farmhand?" he said to Dorothy.

"Better than you'd be at a typewriter."

Leon roared with laughter. "Say, you're right about that! I wouldn't know which end of one of them things to tackle."

Eric drove home and took a hot bath and an alcohol rub-down to ease his aching muscles. In the evening telephone service was resumed, but too late for him to call Irina Lanski or Thompson at their offices. He did not know where either of them lived, nor would he be able to reach them next day, which was Sunday. Unless one of them called him, he would have to wait until Monday to find out what was happening in New York.

XV.

Thompson left an early call for Saturday in order to be on time for his appointment with Claire. He telephoned Emily's hotel, only to be informed that she had left instructions not to be called. He decided against going around to see her. When he got to the office Claire was waiting for him.

"Any news?" she asked anxiously.

"No. I called the hotel, but—" The telephone rang. "All right, put him on." He turned to Claire. "Here's her doctor."

"Good morning, Mr. Thompson," said the doctor. "This is Doctor Thwaite. You may remember my calling you from California when—"

"Yes, of course!" said Thompson impatiently.

"Well, I'm here in Doctor Corcoran's office. He and I have just come from Miss Crandall's and I thought you'd be interested in getting a report."

"How is she?"

"Frankly, she's in pretty bad shape. I was afraid this was going to happen; that's why I came on. I've seen this coming for a long time. In fact, I strongly advised her against undertaking this play, because I was sure she wasn't up to it. She's been under a continuing nervous and emotional strain, worrying about her work and about some distressing personal problems."

"Yes, I know about that," said Thompson.

"She's tried to keep herself going by a constant alternation of sedatives and stimulants—also against my advice, I may say—and the resultant shock to her nervous system has been very severe. My diagnosis, with which Doctor Corcoran is entirely in agreement, is that she is suffering from a psychosomatic condition: an anxiety

205

neurosis accompanied by some rather troublesome functional disturbances."

"Well, I'm sorry to hear it. I suppose that means she won't be able to do the play."

"Oh, that's quite out of the question. This is going to be a long pull, I'm afraid. In fact, hospitalization is absolutely essential. I'm going to put her in a sanitarium in Tucson, where she'll get exactly the care she needs and where I can visit her periodically."

"Is she able to travel?"

"I think so. I've been in touch with Mr. Kipner—I think that's the name—"

"Yes, he's her agent."

"He's making arrangements to charter a private plane, and, of course, I'll go along and see her properly settled."

"Well, if there's anything I can do—"

"Thanks, but I don't think so. Mr. Kipner expects that we'll be able to leave this afternoon, and meanwhile I'm keeping her under sedatives. I probably shan't even tell her what our destination is until we actually arrive. What you could do, if you cared to, is write her a little note expressing your understanding of the situation. She has a feeling of guilt about you, and I think a friendly word from you would have a good psychological effect."

"Yes, I'll be glad to do that. Give me the address, will you?" He jotted it down. "Do you think if I came around to see her—"

"No, I don't recommend that in her present condition. Well, good-by, Mr. Thompson."

"Good-by, Doctor."

He repeated to Claire what the doctor had told him. "I guess I should have seen it coming too," he said. "She seemed awfully jittery when I saw her in Hollywood, but I thought she'd snap out of it when she got to New York."

"It's no wonder, with the lives they lead out there," said Claire pettishly.

"Well," said Thompson, "when you get to looking over the batting averages, you'll find there aren't many .300 hitters in any league."

"What are we going to do?" asked Claire, walking around nervously.

"I wish I knew the answer. Let's get Murray and Doc in here and kick it around."

Winternitz and Fineman listened dejectedly to the news.

"You'd better get out a Monday morning release, Doc," said Thompson. "And try to make it as easy as you can for everybody—including her."

"I've sounded out most of the boys. They'll play ball with us, I think. I don't know about some of the columnists. They don't decontaminate so easy."

"Do we have to say that she's entirely out?" asked Fineman.

"Certainly we have to say it!" said Thompson irritably. "Who the hell are we kidding? It's going to be all over town by tonight."

"Correction," said Winternitz. "Make that last night."

"All right, I just asked," said Fineman.

"What about the play?" said Winternitz. "They're all on me about that."

"Yeah," said Thompson. They all watched him as he sat making crisscross lines on his desk blotter with a paperknife. "You'd better say that I'm considering several other name actresses for the part."

"Are you?" asked Winternitz.

"What's that got to do with it?"

"All right, I just asked." He turned to Fineman. "Any similarity between my line and yours is purely coincidental."

Thompson answered the telephone. "Tell him I'm not in. No, put him on. Hello, Paul."

"I've got some pretty bad news about Emily, Tommy," said Kipner. "She's—"

"I know all about it. Her doctor called me."

"Poor kid! Can you imagine a thing like that happening? She had her heart set on doing this play too."

"Yes, it's tough for all of us."

"Oh, don't think I'm forgetting your end of it. Maybe I can help you find somebody for the part."

"Like who?"

"Well, I haven't really had time to think about it. This thing has hit me like a ball from the blue."

"You mean a bolt from the bull, don't you?"

"How's that, Tommy?" asked Kipner, puzzled.

"Nothing. Just a slip of the tongue. Well, I'm pretty busy, Paul. If you get any ideas, give me a ring."

"I'll do that, Tommy. Oh, while I've got you, what about Emily's contract?"

"Listen, I've got a few other things on my mind now!"

"All right, don't get heated up. All I meant was—"

"See Murray about it next week. Good-by!" He turned to Fineman. "Emily's contract."

"Yes, what do you want to do about it? I meant to ask you."

"What *can* we do about it?"

"Well, we've got a run-of-the-play contract."

"For Christ's sake, Murray! If she had a broken leg would you hold her to a contract? Well, I'd rather have two broken legs than what she's got—and a broken back too."

"All right, he just asked," said Winternitz, rising. "Well, folks, it's been a lovely party, but if you'll excuse me I think I'll go and apply a little confusal oil to my portable."

"You may want to mention that this has hit Kipner like a ball from the blue."

Winternitz shook his head. "Always thinking of the blue balls of his native Scotland."

"The next thing we've got to decide is whether we drop the show or go ahead," said Thompson. "Personally, I think we should try to go ahead."

"How can you go ahead without Emily Crandall?" asked Claire.

"By getting somebody else. The part never was written that only one actress could play."

"Yes, but who?"

"I don't know yet who. Right now I'm toying with the idea of Lily Prengle."

"Who is Lily Prengle? Good heavens, you don't mean that little blonde who's playing Aggie!"

"That's exactly who I mean. Wait a minute!" he said, checking her expostulation. "If you'd seen what I saw yesterday, you'd know what I'm talking about. She stood in for Emily, and I want to tell you she went after that part like a bat out of hell. She had my hair standing up on end, and the cast damn near fell out of their chairs. She's got something, that little lady has."

"Well, I may be talking out of turn," said Fineman, "but that's a hell of a chance to run, shooting your bankroll on a kid that's never done anything."

"Well, that's the kind of business we're in. If I'd never taken any chances or played any hunches I'd still be a stage manager. If the kid clicked it might be something sensational."

208

"And what if she failed?" asked Claire.

"We'd be out of luck. You can't win every time."

"No, but you don't have to take that kind of a gamble."

"What would you do?"

"I'd try to get somebody with a name, and if I couldn't, I'd drop it."

"You mean you're ready to pour twenty grand down the drain, with nothing to show for it?"

Claire turned pale. "Twenty thousand dollars! Why, how can that be?"

"Ask Murray."

"I've been doing a little figuring since I talked to you. It's more like twenty-five," said Fineman.

"I can't believe it," said Claire. "It's impossible."

"Well, I can show you the figures, if you want to see them. First, we've got the costumes—"

"We could call them off."

"Not a chance. They're all cut and we're stuck with them. Anyhow, we've got to pay Louis-Jean's designing fee whether he finishes them or not. And his trip to the Coast wasn't peanuts either. Then there's the scenery—"

"I'm sure that isn't built yet," said Claire desperately.

"A lot of it is, including those two big platforms. And some of it is painted. And we got to pay the scenic designer's fee too—that's a little item of five G's. Then there was Tommy's trip to the Coast and a lot of miscellaneous. When you put it all down and draw a line under it, it adds up."

"I still can't believe it adds up to twenty-five thousand."

"Why go on arguing about it?" said Thompson impatiently. "He knows what he's talking about. And another thing, whose pocket is it coming out of?"

"Whose do you suppose?" said Claire. "The backers, of course. They'll have to pay pro rata, according to their shares."

"You mean you're going to stick the Loftings and Kitty Hines and Louis Greenbaum and all those people for a show that never even gets started?"

"I don't see why not," said Claire defiantly. "They've all made plenty out of Give Them." She was worried about making this embarrassing demand upon her friends and social acquaintances. Such an action would not be likely to encourage them to invest in her future enterprises. Yet it was not easy to pay the entire loss out of her own pocket, on top of what she had already put into the Farow Theater.

"I don't think you could hold them even if you wanted to," said Fineman.

"Why not?" asked Claire angrily.

"All we've got from them so far is pledges. And they're made on the basis of Emily Crandall being in the show. If we don't deliver Emily I don't see where we've got any claim to hold them."

"I think he's right," said Thompson.

"Well, I don't!" she said sharply. "I think we'd better have some legal advice on all this. I'm going to get Tony." Though she loved Thompson more than she had loved anyone else and still hoped he would marry her, she dealt with him at arm's length when it came to business. Afraid the combination of her lover and Fineman would be too much for her, she wanted the help of Anthony Weir.

"I thought he was on his vacation," said Thompson as she put in the call.

"What of it? He can spend a few minutes on the phone. This is important enough. Oh, and what about the theater? You're not going to be ready to open on any October thirtieth, no matter what you do."

"Doesn't look much like it."

"Well, what am I supposed to do about the Farow?"

"You don't have to do anything this minute, do you? We'll know in a few days where I'm at, and if I don't go ahead you've still got lots of time to book something else."

"And meanwhile I may be losing a chance to book something good. I wish I'd never let myself be talked into buying the damn theater."

"Don't look at me. I didn't talk you into buying it," said Thompson, glad that he had always pretended to be indifferent to her acquisition of the theater.

She threw him an angry look as she answered the telephone. "Oh, is that you, Helen? This is Claire Weir."

"Yes, Mrs. Weir," said Anthony Weir's secretary.

"Where can I reach Mr. Weir? There's something very important I have to consult him about."

"To tell you the truth, Mrs. Weir, I don't exactly know where to reach him right now."

"You don't know where to reach him? Why, that's very odd. He told me he expected to go to Asheville. Isn't he there?"

"Well, he was, until last night, Mrs. Weir. But he phoned to say that he was tired of it and was driving south with some people he'd met. He said he wasn't sure just where they were going, but he'd be in touch with me."

"And you have no idea where he might be?"

"Why, no, I haven't. I may hear from him tonight or maybe not until Monday, but the minute I do I'll have him call you. Too bad I didn't know last night that you wanted to talk to him."

"This is something that just came up. When he does call, be sure to ask him to ring me at Poundridge right away, and if I should happen not to be there, tell him to leave word where I can reach him."

"I certainly will, Mrs. Weir. And I'm awfully sorry."

Claire hung up. "I can't understand his going off like that, without leaving some word where he could be reached."

"He's off on a bender," said Fineman.

Claire turned red with rage. "What right have you got to say a thing like that?" she shouted.

Fineman got up, with a shrug. "Maybe I talk too much. Tommy, I'm going to check with Equity on the actors' contracts. I want to find out just how we stand."

"Okay, Murray." He waited until Fineman left the room. "Why pick on poor Murray? It's not his fault that Tony is off on a binge."

"He should mind his own business and not go around spreading tales about people."

Thompson yawned. "You probably knew it all along."

"Would I have called him if I had?" asked Claire indignantly. "Helen told me, after the last one, that she was sure he was cured."

"She's got a tough assignment, that little girl, keeping up a front that fools nobody. Who was it that said the best-kept secrets are the ones everybody knows? Shaw, I guess. Or maybe it was Paul Kipner. Why don't you face it, baby? Tony'll never be cured." He rose. "Well, I'd better go around and talk to the cast."

"Is it all right if I go with you?"

Thompson frowned. "I don't know, dear. This is going to take a little handling and—"

"Yes, I know, and I'd only be in the way."

"I didn't say that. All I meant was—"

"Oh, don't bother about explaining. I should be used to these moods of yours, but it seems I'm not. I guess I may as well go back to the country, since I'm not wanted around here."

Fortunately Fineman returned. "Oh, I just wanted to tell you that I'm seeing Frank Lundwell at Equity at two. Might be a good idea to have one of the cast there."

"All right, I will," said Thompson. He did not allow the door to close behind Fineman.

"I'll wait around, if you want to come up to the country with me," said Claire as she and Thompson left the building.

"No, I can't. I've got a lot of things to do over the weekend. There's a pile of scripts that I have to read. Might be something there I could get started on, in case we do have to drop The Clouded Mirror."

"You could read them in the country."

"Too many interruptions. I'd better stay in town."

"Well, if you do change your mind, let me know, and I'll send the car in for you."

"All right. Well, I've got to run."

"My car's in the Radio City Garage. If you want to wait I'll drop you at the Farow."

"No, it takes too long. I'm an hour late already."

"Well, good-by then." She held up her face to be kissed.

Thompson brushed her cheek with his lips. "Good-by. I'll phone you." He hurried off without looking back.

She watched him for a long moment, then, with a deep sigh, walked to the garage. She was feeling very sorry for herself. She was faced not only with the loss of the money she was pouring into the Farow, but with the entire cost of an abortive production as well. Anthony Weir, whose advice was indispensable, failed her when she needed him most. Worst of all, she could never be sure of Thompson. Why, suddenly, was he talking about entrusting a star part to a little nobody? Did he really think Lily Prengle had that much talent or was there some other reason? She drove home in misery, obsessed by these torturing thoughts.

Thompson found the actors at the Farow listlessly going through the first act, under the guidance of McCarthy. They knew that Richard Ismay had handed in his part, and though there was no news of Emily, no one expected her to return. There was a pervading air of pessimism.

"All right, folks, hold everything," said McCarthy as Thompson entered.

"Hello, boys and girls," said Thompson. "How about if we all sit around and have a little fireside chat." Facetious though his words were, there was no levity in his manner. Thompson swung a chair around and sat facing the cast, his arms resting on the back of the chair.

"I'm going to get right down to Hecuba," he said. "I've had a talk with Emily's doctor and I'm afraid she's out." This was received in dead silence. "I'm not going to go into details, but you can take my word for it that she's in a bad way, and it's going to be a long time before she walks on any stage. If there's any comfort at all in what's happened, it's that it happened here and now and not in New Haven or Boston or the day before we opened in New York." There was a murmur of assent. "But what you all want to know is, where do we go from here? I wish I could give you the answer, but I haven't had time to work it out. What I can tell you is that I want to go ahead, if it's possible to do it. I like this play and I have confidence in it and I don't want to drop it." He looked around into the darkness. "Are you out there, Eric?"

"No, he didn't show," said McCarthy. "I phoned his hotel and he's not there either. That storm hit pretty hard up where he lives, and I figure maybe he went home."

"Well, never mind. To get back to what I was saying, I've got a casting problem on my hands, and it's not an easy one, as you know, especially when I have to work against time. Of course, I could postpone for a month or so, or until I found the right lead and start again from scratch. But I'd rather keep going, if I can, mainly for the reason that I'm very happy with this company and I doubt if I could ever assemble another that I liked as well." Nobody said anything, but he could see that they were pleased. "So I'm hoping that we can work out something together. This is a kind of special case, with a star involved and all, and Murray Fineman is going around this afternoon to get the Equity slant on it. By the way, who's the Equity deputy?"

"I am," said Clark Yardley, a young actor who played the part of a country doctor. The actors' union required every company to elect a deputy from among its members, to serve as a sort of liaison officer between the cast and the union and to adjust any minor differences that might arise backstage.

"Oh, it's you, is it?" said Thompson. "Well, you always struck me as the ward-heeler type. Can you get my grandfather a job in the Sanitation Department?" This brought a laugh. The atmosphere was a little easier.

"I'm incorruptible," said Yardley.

"Well, incorrupt yourself around to Equity at two, will you, to talk it over with Murray and Frank Lundwell?"

"I'll do it."

"Stout fellow. Well, that takes care of that. Now, I know what this means to all of you, not only as actors but as people with responsibilities, and I don't expect you to hang on indefinitely. But unless somebody's got something really hot on the fire, I would like you all to string along for a while and give me a chance to get this thing on its feet."

"Well, I think the least we can all do is give Mr. Thompson a chance," said Florence Fulham. There were several expressions of agreement, but some of the actors, who were less secure financially than Florence, were obviously dubious.

"How long would you expect us to wait, Tommy?" asked Olmsted.

"I'd say a week—ten days at the most. If nothing's cooking by then, I certainly wouldn't want to hold you any longer. Of course, we'll continue rehearsal pay while you're waiting—for whatever cigarettes that's worth."

"Could we have a chance to discuss it among ourselves?" said Yardley.

"I can do a little better than that. Why don't we just let everything ride over the weekend? By that time we'll have the Equity angle and you'll have had a chance to discuss it not only among yourselves but with your wives, ex-wives, future wives, and chiropractors."

"That seems fair enough," said Yardley. "All those in favor raise their hands." Everybody's hand went up. "It's unanimous."

Thompson rose and bowed. "The people's choice. All right, let's make it here on Monday at one. And when I say thank you all very much, I mean thank you all very much."

Several of the actors lingered to assure Thompson that he could count upon them. An elderly man, named James Lawless, grasped his hand. "I just want to say that if all managers showed actors the same courtesy and consideration that you do, this would be a happier profession to be in."

"Well, I'm a frustrated actor myself," said Thompson, touched.

Lily Prengle hovered in the background until everybody but McCarthy had left. Then she came over to Thompson, trembling and hardly able to talk. "Mr. Thompson, could I talk to you for a minute?"

"Yes, sure. Sit down," he said, knowing very well what was coming.

"I'm going upstairs for a minute, boss," said McCarthy tactfully. "Just yell when you want me."

"All right, Galahad," said Thompson. He sat down beside Lily. "Do I think you could play the part of Rhoda, please, Mr. Thompson?"

"Don't laugh at me. I know I have an awful nerve. But I know I could do it. I just know I could. You thought I was good yesterday. And it was the first time I tried it and I was just shaking, with you and everybody watching me. You said I was good."

"Yes, and I meant it too. But that part is quite a lot to bite off for a very small mouth." He took hold of her nose and chin, pulled her mouth open, and peered in. "Not a wisdom tooth in sight."

"I know I'm young and haven't had much experience, but this is one part I'm sure I could play. And with your direction and all. Oh, please, give me a chance! Everybody says how you're always giving young actors chances. So why not me?"

"I gave you a job, didn't I, with a million bloodthirsty females hammering at my door?"

"Yes, you did. And I'll always be grateful to you for it. But this might be the one big chance of my life. It could mean just everything in the world to me."

"It might mean the bailiffs for me, my girl, and a miserable end in the debtors' prison. It takes a lot of dough to put on a show. Say, that's a neat idea for a lyric. I must speak to Sir Arthur about it. What I am talking about, Snow White, is mazuma, sometimes vulgarly referred to as money. The rustle of an angry angel's wings is not a pretty sound. It would be nice if we could all do it just for fun, but under the free enterprise system you can't do things for free." He rose. "Don't be downhearted. You'll go places yet."

She stood up and took his hand. "I want to go now! Won't you at least think it over?"

"Oh, sure, I think about all sorts of things all the time."

"No, I mean seriously. At least give me a chance to read the part for you."

He hesitated. "Well—I'll tell you what I'll do. Let's see what happens Monday, and if we decide to go ahead, maybe I'll let you read for me."

"Oh, thank you! Thank you!" she said effusively.

He laughed. "All right, get out of here now!" He took her by the nape of the neck, held her there for a moment, and then pushed her toward the stage door. She went up the alley with her spine tingling, wishing that she could remember forever the pressure of his fingers on her neck.

McCarthy heard the stage door close and came downstairs. "Do you think she could do it, chief?"

Thompson shook his head doubtfully. "It would be taking an awful chance." They went across the street to O'Leary's, had a drink and something to eat, and reviewed the rehearsal schedule, discussing the various contingencies. In ten minutes Thompson had forgotten all about Lily.

XVI.

His muscles still painfully sore, Eric spent all of Sunday working about the house. The fallen tree had left a gaping hole, which he filled with rubbish, crushing it down with large field stones and leveling it off with several barrowfuls of soil. In the afternoon Irina Lanski telephoned to give him the bad news about Emily. Thompson wanted to see him, on Monday, to talk over the situation. She made no attempt to conceal its seriousness.

Early Monday morning Eric set off for the city once more, on what seemed the most hopeless of all his journeys. The New York paper he bought in Hartford carried the story about Emily substantially as Winternitz had written it. It merely said that she had had a nervous breakdown as a result of overwork, and that rehearsals would be resumed as soon as a suitable substitute could be found. There was no reference to the scandalous incidents at the Farow.

Eric and Irina Lanski arrived at Thompson's office almost simultaneously and were shown in immediately. "Hello, Eric," said Thompson. "How did you find things at home?"

"Nobody hurt luckily. But an uprooted tree tore a big hole in our roof."

"Well, the roof fell in on us here too."

"Yes, I know," said Eric. "But according to the morning paper you're planning to go ahead."

"That's public relations. Like those war communiqués, where our gallant troops are always falling back to more favorable positions."

"You mean you're not going to do the play?" asked Eric, his mouth and throat dry and his eyeballs burning.

"No, I don't mean that. All I mean is that at this moment I don't know where the hell I am. I've just had a session with the cast, and they all want to stick for a reasonable length of time. Frank Lundwell of Equity was there, and we fixed it so that they'll continue for ten days on rehearsal pay. If by then I can't cast the part, all bets are off and nobody's bound. It's a special concession, but Lundwell is sure it'll be approved by the Equity Council. That gives me ten days to turn around in. The next problem is where to turn."

"Don't you think that Miss Prengle could do it?" said Eric. "I liked the way she did it the other day."

"So did I. And I've been thinking it over. She's been on my neck about it, and I'm going to give her a reading. But, Jesus, I don't know."

"Excuse me," said Irina Lanski, "but don't you think that's rather risky?"

"I wish you'd heard her the other day," said Eric.

"I don't question her ability," she said, "but it takes more than just ability to carry a part like that in New York." She had had a full report of everything that had happened from Florence Fulham.

"That's it," said Thompson. "If it were summer stock or even a road company I'd take a chance. But this part calls for experience and for technique, and she hasn't got either. I can give her a lot, of course, but I doubt if she'd ever be able to sustain that long part."

217

"Wouldn't it look rather funny too," said Irina Lanski, "to have an unknown little girl supported by Reggie Olmsted and Flossie Fulham?"

"Yes, it would. I'm not sure they'd do it. Besides, she wouldn't rate any billing—not before we opened anyhow—and that would throw the whole thing out of balance. If we'd started with her it might have been different. But you can't suddenly switch from Emily Crandall to Little Miss Nobody from Nowhere. No, I think we'd better count Lily out."

"Isn't there someone else in Hollywood who—?"

"I've been all over that. I even thought of flying out there again. But it would be a waste of time. I went over the situation pretty thoroughly last summer, while I was waiting for Emily to make up her mind. The girls I can get I don't want, and the ones I'd settle for can't be pried loose. There's just one possibility, and that's May Weeks. Do you know her?" he asked Eric.

"I think I've seen her once or twice in the movies."

"She's not a bad little actress. And she hasn't been out there long enough for it to get her down. Of course, she's not the kind of box-office that Crandall is, but her name would mean something."

"Is there any chance of getting her?" asked Irina Lanski.

"Maybe. I just had her on the phone. She wants to do a play, but she's starting a picture next week and won't be available till the end of the year. That would mean postponing until January."

"January!" exclaimed Eric.

"At the earliest. That complicates things for me. I couldn't hold the cast, of course. Besides, it means that I've either got to sit around and wait or else start work on another show, in which case I probably won't be free in January."

"It doesn't sound very promising," said Irina Lanski.

"No, it doesn't. But I'm air-mailing her a script. I should have an answer by the end of the week. If she wants to do it and we can get together on it, I'll see if I can work out the time schedule."

"What about that Miss Upton?" asked Eric. "I saw her when I was—"

"Yes, I know. I've been thinking about her too. As a matter of fact I tried to reach her, but she's in Chicago, doing a radio show, and won't be back until Saturday. By that time I ought to have some word from May Weeks. If it's no, I'll talk to Ginny. But I don't think she'll want to do it. She's never played anything but comedy, and I'd have a hard time convincing her that this is a comedy."

"Yes, I think you would. But aren't there some other actresses—"

"There are thousands of actresses, but very few of them know how to act. I'm not going to risk my reputation and a bushel basket of somebody's jack by doing this play with some girl I haven't got confidence in."

"No, that would be foolish," said Irina Lanski. "Well, perhaps you will think of someone else."

"I'll keep pegging away," said Thompson. "We're in pretty deep on this thing, and if there's any chance of saving it, I certainly will."

"I guess there's not much use my staying in New York," Eric said, for want of anything else to say.

"Well, not on my account. If we need you we'll let you know. We've had a tough break, but if you're going to stay in the theater there's one thing you'd better learn early and never forget, and that is that there's no law that compels anybody to be a playwright —or a producer."

"Except the divine law that forbids us to kill the creativeness that is within us," said Irina Lanski.

At her suggestion Eric went around to her office with her. Myra Leech looked up from her clattering typewriter to give him a brief nod as they went into the inner office.

"Well," Irina Lanski said when she had lighted a cigar, "I suppose you will think me a fatuous ass if I tell you that you must not give up hope; but, believe me, it is the most important thing that I can say to you."

"It would be all right if that were all there is to it. Or if I had only myself to think of. But I gave up my job so that I could be here for rehearsals. I've been living on the few hundred dollars that I'd saved up, and that's not going to last very long. My father has locomotor ataxia and hasn't been able to work for years, and there's no one but me to look after him and my mother."

"You can't go back to your job? Temporarily, I mean, until we can get a play produced."

"They're pretty sore at me for leaving, and I don't think they'd take me back. I don't want to go back either. I only hung on as long as I did because I had to, but the thought of going back is almost unbearable. I'll go and beg them if I have to—but only as a last resort."

She nodded gravely. "I understand how you feel. When one is burning to create, it is hard to grind one's youth away at sterile work."

"If I could only find something where there was a little chance for initiative, or some hope of getting on to something better. But I haven't any right to bother you with all this."

"Don't talk like a fool!" She pointed to the pile of playscripts on her desk. "Do you see that heap of garbage that I have to wade through, every day of my life—turning the pages with one hand and holding my nose with the other? Don't you think it means something to me to find a young writer with talent? Well, we'll have to put our heads together and think of something."

Her words and the warmth behind them heartened him. "If I could only find a job in New York! Something that had to do with the theater or was related in some way to writing. I don't know just what—a playreader or a job on a newspaper or with a publisher. Do you see any chance of anything like that?"

"I don't know," she said dubiously. "Playreaders hardly exist any more. Those managers who can read do their own reading. The others have their plays read by their telephone operators, their mistresses, their mistresses' mothers, and their barbers. If you went more often to the theater that would be obvious to you. As for newspapers and publishers' offices, there are usually ten applicants for every job. And they don't pay much to beginners. Radio writing, perhaps. I could look into that. But there's no security in that until you are well established, and that takes time of course. How much certain income must you have?"

"Well, to take care of my parents and pay my expenses in New York, at least seventy-five a week." It sounded preposterously high.

She shook her head. "That's very difficult. For someone without special training or experience fifty dollars would be the most you could expect to begin with. Of course, if you had a play running I could get you a Hollywood job at five hundred a week."

Eric laughed ruefully. "If I had a play running I wouldn't need a Hollywood job."

"Exactly. The less you need it, the more they want you. The worshipers of the bitch-goddess Success are not in the market for unrecognized talent."

"I know. To him that hath shall be given, and from him that

220

hath not shall be taken away. Well, I'll go back home and try to think it out."

She extended her hand. "I'll think about it too. And remember, it's too soon to give up all hope about the play."

He pressed her hand warmly. "I don't know how to thank you."

"Thank me when I have really done something for you."

He went to his hotel, feeling a little better for his talk with her. The suspicious manager, accustomed to delinquent guests, was on the point of clearing his room and impounding his belongings. Eric paid what he owed, including that night's rent, for it was too late to start for Coltertown. The stuffy little room seemed drearier than ever. Now that the merciless city was ejecting him and sending him home, in defeat, like so many countless thousands before him, the cacophony of the court seemed like a mocking dirge to his hopes. After a sleepless night he took the first morning train to Hartford.

Eric spent the next few days making arrangements for the needed repairs to the Kenwood house. To his consternation, the cost came to over two hundred dollars. This unexpected inroad upon his fast-dwindling bank account was really alarming. His New York expenses had been considerably in excess of his estimate. The two dollars a day he had allowed himself for food had been insufficient. Cigarettes, laundry, carfares, telephone calls, an occasional drink and other minor incidentals had substantially increased his outlay. The repair bills did not have to be paid immediately, but the money had to be there to meet them eventually, and what was left would barely last another six weeks. Even should May Weeks be available, he had not nearly enough to carry him until January and through the ensuing rehearsal period. It was therefore imperative that he find immediate employment.

Since Coltertown offered little or nothing, he decided after considering every phase of the situation to try to find a job in Hartford, where there were more opportunities. He could continue to live at home, so that his only additional expense would be the cost of transportation.

He bought the Hartford papers every day and carefully read all the help wanted advertisements. There were few jobs for which he was qualified. He had no manual skill and none of the qualities or experience required of salesmen or canvassers. About all that he could hope for was a minor clerical position, and here too a knowledge of stenography, bookkeeping, or the operation of business machines was a requisite. He marked everything that looked even remotely possible and wrote the most persuasive letters of application that he was capable of. Twice he got up at daybreak and drove to Hartford to apply in person, but either the job had been filled before his turn came or he was not satisfactory. The Hartford employment agencies promised to do what they could, though they made it clear that his lack of special training was a serious handicap.

His friend James Duncan, to whom he turned for advice, introduced him to the business manager of the Coltertown Evening Standard, who offered him employment as an advertising solicitor, on a commission basis; but that promised no fixed income. Duncan also suggested that he look into the possibilities of getting a civil service job. As a veteran he had priority, and civil service employment meant security of tenure and slow but certain promotion. Besides, the hours were much shorter than in private employment, a very important consideration, for he was determined to go on with his writing.

He obtained the lists of forthcoming examinations in both the federal and state services. Again, the jobs were mostly of a technological nature, or else called for service in Washington or some remote place where the meager governmental pay would not begin to meet the expense of his living away from home and providing for his family too. The only promising examination was one that was to be held the following week for the job of proofreader on state publications. He registered for the examination, borrowed a manual of proofreading from the Evening Standard, and studied it assiduously.

Amelia, without telling Eric, went to the head of the school board, to ask about the possibilities of her resuming her work as a teacher. She was received with kindness and given a vague promise that an effort would be made to take her on as a substitute after the beginning of the new year. Kenwood was neither sympathetic to Eric's problem nor reticent about condemning him for his rashness and irresponsibility.

It was a black week for Eric, relieved only by the receipt of another installment of his advance royalty, which gave him another two weeks' respite, besides signifying that Thompson had not yet abandoned the play.

To add to his worries, Sylvia was constantly in his thoughts. He could no longer put off coming to a definite understanding with her. Shutting himself up in his room, he spent a whole evening writing her a long and intimate letter. After describing what had happened

222

in New York and explaining its probable effect upon the production of his play, he came to the real purpose of his letter, which was to ask her to marry him. He had always assumed, he wrote, that they would eventually marry; only economic difficulties had prevented their union. It might seem odd therefore, he said quizzically, that he should wait until his prospects were bleaker than ever, but this apparent inconsistency was explicable by his concern about her ambiguous situation. With understanding and tenderness he expressed his feeling that their relationship should be given permanence and public status. The path before them was not easy, but, once married and secure in their mutual love and common interests, they would learn how to overcome the obstacles. He would somehow find a way to make a living; perhaps she would be willing to go on working until he was able to provide for them both. He would not expect her to live under the same roof with his father. But if she wished, he would be willing to move into the Jethrow house, or they could go on living as they were and spend all their non-working hours together. Though far from an ideal arrangement, it would be infinitely better than the present one, for they would be married and working together for a happier future. He wished that he had more to offer her, but hoped she would share his faith in their ability to work things out. Again, he asked her to overlook his past shortcomings, and ended by saying that he eagerly awaited her answer.

Though he could not imbue it with a passion he did not feel, it was a sincere, thoughtful, and deeply felt letter, full of warmth and affection. The writing of it gave him great relief. He sent it off, feeling that he had corrected a grave injustice and fulfilled a deep moral obligation.

XVII.

Claire Weir had no particular fondness for country life, but she could not afford two large establishments. Rather than surrender the beautiful estate she had inherited from her husband, she contented herself with her small apartment in town and made Poundridge her principal place of residence. The Westchester County show place was an important element in the maintenance of her acquired social position, a matter of primary importance to her.

In her more sanguine moments she found satisfaction in the reflection that she had done very well by herself—and with good reason. Born into a dull and undistinguished family, and reared in a small Ohio town, she had upon her graduation from high school taken a year's course in a business school in Columbus and then come to New York in search of a wider life. Attractive, capable, and of an amiable disposition, she had no trouble in finding employment, shifting jobs whenever there was an opportunity for self-betterment. After several years in New York she got a well-paying job in the large cosmetics business of which Charles Weir was the head. Her ability (and her looks) rapidly brought her to her employer's attention. She made good progress in the business and better progress in her personal relationship to him. Nearly thirty years her senior, he was still a handsome vigorous man. She was almost as keenly interested in the business as he, so they always had something to talk about when they were not otherwise occupied and they were never bored with each other. They behaved with great discretion, but complete secrecy was impossible. Charles Weir's invalid wife and his two grown sons, who were in the business with him, knew very well how things stood. However, the wife had nothing to gain from a divorce or a scandal, and the sons thought it better not to bring the subject out into the open; consequently Claire, who was conventional-minded and had occasional moral misgivings, was spared any outward embarrassment.

She made many substantial contributions to the business. For one thing, she persuaded Charles Weir to branch out into the manufacture and sale of theatrical make-up and launched a campaign of exploitation that proved very successful. Part of her promotion plan was to obtain testimonials on the merits of the make-up (which was no better and no worse than competing brands) from theatrical celebrities, which brought her into contact with many famous theater people. She had always been stage-struck—indeed, she had thought at one time of becoming an actress—and this entree into the backstage world filled her with rapture.

From time to time Charles Weir, at his brother Anthony's suggestion, put money into theatrical productions. He never took these ventures very seriously, looking upon them as a rich man's diversion, like betting on the races or playing cards for high stakes. Several of these fliers had paid off well, and under Claire's influence, he began to extend his theatrical investments, with increasingly profitable results. She gave more and more of her time and attention to these activities, and, eventually, when Mrs. Weir died and Charles Weir, allowing a decent interval to elapse, asked Claire to marry him, she gave up her position in the cosmetics business and devoted herself entirely to the financing of theatrical productions.

She had come a long way from her small-town origins, and her new mode of life was far beyond her reasonable expectations. Not only was she married to a very wealthy man with important business and social connections, but she was actually becoming a prominent figure in the world of the theater. She had no interest in the drama as an art, regarding the theater solely as an institution for the amusement of the well-to-do and the pseudo-sophisticated. Her mind was commonplace, her ideas thoroughly conventional, so that her tastes were those of a large part of the playgoing public. If she liked a play the chances were that it contained the elements that made for popular success, and since she was careful to confine her financial support to the productions of well-established managers or in which actors dear to the public appeared, her percentage of correct guesses was remarkably high. In consequence, her prestige and her power were high too. Financially she made a good thing of it. Her indulgent husband gave her a free hand, rewarding her with half his profits, without asking her to share his losses. She became much sought after, on the one hand by producers who wanted her to back their plays, and on the other by her husband's business and social acquaintances who wanted an opportunity to participate in this pleasant form of money-making (and, of course, to meet the stars who appeared in the plays). She was in the enviable position of picking and choosing among the scripts that were sent to her and of deciding which of her importunate friends she should let in on a good thing. It was all very exciting, and she had a thoroughly good time. Her husband had a good time too. Because of his first wife's illness, he had for many years led a quiet life. Now he and Claire attended all the first nights and the parties that followed. They dined and supped at the glittering restaurants and night clubs frequented by the luminaries of the theatrical and social worlds, entertained and were entertained at cocktails and at dinner, and got to know everybody in the theater who was of any importance.

When Charles Weir died after nearly ten years of this amiable married life, he left Claire well provided for. Besides her accumulated earnings from play investments, she had a large cash legacy, the valuable property at Poundridge, and a life interest in one-third of the profits of the cosmetics business. She had long ceased to take any active part in the business and was well content to leave its operation to Charles Weir's two sons, who inherited it. She hardly ever saw her stepsons. There was no open enmity, but she thought them dull and stuffy and their wives even worse; and they could never forget that she had been their father's mistress and, what was more reprehensible, his employee. Beyond an exchange of Christmas cards and an occasional chance meeting, they had little contact with each other. When business matters had to be discussed, Anthony Weir usually acted as intermediary.

Claire had met Leroy Thompson when he was beginning to emerge as a producer. Quick to recognize his potential importance, she had offered to become one of his backers. She continued in this capacity until her husband's death. Then she proposed a more formal arrangement with Thompson—in effect, a partnership. Financial details bored him and he was glad to have a partner who would relieve him of the necessity of raising money every time he produced a play. He insisted, however, that he should be the sole judge of what plays should be produced. Claire made no serious objection to this stipulation. She had great faith in his acumen; in his record as a producer, the successes far outnumbered the failures.

Shortly after they entered into this arrangement the death of Louise

Henry put a sudden end to Thompson's theatrical activities. It was more than a year before he resumed them. When he did, his relationship to Claire became more than a business one. He was desperately unhappy and in need of companionship, and she felt the same need and was strongly attracted to him besides. With her money, social position, and good looks, she could easily have remarried, but Thompson was the only man who had ever stirred her emotions. She knew what Louise Henry had meant to him and that there could be no question of an immediate marriage. But her romantic feeling had outweighed her ever-present preoccupation with expediency and propriety, and she gave herself to him, regardless of conventions and of his instability. However, her objective had always been an eventual marriage. As the years went by and her lover continued to ignore her broad and recurrent hints, she felt that she must bring the issue out into the open and put it squarely before him.

During the week that followed the meeting at Thompson's office she saw little of him. They had several rather impersonal telephone conversations, and once she came to town to attend an opening with him. But they dined in a crowded restaurant and had supper with friends after the play, so that there was little opportunity for private talk. He was reticent about The Clouded Mirror, saying only that he was awaiting an answer from May Weeks. To annoy Claire, he intimated that he was still considering Lily Prengle. He had heard the girl read and, though again impressed by her talent, had decided that she was too inexperienced to be entrusted with the part.

On Saturday afternoon he telephoned Claire that he would like to come up for the weekend. Overjoyed, she insisted on sending the car in for him. She wished she had not invited Whitney and Merle Lofting.

Lofting was second vice-president of a large insurance company and a frequent investor in Thompson's productions. His wife was one of those undistinguished and indistinguishable products of an exclusive finishing school, whose speech, appearance, and behavior are as standardized as those of the heroes of Western movies. The Loftings pounced upon Thompson, eager to learn his intentions about the play and to hear all the details of Emily Crandall's extravagant conduct, to which more than one of the gossip columnists had made reference. He deftly evaded their questions, and they found out little they did not already know. The talk at dinner was light and inconsequential. Afterwards they sat around drinking and listening to the radio and then played contract until bedtime.

Thompson always occupied the room, adjoining Claire's, that had been her husband's. The two rooms, each with its own bath and dressing-room, were in a separate wing of the spacious house. There was a connecting door, so that Claire and Thompson enjoyed unlimited privacy and intimacy while at the same time keeping up appearances—though, of course, the appearances deceived no one.

He got into bed and idled through a bedside book, awaiting her inevitable arrival. Presently, she came in, handsome and seductive in blue silk pajamas.

"Move over, darling," she said. "No sex tonight. I just want to talk to you and be close to you." She nestled against him, kissing and fondling him. "I'm so glad to see you, darling. It's been such ages. Only if I'd known you were coming, I'd never have asked Whit and Merle. And tomorrow there'll be a whole mob, I'm afraid."

"Well, I wasn't sure I could get away until the minute I phoned you. Oh, by the way, Ginny Upton is getting back from Chicago tonight and is spending the weekend at the Mollisons', so I asked Hugh to bring her over tomorrow for a drink. Hope you don't mind."

"Of course I don't mind," she said, trying to brush aside the unhappy thought that this was the real reason for his unexpected arrival. "Only, I must say I don't understand what goes on."

"Goes on where?"

"I mean with that girl and the Mollisons. How can she have the effrontery to go up there and spend a weekend under the same roof with Hugh's wife? And how can Cissie bring herself to put up with such a thing?"

"Maybe she figures she'd never see Hugh at all if he couldn't bring Ginny."

"I don't know why she'd want to see him or go on being married to him. Believe me, I wouldn't stand for anything like that, not if I were twenty Catholics."

"Oh, well, they all seem to take it in their stride. It's what the Salvation Army people call a ménage à trois. Very Continental and all that sort of thing. Anyhow, for all we know, Cissie may be making with the hay while—no, I'd need Doc Winternitz to work that one out."

"That would make it just a little bit worse," she said. "I think the whole thing is just disgusting."

"Get out of my bed!" he said, pretending to push her out.

"Stop being silly! You know there's no comparison. Anyhow— Oh,

228

well, I guess it's really none of my business, so I'll just shut up about it."

"That's the Christian way of looking at it. But it would certainly cramp people's conversational style if generally applied."

"Are you thinking about Ginny for The Clouded Mirror?"

"I don't see any harm in talking to her about it. It's either Ginny or Lily Prengle or nobody."

"Not Lily Prengle, for God's sake!" she said, unable to conceal her irritation at his constant harping upon the young actress, to whom, for no good reason, she had taken a violent dislike.

"Well, then, it's Ginny or we don't do the show," said Thompson, pleased by the effect he had produced.

"Why? Have you heard from May Weeks?"

"Yes, I got a wire this morning."

"Why didn't you tell me?"

"It's the first chance I've had. Anyhow, bad news is always better if it's allowed to age a little."

"What did she say?"

"Oh, just that they're talking to her about doing another picture when she finishes this one. And, anyhow, she's not sure that she's right for the part. I'm not sure that she is either. The whole thing was just a shot in the dark." It was better not to tell her May Weeks thought the play gloomy and unpleasant—that would only supply Claire with additional ammunition.

"Well, I'm not sure about Ginny either," said Claire. "What's more, I don't think she'll want to do it."

"It never hurts to ask."

"And another thing, I don't think Hugh will let her do it. He's often told me he thinks she should play nothing but comedy."

"They're not Siamese twins, for God's sake! Maybe she'll use her own judgment."

"I don't believe she's got any judgment. If she had, she couldn't behave the way she does."

"All right, let's not go through that routine again. What do you want to do, give up the play?"

She sat up and clasped her knees. "I don't know what to say. If we didn't have all that money tied up in it—! But then why throw good money after bad? If I could only talk to Tony! I'll never forgive him for this."

"I wonder if he takes that choker collar off when he lies down in the gutter."

"It's not funny! Helen finally had to break down and admit the truth, but she still swears she doesn't know where he is. I think she does, but that he isn't in any fit condition to talk to anybody."

"Could be," said Thompson indifferently. "Maybe Suzanne Merchant knows where he is."

"Who's she? Oh, you mean that girl that—"

"Yes, the one that Tony sent around to me for the Lily Prengle part."

"Oh, so now it's the Lily Prengle part! I suppose you'll be giving her billing next."

"That's something to think about."

"Goodness, I wish we could find something to talk about besides Lily Prengle."

"All right, let's talk about the Farow Theater. What are you going to do with it if we don't go ahead with the Kenwood show?"

"Don't think I haven't lain awake nights, worrying about that. Every time I look at those bills! I'll just have to try to get another booking, I suppose. Unless you think you can get something else ready."

"You mean right away?"

"Well, it would have to be right away. The damn place eats its head off when it's dark. What about that Miriam Tyler play? I thought it very charming."

"For spring maybe, if she can dig up a third act somewhere. No, I was going to get The Clouded Mirror off my hands and then do a Chicago company of Give Them. And after that, maybe a production of Measure for Measure with Julie Cosgrove. This knocks my schedule higher than a kite. I've gone through about forty scripts this past week, and I can't keep any solid food on my stomach. There ought to be a law making it a crime to operate a typewriter without a license."

"You've got to decide about The Clouded Mirror by Wednesday?"

"The deal with Equity is that I have to be in rehearsal by Wednesday. So it's Ginny Upton by Wednesday or no dice. Unless we switch to Lily Prengle."

She gave him an angry look. "You're strictly a one-gag man, aren't you?" Then, appealingly, "Couldn't you just try to be a little nice to me for a change?"

He fondled and kissed her. "I'm sorry. I've had a lot of things on my mind. What are you crying about?"

230

"Nothing." She wiped her brimming eyes on the sheet. "Only it did hurt a little when you compared us to Hugh and Ginny."

"Can't you take a joke?"

"That's not my idea of a joke. I guess that *is* the way people think about us and talk about us. Tommy, couldn't we get married?"

"Oh, darling, this is so sudden," he said in a falsetto voice, putting a finger in his mouth.

"I wish you'd be serious. I've been thinking about it for a long time. It seems to me you ought to understand that it's not very nice for a woman to be in the position that I'm in."

"Good God, are you going Victorian on me this late in the play?"

"That isn't it at all, and you know it!" she said. "I'm not prudish or conventional or any of those things. But I hate secrecy and pretending, especially when it's so unnecessary. There's no good reason why we can't get married—unless, of course, you don't love me."

"Why say a thing like that?"

"Well, then, why shouldn't we be married?"

"It seems to me we're getting along all right. Why do you have to have a wedding ring?"

"It's not a question of a wedding ring. I want to live the way any two people do when they care about each other. I want us to be together, not leading two separate lives. Oh, it would be so nice, darling! You could make this your home, instead of being just a weekend guest. And for what we're both paying in New York we could have a nice big apartment, for parties and all. And keep a cook, so that we wouldn't have to go running out all the time or eating half-cold food from downstairs."

"I don't think I'm the domestic type," he said. "I tried it once, and look at the damn thing."

"Well, I hope I'm a little different from Isabel," she said indignantly. "You were anxious enough to marry Louise Henry." His grimace of pain made her instantly regret what she had said. But she had been unable to repress her jealousy of the dead girl. "I didn't mean that in a nasty way," she said hastily, trying to make amends. "All I was trying to say was that just because you and Isabel—"

He cut her short. "I'm no good as a husband. I'm selfish and egotistical and I like being on the loose."

"I know all that. I've known you long enough to have a good idea of what you're like. And I promise you, you wouldn't be tied down. I'm not asking you to take on any responsibilities. Thank goodness, I don't need anybody to support me; and at my age it wouldn't be safe to have any children. Though I wish it were," she added with a sigh. Actually children bored her. She had not the least desire for any of her own, but she would have thought it unfeminine to deny the universality of the maternal instinct.

"What's more, I've got a roving eye," said Thompson.

"I know that very well too," she said with a touch of asperity. "But don't you think you've done enough batting around by now? Don't you ever get the feeling that it might be nice just to settle down with one person for life?"

"In a word, no."

She sighed. "Honestly, I don't understand men. If a woman really cares for somebody, why that's all she wants or thinks of. But men don't seem to be capable of any loyalty or any pride. Well, I suppose I could learn to put up even with that, if I had to, just as long as you didn't tell me about it." She waited for his reply, but he lay there in silence. "No answer?"

"Let me think about it."

"That's a polite way of saying no. Well, I never thought I'd live to see the day when I'd be begging a man to marry me—and have him turn me down besides." It was useless to pursue the subject now. Her unfortunate reference to Louise Henry had closed his mind against any argument she could produce. "I think I'll go down to the kitchen for a snack," she said. "Can't I get you something—some cheese or a sandwich or a bottle of beer, maybe?"

"No, thanks, I'm sleepy," he said, yawning.

"Good night, then. And sleep well." She bent over and kissed him. He patted her head perfunctorily. "Good night, dear. Same to you."

After she left the room he put out the light, so that she would think him asleep when she came back from the kitchen. He lighted a cigar and sat by the open window for a long time. Now that Claire had broached the subject of marriage, she would never let it rest. He foresaw a series of long, tedious discussions. It was unlikely, though, that she would break with him, for he was important to her emotional life. What was much more probable was that she would drive him to the point of breaking with her. Of one thing he was completely sure: he would never allow himself to be talked into marrying her.

He slept late, and by the time he put in an appearance the luncheon guests were already beginning to arrive. There were twelve at table, and after lunch more and more people kept dropping in—theatrical and literary personalities and a sprinkling of Claire's prosperous neighbors, including several regular investors in Thompson's productions. The balmy Indian summer weather drew them outdoors, where they scattered over the wide, well-kept grounds, the more active ones amusing themselves with croquet, tennis, and badminton, the others, Thompson among them, drinking and lounging in canvas recliners.

Presently Virginia Upton arrived with Hugh Mollison, in the actor's new convertible. As they walked across the lawn Thompson went to meet them, his practiced eye taking in every detail of Virginia's appearance. He was pleased by what he saw. She was no great beauty, but the impression she made was striking and vivid. Her thick, glossy golden-red hair, which she wore unbound, clustered in natural curls about her long, slender neck. Her skin was fair and delicate, her eyes a yellow-brown with golden flecks. She had a high, thin nose, a full mobile mouth, and square white teeth. Her figure was not particularly good, for she was short-waisted and wide-hipped, but her hands were strong and beautiful, with long square fingers, her legs were straight and shapely, and she carried herself exquisitely. Her clothes were expensively simple and informal. Except for a small emerald ring she never wore any ornament.

"Hello, men," said Thompson, kissing Virginia and punching Mollison in the ribs.

"He thinks you're a man, Huge," said Virginia. (She always called Mollison "Huge.")

"And so I am!" roared Mollison, pounding his chest with both fists.

Claire came over and greeted them with artificial cordiality. "I'm *so* glad you were able to come! But where's Cissie?"

"She told me to say that she's desolate," said Mollison. "But seven or eight of her brothers arrived unexpectedly. Some of them I'd never met before."

"Well, why didn't you bring them along?" asked Claire vivaciously, trying hard to conceal her disapproval of Mollison's open flaunting of his intimacy with Virginia, his desertion of his wife on his one full day home, and, most of all, his alcoholic breath. His drinking was a constant source of worry, for the continued success of Give Them All My Love depended entirely upon the star's fitness to appear.

They joined a group seated around an ambulatory bar, and Claire mixed highballs for the newcomers. After a few minutes of general conversation Thompson said, "Excuse me, folks, but I promised to take Ginny to the orangery and show her the snakes."

"Another drink like this," said Virginia, "and I'll be able to see them from right here."

Carrying their drinks, they went into the house. Thompson led the way to Claire's little writing-room, where they would be undisturbed.

"Is this where you compose your cocktail recipes, maestro?" she asked, looking disapprovingly around the overdecorated room. She cordially disliked Claire and everything about her, not only because she resented the older woman's attitude of moral superiority, but because she thought her vulgar and insensitive.

"Yes, we call it the Stepney gas-chamber, in honor of Professor Moriarity. Tell me, if it's not too personal a question, how the hell do you manage to look so beautiful?"

"It must be this new toothpaste I'm using. It's rich in rancid oils, yet costs only a few cents more."

"You sound as though you'd been doing a radio show."

"Grrrr! Don't speak of it!"

"I meant to listen in," he said. "But I got tied up at the Stuyvesant."

"I'd have busted you in the snout if you had. I don't like people invading my privacy."

"I suppose you've heard that I've been having a little star trouble."

"My little delicatessen man did mention something about La Crandall going berserk on you. Is it true that she insisted upon having Louis-Jean design the padding for her cell?"

"It's nothing to kid about," said Thompson soberly. "She's a pathetic case."

"I'm sorry. I guess I must be developing an allergy to psychiatry; but I'm getting a little tired of people who set fire to day nurseries just because their mummies didn't love them. Personally, I always hated my mother and she returned the compliment, but that doesn't make me go running around biting policemen."

"Well, maybe you're right. But to hell with all that. What I want to talk to you about is playing that part for me."

"Oh, I see! So that's why you lured me in here!" She had known all along that that was what he wanted to talk to her about. "You're all alike, you men—always ready to take advantage of a young girl's innocence. You're not serious, are you?"

"Yes, darling."

"You must be going bats too. How do you figure me to step into Missy Crandall's panties? I'm not worth a good five-cent cigar at the box-office."

234

"You know damned well you are. Anyhow, that's not what interests me. I want an actress."

"There's even some difference of opinion about that."

"Stop fishing," he said. "Would I ask you to play the part if I didn't think you were right for it?"

"People do all sorts of things out of sheer desperation. From what my spies tell me about the part, I'm not the least bit right for it. I understand that she's a hare-lipped girl who makes love to all her relatives, regardless of sex, and then finally mows them down with a tommy gun and serves them up in a pie."

"You've been talking to somebody who read the expurgated version. As we do it, she uses poison gas, and wind machines blow it out into the audience. But for your private ear, it's the best new play I've read in two years and something you shouldn't pass up."

"I'm supposed to be a comic," she said. "When I come on people go 'Ha! Ha!' and fall out of their seats."

"Well, this time they'll go 'Boo-hoo!' and stay in their seats clapping when the curtain comes down. Where's the law that says you always have to play comedy?"

"There's an unwritten law, pardner, that says you shouldn't go out and make an idiot of yourself in public if you don't have to."

"If I weren't sure you'd score in this part, I wouldn't offer it to you. I'm not anxious to make an idiot of myself either. I saw my doctor yesterday, and his diagnosis is that I'm not in this business for my health."

"You should try Yoga. That's that curdled milk stuff that does things to your intestines. I think I'd better sit this one out, Tommy."

"You might at least read the script, before you decide."

"Oh, is there a script? I thought maybe you made it up as you went along. You know, the Stanislavsky method. All right, I'll read the script if it'll make you happy."

"It will, because I think, when you've read it, you'll want to do it. Only I'd like an answer tomorrow. Can you read it tonight?"

"Don't high-pressure me, Thompson. Sure, I guess so. I'll give Huge his bottle and sneak off and read it in bed."

"Nice girl!" he said, patting her head. "Only I'm not too happy about that bottle angle. He's supposed to go on six nights a week, and Wednesday and Saturday matinees."

"He hasn't fallen down on his face yet, has he? All right, I'll try to sober him up a little for you."

"And another thing. Don't let him talk you out of doing that play. Use your own bean. That's what it's there for."

"Well, that clears up a long-unsolved mystery! All right, professor, whatever you say."

She went out to rejoin the others. Thompson went to his room to get the script, which he put in the car for her. The guests were beginning to leave; learning that the Loftings were driving to New York, he decided to go with them. He pleaded an early morning engagement to Claire as an excuse for not staying overnight.

XVIII.

Claire was not the only one who found the relationship between Hugh Mollison and Virginia Upton a little shocking. What scandalized people was their openness and indifference to public opinion. It was not a question of morals but of convention. Their irregularity would have been readily accepted, if they had taken the trouble to cloak it in the appropriate semblance of secrecy. But Virginia was too honest and Mollison too lethargic to play the elaborate game of false pretenses. They did as they pleased, careless of the disapproval of their more conservative acquaintances.

They were an oddly assorted pair. Mollison, who came of a long line of well-known actors, had been on the stage since early childhood. He had had little formal education; indeed, little education of any kind. He knew and cared almost nothing about the world outside the theater. He was charming, amiable, generous, and not without humor, but, like many actors, childishly vain, psychically insecure, and emotionally immature.

Both in background and in character Virginia was almost his complete antithesis. Born in San Francisco, she was the descendant of a Forty-Niner who had struck it rich and laid the foundations of a considerable fortune. Her father, Phelps Upton, an overbred and over-educated introvert, without any particular ability or ambition, had set himself up as an investment counselor. He lacked both training and initiative, but he had the right connections. His social acquaintances gladly entrusted their money to him, on the theory that wealth breeds wealth, and that a man of his status must necessarily have the golden touch. His wife, a selfish, calculating woman, who had married him for his money and position, divided her time between sports and presiding over the great house in San Francisco and the country place on the Peninsula. Virginia, unwanted and unloved, was entrusted to governesses and tutors until she was old enough to be sent to boarding-school. Between her and her father there was a vague kind of affection. But he saw little of her; when he did, he never quite knew what to say, and her instincts told her that he was not to be depended upon. Left to her own resources, she grew up self-willed, headstrong, proud, and fiercely independent.

In her middle teens she was sent to a girls' school in Lausanne, and the weak family tie was almost entirely dissolved. Europe was an eye-opening adventure. She had aptitudes for all the arts, and the school encouraged her to develop them. She painted, wrote poetry, studied the piano, acted in the school plays. On the conducted holidays she attended performances at Salzburg, La Scala, the Comédie Française and the Old Vic, and became well acquainted with the treasures of the Louvre, the National Gallery, the Uffizi, the Pitti, and the Borghese. As her graduation approached she hesitated between studying painting in Paris and architecture in Rome. But Hitler's march into Poland sent her scurrying back to the United States. Unwilling to live at home, she decided to spend a year at a fashionable school in Maryland in order to complete her college-entrance requirements.

She had not been back long when a family catastrophe completely altered her life. A suspicious client of her father's had inquired into Phelps Upton's affairs and discovered gross misappropriations. Upton had not intended to defraud anyone, but he had taken to drawing upon the money entrusted to him, always with the intention of repaying it. When exposure came, he freely admitted his guilt, glad to be relieved of the burden of responsibility he had been carrying.

Nobody took the trouble to inform Virginia of the scandal. She read it in the newspapers and went home immediately, feeling that she should make the gesture of standing by her father. He had thought it necessary to make the gesture of taking his own life, but, like everything else he had attempted, it was vague and unsuccessful; the heavy dose of sleeping tablets had merely induced a violent attack of vomiting. He was faced with the prospect of a long prison term. But the district attorney was persuaded to hold off long enough to give the family a chance to make good the losses. By means of an enforced levy upon all the wealthy connections, the creditors were satisfied and the disgrace of having an Upton in a convict's uniform was averted.

The result was the complete disruption of the Upton household. Mrs. Upton promptly divorced her husband and married a moneyed Army officer, who had been stationed at the Presidio and was presently transferred to an important post in the Canal Zone. Upton, unable to face his former friends, went to live with his father, who had vast citrus-fruit interests in Southern California.

Virginia, having made her gesture, returned to the East. She had only a small income from a family trust fund. Her grandfather had offered her an additional allowance, but preferring to be independent, she decided upon a stage career. For her, it was not too difficult to overcome the obstacles that beset the ordinary beginner. She used her social connections to obtain introductions to important producers, and they were impressed by her striking appearance, cultivated manner, and natural grace. Having a real talent for acting and considerable amateur experience, she quickly demonstrated her ability. Fortunately, too, the first play in which she appeared was a hit, and though her part was a small one, it enabled her to be seen by all the producers and directors. Her progress was not sensational, but steady, and she soon began to be known as a promising young actress.

Then, yielding to an impulse, she answered a call for volunteers and joined a U.S.O. unit that was going out to tour the South Pacific battlefronts. The company was headed by Hugh Mollison, already well established as a star, who felt it his patriotic duty to help entertain the fighting services. He and Virginia were strongly attracted to each other. Since they were constantly together, living in a perpetual state of excitement and tension, it was not surprising that a love relationship developed. It may have been their very unlikeness that gave them a piquant interest in each other. Unconsciously, too, she may have identified him with her father, for the two men had the same sort of affableness, impracticality, and appealingly boyish irresponsibility.

When the South Pacific tour ended Mollison returned to the Broadway stage. Virginia was induced to make another tour, this time of the home camps, in the course of which she had visited the camp where Eric had seen her perform.

Upon her return to New York she rented a small, attractive apartment, so that she and Mollison could see each other freely. He could always find convenient excuses for remaining in town, so that he spent more time at Virginia's than he did in New Canaan. But as she matured, she became increasingly conscious of his immaturity. Once the first rapture of physical passion had abated, she was no longer blind to his inability to stimulate her mind and kindle her imagination.

On the afternoon following their visit to Claire's, Virginia and Mollison drove in to New York. They were having early dinner in town, to enable him to get to the Stuyvesant in plenty of time for the evening performance. They were both in a bad mood. Mollison, who had been drinking steadily over the weekend, was feeling the effects of it. Virginia was bored and irritable. She resented the casual way in which the Mollisons accepted her as a member of their household and their assumption that she was as much interested in their domestic problems as they were. All through lunch she had sat silent while Mollison and Cecelia argued about their laundry troubles. He complained about the damage to his shirts and urged the advisability of engaging a laundress, while Cecelia enlarged upon the complications that would be created in the kitchen by the introduction of yet another person. The discussion went on interminably and with maddening repetitiousness, neither of them paying the slightest attention to Virginia. After lunch Mollison retired to the bar to read Eric's play and stayed there until it was time to leave for New York. Meanwhile Virginia had to listen to Cecelia's account of the difficulties she was having with her adopted children, who were now at the troublesome stage of early adolescence. Mollison had always found it easiest to humor them, and Cecelia, a stout, lethargic, literal-minded woman, was too phlegmatic to exercise any real authority. Virginia, who thought them ill-mannered and insufferable brats, finally took refuge in the bathroom to escape the detailed description of their unreasonable behavior.

When Mollison appeared he said nothing about the play. He was waiting for Virginia to ask his opinion, as she usually did when she was offered a part. She was determined, however, that the initiative should come from him. So they drove along the Merritt Parkway in silence, until his reckless weaving through the traffic got on her nerves.

"On Mondays you're not supposed to go over a hundred and ten," she said as they shot past another car on a curve.

"Oh, am I going too fast? Sorry!" He slowed down from sixty-five to sixty. Then, after another five minutes of silence, "I read that play."

"Oh, is *that* what you were doing with it?"

"Tommy must have been kidding when he asked you to play that part."

"Well, he wasn't laughing," she said, "so I wouldn't know, I guess."

"In the first place, the play hasn't got a chance."

"Tommy seems to think it has."

"The hell he does! He saw it as a vehicle for Emily Crandall, and now that she's out he's stuck with it."

"Thanks, chum!"

"What do you mean by that?" he said. "Good God, you're not going sensitive on me just because I happen to say you haven't got Crandall's draw! Why, I haven't either for that matter."

"Come, come, don't exaggerate! And don't you think it's just a little dogmatic to say that the play hasn't a chance? How do you happen to know?"

"All anybody has to do is read it."

"I've read it and like it."

"What, all that morbid, unhappy stuff? What do you like about it?"

"It's damn well written," she said. "And it's about life. Didn't your mummy ever tell you about life? That's morbid and unhappy too."

"All the more reason nobody wants to see it in the theater. People pick their noses in real life too, but who's going to pay four-eighty to see it on the stage?"

"I'd just as soon see that as some of the little numbers I've sat through recently. And I don't subscribe to the theory that nothing goes but prat-falls."

"People go to the theater to be entertained and have a good time, not to listen to a lot of gloomy, tragic stuff."

"Alas, poor Ibsen!"

"All right, I'll take you up on that," he said. "When did Ibsen ever make a dime for anybody?"

"I wasn't thinking about dimes when I read it. I was just thinking about what an interesting play it is and what a good acting part."

"But not for you."

"Why not for me?"

240

"Because you're a comedienne."

"A guy out in Des Moines once told me that I'm an actress. But I guess maybe he was crocked."

"An actress who knows her business finds out what she can do and sticks to it. You've built yourself up as a comedienne, and that's what the public expects of you. So why not do the smart thing and cash in on it, instead of making a stab at something that's not up your alley?"

"Or, to translate freely, you think I can't play the part." She had her own doubts about playing it but resented his doubt.

"I'm not saying you can't play it—" he began, feeling he had been a little too blunt.

She did not let him finish. "The part where she sleeps with a married man, I could play that good."

He gave her a hurt look. "What kind of a remark is that?"

"It's the kind of a remark a girl makes when she begins to get fed up with being the family concubine."

"Jesus, you can dish it out, can't you?" He swerved sharply back across the white line to avoid an oncoming car.

"Look," she said, "either let me drive or let me thumb my way back to town."

"All right, I'll slow down." They drove on in silence for a while. "What do you want me to do?"

"Maybe you could take me on as a laundress. I once played Little Eva, so I ought to get along fine with the plantation hands."

"Oh, so that's what's eating you! I didn't know you expected us to put on a floor show for you. All right, from here on out we'll talk strictly about James Joyce and grand opera."

"Good. But I think we should decide first whether Kitty is old enough to wear lipstick."

"What's wrong with a woman being interested in her children?" he said.

"Nothing in the world. Maybe that's what's the matter with me. Maybe I wish I had some to be interested in. Only I think I'd prefer the homemade kind. It's more work, but they taste better."

"That's a dirty crack. We tried and couldn't. If you ask me, I think Cissie's been a pretty good sport about everything."

"Yes, I know. That's the Claire Weir view of it. Otherwise known as the Westchester County gambit. But from where I sit she's in a very cushy spot. Papa isn't around enough to interfere with her herb garden and gin rummy and Parent-Teacher Association. And meanwhile she's playing the understanding little woman to a fare-you-well, knowing damn well that if you conk out on her she's got the house and the annuity and the family jewels and top billing at the funeral."

"You're always telling me you're not interested in jewelry."

She shook her head. "If that's an example of masculine logic, give me the old-fashioned nightshirt."

"She'll never agree to a divorce, you know that. And I'd feel like an awful heel trying to get one without any grounds."

"When did I ever say anything about divorce?"

"Then what *do* you want?"

"If I knew I'd go out and get it. Only I'm coming to the conclusion that what I don't want is just sex in the afternoon."

Deeply troubled, he did not answer. It was not the first time she had expressed her dissatisfaction with their relationship, but she had never gone quite so far. What disturbed him most was that his marriage was not the sole, or even the chief, reason for her discontent. He was intuitive enough to understand that she felt she had outgrown him. There was nothing he could do about that. Always in awe of her superior education and intellect, he had relied upon his personal charm and bluff air of worldly wisdom to make up for his deficiencies. But the charm was fading and the wisdom was a pretense and he had nothing more to offer her; whereas the growth and development in her had made her increasingly attractive. Though he sensed all this, he lacked the courage to face it squarely and accept it. Indeed, the prospect of losing her was something he could not even contemplate. He evaded the issue by telling himself that she was merely going through a phase of typically feminine instability; if he just let matters rest, they would eventually adjust themselves.

They dined at Pinelli's, where they were kept too busy chatting with acquaintances to continue their personal discussion. After dinner she walked around to the Stuyvesant with him. He suggested that they meet at a bar after the performance, and she quickly agreed. She could see how she had hurt him and felt very penitent. Thompson had said that he would call her at nine, and since there was still an hour to spare she walked slowly to her apartment in the East Sixties, brooding over what had happened and wishing that she had expressed herself with less bitterness.

XIX.

Eric had had no further word from New York. Several times he was on the point of calling Irina Lanski, but he knew that if there had been any encouraging news he would have heard from her.

On Tuesday, the day before the expiration of the ten-day period of grace, he was listening to a broadcast of a World's Series game. This was the high point of his father's year, even though the Red Sox were not involved. Eric felt rather guilty about idling, but he had done all he could in the way of job-hunting, and next day he was going to take the proofreading examination. Baseball was almost the only subject he could discuss with Kenwood without becoming involved in a bitter argument.

While they were exchanging comments on the game the Western Union operator rang up. When she told Eric that she had a message for him from New York, he could hardly find the courage to ask her to read it. It was from Leroy Thompson, notifying him that Virginia Upton had been engaged and rehearsals would be resumed next day at the Farow. Not trusting himself to believe that he had heard aright, Eric, with the receiver pressed close to one ear and his finger in the other, asked the operator to repeat the message.

As he started for his room his father shouted, "Who was that?"

"A telegram from New York. We've got a new actress for my play and rehearsals are starting again tomorrow."

Kenwood did not understand what he was saying, and Eric had to come close to him and yell into his ear.

"Jesus Christ!" screamed Kenwood angrily. "Are you starting with that again? Why the hell don't you go out and find yourself a job, instead of wasting your time with that goddam crap?"

Eric started to reply, but the game entered an exciting phase and

Kenwood motioned him impatiently to silence. "Shut up! If you want to be a loafer and starve us all to death, go ahead!" He leaned forward in his chair, shouting curses at the players.

To get to rehearsal on time Eric had to be in New York that night, which meant getting the four o'clock bus to Hartford. While he was packing it occurred to him that if he left now, he would miss the examination. What he had already gone through warned him that he had better make what provision he could against another unpredictable accident. He was eager to see Virginia Upton in action, but decided he could better afford to miss the first day's rehearsal than forego the examination.

When the ball game was over Eric sent Thompson a telegram, telling him that he would be delayed until Thursday. He smiled inwardly as he gave the operator the message, for he knew that the less of him the director saw at rehearsals, the better Thompson liked it.

Then he called Great Barrington, anxious to know why he had received no reply from Sylvia. Muriel Davis, Sylvia's hostess, answered. A Coltertown girl, she had known Eric since childhood. She had always heartily disliked him, and her manner was cold and hostile. After a considerable interval she came back to the telephone and said that Sylvia was out and would not be back until late that night. Obviously she was lying. Eric hung up, worried by Sylvia's unwillingness to talk to him.

Next day, as Eric was leaving for Hartford, the postman arrived with a bulky letter from Sylvia. Eric put it in his pocket without opening it. He wanted to keep his mind as clear as possible for the examination.

He checked his valise and sat in the station, reading the proofreader's manual until it was time to walk around to the high-school auditorium where the examination was being held. There were more than two hundred applicants, so that anyone's chances seemed very slim. However, Eric had prepared himself carefully, and with his veteran's priority his prospects were quite good. He hoped though that he would never be obliged to take the job.

On the way to New York he read Sylvia's letter. He was prepared for an evasively argumentative reply, even an outright refusal of his offer of marriage, but not for the virulent tirade with which she answered his warm and heartfelt missive. In language melodramatic to the point of hysteria, she accused him of bad faith, cruelty, irresponsibility, callousness, shiftlessness, and hypocrisy; of keeping her dangling, using her or neglecting her as suited his convenience; of frivolously throwing away economic security to follow a selfish whim; of making a recluse of her and ruining her chances of meeting other men; of deliberately postponing the question of marriage until he had nothing to offer her but a life of drudgery. She did not say, in so many words, that he had taken advantage of her virginal innocence only to betray her, but the implication was unmistakable. She did say that she thought him a waster and a coward; that in her opinion he had no future as a writer; that she would rather spend her life in solitude than marry him; and that she never wanted to see him or hear from him again.

This outburst of Sylvia's was caused by a combination of circumstances, connected with her visit to the Davis household. From the moment of her arrival, Sylvia's pleasure in seeing Muriel had been overshadowed by her envy of her friend's happy situation. Muriel's husband owned one of the largest automobile agencies in the Berkshires. With her lavish house, her garden, her servants, her cars, her New York clothes, her social set, to say nothing of her handsome, worldly husband and lively six-months-old son, she lived a life that was very unlike Sylvia's own drab existence. Muriel's prospects in Coltertown had not seemed much better than Sylvia's, and still dazzled by her own good fortune, she lost no opportunity to show off her acquisitions.

Sylvia, in a desperate effort to offer some competition, enlarged upon Eric's happy prospects of success and her expected participation in it. She painted a glowing picture of Eric, as the author of a Broadway hit, establishing her in a New York apartment, where she would play hostess to the celebrities of the theater. In fact, she would soon be going to New Haven to attend the tryout, and she intimated that she would see a good deal of Emily Crandall, who, she said (carried away by her own fantasies), had told Eric that she was looking forward to the meeting. Muriel, impressed by Sylvia's glamorous inventions, saw her friend in a new light. The shabby, frustrated, small-town girl, before whom she took such pleasure in preening, now appeared as the potential occupant of a Park Avenue apartment and the intimate of movie stars. That made even a sumptuous life in the Berkshires seem a little prosaic. Sylvia, pleased by the effect she was making, expatiated upon Emily Crandall's rather spectacular professional and marital life with the air of having obtained her information from some very private sources rather than, as was the case, from a careful study of the movie magazines.

The first thing that clouded Sylvia's dream world was the arrival of a letter from her mother, caustically describing Eric's visit and emphasizing the fact that he had waited until the day after his arrival to come around. When she came to her mother's characterization of Eric as looking "like some filthy hobo," she involuntarily glanced across the bright breakfast table at the well-tailored, well-barbered husband of her friend. And, a moment later, her fabricated structure collapsed when Muriel, looking up from the New York paper, exclaimed almost jubilantly, "Well, listen to this, will you? Emily Crandall's had a nervous breakdown and she's out of Eric's show."

"Oh, that can't be true!" said Sylvia desperately.

Muriel handed her the newspaper. "Here it is, right in the paper! And Eric didn't even take the trouble to let you know?"

Her friend's tone told Sylvia that the aura had faded and that once again she was only the pathetic little school chum from Coltertown. "It probably just happened," she said, fighting back the tears of anger and chagrin. "Or it may not even be true. The papers always print all sorts of made-up stories, especially about celebrities."

So great was Sylvia's humiliation that she was tempted to invent some excuse for going back home. But no excuse would have been plausible; besides, she was too practical to rob herself of a luxurious vacation, even at the price of being patronized by her friend.

Muriel, convinced that Eric was not a fit husband for any girl and intent upon making a suitable match for Sylvia, introduced her to Alden Greer, a business associate of her husband's, and arranged for them to be together frequently. Greer was attracted by Sylvia's prettiness and coyness; Sylvia was flattered by Greer's attentions and impressed by his glib patter, so unlike Eric's fumbling inarticulateness. She began building a fine house of her own, on a hill overlooking the Davis place, and superior to it in many respects, thanks to her finer taste.

This was her state of mind when Eric's letter arrived. She read it with feelings of outrage and self-pity. His offer of marriage struck her as a shameless attempt to enslave and victimize her. In contrast to the life of ease she had been envisioning, his suggestion of a union that entailed dreary discomforts and perpetual uncertainty seemed downright insulting and inexcusably selfish. He was trying to use

246

her for his own ends, demanding that she sacrifice her whole life to his irresponsible whims.

Muriel, finding her in tears and learning the cause of her distress, proceeded to aggravate Sylvia's anger. She urged Sylvia to lose no time in breaking completely with someone so thoroughly incompetent and untrustworthy.

This was exactly what Sylvia wanted to hear. Basically literal-minded, she accepted the clichés of melodrama at their face value and saw herself romantically embodying virtue and righteousness, constantly menaced and victimized by the evil-hearted. In her world, there were only black and white, only guilt and innocence, and every situation had to have its villain and its hero. By the time she finished writing to Eric, she actually believed her own inventions.

Eric read the letter in stunned surprise. Always dissatisfied with his failure to live up to his ideals, he asked himself if Sylvia's accusations were justified, if he could really be the unprincipled scoundrel she portrayed. His objectivity and his sense of humor came to his defense. Sylvia's case was completely vitiated by her gross distortions and fantastic exaggerations. Temperate reproaches might have aroused his sympathy and made him feel guilty; this diatribe merely disgusted him with her complete failure to evaluate the honesty of his letter.

He had not wanted to return to the hotel where he had been so uncomfortable, but he was too upset to undergo the ordeal of trudging the streets for hours, so after being refused two or three times he went back to the old place. He was given an even stuffier and noisier room. Choked with emotion and impelled to strike back and hurt Sylvia, as she had hurt him, he sat for two hours, with a tablet on his knees, writing furiously, sarcastically refuting her charges and meeting her attack with calculated and searing ridicule. He went to bed, emotionally spent but relieved by this venomous discharge.

The next morning he reread what he had written, tore it into bits, and threw it into the waste basket. Then, afraid he might be tempted to read Sylvia's letter again, he tore that up too. After all, it called for no answer: she said that she never wanted to hear from him again, and he would comply with her wishes.

It was good to get back to the Farow. He walked briskly down the alley, opened the stage door with an air of easy familiarity, and shook hands cordially with the old doorman. The members of the cast asked solicitously about the damage to his home. McCarthy introduced him to the only stranger, Forrest Norman, who had been engaged to replace Richard Ismay. It was like a happy homecoming, and he had the warm feeling of being welcome among old friends.

When Virginia Upton came in he went over to her with uncharacteristic boldness. "Hello, Miss Upton, I'm Eric Kenwood. I was in Camp Wendell, with a broken leg, when you played there."

"Yes, so I understand," said Virginia, quickly taking in his illfitting clothes, his shaggy hair, and his myopic eyes behind thick lenses, and deciding that she was going to like him. "You must have been slightly delirious or you never would have wanted me in your play on the basis of that exhibition. Leg all right now?" She looked questioningly from one leg to the other.

Eric laughed. "Oh, yes, it has been for years. I hardly remember which one it was." She was even more attractive than he had remembered.

The rehearsal was pervaded by an entirely new spirit. Instead of uneasiness and uncertainty, there was a general air of confidence and alertness. Virginia was not only quick to learn but anxious to make a good impression upon Thompson, Eric, and her fellow players. With her keen mind and her thorough understanding of her craft, she responded smoothly and creatively to Thompson's directions. In two days she had progressed farther than Emily had in five. What pleased Eric even more was the justification of his belief in her rightness for the part. She read with sensitivity and a feeling for values; already the character was adumbrated as the tragic figure Eric had conceived rather than the melodramatic one indicated by Emily's more obvious approach to the part.

When the company was dismissed for the day Eric summoned his courage again and went up to Virginia. "I think you're going to be wonderful," he said.

She flushed with pleasure. "Are you sure your leg is all right?" she asked with mock anxiety.

"Yes, quite sure. And I'm sure you're all right too. You're just the way I imagined the girl to be."

"Do you mind putting those words in writing? Just so you have them handy to eat when you read my notices."

When she left the theater, Thompson, who had been talking to McCarthy, came over to Eric. "Well, you seem to like her."

"I think she's going to be just right, don't you?"

"She knows her business. And she's got a quality. Only she's so used to playing comedy that it's going to be a job to get her to loosen up emotionally. But I think I can get her to do it."

"Well, I think she's much better than Miss Crandall," said Eric.

"I hope the cash customers take your artistic view of it. However, we haven't got Emily Crandall, so let's see where we can get with Ginny."

XX.

The resumption of rehearsals had entailed much more than the engagement of Virginia. There were a great many productions in preparation and it was not easy to get out-of-town bookings. Thompson wanted to revert to his original plan of opening in New Haven, but the town's one theater was solidly booked until Christmas. Boston was heavily booked too, and it took all of Murray Fineman's persuasiveness and Thompson's prestige to get the booking office to rearrange its schedule and assign him to a smaller and less desirable theater two weeks later than the original date. That meant an over-all rehearsal period of six weeks. Equity, in view of the troubles with Emily Crandall, had agreed to an extra free week but had insisted that for the sixth week all members of the cast, except the newcomers, receive full salaries—a heavy and unforeseen expense. Furthermore, all the costume expenditure was wasted. Virginia declined to wear Emily's half-finished clothes, on the reasonable ground that neither the cut nor the colors suited her. She would have liked to have Louis-Jean design a new set of costumes for her, but she could not demand that and had to be content with a less expensive costumier.

In the continued absence of Anthony Weir, Claire had to make the decision to hold the Farow Theater until The Clouded Mirror was ready to open. She could not do otherwise without antagonizing Thompson; nevertheless, she was disturbed about the cost of keeping the theater dark for another two weeks, particularly since she had little hope that the play would be a success without Emily Crandall.

When Weir returned to his office a few days after rehearsals were resumed, he agreed that, in the circumstances, there was nothing else Claire could have done. He made no reference to his absence. She dared make none either, dependent upon his advice as she was, and a little afraid of him besides.

Thompson usually stopped at his office on the way to rehearsals, to look at his mail and attend to other business matters, and several days after Weir's return Murray Fineman came in, carrying some papers and obviously agitated.

"Have you got a minute, Tommy?" he asked.

"What's wrong now, Cassandra?"

"Well, I just got the theater contracts from Tony Weir. And he's not giving us much of a break on the terms. I talked to him before he went off on that binge and we agreed on seventy-five per cent straight. Now, I get these contracts and—"

"That was on the basis of Crandall," interrupted Thompson. "We can't expect the same deal with an actress that has no draw."

"Sure, I know that. But he's cut us away down to sixty on the first fifteen thousand, sixty-five to twenty, and seventy over that."

"The hell he has!" said Thompson angrily. "Why, that's no better than we'd get from the booking office."

"Not a bit," said Fineman. "And he's cut us down on stagehands and advertising allowance too. And a sixteen thousand stop clause."

Thompson got up and walked around, fuming with rage. "The double-crossing old bastard! Have you talked to him about it?"

"No, these just came in. Anyhow, I think this is something you'd better handle yourself. I wouldn't be able to get to first base with him. He's got us in a spot and he knows it."

"The son of a bitch! All right, I'll talk to him." He told his operator to call Weir. "How much is our nut?" he asked Fineman.

"Well, I figure we can break on about fourteen. Maybe a little less once we get running and get our prop and electrical rentals paid off."

The telephone rang. "Hello, Tony," said Thompson. "Say, I wonder if I could see you for a few minutes."

250

"Why, certainly, Tommy. Whenever you say."

"Well, how would it be if I came right over?"

"Fine! I'll be waiting for you."

Thompson hung up and looked at his watch. "Call the Farow, will you, and tell Mack to take the rehearsal till I get there."

"Okay. Try to get at least sixty-five straight on the first fifteen and seventy straight if we go to twenty. And cut down that stop clause."

"This is going to be tough. What are the chances of getting another theater?"

Fineman looked worried. "Do you want to postpone again?"

"No, of course not! We can't afford any more postponements."

"Well, that's what I thought too. I'm pretty sure there's nothing open right now—nothing that you'd want, that is. Anyhow, how would you square it with Claire?"

Thompson, who had been thinking of that too, did not answer. "Give me those contracts," he said.

He walked around to Weir's office, trying to control the anger that the lawyer's sharp business methods had aroused in him.

The usual contract between a producing manager, like himself, and a theater owner, provided for a division of the gross weekly box-office receipts on a percentage basis, the major share going to the producer, since his expenses were far heavier than those of the operator of the theater. There was considerable latitude in the fixing of these percentages, the determining factors being the popularity of the principal actors, the prestige of the producer, the current demand for theaters, and the bargaining abilities of the respective parties. To the producer of a play that was only moderately popular, a difference of ten, or even of five, per cent in his share of the revenue might mean the difference between profit and loss and might seriously affect not only the play's success but the value of the motion-picture and other subsidiary rights, which often depended upon the length of the play's run. Consequently the terms of the theater contract were a matter of the greatest importance.

Helen Jacoby, Weir's secretary, averted her eyes as she told Thompson to go right into the lawyer's private office. Her employer's periodic alcoholic escapades were a source of grief for her. Whenever they occurred she could hardly bear to face his friends and clients.

Weir and Thompson greeted each other with a cordiality neither

251

felt. The lawyer was as meticulously dressed and as self-possessed as always. Except for his leaden eyes and a slight huskiness in his voice, there was no outward evidence of his recent debauch. "Well, sonny, what's on your mind?" he said with that air of benign joviality which always infuriated Thompson.

"It's this Farow contract," said Thompson, coming straight to the point. "Murray thinks you're crowding us pretty hard on the terms, and I must say I agree with him."

Weir raised his eyebrows in mild surprise. "Do you, Tommy? Well, I'm sorry to hear that. Of course they're not the terms we agreed on while Emily Crandall was still in the picture. But there we had a great box-office name and the practical certainty of capacity business, for at least ten weeks anyhow."

"I understand that," said Thompson, finding it hard to conceal his irritation. "Naturally I don't expect the same terms now. But there's still a hell of a spread between that and what you're offering us."

"Well, I just assumed that under the present setup we'd go along on the usual terms for a dramatic show. Isn't that what the contract provides for, or is there some mistake?"

"I guess the mistake is mine in thinking that I'd get a little better break on the Farow than I would from the booking office."

"Well, that puts me in a rather awkward position, Tommy," said Weir, assuming a frank man-to-man manner. "I need hardly tell you that both for personal and professional reasons I'd like to give you every break I can. But I'm acting here for the Farow Theater, that is to say, for Claire, who has the majority interest in it. She's in pretty deep in this thing, much deeper than she anticipated, due, of course, to unfortunate and unforeseen circumstances over which none of us had any control. Now she has to keep the theater dark for another two weeks, and, of course, she's perfectly willing to do so. But all that means that she's got a long, hard row to hoe. In order to see daylight, she's got to handle her bookings on a business-like basis."

Thompson waited impatiently for this long harangue to come to an end. "She's heavily in the show too. What difference does it make to her whether she takes her profit on the theater or on the show?"

"That cuts both ways, my boy. You're in on the theater too."

"How do you figure that? I don't own any stock in the theater."

"True. But you're an officer and director. If the theater prospers,

252

we'll pay substantial salaries before we declare a dividend on the stock—for tax purposes, if for no other reason."

"I'm a little young to be thinking of an old age pension," said Thompson.

Weir ignored the sarcasm. "This is the way we have to look at it," he said urbanely. "In spite of the community interests and all the personal considerations, the theater and the production are separate entities, and as I think I suggested to you before, the only way we can avoid a lot of troublesome complications is to treat them as such and to let each enterprise stand on its own feet. This is not an unusual situation. People who are in business together often find themselves confronted with a conflict, or, let us say, a disparity of interests, and what they have to do is act as though there were no interrelationship. Let me give you an example. Suppose a corporation, in which I am a large stockholder, asks me to represent it in a law suit. Well, what I have to do is fix my fee in accordance with my usual scale, regardless of the effect upon the finances of the corporation and my own interest as a stockholder. Do you see what I mean?"

"Yes, I see what you mean all right. But what I don't see is where it's any advantage to me to go into the Farow if I don't get a break in the terms."

Weir looked at him in mild surprise. "Well, I should say it's the difference between being in your own home and living in a hotel. After all, you and Claire are closely associated in a continuing business relationship." He put the faintest emphasis on "business."

"You just finished telling me that we have to forget that and act as though we were separate entities. I think entities was the word."

"Exactly," said Weir. "As far as terms are concerned. But I don't have to tell you that there's more to show business, or any business for that matter, than just dollars and cents. In fact, I often think the personal element, the teamwork and the give and take, are more important than the money end of it."

"What about that stop clause?" asked Thompson, weary of this meaningless palaver. "Sixteen is pretty stiff, it seems to me."

"About normal, I should have said. What's your nut?"

"Around fourteen, Murray figures."

"Well, the house could just about squeak by on that even on the terms I've indicated. However, if the terms stand, we might cut down the stop to fifteen and go a little further on stagehands and advertising allowance. I'm sure Claire will do anything within reason to make you happy. Have you talked to her about this?"

"No, I haven't."

"Why don't you? After all, this is up to her. I'm only acting in the capacity of an attorney, and whatever she says is what counts. My suggestion is that you go over the whole thing with her, and then just let me know what you agree upon."

"All right, I will," said Thompson, rising.

Weir rose and extended his hand. "We'll work it out, my boy. The important thing is for everybody to be happy. After all, we pass this way only once, and if we don't make the most of our human opportunities we'll never have another chance. How is little Virginia Upton going to be?"

"She'll be all right."

"Well, I'm delighted to hear it. She's a fine little actress in my opinion, but, of course, she hasn't the following of Emily Crandall. Well, that can't be helped. What's that old saying? The best-laid plans of mice and men—"

Thompson left Weir's office, smarting under the consciousness of defeat. What made it hardest to bear was that it was his own fault. Behind the lawyer's economic ruthlessness was his determination to revenge himself upon Thompson for the latter's refusal to give Suzanne Merchant a part in the play. Not only had Weir looked upon it as a personal slight, but he had probably suffered a considerable loss of prestige in the girl's estimation. Now that he was in a position to pay Thompson back, he was taking full advantage of it.

At dinner that night, when he complained to Claire about the contract, she pretended that this was the first she had heard of it. She was not a very good actress, and Thompson rightly assumed that she had been fully informed by Weir of the morning's conversation. More than that, Weir had strongly urged her to stand fast by her economic interests and not to be swayed by sentiment. Left to herself, she might have yielded to Thompson's arguments; fortified by Weir's firmness, she evaded the issue and took the line that the contract was a mere formality, that between people as closely bound as they were, legal arrangements were not worth talking about.

"Good heavens, Tommy," she exclaimed, "anyone would think we're strangers to each other, the way you go on about terms and

254

clauses. We're all mixed up in this together. What difference does it make what's in some old contract? You know that I'm as much interested in the show as you are and that we're both going to do whatever we can to make it a success. So why waste time trying to battle that legal mind of Tony's? Why not just sign the old thing, and when the time comes, you and I will work it out the way we think best."

Thompson saw that further argument was useless and that he would simply have to depend upon his ability to influence Claire to modify the terms of the contract, if the situation demanded. So, next day, he instructed Fineman to sign the contracts, with the minor modifications to which Weir had agreed, and dismissed the matter from his mind.

XXI.

Eric was having a happy time, finding at last the aesthetic and mental stimulation of which his life in Coltertown had been so barren. As rehearsals progressed he began to grasp something of the essentials of acting and to understand the creative elements that went into the transference of a play from the typed page to the stage. Winternitz provided him with free seats for several plays that were not selling out, and though they were rather inept pieces he enjoyed the unaccustomed experience of theatergoing. Their very mediocrity threw into relief the excellence of his own cast and the directorial skill of Thompson.

He no longer suffered from loneliness either. Almost every night he had dinner with Peter Quirt, Lily Prengle, or some of the other younger members of the company. Sometimes three or four of them would dine together. He learned of the backgrounds and struggles of his new friends, most of whom, like himself, had come from small communities and had had to fight their way into the professional theater. He was eager to become better acquainted with Virginia Upton, but he was afraid that if he asked her to go out she would invent some excuse or accept from mere politeness. Besides, her relationship to Hugh Mollison made him feel inexplicably self-conscious.

His intellectual horizon widened too. One night Irina Lanski asked him to accompany her to a dinner party at the home of some friends. The host, a successful lawyer, had written some excellent verse, and his wife was the author of several quiet, sensitive novels. They lived near Washington Square in a pleasant old house where books and pictures were not merely ornaments but an integral part of the fabric. The others at dinner were an architect with a passion for city-planning; his wife, a compatriot of Irina Lanski's and an accomplished amateur pianist; a well-known publisher; and a woman anthropologist.

The dinner was first-rate and tastefully served, and there was enough good wine to loosen everyone's tongue. Eric had never been in such a house or met such people. Everyone but himself was widely traveled, and the talk roamed the globe, opening to him the possibility of a whole new range of experiences. Music and art and literature were discussed too; and the unhappy state of the world and the pathetic struggle of the human race to rise above its baser instincts and to realize its inherent godliness. At first Eric was too awed to take part in the conversation, but the others unostentatiously put him at ease; before long he found himself expressing thoughts and opinions which he was formulating clearly for the first time.

After dinner the architect showed them some plans he had drawn for a model housing project. He spoke with deep feeling of a future society, in which squalor and ugliness would be obsolete; in which spacious and beautiful dwellings would house spacious and beautiful lives. Then his wife sat down at the piano and played Chopin and Rubinstein and Debussy.

At parting, Eric's hosts wished him success and expressed a desire to see him again. He said heartily that he had never spent a more enjoyable evening. In the taxi he thanked Irina Lanski profusely for having brought him along.

"Well, I'll tell you the truth," she said. "If I didn't now and then have an evening like this to wash my soul clean of the filth of Broadway, I would long ago have been in a strait jacket."

He left her at her apartment house in the Forties, near the East River and walked the two miles to his hotel in a state of exhilaration, conscious that he had made a good impression and that Irina Lanski was pleased with him. Too stimulated to sleep, he lay awake half the night, thinking of the people he had met and of the things they had said, oblivious for once to the uproar of the hotel court.

The first run-through of The Clouded Mirror took place on the second Friday after the resumption of rehearsals. To a director of Thompson's stature, this was an important milestone in the progress of a production, for it was his first opportunity to see the play as a whole, substantially as it would be presented to audiences. It was important to the actors too, for it offered them their first chance to give a sustained performance. Consequently everyone was keyed up and nervous, anxious for the outcome of this preliminary test of play, players, and direction.

Ordinarily Thompson did not allow anyone to be present at rehearsals, but on this occasion he wanted a few spectators, to enable him to judge the effect of the play upon those who were not too familiar with it. Claire, Winternitz, and Fineman were there as a matter of course; he also invited Irina Lanski, Arthur Eckstein, the scenic designer, Samuel Rothberg, the company manager, Cleveland Dean, the house manager of the theater, John Beeman, Winternitz' young assistant in the press department, Felix Obermeyer, who was to do the publicity photographs, and Anthony Weir. He had been inclined not to ask Weir, but thought it impolitic to offend him further. Virginia's theater maid, Pearl Dunlop, was also present, in order to familiarize herself with the sequence of scenes and to see how much time she would have for the numerous costume changes. Thompson had deliberately set the run-through for an hour when Hugh Mollison would be rehearsing a radio show, for he did not want the actor, at this stage of rehearsals, to make suggestions to Virginia that would conflict with his own conception of how the part should be played.

Knowing that Thompson was a stickler for punctuality, everyone arrived a few minutes before the appointed time. Promptly at four o'clock he assembled the cast on the stage and addressed them briefly.

"All right, children," he said. "What we want to do today is see what we've got. We'll go right straight through, with a five-minute break between acts and just enough time between scenes for the stage managers to shift the props. And I don't want to see anybody come on with a part in his hand. You've all had time to learn it, so just go ahead and make a stab at it. If you dry up, the boys will throw you a line. But don't stop or go back. Just keep going as though it were a performance. And give it enough projection so that we can all hear it out there. I think that's all I have to say. Oh, just one other thing," he added, as though it were an afterthought. "If you show me a little something, I won't be too annoyed."

He came down into the auditorium and sat directly behind his secretary, who had a blank book and a tiny flashlight, ready to take his notes. "All right, Mack," he said, "whenever you're ready."

"Heads up, everybody!" rasped McCarthy from his table behind the proscenium. "And watch that offstage talking. All right! House lights down. Curtain going up!"

The performance began, and there occurred one of those minor miracles that, to the people of the theater, are more than adequate compensation for all the uncertainties and disappointments, the anxieties and the heartbreaks, with which their lives are beset. Stimulated by the presence of even a handful of spectators and by Thompson's broad hint that he expected something of them, the actors threw themselves into their parts with fervor and vitality. Without benefit of costumes or make-up, with no scenery, no furniture but kitchen chairs and rickety tables, no illumination but the single work light overhead, they imbued the play with vibrant life, creating an illusion of reality that made all the trappings of the stage a superfluity. It was a performance such as no lay audience ever sees. While it lacked the technical perfection of the finished product, it had the excitement of creativeness and the freshness of improvisation. The actors made a few mistakes and several of them required prompting, but these minor slips did not affect the over-all sweep and surge of the performance.

At the end of the first act Thompson jumped up and hurried down to the lounge to avoid hearing any comment until the performance was over. Eric had sat forward in his seat, spellbound, as the characters he had imagined became flesh and blood. His heart was pounding by the time McCarthy shouted, "Curtain! Five minutes, everybody, and don't make it any more," and he leaned back and looked at Irina Lanski, who sat beside him, wiping her eyes.

"It's good! Very, very good!" she said, squeezing his hand. "It should make you very happy."

258

"Yes," said Eric, "it does." It was the fruition of what had been germinating so long, the moment when, like the Maker of the universe, he looked upon what he had created and saw that it was good.

He heard someone sniffling behind him. Turning his head, he saw Virginia's maid blowing her nose. The middle-aged Negro woman was his first audience, and he was profoundly grateful for the unspoken tribute.

Claire came up the aisle. "Well, what do you think?" she asked Irina Lanski, giving Eric a cold nod.

"I think definitely yes."

"Tommy's done a beautiful job, hasn't he?"

"Yes, beautiful," said the agent, kicking Eric's foot.

He was both piqued and amused by her giving Thompson all the credit. Yet he had to admit that the director deserved the praise. The insistence upon mechanical details, which had seemed so tedious to Eric, had resulted in a perfect coordination of words and action, so that the players moved through their laboriously rehearsed stage routine with the appearance of complete spontaneity and naturalness.

Thompson reappeared and gave McCarthy the signal to begin the second act. It proceeded with the same verve and tempo as the first, building to a fine, stirring conclusion. When the last line was spoken the spectators burst into applause. The clapping of a dozen pairs of hands was a thin sound in the large theater, but to the eagerly receptive ears of the actors it thundered like a mighty ovation.

Thompson rose abruptly and turned to those who were seated behind him. "That's the best goddam performance of *that* play that anybody will ever see," he said, his face flushed with excitement. "If we run eleven years we'll never top that." Then, going down to the rail, he called, "Everybody on, please."

"Onstage, everybody!" shouted McCarthy. The actors gathered in a group behind the footlight trough.

"All right, kiddies," said Thompson. "That wasn't too bad. In fact, I'm going to stick my neck out and say it wasn't bad at all. I've got a few notes—not more than a thousand or so—and we'll check over them tomorrow at twelve. That's all for today. You can all go out and get as drunk as you like, provided you take damn good care to stay sober."

259

The actors laughed happily, pleased with themselves, pleased with the applause, and pleased with Thompson's praise. Eric came quickly down the aisle, trembling with nervousness. "May I say a word, Tommy?" he said in a choked voice.

"Ladies and gentlemen, the author!" said Thompson with a flourish.

Eric cleared his throat. "Well, all I want to say is that I think you're wonderful and I—well, I just want to say thanks, that's all."

"And thank you for a beautiful play," said Florence Fulham, and the other actors applauded.

"Why, it's turning into a love feast," said Thompson, enchanted with everybody. As he started for the stage he encountered Anthony Weir.

"Well, that looks finè, Tommy," said Weir. "You've got a wonderful cast. But I hope you won't mind one tiny little suggestion."

"Of course not," said Thompson impatiently.

"Well, it's just that maybe you could get that little girl in the first act—I don't know what her name is—to talk up a bit. I could hardly hear her, even in the fourth row."

"She'll be all right. She was just a little nervous, that's all. It's the first part she's ever played." And then, afraid that he might lose his temper, "Excuse me, I've got to talk to some of the people before they get away."

He went up on the stage, his jubilation somewhat marred by Weir's thrust. It was true that Lily Prengle, in her inexperience and nervousness, had not projected her voice enough; but Thompson knew that Weir was merely reminding him that he had not forgotten the rejection of Suzanne Merchant.

"What do you think, Murray?" Claire asked Fineman.

"Great! Great! A beautiful, artistic job. The only question is, will they buy it."

"Yes, that's what I'm worried about too," she said.

Several of those present were thoughtful enough to congratulate Eric, among them Winternitz. "Eric, my bucko," he said with a warm handshake, "it's the first time I've cried since I heard the news of Hoover's election."

"Well, I hope that doesn't mean we're headed for another depression," said Eric, laughing.

He walked gaily up the alley. As he came through the gate he saw Virginia getting into a taxi. "Oh, Miss Upton!" he called impulsively.

She turned. "Well, if it isn't Ben Jonson!"

"Can I get in with you?"

"Please do. That is, if the driver doesn't mind."

"It don't cost no more for two than for one," said the driver.

"Yes, it's sort of like marriage, isn't it? Where are you headed for?"

"Nowhere in particular," said Eric. "I just wanted to talk to you."

"Well, I'm glad we're still on speaking terms. Pinelli's, please," she said to the driver.

"I want to tell you again how wonderful I think you were."

"I hoped you were including me in that nice little curtain speech. Personally, I thought I stank, fluffing all over the place and going higher than a kite about a dozen times."

"I can't imagine anybody being any better." He went on singing her praises with a fluency that was new to him. He was disappointed that the ride to Pinelli's was so short. When they arrived he said, "I think I'll get out here too." Then, with another sudden impulse, "Are you having dinner with someone?"

"Not a soul in the world—unless the fleet's in."

"Well, I used to be in the Army," he said, "so maybe you'll have dinner with me." He trembled at his temerity, afraid that she might think him pushing, and thinking of his slender purse too. But he wanted to celebrate and could have thought of no better way of doing it than by dining with her, in this famous Broadway restaurant, for twenty years the favorite eating-place of theatrical folk.

"But with pleasure!" she said. "I've been mighty depressed about spending the evening alone with a mixed salad." She usually dined with Mollison, but this evening he was busy with his radio rehearsal.

Pinelli's was jammed. About twenty people were waiting for tables, but Ricardo Pinelli, the proprietor, a small, thin man with a dyed mustache and a toupee, saw her enter and beckoned to her. "Right this way, Miss Upton," he said. "I've got your table all ready for you."

They pushed their way through the waiting crowd to one of the tables that he always reserved for his professional regular customers, compelling the laity, who came to gape, to wait its turn.

Eric looked around with great interest at the restaurant of which he had heard so much. The tables were close together, and the clientele was mostly theatrical. Virginia seemed to know everybody. As their table was on the central aisle, she was kept busy exchanging greetings with the passing procession of actors, directors, agents, authors, and columnists. Those who lingered for a moment she introduced to Eric. Some had familiar names, a few others he recognized as actors in Give Them All My Love or in other plays he had seen, most were unknown to him. He marveled at the extent of Virginia's acquaintanceship. They had a cocktail and drank to each other and to the success of the play.

"Are you up there?" asked Eric, his eyes roving the walls, which were covered with framed caricatures by a Mexican artist.

"I think you'll find me between Edwin Booth and Rin-Tin-Tin," she said.

"I'm afraid that doesn't help me much."

She leaned forward and whispered. "The third row, second from the left, if you insist. Only don't look now."

"Why, it looks nothing like you," he said.

"You have a little way with you, haven't you? But if you'd said anything else I'd have bopped you."

After a second cocktail Virginia said she was getting hungry. The head waiter brought them the huge menus. Eric turned pale at the prices. While Virginia was ordering oysters, a steak, two vegetables, a salad, and a sweet, he looked in vain for something cheap. He could not sit there, eating a sandwich, while she went through a large dinner, so, stimulated by the run-through, the cocktails, the lively restaurant, and Virginia's company, he cast away discretion and matched her order. They kept up an animated conversation and in spite of frequent interruptions learned a great deal about each other's backgrounds. Eric was dazzled by the extent of Virginia's travels and the variety of her experiences. It would have surprised him to know that she, in turn, envied him his simple home life and close family relationships.

After dinner she ordered a brandy and then another. It was nine o'clock before they were ready to go. The check with the tip came to over fifteen dollars—a whole week's food allowance gone for one meal.

"Do you want a taxi?" he asked as they left the restaurant.

"I think I'll walk home," said Virginia.

"Would you let me walk with you?"

"Well, if you can stand any more of me. Only don't do it just because you think I need protection."

"No, you look as though you're able to take care of yourself."

"I'm not sure whether I like that or not. As a matter of fact, when I first came to New York I was prepared to defend my honor at every street corner. But in all the years I've been here no one has ever accosted me except a few old ladies who wanted to know how to get to the Woman's Exchange."

"I don't believe that."

"Where I come from, no gentleman calls a lady a liar. He just takes it for granted that she is."

Eric laughed. "When I first came to New York I was scared to death of everything and everybody. I still am, in a way, but it's beginning to wear off a little. Did you feel the same way?"

"Not exactly. New York just seemed to me to be a bigger, noisier, and uglier San Francisco. But I know what you mean. And a good way to get over it is always to keep in mind that nine-tenths of the people you meet are as scared of you as you are of them."

"Thanks. I never thought of that. It may help."

When they reached her door Virginia asked him up for a drink. She lived in a house that had been converted from a private residence into small apartments. Hers consisted of a large living-room with a fireplace, a good-sized bedroom, a small kitchen, and another small room, intended as a dining-room but which she had made into a spare bedroom, as she almost never ate in. To Eric, the charmingly furnished apartment seemed quite luxurious and elegant, but for her, it was a very modest place indeed, after the great houses to which she had been accustomed.

While she mixed highballs Eric looked at the paintings with which the walls were hung. There were several originals by Klee, Miro, and Picabia and good reproductions of Braque, Picasso, and Rouault. Eric, who was beginning to appreciate Cézanne, Degas, and Manet, was puzzled by these works of the twentieth-century abstractionists and surrealists. He asked Virginia to explain to him what she saw in them, and she launched into a disjointed but eloquent discourse on non-representational art, trying to make him see that he was making the mistake of looking at painting from a literary point of view, instead of thinking of it in terms of its plastic elements of form, design, and color, and of the artist's attempt to reproduce his subjective response to his material rather than its external reality. Eric listened with interest, not fully grasping her argument but beginning to understand that modern painting was influenced by the same principles that underlay much of the modern literature he had read. Indeed, his own play to some extent reflected these tendencies.

From painting they went on to poetry, in which they were both widely read. Virginia was particularly fond of the late Victorians —Browning, Swinburne, Matthew Arnold, and Francis Thompson— and had committed long passages to memory. She replenished the highball glasses, then put on some records of de Falla, Albéniz, and Granados, none of whom Eric had heard of. They were both enjoying themselves thoroughly. Virginia, however, was relieved when Eric said he thought it was time for him to go. She did not particularly want him to meet Mollison there.

Just as Eric was saying good night a key turned in the door of the apartment. Virginia bit her lip in vexation. She had repeatedly asked Mollison to ring the doorbell and to use the latch key only when she was out, but he frequently forgot.

"Hi, Ginny!" Mollison shouted. He burst into the living-room, then stopped short as he saw Eric.

"Why, if it isn't Huge himself!" said Virginia with affected casualness. "This is Eric Kenwood, who wrote all those words I can't seem to remember. Eric, Mr. Huge Mollison, star of stage and rodeo."

"Mr. Kenwood, it's a pleasure," said Mollison, pumping Eric's hand with excessive heartiness. "Ginny, you left your keys in the door." He put his own bunch of keys on the marble mantlepiece.

"No, not again!" said Virginia, forced to play up to his transparent fiction. "Some people never seem to learn." Sure that Eric had seen her put her own keys back into her handbag, she inwardly cursed Mollison for making matters worse with his clumsy subterfuge.

"Sorry I couldn't get to the run-through," said Mollison. "How did it go?" He went to the cellarette and mixed himself a drink. Eric did not fail to note how completely at home he was.

"Well, the author attempted suicide but failed," said Virginia, trying desperately to make the best of the situation. "So maybe that's a good sign." Eric's frozen silence was painfully evident. She was annoyed at him, too, for not showing a little more social grace.

"Sounds to me like a hit," said Mollison. "Mr. Kenwood, can I assemble a drink for you?"

"No, thanks, I was just leaving."

"Won't you have one little one for the road?" asked Virginia.

"No, I really can't. I—I have to write some letters before I go to bed."

She made no further effort to detain him. He was feeling slightly ill. When he got downstairs he stood for a few moments on the stoop, filling his lungs with the cool night air. He did not have Virginia's capacity for alcohol, and his head was reeling. The joyous day had come to a miserable end. The dazzled delight with which he had regarded Virginia gave way to a feeling that was almost hatred. It was wholly irrational, for her relationship to Mollison was a matter of common knowledge and she was not to blame for the actor's bungling entrance. But the sudden and brutal visualization of their intimacy shocked Eric's sensibilities and belied his idealization of her.

The next morning Virginia, usually very prompt, was fifteen minutes late at rehearsal, purposely delaying her arrival in order to avoid conversation with Eric. She bustled in, profusely apologetic, and slipped into a chair among the other actors.

Thompson began to go over the typed-up notes he had made at the run-through. Eric was again amazed by the acuteness of his observation and the sensitivity of his perception. Thompson had noted every minute defect, every false intonation and gesture, every slurred line and overlong pause. He had some suggestions for textual changes too, and after he had finished with the actors he turned the rehearsal over to McCarthy and went down to the lounge with Eric. Most of the proposed changes were of a minor nature, and Eric readily agreed to make them. Several, however, entailed a good deal of rewriting. Eric demurred a little but finally gave in. Since their first meeting his respect for Thompson's judgment had increased enormously.

He was glad to be kept busy, for it would have been painful to sit all day watching Virginia, with the memory of last night still so vivid. Since it was impossible for him to concentrate in his room, he went to the main reading-room of the Library, and with a few books propped up before him to give the appearance of research, worked away at the revisions until closing time. On Sunday afternoon, when he finished, he called Thompson at his hotel.

The director invited him to supper in his suite, and they spent the evening going over the revisions, arguing about the use of words, and the exact shade of meaning to be conveyed by this or that speech, until they reached an agreement on all the disputed points.

Again Eric was struck by the contrast between his own dismal cubicle and the roomy, attractive quarters of his new friends. He had no craving for luxury, but he was sensitive to his surroundings and wished he could afford to live tastefully and with a certain degree of comfort. He contrasted, too, what life would be like with Sylvia, on the one hand, and with Virginia, on the other, but dismissed these speculations as wholly idle.

XXII.

Two weeks remained before the departure of the company for Boston. Thompson, working like a sculptor, devoted this period to giving his production its final form. The solid mass had been hewn into shape, its balance and design had been tested; what remained was the pointing up, the refinement of detail, the delicate and laborious polishing of the surface. With the unwearying patience of a perfectionist, he went over and over the play, scene by scene and line by line, modulating, trimming, intensifying. He had an almost musicianly ear for timing and phrasing; he knew exactly where the values were and where the emphases should fall and, to a split second, how long a pause would hold. His influence upon the actors was almost mesmeric. They responded to his touch like the strings of a perfectly tuned instrument.

Sometimes, indulging his irrepressible yearning to act, he got up on the stage and assumed this role or that, demonstrating how he wanted it played, while the displaced actor stood aside and watched. He never knew the lines, but he had the knack of improvising in a way that conveyed accurately the sense of the scene; his intentional exaggerations served as vivid illustrations of the quality he wanted from the actor.

This concentrated activity consumed only a part of the rehearsal time. When each new point had been made, it had to be repeated, over and over, until the actors had thoroughly assimilated it. During these necessary but boring repetitions Thompson left the stage, sometimes retiring to the lounge to smoke a cigar or relax for half an hour on one of the long divans, sometimes roaming aimlessly around the dark, empty theater. Claire dropped in for an hour occasionally, or one of his staff would come in to consult him about some business or technical detail. Usually there was no one in the auditorium except his secretary and Eric.

The only other exception was Lily Prengle. Thompson had made her Virginia's understudy, partly to soften her disappointment at not getting the role, partly because he thought her capable of going on, in the event of Virginia's indisposition. The public would not have accepted a substitute for Emily Crandall, but it was quite feasible to make a temporary replacement for an actress of Virginia's lesser eminence. Since Lily had only one scene of her own, she had asked permission to watch the rehearsals from the auditorium when she was not needed on the stage. Thompson did not like to have actors sitting out front and seldom permitted it, but Lily had very sensibly pointed out that she could get a much better understanding of the part if she could watch Virginia's performance from the front. He had finally consented, warning her, however, to make herself as unobtrusive as possible. So she would slip through the pass-door and steal quietly up the side aisle. In his peregrinations he would see her dark silhouette as she stood motionless at the back or sat in some side seat. Actually it was a relief not to have her on the stage. He was beginning to get a little tired of her silent adoration. Every time he looked in her direction he could see the undisguised worship in her large, pale blue eyes. He was quite accustomed to having the women in his companies fall in love with him—a psychiatrist friend had once explained that it was a form of father fixation—and not infrequently he availed himself of their emotional receptiveness. But he found Lily's mooning, humorless, adolescent homage something of an annoyance—especially since he was not particularly attracted to her.

The hours he spent in the dark auditorium always aroused in

him a strange excitement. He roved the blackness with feral enjoyment, like some solitary beast of prey prowling the midnight jungle of which he was undisputed king. He would creep stealthily up the carpeted stairs to the balcony and then up the steeper stone steps that led to the gallery. Here the proscenium arch cut off the rehearsal light, and as he went down the sharp gradations of the gallery aisles he had to proceed with extreme caution. A misstep might mean a broken limb or a fractured skull. He seldom used the small flashlight he carried hooked on to his breast pocket like a fountain-pen, preferring to feel his way through the darkness. As he moved around he could hear the lines spoken on the stage, and the actors were often startled as he boomed directions from an upper box or the gallery rail. Sometimes he even climbed up to the big rehearsal room and peered out through the peephole from which Oscar Farow had spied upon him so many years ago. From that great height he watched the foreshortened and diminutive actors with the satisfaction of a puppeteer who sees his dolls respond with great precision to his invisible manipulations.

On the last Tuesday of the rehearsal period he was awakened at six o'clock by the ringing of the telephone. He fumbled sleepily for his bedside lamp and picked up the receiver.

"Hello, Tommy, this is Isabel." Before he could lash out at her for calling him at such an hour, she went on in a voice full of anxiety, "I thought I'd better let you know that Doris is in a critical condition."

Instantly Thompson was wide awake. "What is it?" he said in great alarm.

"She woke up about an hour ago screaming with pains in her abdomen. Doctor Wolfe is here and he says it's an acute appendix. We're rushing her to the Metropolitan Hospital just as fast as we can." She was weeping now. "If we can only get her into the operating-room before it ruptures!"

"Have you got a good surgeon?"

"Doctor Simmons. Doctor Wolfe says he's the best."

"Maybe I'd better come around to the hospital."

"No, that won't do any good. I'll call you when the operation is over. Only this is going to be a terrrible expense, Tommy, and I can't—"

"To hell with that!" said Thompson angrily. "Just see that she has the best of everything and send the bills to me."

268

"I don't know what I'll do if anything should—" sobbed Isabel. "Wait, there's the doorbell. That must be the ambulance now. Good-by. I'll call you later."

Unable to go back to sleep, he pulled up the shades, bathed, shaved, and made himself some coffee. Then he tried to read, but he could not put his mind to it. He sat with the book open on his knees, smoking one cigarette after another, and drinking brandy to fortify himself. Since his divorce he had seen less and less of his daughter. It had been part of his agreement with Isabel that he should have the child to himself one day a month; but she was usually away for the summer and sometimes he was off on a business trip or a vacation, so that actually he saw her only five or six times a year. On their days together he would take her to lunch and then to a movie or the circus, striving to find ways to please her and using all his charm in an effort to recapture the affection she had had for him before the divorce. On Christmas and her birthday he sent her lavish gifts, and every now and then he would write her a little note or send her a box of sweets. But she was, of course, completely under her mother's influence, and he could not combat Isabel's systematic campaign of alienation. Each time he was with the child he was more conscious of the growing estrangement. It saddened him, for she was one of the few people he had ever loved. Always afraid of pain, he had rationalized his grief into an attitude of cynical indifference. Now that she was seriously, perhaps even mortally, ill, all his love for her came back with a rush. He remembered the feel of her little arms about his neck and her babyish delight in his pranks and foolery. The thought that she might die without his seeing her again was unendurable. He had an impulse to rush to the hospital, but she would be in the operating-room by the time he got there. He threshed about the room, looking at his watch every five minutes, finally picking up a magazine, which he systematically cut into ribbons with a paperknife.

Shortly after nine the telephone rang and he leaped to answer. It was Isabel. "Well?" he asked breathlessly.

"Thank God everything is all right. We got her here just in the nick of time. The thing burst when they started to remove it, but they were able to clean it all out. If it had happened any sooner it might have gone into peritonitis. Oh, God, what I've been through since five o'clock!"

"How is she now?"

"Well, she's just coming out of the anesthetic. The doctor says she may be uncomfortable for a few days, but there's no danger."

"Can I come around to see her?"

"Just a minute; I'll ask Doctor Simmons. He's right here." There was a brief pause. "He says if you want to step in around twelve it will be all right. But only for a few minutes."

"Okay. I'll be there."

On his way to the hospital he stopped at a toy shop and bought a large china doll in an exquisite hand-sewn silk dress. He tapped lightly on the door of Doris's room. After a moment a nurse opened it softly. "I'm Doris's father," he said with the inevitable flash of anger as the nurse's eyes involuntarily went to his disfigured face.

"Oh yes. Come in."

"Hello, Tommy," said Isabel, assuming the madonna-like air that was appropriate to the occasion.

"How is she?"

"Oh, she's coming along fine," said the nurse.

Thompson tiptoed over to the bed. Doris was lying on her back, her eyes closed, breathing rather heavily. As he looked down at the flushed face and the twitching lips a swift rush of love and pity went through him.

"She's not asleep. You can talk to her," said the nurse.

Thompson bent over her. "Hello, sweetheart," he said tenderly. "How's the old pain in the neck?"

The child opened her eyes, looked up at him, and closed them again without answering. Thompson removed the wrappings from the doll.

"Oh, isn't that beautiful!" said the nurse. "Look what your daddy brought you, honey."

Again the child opened and closed her eyes.

"Just a little girl friend to keep you company," said Thompson. "She's not feeling so well either, so I guess we'll put her right into bed with you."

He put the doll on the pillow beside her. Doris opened her eyes and turned her head slightly. Then she gave the doll a violent shove. It fell to the floor, the head cracking on the cement. "Get out of here!" said the child hysterically. "I hate you and I hate your ugly face."

"Why, Doris!" exclaimed Isabel.

"Oh, dear, what a shame!" said the nurse, picking up the doll and examining the damaged head ruefully.

270

The port-wine stain had turned a deep purple. "I guess I've worn out my welcome," said Thompson.

"I'm terribly sorry, Tommy," said Isabel. "The poor child doesn't know what she's saying. I'm sure if she did—"

Thompson cut her short. "Let me know how she's getting along, will you?"

"Yes, of course I will."

He emptied his brandy flask in the taxi and stopped on his way to the theater to replenish it. McCarthy was taking the company through the second act. Telling them to go right on, Thompson went down the steps and walked up the aisle. Lily Prengle was standing at the back, behind the last row of seats, leaning her arms on the half-partition. Thompson nodded to her, walked around to the other aisle, and took a seat halfway down. He tried to concentrate on the rehearsal, but he could not shut out the memory of the detestation in his daughter's voice, the gleam of triumph in Isabel's eyes, and the nurse's clumsy embarrassment. He reached for the brandy bottle and swallowed a huge mouthful. Unable to sit still, he got up and walked up the aisle again. As he saw Lily standing there immobile, her eyes glued to the stage, he had a sudden vivid image of Emily Crandall slapping the girl's face and screaming insults at her. Lily, too, had known humiliation and hurt, and recalling how she had clung to him afterwards and the feel of her soft, yielding body, he had a sense of kinship for her and a desire to seek some assuagement of his pain.

He walked over toward her. She knew he was there but gave no indication of it. He stepped softly behind her and, circling her with his arms, cupped her unbound breasts in his hands, pressing his blemished cheek against hers. He could feel the pounding of her heart and the tensing of her muscles. He held her closer against him, thinking irrelevantly that with her long-lashed blue eyes and silken yellow hair she was not unlike a doll.

"Half a moment, dear," said Reginald Olmsted to Virginia, with whom he was playing a scene. Stepping down to the footlights, he peered out into the darkness. "I say, Tommy, are you there?"

"Always at your service," said Thompson, leaving Lily instantly and walking down the aisle. "Something troubling you?"

"Well, I don't want to be a bother, but it's just that I feel that this speech in which he goes on about the different varieties of slut she is, is just a little too much of a muchness, even for a loving father. I always feel I should play it with my fangs dripping blood."

"Good!" said Thompson. "Mack, get Mr. Olmsted a set of fangs and a pint of blood."

The actors laughed. "Yes, sir," said McCarthy. "What size fangs do you take, Reggie?"

"No, but seriously, old boy," said Olmsted. "Don't you think it could be toned down a bit. I don't mind being a wolf, but, somehow, I don't quite fancy myself as a werewolf."

"How about it, Eric?" said Thompson. "Do you think you can get the were out of the werewolf?"

"Yes, I guess I could tone it down a bit," said Eric.

"Well, go to it, will you?"

"Thanks awfully. Sorry to be a nuisance," said Olmsted.

Eric went up to one of the dressing-rooms to work over the speech, and the rehearsal was resumed. Thompson sat down and took another long drink. It had been a strain for him to keep up his customary badinage. The alcohol was beginning to mount to his brain, and he got up to go to the lounge. Lily had disappeared.

In the lounge he noticed a light shining through the transom of the women's room and came to the conclusion that Lily must be in there. Claire was in the country and his secretary was at home with a cold. So it must be Lily. A strict rule forbade the members of the cast to use the toilet facilities at the front of the house, but a novice would probably not be familiar with this regulation.

He started for the men's room, then stopped and strode over to the women's room, pushed open the door, and entered the anteroom, which was furnished with several dressing tables, full-length mirrors, and a chaise longue. He let the door close behind him and stood looking around uncertainly. Behind the latticed swinging doors he could hear Lily clearing her throat and the sound of water spurting into a wash basin. Then he heard the rip of a paper towel, pulled from the container, and the crumpling of it as she dried her hands. Presently the door swung open and she came out. She stopped short with a gasp of amazement, terror in her eyes. Staring fixedly at her, he took a swift step backward, groped behind him for the wall switch, and turned out the lights.

"Oh, no, no! Please! Please!" cried Lily as he came toward her in the darkness. His arms went around her and his mouth smothered her outcry.

When Thompson returned to the auditorium Eric was waiting for him on the stage with the revised speech. They went over it with

Olmsted, who still offered a few objections. After some discussion it was put into a form that satisfied everybody. While they were talking Thompson saw Lily come through the pass-door onto the stage. Without looking in his direction, she went swiftly to a far corner, sat down, and turned the pages of her understudy part. It was now almost half-past three. Thompson halted the rehearsal for the usual midafternoon interval. The instant he gave the signal for dismissal, Lily got up, without a word or a glance, and was the first one out through the stage door.

Thompson's temples were throbbing and his eyes were heavy from lack of sleep. He wanted to leave the rehearsal to McCarthy and go to bed. Unfortunately he had scheduled a run-through for four o'clock and had invited Mollison, unable to evade any longer the actor's insistence. It would be rude of him to absent himself; besides, he was worried about what Mollison might say to Virginia about her performance if he were not there. So he went to the lounge and lay down, dog-tired and headachy and furious at himself for his lack of self-control. He had no feeling of guilt. Lily was old enough to know how to look out for herself, and no girl yielded to a man unless she wanted to. Indeed, she had incited him with her fatuous, unconcealed adoration. What angered him was his folly in getting himself involved with this half-baked little actress, in whom he had no interest and who was obviously not the sort who could surrender to a quick impulse and then as quickly forget about it. Her romantic, febrile nature would undoubtedly endow it with the dimensions of a grand passion. He foresaw that she would be a problem. With the heaviest part of his work still ahead of him—the dress rehearsal, the tryout, the preparations for the New York opening—he did not want to have her hanging around his neck, or, in fact, anywhere near him. It occurred to him that the simplest way of disposing of her would be to give her her notice, pay her the required two weeks' salary, and be done with her, once and for all. He would not even have to take her to Boston. It would be easy to get up somebody in that small part, in two days, and to find another understudy for Virginia. With grim humor he contemplated engaging Suzanne Merchant. That would make Anthony Weir happy and might turn out to be a good stroke of business. But even while he was weighing it he knew he would not do it. He could be brutal on occasion, but not to someone as ineffectual and as defenseless as Lily. She was no challenge to him in any sense, and his self-esteem would not permit him to use his power against one so helpless. Nor could he bring himself to rob her of the professional opportunity he had so generously given her and of which she had proved herself so worthy. No, there was nothing to do but to accept the situation and find a way to wriggle out of it. With this bitter reflection he fell into a troubled sleep, from which McCarthy apologetically awakened him at four-fifteen.

The run-through was listless and pedestrian. The company was going through the period of lethargy that usually precedes the final tuning up. Besides, word that Mollison was there spread, and it made them self-conscious to perform under the critical eye of an actor of his importance. That was particularly true of Virginia, who always set great store by his judgment of her performance. Though she had accepted this part largely as an assertion of her independence of him, she was afraid of his criticism. She found it impossible to surrender herself and merely walked mechanically through the part. The other actors took her mood, and the result was a dull and uninspired exhibition. As for Lily, she did little more than repeat her lines automatically, hardly knowing what she was saying or doing. Thompson sat inattentively through the performance, too indifferent to make notes. The moment it was over he dismissed the company without a word of comment.

XXIII.

The final days of rehearsal were trying ones for Virginia, crowded with shopping and packing and tiring costume fittings and then the costume parade, always an ordeal. The clothes never seemed to turn out right, and there were heated discussions and hurried last-minute alterations. Claire's hovering presence did not help matters. She had very definite ideas about clothes, which she did not hesitate to express. Virginia resisted her every suggestion, and there were lost tempers,

274

sharp words, and tears. It took all Thompson's diplomacy and authority to prevent a serious quarrel.

Worst of all was Mollison's meddling. Thompson's fears of the actor's influence upon Virginia had been more than justified. The ragged run-through had confirmed Mollison's dislike of the play and his conviction that she was unsuited to the part. All through rehearsals she had felt very happy and very sure of herself; now she was so discouraged by Mollison's antipathy to the play and his caustic criticism of her performance that she actually asked Thompson to release her. His reassurances, together with those of Eric, Olmsted, and Florence Fulham, finally persuaded her to go on, but did not succeed in fully restoring her confidence. She approached the Boston opening with even more than the usual uneasiness.

Added to her other difficulties was the problem of Mollison himself. Though she had superficially patched up her differences with him, she had, after many doubts and waverings, come to the conclusion that she must terminate their intimate relationship. The meaning had gone out of it for her; it seemed senseless to go on with it. (There was another deeper reason for her decision, but she was not yet ready to admit it even to herself.)

But it was one thing to decide to break with Mollison and another to put her decision into effect. His feelings for her were unchanged—if anything, he was more dependent upon her than ever—and she could not bring herself to tell him bluntly she was through with him. That would be too severe a shock to his emotions, too crushing a blow to his pride. Of late he had accused her more and more of thinking herself superior to him, and a curt dismissal would be a humiliating confirmation of his misgivings. (That she really did feel superior merely made matters worse.)

To spare him a sudden, cruel blow and herself the degradation of a sordid quarrel, she decided to try to free herself by a process of gradual extrication, so that when the break finally came it would be made easier by long preparation. The first logical step in this campaign was to make it more difficult for them to be together. However, as long as Mollison had free access to her apartment there was no keeping him away. In fact, her chief reason for taking it had been to give him unlimited opportunity to be with her. She could give up the apartment, but she was unwilling, except as a last resort, to move from her charming and comfortable home into a cheerless hotel.

She decided instead to take someone in to share the apartment with her. The prospect did not delight her, but it seemed the most effective way of dealing with Mollison. Besides, once the breach was complete, she could easily get rid of her tenant. She ran over the list of her acquaintances, looking for the most likely person, and finally hit upon her cousin, Marion Sweet. Marion was a San Francisco girl, who had recently come to New York to enter Columbia University Law School, after taking her bachelor's degree at the University of California. She was a serious, studious young woman, tall, square-shouldered, deep-voiced, and thick-ankled. Except that she was intelligent and well bred, she was about as different from Virginia as could be imagined. This very disparity made her all the more desirable. Their interests were so unlike that there was little probability of their getting in each other's way. Furthermore, Marion would be up and off to classes while Virginia was still asleep, and by the time Marion came home Virginia would be almost ready to leave for the theater.

Virginia sounded out her cousin (without, of course, disclosing her reason for making the proposal), and Marion leaped at the opportunity to leave the unattractive university dormitory for Virginia's bright apartment, although it meant a long trip to and from classes She even offered to prepare dinner for Virginia whenever she wanted it, and Virginia, who knew that her cousin was an excellent cook, was pleased with the suggestion. She could hardly manage to boil an egg for herself and got tired of going out for all her meals. This way, instead of meeting Mollison at Pinelli's or some other restaurant, she could invite him in, confident that Marion's conversation and restraining presence would not encourage him to accept too often.

It seemed an ideal arrangement, and the best time to put it into effect would be when she left for Boston. She could then present it to Mollison as a temporary loan of the apartment to Marion, and upon her return to New York invent some excuse for her cousin's continued occupancy.

On Saturday, between the matinee and evening performances of Give Them All My Love, she had dinner with Mollison at Pinelli's. As they were sipping their coffee she said, "Oh, by the way, I'm lending my apartment to my cousin Marion while I'm in Boston."

"Your cousin Marion? Is she anybody I know?"

"I think you met her one day at cocktails. My hunch is that you were not smitten with her."

"Oh, I think I know. She's trying to discover radium or something."

"That's the general idea. She's a law student at Columbia."

"The one with the big bozooms and a voice like a bullfrog?" He gave an exaggerated imitation of Marion's husky voice.

"You're getting warmer every minute."

"What's the idea?"

"Well, I thought it would be a nice change for her. Have you ever tried living in a girls' dorm?"

"Not that I remember."

"It's not an experience that a man would be likely to forget."

"When is she moving in?"

"Tomorrow, after I leave."

"Nuts!" he said sulkily. "I was figuring on dropping in once in a while myself."

"Well, I'm sorry. But I guess you'll just have to live at home for those two weeks. It'll be a nice change for you too."

"I don't see why you had to do that," he grumbled.

"I didn't have to. I just thought it would be a friendly thing to do. Which reminds me, you'd better give me the keys."

"Can't you give her yours? You won't need them in Boston."

"That's not the point."

"What is the point?"

"Well," said Virginia, "she's a simple girl, and she might not understand your barging in while she was cutting her corns or fighting her way out of her girdle."

"What the hell makes you think I'd go near the joint with that ape-woman in it?"

"Oh, I don't know. Force of habit. Conditioned reflexes. The murderer returning to the scene of the crime. The dog returning to his vomit."

"You have a nice refined way of expressing things."

"That's on account of my having gone to the very best schools. With washing and French extra."

"I'm glad to hear it."

"Oh, go on with you! You knew it all along." She held out her hand. "The keys, please."

"I haven't got them on me. I'll give them to you tonight, after the show."

"So you'll have time to have duplicates made?" She looked at her watch. "Well, I guess that still gives *me* time to have the lock changed."

"God, you certainly trust me, don't you?" he said angrily. He reached into his back pocket, produced his key ring, and started tugging at it.

"Not in full view of the Actors' Equity Association, if you don't mind!" said Virginia, enraged. She snatched the keys from him and, putting them in her lap, worked loose the ones to her apartment, breaking a nail in her haste and anger.

Mollison beckoned to the waiter. "Give me a double brandy."

"Not right before the show, Huge!" said Virginia, unable to suppress her anxiety.

The waiter, about to go, hesitated.

"What's the matter?" asked Mollison. "Didn't you hear me?"

"Yes, sir, Mr. Mollison!" said the waiter, hurrying off.

"And make it quick. I've only got ten minutes," Mollison called after him. "If you don't mind, I like to do my own ordering."

"I'm sorry, Huge," she said. "It slipped out before I—"

He cut her short. "When is that zombie getting out of there?"

"I told you I invited her to stay while I'm in Boston," said Virginia, trying to avoid a direct lie with which he could charge her later.

The waiter brought the brandy. Mollison swallowed it in three gulps. Virginia, who usually walked around to the Stuyvesant with him, excused herself on the ground that she still had a lot of packing to do. She sank back in her taxi, exhausted from the trying scene and very much worried about Mollison, but thankful that she had been able to get possession of the keys so much more easily than she had expected.

At half-past eleven Mollison rang the doorbell. He was silent and sullen; but under the influence of her warm vivacity and of numerous highballs he thawed out, and they were soon on their old, easy, intimate footing. Having won her first point, she could well afford to relent a little. When, at three o'clock, he yawned loudly and said that it was time for bed, she made no attempt to send him away. Indeed, the thought that this might be the last night he would ever spend there filled her with sentimental sadness and kindled a warmth she had not felt in a long time.

XXIV.

As the rehearsal period neared its end Eric grew more and more worried about money. His bank balance was down to three hundred dollars, and more than two hundred had to be reserved for the repair bills. He did not see how he was going to meet his Boston expenses and wondered if he dare ask Thompson for a loan. But if the play failed, he would be unable to pay it back. He had never borrowed a penny from anyone, and the prospect of going into debt was repugnant to his New England conscience. Besides, he was reluctant to reveal his extreme need. He was on the point of asking Irina Lanski's advice, but before he could bring himself to do even that, Samuel Rothberg, the company manager, talked to him about his Boston living arrangements.

"I reserved a room for you at the Marlborough," he said. "I figured that's where you wanted to stay."

"Well, I don't know," said Eric nervously; then, summoning his courage, "Do you know how much it will cost?"

Rothberg stared at him in surprise. "Well, it depends on the room. Eight or ten bucks a day, I guess."

"Eight or ten dollars just for the room! I can't possibly afford that."

"Well, as long as you don't have to pay for it," said Rothberg, eyeing him suspiciously. Not too quick-witted, he thought this might be some joke that was over his head.

"What do you mean?" asked Eric, puzzled.

Rothberg gave him another sharp look. "It's on the management."

"You mean the management pays for my room?"

"Why, sure. The management always takes care of the author's out-of-town expenses. It's in your contract."

"I guess I should have known that, but I didn't," said Eric, overjoyed by this unexpected windfall.

"If you eat at the hotel, just sign for it, and I'll pick up your bill when you check out," said Rothberg, still suspecting that Eric might be pulling his leg. "And any cash expenses, just give me a memo of it. We're leaving Sunday on the noon train and I'll have your transportation for you Saturday."

With this major worry disposed of, Eric looked forward eagerly to the trip to Boston. The last day of rehearsals was a tedious one. Thompson, McCarthy, and Peter Quirt had already left for Boston to supervise the setting up of the scenery, and the actors were left in the very unfirm hands of Gladys Kaye. They were all just marking time. After a few hours of perfunctory rehearsing they went home to finish packing.

Sunday morning Eric checked out of his hotel with the feeling that he was being released from a prison, or, more properly, a madhouse. He was almost at the end of his endurance and made up his mind that he would never again return to that dismal, nerve-wracking place.

He had a seat in a parlor car—a novel experience for him. Olmsted, Florence Fulham, and two or three other members of the cast were in the car. The management provided coach transportation and those who wanted to travel first-class did so at their own expense. Pearl Dunlop, Virginia's maid, was there too. Virginia arrived a few minutes later, accompanied by a station porter, who carried two large, stylish suitcases. Eric was delighted to discover that she had the seat next to his. He had had no opportunity to be alone with her since the night they had dined together. Several times during rehearsal he had had coffee or a drink with her at O'Leary's, but always with other members of the company present. He had not asked her to go out with him again, partly because he could not afford it, and partly because he was not sure that she would welcome the invitation.

She waved to her fellow players and had just got herself settled, with the assistance of her maid and the porter, when Hugh Mollison came up the aisle, carrying a large package.

Virginia found it hard to conceal her anxiety. Mollison had taken her to the station and had kissed her good-by at the train gate, telling her that he was leaving shortly for New Canaan. She had boarded the train, happy in the thought that she would not see him again until her return to New York, for his engagement at the Stuyvesant made it impossible for him to attend the Boston performances. Now, here he was, bobbing up again. She was afraid he meant to go to Boston, to spend the night and see at least part of the dress rehearsal. It was just the sort of thing he was capable of.

"Hi, Ginny," he said, nodding to Eric. "Just thought I'd say good-by and good luck." He put the package in her lap.

"What's in there, for God's sake, the torso of a traffic cop?" said Virginia, relaxing. His presence there was bad enough, with everyone's eyes on him, but not as bad as having him come along.

"Just some chocolates in case you get hungry," he said.

"And a pair of scales, I hope." Then as the conductor shouted "All aboard!" she said, "Hey, get off, or you'll have to thumb your way home from New Haven." To prevent his kissing her she pushed back her hair, so that her hand covered her face.

"Okay! Good luck, Flossie! Good luck, Reggie!" he called to Florence and Olmsted. "Good luck, Upton!" He patted her head, said good-by to Pearl, and then, as an afterthought, "Good luck, Mr. Kenwood."

"Hurry up!" said Virginia anxiously.

He dashed up the aisle and out of the car just as the porter was about to close the door. Then he tapped on Virginia's window and, as the train began to move, stood there waving and blowing kisses to her.

"Pearl," said Virginia, "take this ton of calories away from me. Eat it or drop it out of the hotel on somebody's head or whatever you like. I don't care what you do with it. But if you ever let me see it again, I'll roast you over a slow fire."

"Okay, Miss Ginny. I don't mind eatin' 'em. My figger's one thing I don't have to worry about, I'm thankful to say. Only don't come askin' me tomorrow, 'Pearl, what ever happened to that box of choc'lates?'" She lifted the box. "My goodness, must be a good five pounds."

"You go back to your mystery story," said Virginia, "and let me hear no further speculations on the subject of poundage. And now," she said to Eric, "for the grim ordeal of the Sunday paper. But you haven't got one! Here, take one of mine."

Eric tried to busy himself with the paper. The joy of being with Virginia had gone out of him again. He had an uncontrollable feeling of bitterness and, at the same time, was angry at himself for this irrational resentment. After all, Virginia owed him nothing and her private life was her own business. Besides, she had been obviously upset by Mollison's appearance and had carried off her embarrassment with the best grace possible. He wished that he could display the tact that the situation demanded instead of letting her see his sulky displeasure, making matters more difficult for her.

It was she who had to smooth things over. When they had gone as far as Stamford, with hardly a word, she said, "My gastric juices are clamoring for a salmi of grouse. How's about you?"

He accepted with alacrity. When they had ordered Virginia brought the conversation around to the safely impersonal subject of modern painting. At her suggestion Eric had paid several visits to the Museum of Modern Art and had become acquainted with the works of many contemporary painters. A lively discussion carried them through lunch, and when they returned to the parlor car they were on easy terms again.

Most of the actors—several of whom had brought their husbands or wives—got off at the Back Bay station. But only the principals could afford to stay at the Marlborough; in fact, the tryout was an unprofitable excursion for the minor actors, since their salaries barely covered their out-of-town living expenses.

Eric taxied to the Marlborough with Virginia. (Pearl went on to South Station, for she had to stay at a remote hotel, where Negroes were acceptable.) The Marlborough was one of the finest hotels in the United States, if not in the world, and Eric was shown to a large, charmingly appointed room, high up, with a fine sweeping view of the Common. He was dazzled by this unaccustomed splendor and grinned with amusement as he hung his one extra suit in the huge closet and distributed the rest of his scanty wardrobe through the commodious chest of drawers. He tried to imagine himself owning enough clothes to fill all that space but gave it up as a fantastic speculation.

He answered the buzzer to admit Winternitz, who had an armful of newspapers. "Greetings from the Beacon Street soviet, comrade," he said. "What are your impressions of the Athens of the West?"

"Well, I haven't had much time to look around," said Eric.

"I feel the same way myself." He put the newspapers on the bed. "I've brought a culling of the dominical feuilletons for your delectation. The tidings of our cultural activities receive modest attention. We are competing for the encomia of the multitudes with a lyrical divertissement alliteratively entitled Gotta Get That Gal. It is, I surmise, a callipygian étalage, and since the Pilgrim Fathers have an amiable predilection for the nether extremities of the shapelier sex, it

282

follows that your lucubration is relegated to a position squarely behind the eight ball. However, I have achieved the possible, without benefit of cheese cake. Further, I have arranged to have you catechized by Daniel O'Fallon, who vivisects the dramaturgic art for the Evening News, an estimable diurnal publication somewhat morbidly preoccupied with ax murders and Hollywoodian—or should I say Hollywooden?—adulteries. The bar at six is the place and time."

"What am I supposed to say to him?" asked Eric nervously.

"Anything, my lad, anything—as long as you eschew polysyllables and keep your opinion of the Franco government to yourself. I am trying desperately to build you up as a clean-cut, wholesome American youth. Alors, mon vieux, jusqu'à six heures!" With a wave of the hand he was off.

Eric went through the Boston papers, all of which contained publicity material about his play. As Winternitz had pointed out, it was hard for a serious play, written by an unknown author and performed by relatively unknown actors, to compete for space with a musical comedy that offered a popular comedian and a dozen shapely girls. But he had managed to place several news stories about the play, the cast, and Thompson, as well as photographs of Virginia, Florence Fulham, and Reginald Olmsted. Each paper also carried a large advertisement of the opening (the quid pro quo of the publicity material), and he was pleased to see his play's name and his own in bold type. He carefully clipped out all the items and put them in an envelope for his mother.

He went down to the bar at six, a little shaky about the interview; but it passed off smoothly enough. O'Fallon was bored by this routine Sunday assignment and would far rather have been playing poker or golf, but he was cordial to Eric and tried, with the help of Winternitz, to find something on which he could base a readable story. From a reporter's point of view Eric was not very promising material. He was not married or engaged, his war record was negative, and he had never done anything in particular, except live the life to which he had been born and try to find his way to a better one. At last, however, when Winternitz, who had been racking his brains, pointed out that Eric was a New Englander, O'Fallon brightened and said, "Well, that's an angle!" and proceeded to question him about his home town and family background.

"Was I all right?" asked Eric when O'Fallon had left.

"My boy, you were superb," said Winternitz, wringing his hand.

283

"Transliterated by the inattentive O'Fallon, your profound inconsequentialities will assume an even more exquisite banality."

Eric went back to his room and called his mother, attempting once more to persuade her to come to Boston for the Tuesday night opening. She insisted that it was impossible for her to get away and promised to try to get to New York for the opening there.

He had dinner alone in the hotel restaurant. Virginia was at a table, at the other side of the room, with Winternitz and a woman columnist; but she left without having seen him. The hotel had an excellent cuisine, very different from the cheap restaurants to which Eric was accustomed, and he enjoyed the novelty of ordering what he liked without thinking of the cost.

After dinner he walked across the Common to the Mayflower Theater where The Clouded Mirror was to be presented. The front of the theater was dark, and the electric sign above the marquee still bore the name of the play that had closed the preceding night. Accustomed now to the ways of theaters, he walked down the alley (which was even dingier and dirtier than the Farow's).

The stage was seething with activity. Everything appeared to be in a state of hopeless confusion. Fifteen or twenty stagehands were moving around, climbing up and down ladders, setting up the false proscenium, hooking up portable switchboards, laying linoleum tracks for the movable platforms. Sections of painted scenery were propped against the back wall or lying flat on the stage, and there was a bewildering clutter of furniture, properties, and large packing cases in which the costumes, draperies, and electrical equipment had been shipped.

In the midst of all this hubbub McCarthy, shirt-sleeved, haggard and unshaven, was bustling about, trying to bring some order out of the chaos. He was in general charge of the setting up and gave instructions to Harry Baumrucker, Charles Ankrim, and Ira Whitestone, the house crew of the Farow (acting as road crew during the tryout), who relayed them to the men in their respective departments. The rules of the stagehands' union strictly defined the duties of the three departments, so that no property man could handle scenery, no carpenter could touch a piece of furniture, and the electricians could deal with nothing but lighting equipment. Hence three groups of men were attempting to perform, simultaneously, three different sets of operations, and were forever getting in each other's way or having

284

to stand aside because of some activity that was obstructing their own.

This was only one of the problems that harassed a meticulous producer like Leroy Thompson. What worried him most was the time element. Ordinarily the play would have opened on Monday night, for the actors were on full salary whether they played or not. With a complicated production such as this, a Monday opening was out of the question. The scenery and properties, which had arrived in Boston on Friday, had to be kept in the freight cars until the theater was available. Since the preceding production could not be moved out until after the Saturday-night performance, the moving in had to be delayed until early Sunday morning. Skillful workmen though most of the stage crew were, they were seeing the scenery and equipment for the first time, and they had to devise the means of assembling the unfamiliar material and of stacking it in a way that would facilitate the scene changes. The lights presented another problem. In the interests of efficiency and economy every theater should have been equipped with a permanent lighting system and a comprehensive switchboard, adequate for the lighting of any production. Yet each play carried its own special lamps and portable switchboards, which had to be dismantled, packed, and shipped when the production moved out, only to be replaced immediately by almost identical equipment when its successor moved in. Worse yet, the electricians could not hang the overhead lamps until the carpenters and property men had cleared the stage to make room for the towering ladders. Delay followed delay, time and money were wasted, everybody's nerves were frayed, and sometimes the very success of the play was jeopardized by the insufficiency of its technical preparation.

As Eric stood observing the disordered scene a sharp voice behind him said, "Watch it, buddy!" He stepped aside quickly to get out of the way of two property men who were trying to maneuver a large sideboard through the maze of obstructions.

"You better get off the stage, Eric," said Murray Fineman, with whom he had almost collided. "You're liable to get hurt here. There's a pass-door on the other side." The business manager was nervously chewing an unlighted cigar. The stagehands received double pay on Sunday, and every extra hour meant at least a hundred dollars in labor costs.

As Eric worked his way carefully across the stage he saw Peter Quirt. "Hello, Pete," he said. "You look all in."

"We've been here since seven this morning and I guess we'll be here all night," said Peter. "At this rate we'll be lucky if we open by Christmas."

Thompson was sitting in the third row with Arthur Eckstein. The scenic designer gave Eric a friendly greeting, but Thompson was obviously not pleased to see him there. He did not like having anyone about who was not useful, particularly when he was in a state of tension.

"Eighty-thirty," said Thompson, looking at his watch. "How much time do you need for the lights?"

"Well, I really need a day and a half," said Eckstein. He was a tall, heavy man, phlegmatic, deliberate, and slow of speech.

"You know damn well you can't have a day and a half," snapped Thompson.

"Well, I think we'd better let the carpentry and prop departments go at ten. They're dead on their feet right now, and not much good for anything. We'll start hanging then and knock off at two. The boys need at least six hours' sleep. So we'll come back at eight. When do you want the stage?"

"I've called the company for two," said Thompson. "And I'd like to get started by three. We've got a hell of a lot of work to do."

Eckstein shook his head. "It's going to be tough. I'll do the best I can, but I warn you it's going to be mighty sketchy, so don't expect too much."

"How long will the dress rehearsal take?" asked Eric, regretting the useless question the moment he had asked it.

"That's a good question to send to some quiz program," said Thompson irritably. "Maybe you'll win a free trip to the Virgin Islands." He walked down to the orchestra rail and called McCarthy. Eric, not wanting to be in the way, zigzagged across the stage again and left the theater. The weather, which had been mild, had suddenly changed. The temperature had dropped sharply, and a cold rain was falling. He could not get a taxi and walked back to the hotel in the drenching downpour.

XXV.

Eric woke up with a cold in the head. Feeling miserable, he had breakfast sent up, telephoned the drugstore for aspirin tablets, and spent the morning in his room. Irina Lanski called him when she arrived and at one he went down to the dining-room to have lunch with her. It was still raining hard. But unwilling to miss the dress rehearsal, Eric ignored her advice not to venture out. They taxied to the theater, and she suggested that they go in through the lobby instead of going down the long, exposed alley with its deep puddles. The name of the play was being put on the big electric sign, and Eric felt a shiver of excitement at this evidence of the nearness of the first public performance. The box-office was open, but there was no one at the window. Irina Lanski identified herself and Eric, and the treasurer pushed a button that unlatched one of the entrance doors.

It was a little after two. The stage was still crowded with workmen. The electricians, on their tall ladders, were angling lamps and inserting sheets of colored gelatin; in the background the carpenters were hammering. Eckstein sat in the middle of the auditorium, behind a large drafting board, which was equipped with a telephonic device that had a backstage connection through which he gave instructions to the stagehands. As the lights went on and off, bank by bank, he consulted his lighting plot, on which each lamp was numbered, and ordered modifications in position, color, and intensity. The sound effects were being rehearsed simultaneously, and he regulated their volume and the position of the loudspeakers through which they were amplified.

Winternitz was talking to Felix Obermeyer and his assistants, who were ready with their elaborate photographic equipment to take scene pictures as the dress rehearsal progressed. Claire and Fineman were moving around restlessly, worrying about the ever-mounting labor costs and even more about the weather. The advance sale had been light, and the predicted continuance of the downpour destroyed the hope of any last-minute demand.

Thompson saw Eric and Irina Lanski enter and strolled up the aisle. "Howdy, folks," he said. "Well, you're in good time. This thing won't start for hours." Then, as Eric sneezed convulsively, "For God's sake, keep away from the cast with those sneezes. Two or three of them have got the sniffles already, and, just to keep things lively, Ginny has come up with an attack of laryngitis. There's never a dull moment with this opera."

The night before Virginia had gone to visit friends and had caught a chill on her way home. Like most actors on the eve of an opening, she was in a tense and nervous state, which made her abnormally susceptible to any ailment. On awakening, she had a slight fever and an aching throat. She had sent for a throat specialist, who had advised her to stay in bed. But as she could not open in the play without a dress rehearsal, she had insisted upon coming to the theater.

Eric heard this news with consternation. "Where is she?" he asked.

"In her dressing-room. We put a cot in there for her, and she's trying to get some sleep. So don't go back there."

"No, of course not," said Eric, annoyed by Thompson's imperious manner.

"Can she get through the dress rehearsal?" asked Irina Lanski.

"Well, if she doesn't, there's no show. I think she'll make it. I've told her not to use her voice, and if necessary we'll have the whole faculty of the Harvard Medical School in, to goose her up."

"But what about tomorrow night? If she can't use her voice—"

"We'll open, come hell and high water. I'm not having any more postponements. If I have to I'll open with Lily Prengle."

"Do you think that's wise?"

"Well, wisdom is not what I'm famous for. All I know is that I've got to find out what this goddam thing looks like, and I'd rather see it tomorrow night with Lily than wait another two or three days. We're not going to do any business here anyhow, so it doesn't make much difference. If I ever get this one opened in New York I'm going to retire to a grapenuts farm in South Dakota."

"If you don't mind," said Irina Lanski to Eric as Thompson stalked down the aisle, "I think I'll go back to the hotel and lie down for an hour. My old bones don't travel as happily as they used to. And I advise you to go back too and get into bed. You are not needed here, and what you see will only discourage you, especially if Ginny can't use her voice."

"I guess you're right, but I think I'd rather stay."

She shook her head. "I don't know which is worse, the stubbornness of young writers or the cynicism of old ones."

Eric took two aspirin tablets and then stretched out on a leather sofa in the smoking-room. He was anxious about Virginia and wanted to go backstage to see her. Since she was already infected, there seemed little likelihood that his visit would do her any harm. But he did not want to incur Thompson's displeasure, so he lay there for an hour, sneezing and squirming uncomfortably. At half-past three he went upstairs again. The stagehands were still busily at work. Irina Lanski returned shortly after four, and a few minutes later Thompson ordered the work to stop. The electricians took down their ladders and two property men began to clear away the debris and sweep the stage.

"All right, Mack," called Thompson. "Take in your curtain, give us the house lights, and let's get going."

The heavy curtain came down slowly, the lights in the auditorium came up. Eric was suddenly aware that he was sitting in a lighted theater, waiting for the curtain to rise for the first time on the play that he had written.

There was another long wait; it was almost five when the house lights slowly dimmed out. After five seconds of darkness the curtain went up on the first scene of the play.

Eric's excitement soon subsided. What he saw bore no resemblance to the performance of a play. From the very beginning everything went wrong. Every few minutes Thompson interrupted the actors to correct a mistake, clear up some unforeseen difficulty, or demand an explanation for an exasperating delay. The actors were fumbling and jumpy. They were depressed by the weather, worried by the proximity of the opening, and tired from sitting idly for hours in their costumes and make-up. Because of the absurd method of rehearsing a play without the use of any of its appurtenances, they had to readjust themselves constantly to their unfamiliar surroundings. The actual furnishings took up much more space than the rehearsal make-shifts, so that there was less room to move around in. The chairs and sofas were either higher or lower than the stock kitchen chairs, or else so soft that it was difficult to get out of them gracefully. Drawers stuck, doors opened with a suddenness that catapulted the actor onto the scene or refused to close behind him. Properties were missing or were of an unexpected shape or size. Sound effects did not come on cue and were too loud or too prolonged. And offstage there was a hubbub that drove the actors to distraction, as the stagehands, themselves exhausted, and working in semi-darkness, shouted to each other and knocked things down in their efforts to get the next scene ready.

To add to the confusion the quality of the lighting kept changing as Eckstein telephoned instructions to the electricians to alter the reading on this lamp or that. As always there was a sharp though concealed conflict between the scene designer and the actors. The designer, naturally anxious to have his settings make a favorable impression and knowing that bright lights tended to reveal the bolts and seams and paintiness of canvas scenery, tried to produce an illusion of reality by toning down the illumination and deflecting it as much as possible from the painted surfaces. The actors, on the other hand, liked the stage to be flooded with light, not only because a bright stage holds the attention of the audience more readily than a dim one, but in order that their facial expressions, which were an integral part of their performances, could be clearly seen. Thompson was inclined to side with the actors, though he did not go to their extreme. Scenery was important, but an audience hardly looks at it two minutes after the curtain is up; it looks at the actors all through the performance. Experience had taught him that the best way to handle Eckstein, for whom he had great admiration, was to let him have his own way at the beginning, and then bit by bit coerce him into intensifying the lighting. If Eckstein offered too much resistance, Thompson would wait until he went back to New York and then simply instruct the head electrician (frequently a lighting expert himself) to step up the readings to the desired brightness. In the meantime, however, the actors suffered agonies, complaining bitterly that they were invisible in the gloom that pervaded the stage, and constantly tried to edge their way into any bright area that they could find.

Eric waited anxiously for Virginia's first entrance. He was amazed by her fresh and girlishly healthful appearance, forgetting to take into account her skillful make-up and the flattering lights. But he soon saw evidences of her illness. Drugged and feverish, she moved sluggishly and spoke in tones that even the actors could hardly hear and that were completely inaudible to those seated out front.

It took nearly an hour to get through the first scene of the play. Then began the problem of speeding up the scene changes. The play was in eight scenes—four in each act—and required five sets of scenery. To quicken the changes, a device known as a jack-knife stage was employed. This consisted of two platforms, set on casters, on either side of the false proscenium and at right angles to it. They were alternately used, so that one could be reset offstage while the other was in view of the audience. As each scene was finished the curtain was lowered and one platform was pivoted back a quarter-circle to its offstage position while the other was pushed on into the vacated space in the proscenium opening. The platforms were simultaneously in motion and their movement resembled the opening and shutting of the blades of a pocketknife. Speed was of the utmost importance, for it is hard to hold an audience's attention in a darkened theater, and the cumulative effect of the play depended largely upon a continuing maintenance of interest. The production had been planned with a view to making these changes in thirty seconds; but when the curtain fell on the first scene, more than four minutes elapsed before it rose again.

Thompson, watch in hand, stood tensely in the aisle. "Hold it, Reggie!" he called as Olmsted began to speak. "Well, Arthur, what about it? Nearly four and a half minutes."

"It's the first time they've done it," said Eckstein. "And they're punch-drunk besides. Ask Harry to come on," he said into the telephone.

Harry Baumrucker shuffled onto the stage, trying not to show the aching weariness of his old body.

"What went wrong, Harry?" asked Eckstein quietly.

"Well, it's the first time through," said Harry, shielding his one good eye from the blinding front lights. "The boys got a little mixed up."

"Over four minutes," said Thompson. "If that happens tomorrow night, we're up the creek." It was not the fault of the overworked men, but he had to keep the pressure on until after the opening.

"Can you give me five minutes to routine it?" asked Harry. "We'll get it down for you once we get it rolling."

"All right, go ahead, and then let's take another crack at it."

"Take it back, boys," shouted Harry.

The platform swung back, and the first scene rolled into place again. The actors slumped wearily in the chairs—all but Virginia, who had gone back to her dressing-room. Instead of five minutes, it took Harry twenty-five to get his men properly organized. Then Virginia was summoned, the end of the scene was repeated for the curtain cues, and the change was made again. This time it took a little less than two minutes.

"That was better, wasn't it?" said Harry, coming on.

"Still not good enough," said Thompson.

"We'll get it licked before tomorrow night. Do you want to try it again?"

"Yes, but first we're going to take pictures of this scene."

Felix Obermeyer and his assistants set up their cameras and flood-lights and posed the actors in the situations Winternitz had selected as the most effective for publicity purposes. It was a tedious process. The actors resignedly submitted to the photographer's very precise requirements and tried to give an appearance of animation they were far from feeling. When the photographic apparatus had been cleared away the end of the scene was played once more. This time the change took only a little more than a minute. That was good enough for the present, and Thompson went on with the second scene. Again there was a series of delays, miscues, omissions, and misunderstandings, again the change to the next scene had to be gone through several times and the photographs taken. It was nearly half-past eight when the third scene was finished. Thompson called an hour's halt to give the cast and crew a chance to eat and snatch a few moments' rest. He had sent for great quantities of coffee and sandwiches for the actors, so they would not have to go out in the rain.

Eric and Irina Lanski went to a sea-food restaurant, next door to the theater. A few minutes later Claire came in with Winternitz and Fineman. Nobody was in a mood for conversation, and they went on to a table at the back. All through the rehearsal Claire had turned to glare at Eric each time he sneezed. Thompson had stayed in the theater to talk to Eckstein and to avoid Claire. Her exaggerated worry over every mishap and delay was an added annoyance; he wished he could think of some way of getting her to leave, but he knew she would stay to the bitter end.

Eric and Irina Lanski ate in silence. When dinner was over she said, "Perhaps I am just a self-indulgent old woman, but I don't see what good I do by sitting in that theater, so I am going to my room and get into bed. And if you'll take my advice, you'll do the same thing."

"Thanks, but I think I'll stay. I'm worried about Ginny. Do you think she'll be all right?"

"Well, I hope so. But I don't see how sitting there will help her, any more than an expectant father pacing a hospital corridor helps the screaming woman in the delivery room."

Eric smiled. "I guess you're right. But in all the stories I've read, the father goes on pacing until the baby is born."

He helped her into a taxi and went back to the theater. As he sat sneezing Thompson came up to him. "Why don't you go to bed, Eric? There's nothing for you to do around here. We've just got to sweat it out and hope to Christ we can give a show tomorrow night."

"Well, I may, in a little while," said Eric, without the slightest intention of complying. "How is Ginny?"

Thompson gave him a withering look. "How old is Ann?" he said and walked away.

It was nearly ten before the rehearsal was resumed. It dragged on in its dreary course, hour after hour. Tempers snapped under the strain of aching muscles and taut nerves; there were sharp words and tears. Even Florence Fulham lost her habitual poise and bristled angrily when Thompson asked her to repeat a complicated piece of business. The final curtain did not fall until half-past two, and Thompson ordered it raised immediately and told McCarthy to call the company onstage. "Everybody but Ginny. Tell her I'll be back to see her in a minute."

The actors came on, dragging their feet and sagging wearily against the furniture.

"I won't keep you a minute," said Thompson. "I'm sorry it had to be this way, but it's one of those things, and this is the way it had to be. We're a long way from home yet, and much as I hate to do it we've got to have another technical run-through tomorrow."

The actors groaned in protest. "Are you expecting us to give a performance tomorrow night?" asked Olmsted acidly.

"There can't be any performance without a run-through, I can tell you that. We're going to have the critics in here tomorrow night, and I'm not going to kick our chances away with a ragged production. So we'll just have to grit our teeth and go through with it. I know you didn't ask to be born and neither did I, but that's the kind of business we're in. I'll make it as easy as I can for you. No make-up, costumes, or acting; but everything else—lights, props, effects, and scene changes. We'll start promptly at two, and I promise to get you out of here by four-thirty And thanks for everything so far. All right, that's all. Merry Christmas to all and to all a good night."

The actors scattered to their dressing-rooms, bemoaning the day they had first set foot upon a stage.

"The front of the house is locked, folks," called Fineman to the people out front. "You'll have to go out through the stage door."

They all moved over to the side aisle and up through the pass-door. Eric saw Gladys Kaye and asked her where Virginia's dressing-room was. As he approached it he saw Thompson going in and decided he had better keep clear of him. He groped his way through the tangle of scenery to the stage door. It was raining steadily, and he had difficulty in avoiding the alley's deep puddles. The street was deserted. He did not dare take the long walk back to the hotel, so he stood under the marquee, determined to wait until a taxi came along. After about fifteen minutes one pulled up in front of the theater. As he started for it, McCarthy got out. "Don't take that," he said. "It's for Ginny."

McCarthy hurried down the alley. A few minutes later, Thompson came out carrying Virginia, with Claire following. Eric felt a sudden pang when he saw Virginia in Thompson's arms, her head on his shoulder. As Thompson put her down she noticed Eric and beckoned to him to get into the cab. She and Claire got in and Thompson followed. "Well, come on!" he shouted impatiently as Eric stood hesitating. Eric got in and put down one of the jump-seats. He turned to look at Virginia. She had not removed her make-up, but beneath it she was pale and her eyes were dull and heavy.

"How are you?" he asked.

She shook her head and put her finger to her lips.

No one spoke during the ride to the hotel, nor in the elevator. Eric was the first to get out. He took Virginia's hand. "I hope you'll be better," he said. She nodded but did not answer.

He staggered down the corridor to his room, let his clothes lie where they fell, and tumbled into bed, breathing heavily and almost hysterical with fatigue. Brooding over Claire's cold hostility, Thompson's contempt, and his own unimportance to Virginia, he was overwhelmed by self-pity. As for his play, he saw no possibility of its opening in eighteen hours; in his unhappy state he did not care whether it did or not.

XXVI.

Eric slept fitfully and awoke at noon, depressed and achy. The rain was still falling from a leaden sky. He tried to call Virginia, but the operator had instructions not to disturb her. He hesitated about calling Thompson, fearing another rebuff, and while he was debating it Irina Lanski called him. She had just learned from Thompson that the doctor was reasonably sure that if Virginia spent the day in bed she would be able to go on that evening. Thompson had instructed McCarthy to have Lily Prengle stand in for her at the run-through. The agent urged Eric to stay in bed too, since he was not needed at the theater. He gladly agreed, arranging to have dinner with her at half-past six.

When Thompson arrived at the theater Richard Ismay, the actor who had handed in his part at the time of Emily Crandall's collapse, was waiting for him. The play in which Ismay was appearing had opened in Boston the week before and was playing its second week.

"Hello, Mr. Thompson," he said self-consciously.

"Oh, hello, Dick," said Thompson, suspecting why he was there.

"I know this is no time to bother you, but I just wanted to ask you to keep me in mind in case there's any change."

"I thought you were in that Jack Homburg show."

"I am," said the actor ruefully. "Or rather I was. The notice went up last night."

"It's not opening in New York?"

"It never should have opened in Boston. We got panned from hell to breakfast, and the business has been brutal. They shot a deer in the balcony at the Saturday matinee."

"Well, imagine that happening to a Homburg production!" said Thompson with more than a touch of malice.

"I guess you think I was a dope for not sticking with you and

I damned well know I was. But I thought you might not go ahead, and, Mr. Thompson, I've got grocery bills like nobody's business."

"It's too bad," said Thompson. "I wish I could help you out. But I'm pretty sure I won't be making any changes."

"I figured you wouldn't, but I thought I'd ask, just in case. Well, maybe next time."

"Oh, sure. Come in any time I'm casting."

"Thanks, Mr. Thompson. And believe you me, next time I'll stick." He extended his hand. "All the good luck in the world to you for tonight. I hear it looks great."

"I hope you heard right. And good luck to you."

"Thanks a lot. I sure need it. I haven't had a break in three years."

As Ismay went dejectedly out into the rain-swept alley Thompson felt a twinge of sympathy for him. He was an exceptionally capable actor, but the theater offered him no security or continuity of employment. He was a counter in a gambler's game, and the energies that should have gone into the development of his talents were expended in the frantic struggle to meet his family responsibilities. Thompson had little interest in economic theories, but he reflected that there must be something wrong with a system that squandered and wasted good human material.

He had given strict orders that the run-through was to begin at two, to give the actors at least three hours' rest before the evening performance. The stagehands had come back at nine and had spent a busy morning, putting things in order and devising means of correcting the defects the dress rehearsal had revealed. Eckstein was out front, still working on the lights. He was seemingly tireless and never got ruffled no matter what the provocation. Promptly at two Thompson had the company called. He eyed them quickly as they came on. They were silent and in low spirits, but a night's rest had relaxed them somewhat; they were no longer at the explosion point.

"Well, here we are again," said Thompson. "First of all, I want to tell you that Ginny's medicine man is quite sure she'll be able to go on tonight." The cast brightened perceptibly. Glancing quickly at Lily Prengle, he saw that she was half relieved, half disappointed. "This is just technical today, and we're going right through, no matter what happens, so if anything goes wrong, just crash right ahead as though it were a performance. Don't use your voices and never mind the acting. All right, we'll start right away, and I'll guarantee to have you out of here by four-thirty."

He started for the pass-door as the actors dispersed—all but Lily, who stood looking at him with languishing eyes. He had to say something to her. "Gladys is on the book, so if you need any help, just yell for it," he said, pressing her arm.

She trembled at his touch. "I won't need it," she said almost inaudibly.

"Good girl," he said, walking away quickly.

After the episode at the Farow, Thompson had deliberately avoided being alone with Lily and barely spoke a personal word to her. He was uncomfortably aware that her eyes were always on him; but by maintaining an appearance of constant preoccupation with the play he made it almost impossible for her, as a minor member of the cast, to approach him. At the day's end he checked over notes with the principals or with McCarthy until Lily had gone; and he left with someone else in case she might be waiting outside. He kept away from his hotel until late at night, afraid that she might call. Twice he did find messages from her; he made no reference to them, and she did not either, merely gazing at him in reproachful despair. He could not go on like this indefinitely; since only three days remained before his departure from New York, he succeeded in carrying it off. As it was, he left for Boston somewhat sooner than was absolutely necessary, merely to be out of her way. He was quite certain that she could not afford to stay at the Marlborough, but consulted Rothberg's list of hotel reservations to reassure himself. In Boston the pressure of work made any personal contact impossible, at least until after the opening, and that gave him another three or four days' respite.

The problem of what to do about her was a constant irritant. Daily and hourly he cursed himself for his act of folly. For want of a moment's judgment, a moment's self-control, he had become involved in a situation from which he did not know how to extricate himself. The simplest and most honest course would be to ask her forgiveness for his failure to resist an irresponsible impulse and to tell her, bluntly, that since there was no possibility of any future relationship between them, the best thing for her would be to forget what had happened as quickly as possible. But that would mean a long, harrowing scene; reluctant either to bear pain or to inflict it, he shrank from the tears, the reproaches, and the pleadings of adolescent agony. Besides, there was always the possibility that her humorless, intense nature might drive her to suicide. Years ago he had

297

had a somewhat similar experience, and he shuddered as he remembered the narrow margin by which a tragedy had been averted. To go on with Lily, however, was impossible, for they lived on different planes of thought and feeling, and, as far as he was concerned, even the physical attraction was not very strong. If she could take it all lightly and casually, he might be willing to go on until they tired of each other. But it was evident that she believed herself to be in the throes of a grand passion, and he knew that nothing was more boring and distasteful than being the object of an unrequited infatuation. He put off facing the situation, hoping that when at last he was forced to, the day would be saved by some happy improvisation or unexpected turn of events.

In contrast to the stumbling dress rehearsal, the run-through proceeded with smoothness and dispatch. Eckstein and the three veterans of the Farow Theater had straightened out the snags and coordinated the various elements of the production. Everything was in place and on time, the lighting had been vastly improved, and the scene changes cut down to about a minute. Thompson made numerous notes, most of them dealing with easily correctible errors. When the final curtain fell and the company rehearsed the curtain calls, which he had carefully planned, he said a few words of encouragement and dismissed them.

"Just a moment, folks," said McCarthy as they started to leave the stage. "I just want to say that curtain time is eight-thirty and I want everyone in the theater by half-hour. The acts will be called but not the scenes. We've got all we can handle here as it is. So it's up to everybody to watch their own cues and be responsible for being on time. And when you finish a scene, kindly leave the stage. We're so jammed up here we couldn't get anything else on with a shoehorn, so let's not have anybody around who isn't needed. And, one more thing, watch the offstage talking. We've got a lot of fast and tricky cues that are hard to pick up, so please, everybody cooperate by not talking. Okay, that's all I've got to say and thank you."

When the actors had left Thompson called the crew on. They filed onto the stage, sixteen tired men in overalls and work clothes.

"That was very good, boys," said Thompson, "and I want to thank you all for a swell job. I know it's been a tough one, but I think we've got it licked, and if we're that good tonight there'll be no kick coming."

"We'll be better tonight," said Harry Baumrucker.

"That'll be all right too. I've got a few notes for you, Harry, and for Charlie and Ira. But that's all for the rest of you, and thanks again."

The men filed off impassively. His words strengthened their morale, a factor whose importance Thompson never minimized. One reason his productions functioned smoothly was that he saw to it that his stage crews were friendly and cooperative, instead of sullen and indifferent.

The stagehands were, in a sense, the black sheep of the theater. Because they were invisible and anonymous, the value of their contribution often went unrecognized. Managers, authors, and actors had a tendency to look down upon them and to charge them with laziness, malingering, stupidity, and incompetence. But directors like Thompson and scene designers like Eckstein, who worked in close collaboration with the stagehands, knew that many of them were highly skilled artisans whose ingenuity and resourcefulness were invaluable in the solution of difficult technical problems. There were bunglers and misfits among them, to be sure, but there were also actors who did not know how to act, authors who did not know how to write, and producers who did not know anything.

Undoubtedly instances of "feather-bedding" and even racketeering could be found among the stagehands' union's practices, and the inflexibility of its regulations often imposed needless hardships upon productions that were struggling for survival; but these abuses were often over-emphasized by those who would have been only too ready to take advantage of the workmen if they had not the protection of a strong organization.

Superficially, it seemed anomalous that an industry which, on its managerial side, was unorganized, wasteful, inefficient, and chaotic, should be, on its operational side, one of the most tightly organized in the American economy. The incongruity was more apparent than real, for the restrictive unions had developed as a measure of self-defense on the part of workers who had been consistently sweated, underpaid, and even swindled by unscrupulous managers. The result was a condition under which honest and fair-minded employers had to bear burdens that could have been eased if they had had the foresight and initiative to establish and enforce a code of ethics that would have put the crooks and the exploiters out of business.

As it was, the failure of the managers to regulate and stabilize the industry and to provide security and continuity of employment forced the workers to do what they could to protect themselves against the economic hazards of their occupation. Since employment in the theater was sporadic, seasonal and of uncertain tenure, the unions had adopted abnormally high wage scales in an effort to provide their members with an adequate annual income. Consequently the peak load of labor costs had to be carried in the weeks of active production instead of being distributed over a period of continuous operation, so that many plays had to close while there was still an active popular interest in them, thus creating more unemployment and demands for yet higher pay to bring up the weekly average.

A closed shop was enforced not only by the stagehands but by the actors, the musicians, the scenic artists, the scene painters, the press agents, the company managers, the box-office employees, the wardrobe women, the truckmen, and the maintenance men. The Dramatists' Guild too, while not a labor union, required membership of everyone professionally engaged in writing, translating, and adapting for the stage. Unfortunately all this organization was on a craft and not on an industrial basis. Though each union was justifiably concerned with the welfare of its own members, all ignored the primary and paramount fact that they had a common interest in establishing a sound and efficient economy. A body representative of all the crafts could undoubtedly have found solutions for many of the over-all industrial problems affecting everyone, but the American prejudice against "planning" could not be overcome; so the American philosophy of every man for himself and the devil take the hindmost prevailed.

After the run-through Thompson went backstage to go over his notes with the three heads and McCarthy. It was more than a half-hour before he was ready to leave. He assumed that Lily had gone long ago; but when he got to the stage door she came running down the stairs from the dressing-rooms and caught up with him.

"Hello, Lily," he said, taking her arm. "Have you got those first-night jitters?"

"Yes, I guess I have," she said, pressing close against him. "Though I don't know why, with the little I have to do."

"Everybody has them. Even the wig-maker is out there biting his nails and hoping the star doesn't knock the heavy's toupee off.

Look out for that puddle!" She was paying no attention to where she was going, oblivious to everything but his nearness.

He hailed a passing taxi without stopping to think that he could not very well leave her standing there, particularly since the streets were still wet. "Can't I give you a lift?" he said, making the best of it.

"If it isn't out of your way. I'm at the Bay State."

"The Bay State first and then the Marlborough," he said to the driver.

The moment the cab started she threw herself against his shoulder. "Oh, I've been so lonely! A whole week, and you haven't said a word to me or even noticed me."

He put his arm around her. "Well, I've been a little bit busy, honey. This is a tough show to get on."

"Oh, I know that! All I wanted was just a look or a smile. Oh, kiss me, darling, please kiss me!" As he bent his head she glued her lips against his. He responded automatically—not without an involuntary glance at the driver's immobile head.

"Oh, thank you, thank you!" she said. "Am I never going to see you again?"

"Well, that's a silly question," he replied, not urgently. "But give me a chance to get this show open."

"Couldn't you get out with me now? Or let me go with you just for a few minutes. I'll leave the minute you tell me to."

"I wish I could, dear, but I've got some newspaper people waiting for me at the hotel," he said, snatching at the first excuse that occurred to him. Fortunately the Bay State Hotel was only three blocks from the theater, and they were already there. "Anyhow," he said, opening the door of the cab, "you'd better be concentrating on your work. I don't think Ginny will be up to two performances tomorrow and I may want to put you on at the matinee."

"Don't worry about me. I'll be ready. And I won't let anything interfere with my work."

"I'll see you later."

Lily walked quickly to the hotel entrance. As the cab moved away she turned and threw him an agonized look. He leaned back and closed his eyes, wishing he had given the part to Suzanne Merchant. It was not likely that he would have been tempted by her; if he had been, he certainly would not have found himself in his present situation.

XXVII.

Eric got up at six, feeling much the better for his day's rest. Before going down to dinner he called Virginia's room; there was no answer. He wondered where she could be. Irina Lanski quickly reassured him. She had met Virginia in the lobby, as she was leaving for the theater. She wanted to make up early, so that she could have an hour's rest in her dressing-room before the performance.

The agent had attended the run-through and gave Eric an encouraging report. "I think everything will go quite smoothly tonight. So all you need worry about now is the play."

"That's not much, is it?" said Eric with a weak smile, breaking into a cold sweat.

"I suggest that you take a cocktail, or, better still, two cocktails, to fortify yourself for what is journalistically known as your baptism of fire."

When the cocktails were brought she raised her glass. "To the success that you deserve and that I hope will be yours! But if you will take my grandmotherly advice, you will not expect too much either from the audience or from the press. In fact, even an enthusiastic reception will mean very little as far as New York is concerned."

"Then why go through all the expense and agony of a tryout?"

"That is a question I have often asked myself," she said. "The managers will tell you that the actors need the experience of playing before audiences before they face the New York first-nighters, and that it allows time to correct weaknesses in the play. In my opinion, a half-dozen previews in New York would accomplish the same purpose at no greater cost and at an enormous saving to everyone's nervous system and disposition."

302

While they were having a second cocktail Claire came into the dining-room with Anthony Weir and another man, who smiled and waved to Irina Lanski.

"This is Freddy Haig," she said to Eric as the man came over to her. He was slender and stoop-shouldered, with graying hair and gold-rimmed spectacles. There was a perpetually quizzical smile on his deceptively youthful face.

"Irina, my darling," he said, stooping to kiss her cheek, "how are you? And why do I see you only in moments of crisis?"

"Perhaps it is because my life consists entirely of moments of crisis. Do you know Eric Kenwood?"

"I do now," said Haig, beaming at Eric and extending his hand. "May I say that I admire your fortitude, Mr. Kenwood, in sitting at table on such an occasion? I usually spend my first nights supine in an oxygen tent, desperately dictating codicils, while a fully accoutered cleric hovers about, prepared to administer the last solemn rites."

"Maybe that's what I'll be doing when I've had a little more experience," said Eric.

"No, I think you are made of sterner stuff. Well, I hear wonderful reports and I'm well equipped with soothing lotions for my smarting palms. But I must return to my hostess. Poor, dear Claire! I always feel for her on a night like this! For what is the tug at our heart strings compared to the pull on her purse strings? The best of everything to you, Mr. Kenwood. And the customary ten per cent of the best to you, Irina." He beamed at them both again and went over to join Claire and Weir.

"Does he always talk like that?" asked Eric.

Irina Lanski smiled. "I'm afraid poor Freddy is an acquired taste. You probably don't like truffles either."

"I've never had any. Do you think he came all the way from New York just to see the play?"

She nodded. "At Claire's insistence, I'm sure. She is a great gatherer of expert opinions, especially when they cost her nothing."

Feeling as he did about Frederic Haig's plays, Eric was far from pleased to have Haig called in to sit in judgment on his own work. He already was conscious of an anticipatory emotional resistance to any suggestions that Haig might see fit to make.

Eric had eaten little all day, and the cocktails went to his head. He had no appetite and hardly touched the substantial dinner he had ordered. When he had finished his second cup of coffee it **was** yet an hour until curtain time. He could sit still no longer. Besides, he wanted to try to see Virginia before the play began. He and Irina Lanski were sitting together; after asking her to meet him in the lobby ten minutes before curtain time he hurried out of the dining-room. She went over to join Claire's party.

His heart leaped as the taxi turned a corner. Far down the street was the name of his play in bright lights over the marquee of the theater. He went up the dark alley and onto the stage. The first scene was already in place behind the lowered curtain. The property men were carefully placing the furniture in the exact positions indicated by chalk marks on the floor. On the offstage platform the carpenters were setting the second scene.

Eric went to Virginia's dressing-room and knocked timidly. The door opened a few inches, and Pearl's face appeared, looking far from friendly.

"Hello, Pearl," said Eric. "Can I see Miss Upton?"

"Well, she's layin' down right now, Mr. Kenwood, tryin' to get a little rest."

"Come in, Eric," called Virginia.

Pearl opened the door disapprovingly. Virginia got up from her cot. She was wearing an old dressing gown, streaked and spotted with make-up.

"Oh, please don't get up," said Eric.

"No, it's time I got on my bicycle," she said. "How are you?" She went to the dressing table and began brushing her thick red hair with a long, sweeping motion.

"How are *you?* That's the important thing."

"Couldn't be lousier. I hope you don't hate me for being such a drip."

"I've been terribly worried about you. Are you sure it's all right for you to go on?"

"The old vet was just in to give me another working over, and he says he'll get me through it. But I'd go on anyhow, even if I had to use a megaphone. No Baby Blue-Eyes is going to do any first-night pinch-hitting for me. Let the younger generation knock at somebody else's door."

"Don't forget what the doctor said about not talkin' when you don't have to," said Pearl, who was hanging up clothes and putting things in order.

304

Virginia thumbed her nose at her and motioned to Eric to sit beside the dressing table. He looked around the long, narrow, cheerless room. The plaster was peeling off the grimy walls; exposed steam-heat pipes ran along the ceiling. Virginia's smart wardrobe trunk filled one end of the room; at the other end were several unopened boxes of flowers and an enormous beribboned, flower-filled gilt basket that Eric was sure had been sent by Hugh Mollison. On the dressing table was a heap of unopened telegrams. It had not occurred to Eric to send flowers, and he wondered if Virginia would be offended by his neglect.

Virginia glanced at him and saw his uneasy look. "The doc didn't say anything about you not talking," she said.

"I guess I don't know what to say. This is my first opening night."

"Poor baby! Well, cheer up. They get worse as you go along."

There was a knock at the door. "Half-hour, Miss Upton!" called Gladys Kaye.

"Okay," said Pearl. She turned briskly to Eric. "You'll have to excuse us, Mr. Kenwood. We gotta get dressed."

Eric rose quickly. "Yes, of course."

"Good luck, Eric," said Virginia, holding up her face.

"Good luck to you, Ginny," he said, kissing her. "And I hope you'll be all right."

He left the dressing-room, and Pearl closed the door almost on his heels. Embarrassed and afraid of impairing Virginia's make-up, he had barely touched his lips to her cheek, but even that light contact had made him tingle.

Most of the actors who appeared in the first scene were already on the stage, looking like painted dolls under the overhead work lights. They tiptoed about and spoke in whispers, though there was no need for silence yet. They smiled nervously at Eric and wished him luck. As he grasped their hands he had an eve-of-battle feeling that was compounded of fear and a warm sense of comradeship in a perilous adventure. He went onto the set again. Reginald Olmsted was pacing back and forth, murmuring his lines, and McCarthy was looking at the audience through a peephole in the curtain. "Hello, Eric," he said as he turned away. "They're beginning to come in. Want to take a look?"

"Yes," said Eric eagerly. He applied his eye to the peephole and looked at his first audience slowly assembling. Some of the spectators were already in their chairs, talking or reading their programs;

others were following the ushers down the aisles. Through the curtain the buzz of conversation and the clatter of seats could be plainly heard. Eric gazed out at this gathering of casual strangers who were so soon to sit in judgment upon his play, envying them their detachment and almost hating them for it, like a prisoner on trial for his life who covertly eyes the jury upon whose verdict his existence depends.

As he left the set he encountered Thompson. "Well, Eric, think you'll live through it?"

"I doubt it."

"Well, good luck!" said Thompson, extending his hand.

Eric grasped it warmly. "Good luck. And thanks for everything," he remembered to add.

Gladys Kaye was making the rounds again, calling, "Fifteen minutes!" She knocked on Virginia's door, then went up the iron stairs to the upper dressing-rooms. On his way out Eric saw numerous telegrams thumbtacked to the call board, expressions of good wishes to the cast from Thompson, Claire, Irina Lanski, and several others, including one from Tucson, Arizona, that read: "My heart is with all of you tonight." It was signed "Emily Crandall." He was mortified by his own omission and hoped the cast would understand that it was due to his ignorance of theatrical customs and not to thoughtlessness or ingratitude.

Irina Lanski was waiting for him in the crowded lobby. They shuffled along slowly into the well-filled auditorium. Eric did not know that half the audience was there by invitation. The press had been liberally supplied with seats by Winternitz, and, in addition, Fineman had judiciously distributed enough tickets to ensure the presence of a large audience. The giving out of tickets for tryout performances was a source of continual conflict between the producing management and the theater management. The producer, knowing how greatly the cast was affected by the volume of applause and laughter, was always anxious to have the house packed, while the theater owner was fearful of establishing a precedent that might interfere with the sale of tickets for future productions. Fineman, by stubborn persistence, usually had his way on opening nights, but for subsequent performances he could seldom overcome the opposition of the theater manager.

Eric and Irina Lanski had seats in the fourth row on the aisle. With trembling hands he opened his program and turned the pages slowly until he came to the playbill. He tried to read it, but all that was visible was his own name, which leaped out at him from the printed page. Glancing across the aisle, he was startled to see Daniel O'Fallon sitting in the third row. A report of his interview with Eric had appeared in the Evening News the day before. It was an innocuous piece that dwelt a little too much, Eric thought, upon his youth and inexperience. "There's Mr. O'Fallon, one of the critics," he whispered. Irina Lanski merely nodded.

At half-past eight the audience was still coming in. Eric kept glancing anxiously at his watch. A few minutes later the members of a small orchestra squirmed through a little door under the stage and, taking their places in the pit, began to play a medley of airs from The Pink Lady. It was a ragged and spiritless performance; as Eric listened, he reflected that nothing could have been less likely to put the audience in a proper mood for his play. However, he was apparently the only one who was paying attention to the orchestra. He sat in an agony of suspense for what seemed a half-hour; actually the musicians played for only six or seven minutes. The performance finished with a feeble flourish, and the conductor bowed profoundly in response to feebler applause. "I come here every time convinced that they could not play worse than the last time," said Irina Lanski. "And, every time, I find that I am wrong."

Eric hardly heard her, for the lights were beginning to dim. As they slowly faded out and the buzz of the audience subsided, Eric dug his nails into his palms and caught his lower lip between his teeth. Irina Lanski pressed his knee with her hand, and he welcomed that friendly touch. After ten interminable seconds of darkness the curtain rose slowly. With perfect synchronization, the balcony spotlights were brought up the instant the curtain had cleared the path of their radiance. There was scattered applause for Arthur Eckstein's fine, atmospheric setting; then the first actor entered, went to the telephone, dialed, spoke his first line. The play was under way.

Florence Fulham's entrance evoked a round of hearty applause, mostly from the gray-heads, who remembered the days of her stardom. There were a few handclaps for Olmsted too. (He explained, later, that they emanated from his creditors, who were anxious for the play to succeed so that he could pay what he owed them.) Eric waited anxiously for Virginia's entrance, and she too was greeted with warm applause. She was not generally known to theatergoers,

307

but she had many friends in Boston and a considerable number of them had come to the theater. There was no sign of her illness. She looked fresh and charming and moved with briskness and authority, taking instant command of the stage and making that vivid first impression that is so important for the actor and for the play. Her voice sounded clear and unforced. But Eric, whose eyes never left her, saw her glance for reassurance toward the stage box, beside the pass-door, where her throat specialist was seated, prepared to go backstage on a moment's notice.

As the performance progressed Eric's feverishness mounted. Without knowing what he was doing, he repeated every line of the play to himself and shook his head disapprovingly at every slight omission or error, though the audience, of course, was entirely unaware of the minor lapses. Nor were he and Virginia the only ones who had been affected by the wet weather; every time there was a cough or a sneeze he turned his head impatiently in the direction of the sound. Frequently he glanced across the aisle at O'Fallon. Except for an occasional nod or shake of the head in response to a whispered comment from his female companion, the critic maintained an air of impassivity. Eric wondered anxiously what he was thinking.

When the curtain fell on the first scene Eric clutched the arms of his chair, fearful of a long delay. The change was made swiftly, and he breathed a sigh of relief. In fact, the whole act moved with technical perfection and the actors seemed at ease. Several times he was surprised by the audience's laughter. There was almost no humor in the play, but Thompson, knowing the importance of an occasional break in an audience's tension, had taken advantage of every idiomatic turn of speech and every oddity of small-town characterization to produce a healthful comedic effect. Occasionally, however, when there were laughs where none were intended or desirable, Eric squirmed unhappily.

At the end of the first act there was general applause. As the house lights came up Eric leaned back to relax his tensed muscles. Half the spectators left their seats and filed up the aisles to the lobby for a stretch and a smoke. The throat specialist got up and disappeared behind the curtains of the box. Eric, with Virginia very much on his mind, wanted to go back himself but was afraid he would only be in the way.

"It went very well," said Irina Lanski.

"Do you really think it did?" Eric asked.

308

"Yes. For a first performance far better than I expected. Why don't you go out and smoke a cigarette? You worked harder in that act than any of the cast."

Eric laughed. "I guess I did. Don't you want to come along?"

"No, I'll stay here if you don't mind. I find that I no longer enjoy these mass migrations."

Eric joined the slow procession. The beneficial effect of his day in bed was beginning to wear off. He felt congested and heavy-limbed. In the lobby he moved about from group to group, keeping his ears open for comments about the play. He heard only exchanges of social pleasantries or snatches of conversation about business, the weather, and the day's news. He went to the men's room to take an aspirin tablet, and it was there that he heard the only reference to the play.

"How do you like that little red-headed number—what's her name?" a man asked his companion.

"I don't know—Virginia somebody-or-other. Very snazzy. She can come and play in my back yard any time she wants to."

"Listen, feller, she's welcome right in my front parlor—on Mabel's bowling nights, of course." They both laughed and then, as the warning bell sounded, moved toward the stairs to the lobby. "What is there, just one more act?"

"Yes, and I think that's going to be plenty."

Eric followed them up the stairs, not cheered by their remarks. In the lobby he was surprised to see James Duncan. "Hello, Jim!" he said. "What are you doing here?"

"Hell!" said Duncan, "Don't you know a dramatic critic when you see one?"

"You mean you're going to review the play for the Standard?"

"What else? You're practically Coltertown's leading dramatist, and the Standard gives its readers complete news coverage regardless of expense. You look terrible. How do you feel?"

"Terrible!" They were at the back of the auditorium and the lights were dimming. "Will you meet me afterwards?"

"Can't. I have to drive back home tonight."

"Well, I'll be seeing you."

"You betcha."

Eric hurried down the aisle, flustered by Duncan's presence and disappointed by his friend's failure to express an opinion. He did not understand that Duncan, somewhat inflated by his mission, was intent upon preserving his journalistic integrity and objectivity regardless of friendship.

"Well, I'm glad you decided to come back," whispered Irina Lanski as Eric dropped into his seat just as the curtain was rising.

The second act was a worse ordeal for him than the first. He found it hard to breathe, and the strain was beginning to tell. Every cough, every sign of inattentiveness, every minute defect in the performance, took on an exaggerated importance. He sat hunched up, wondering dismally if the play would ever come to an end.

At last the final curtain fell. Before it had touched the stage numerous spectators—including, Eric noticed, Daniel O'Fallon—hurried up the aisles. The majority remained to applaud as the curtain rose again to reveal the entire cast lined up behind the footlights. The calls followed the usual procedure: first the whole company; then the secondary players, and finally the principals. If Emily Crandall had been in the play she would have taken the last call alone, an honor accorded to a star or solely featured player. Virginia would have liked to take a solo call, for the importance of her part warranted it. Thompson was inclined to give it to her, but the contracts of both Florence Fulham and Reginald Olmsted provided that they were to receive equal prominence with anyone but Emily Crandall. The appearance of the three together evoked a burst of genuinely enthusiastic applause and even a few cries of "Bravo!" Eric felt a flush of exaltation, as he gazed at Virginia standing there, smiling and bowing gracefully, so vivacious and self-possessed.

The curtain fell on the trio, the house lights came up, the orchestra launched into a funereal rendition of a Sousa march, the audience crowded into the aisles. It was over!

"Good!" said Irina Lanski. "Very good!" Eric, numbed and weak, felt only a desire to get out of the theater.

The pass-door was on the opposite side, and it took them fifteen minutes to work their way around the back and down the side aisle. Virginia's door was open. She had changed to an exquisite negligee of dark green crepe de chine. A dozen friends, the women in long dresses and fur capes, the men mostly in dinner jackets, were showering her with compliments, and she was talking excitedly to everybody at once.

"Come in! Come in!" she called to Eric and Irina Lanski. "There's always gloom for one more."

The visitors made way for them. Irina Lanski threw her arms

around Virginia and kissed her. "You were beautiful, darling! Simply beautiful!"

"Well, I managed to say all the words, and that's about all. Eric, if you're thinking what I think you're thinking, have a heart and don't say it."

"I think you were wonderful," murmured Eric. He wanted to kiss her too, but did not dare with all those curious eyes on him. A quick look at Virginia's face told him that her vivacity was assumed and that she was dead tired.

"People," said Virginia, "this is Irina Lanski, and this valiant youth is the father of it all—Eric Kenwood, the author." She rattled off a string of names, none of which Eric in his self-consciousness could connect with these nonchalant men and elegant women who stood gazing at his inflamed nose and bleary eyes, his tousled hair and ill-fitting clothes. A few shook his hand and offered congratulations, but he did not know what to say to them. Making way for some new arrivals, he edged his way out of the room almost unobserved. He wanted to get back to the hotel, but Irina Lanski told him that he must not neglect the other actors. Dutifully he made the round of the dressing-rooms with her. It was worth the effort, for they were all obviously hungry for praise.

Thompson had asked him to come to his suite after the performance for a general conference. When they reached the hotel Irina Lanski suggested that he rest a half-hour first, warning him that the session would be a long and tiring one. Eric followed her advice. His whole body ached and was damp with perspiration. He undressed, took a warm shower, and got into bed, brooding over his inability to get really near Virginia. The sight of her in the midst of those well-to-do and sophisticated people with whom she was so much at home made him feel, more than ever, that she inhabited an alien world in which he had no place. He closed his eyes and wished that he could sleep for a week, or perhaps forever. After ten minutes of this desolate yearning for oblivion he threw off the covers, put on fresh clothing, and went to Thompson's apartment.

Thompson's secretary opened the door for him. "Oh, hello, Mr. Kenwood. Come right in."

As Eric entered the large sitting-room Thompson came forward, a highball in hand. "Here's the goddam author now," he said. "We thought you were riding the rods back to Connecticut."

"I'm sorry if I'm late but—"

"Never mind the alibis. Katie, give him food and drink. We may as well fatten him up before we take him apart."

"What will you have, Mr. Kenwood? Scotch, bourbon, beer?"

"Scotch, please."

She went to a table which was loaded with bottles, glasses, ice-buckets, and platters of sandwiches.

Irina Lanski, Claire, Fineman, Weir, and Eckstein were all there, and, to Eric's dissatisfaction, Frederic Haig.

"Scotch," said the secretary, handing Eric a drink, and then, as she hurried to the door in answer to the buzzer, "Help yourself to a sandwich."

"Thank you," said Eric, suddenly aware that he was very hungry. Everybody else was already supplied, Weir being conspicuous with a large glass of tomato juice.

Katherine Swayne came back, followed by Winternitz. "Peace to all here," he said, bowing, his palms downspread. "May the Lord make His countenance to shine upon you."

"Any dope on the notices, Doc?" asked Thompson.

"He hasn't had time to write them yet," said Weir with his loud, mirthless laugh, in which no one joined.

"Nothing very specific," said Winternitz. "I met Jerry Walters of the Eagle as he was rushing for his deadline, and he said he thinks I've put on a little weight."

"Well, that's encouraging," said Thompson. "All right, kiddies, let's get down to business. But before we get into a general brawl, I'd like to give everybody a chance to speak his piece. Katie, get out your notebook and be sure you get every point. First of all, I'd like to hear from Freddy, since he saw it for the first time and is fresher on it than anybody else."

"Would you think it very fresh of me," said Haig, beaming at everyone, "if I just recited Danny Deever? I do it awfully well, won a bronze medal for it at prep school."

"No, come on, Freddy! Do something to earn your keep, for Christ's sake. As it is, Murray is griping about paying your fare and room rent."

"Wisecracker!" said Fineman, shaking his head.

"I'll forego my customary porridge and breakfast frugally, Murray," said Haig. He peered around with his alert, birdlike air. "Well, since I have been thrust upon the podium, I must compliment Mr. Kenwood for his fine play. Very direct, very forceful, very intense.

I found myself all eyes and ears, quite stirred and shaken; in fact, if Mr. Kenwood will forgive me, perhaps too shaken."

"You think the end is too melodramatic?" asked Thompson.

"Well, too something. Perhaps I haven't an adequate capacity for carnage. My doctor hints at a deficiency in my blood count. The fault is mine, I have no doubt."

"I agree with Freddy," said Claire. "I always felt that about the end."

Thompson glanced at her in annoyance. "Freddy may be right about that," he said to Eric.

"No, no, quite wrong, I'm sure!" said Haig with a deprecatory flutter of his hands.

"The whole play points to that ending," said Eric, his voice trembling. "And there's no possible way of changing it." He resented not only the older playwright's thinly disguised dislike of his play, but the deference that everyone paid to his opinion.

"It's possible to change anything," said Thompson with a shade of irritation. "Besides, who said anything about a different ending? It's a question of doing it in a less obvious way, that's all."

"Well, I don't think there is any other way of doing it without weakening the play," said Eric, stubbornly.

"And, of course, you couldn't be wrong, could you?" said Thompson sarcastically.

Eric felt Irina Lanski's restraining touch on his arm and checked an angry retort. "Yes, I could be," he said sulkily, "but I don't think I am."

"Excuse me for butting in," said Weir, "but I felt the need of a little comedy here and there. Of course, I'm only a layman, but then so is the average man out there in the audience. I've been thinking that if Freddy happened to have a few good laugh lines up his sleeve, why, it might not hurt a bit."

"Absolutely!" said Claire.

"A few laughs would help," said Fineman.

"Laugh lines, my dear Tony," said Haig, "are not, unfortunately, the product of legerdemain but of profound visceral agonies in the small hours of sleepless nights."

Weir laughed loudly. "I stand corrected! But I'm still for getting those laughs in. Don't you agree, Tommy?"

Eric waited tensely for Thompson's reply. He was determined not to let Haig tinker with his play, no matter what pressure was

313

brought to bear upon him. In his self-absorption it did not occur to him that Haig was there only because Claire had so persistently urged him to come, and that he had not the slightest interest in making any contribution to the play.

"No, I don't agree," said Thompson. "Let's face it. The play is a tragedy, and it's got to stand or fall on what it is. If we try to gag it up now, it's going to look like just that, and we'll be doing ourselves more harm than good."

"I think you are entirely right, Tommy," said Irina Lanski. "If they want jokes, let them go to Gotta Get That Gal."

"Or to Give Them All My Love, matinees Wednesdays and Saturdays, you might have added, my dear Irina," said Haig, shaking his forefinger at her.

"Well, I don't think it necessary to say what everyone knows, Freddy."

"That is why you are not a successful playwright, darling. But I am entirely in accord with you and with Tommy. As a pastrycook of sorts, I can tell you that the spices must be baked into the cake and not sprinkled on at table."

"I don't think they should laugh in the third scene," said Claire irrelevantly, "when Ginny says to her father—"

Thompson interrupted impatiently. "Yes, I know, I know. There were a half-dozen bad laughs. I've got notes on all of them and I know how to kill them." He got up and mixed another highball. "Have you got any notes on the performances, Freddy?"

"Well, I did venture to jot down a few minor observations," said Haig, taking a sheet of paper from his pocket. "I hope I can read them. I am not at my happiest when I write in complete darkness."

"Apparently you have never been a press agent," said Winternitz.

Thompson listened attentively to Haig's comments. And though Eric felt an instinctive hostility to everything Haig said, he had to recognize the acuteness of the playwright's observation and his sensitivity to false values that Eric himself had not noticed.

In turn, Thompson called upon the others for their notes. In the course of the ensuing discussion a hundred details were debated. The lighting, the costumes, the stage business, the actors' readings, the content and meaning of certain scenes, all were subjected to critical comment and analysis. Some of the criticisms Thompson accepted immediately; others he brushed aside; still others led to long and acrimonious arguments. Under the influence of alcohol and

314

the stifling air of the smoky room, tempers quickened and voices became blurred. In an effort to fight off fatigue Eric devoured sandwiches and repeatedly filled his glass. As hour after hour dragged by he was less and less able to attend to what was said and was conscious only of an indistinct babble of voices heard through a suffocating fog.

It was after three when the conference came to an end. Winternitz had long been dozing; the others were drooping from exhaustion. Eric staggered to his room, dizzy and nauseated, and soon fell into a drunken sleep.

XXVIII.

He was awakened at half-past ten by the ringing of the telephone. Barely able to open his eyes, he groped for the instrument. With difficulty he grasped that Fineman was inviting him to breakfast in Thompson's apartment. He fell back upon the pillow, struggling to recall where he was and why he was there. At last he forced himself out of bed, his head splitting and his mouth dry and bitter. A cold shower revived him somewhat, and he hurried into his clothes, suddenly remembering that he had not seen the reviews of his play.

Thompson's sitting-room had been put in order and ventilated. He was seated at a large, round table, breakfasting with Claire, Fineman, and Irina Lanski. They were all reading the morning papers.

"Hello, Eric," said Thompson. "You look like one who is hanging over."

"I guess I am, a little." The director, in his handsome brocade robe, appeared amazingly fresh. The others too showed no sign of indisposition.

"Well, how do you like your notices?"

"I haven't seen them."

"Now, there's a blasé young author for you! I expected you to be up all night, haunting the newsstands."

"Are they good?" asked Eric.

"Not bad," said Irina Lanski. "Kendall Petrie is quite good, Walters on the good side, and the others neither one way or another. Here, you'd better read Petrie first."

Claire excused herself and left the room as Irina Lanski handed the paper to Eric. He read the review with eager attention. Kendall Petrie was known to Eric by reputation. He was the oldest and perhaps the most influential of the Boston critics. A man of considerable learning and intelligence, he was noted for his long, analytical critiques of books and plays, written in a style that was epigrammatic and slightly Victorian. His review was lively and appreciative. He understood the tragic intention of the play and praised it for its integrity, dramatic effectiveness, and essentially poetic quality. He had his reservations too, and his caustic references to immature writing and to what he considered lapses in taste made Eric wince. He had yet to learn the rarity of unqualified praise.

"Well, he does say some good things about it," he said when he had finished reading the review.

Thompson laughed. "I'll settle, right now, for three or four like it in New York."

"Yes, I agree," said Irina Lanski.

Eric read the other reviews. Gerald Walters wrote approvingly too, but in rather superficial terms and with a tendency to facetiousness. The others were evasive and noncommittal. They pointed out that the play had many merits and many defects, that it was still in a "rough state" and needed "lots of work," "pulling together," and "polishing."

"They don't say anything very much, do they?" said Eric.

"It's a technique," said Irina Lanski. "If the play succeeds in New York, it is because the necessary work has been done; if it fails, it is because it has not. Either way, they cannot be wrong."

"Don't be cynical, Irina," said Thompson. "It doesn't become you." The buzzer sounded. "That's probably Doc with the afternoon papers."

Fineman opened the door for Winternitz, who had a stack of newspapers under his arm.

"How are they, Doc?" asked Thompson.

316

"Passionate affirmations of negativity," said Winternitz, giving them each several papers. "All but Korpsbruder O'Fallon, whose eulogies are somewhat muted. In fact, he seems to confuse Eric with Jack the Ripper. A condonable error, if you will forgive my saying so," he said with a deep bow to Eric. "And now, by your leave, friends, I'm off to a rendezvous with a lady journalist who wishes me to discourse on the woman's angle—though, personally, I detest angular women."

They were all reading the papers and paid no attention to his departure. Eric reddened with anger at O'Fallon's virulent denunciation of the play. He called it immoral, indecent, morbid, offensive, and an affront to womanhood, a play that no father would want his daughter to see.

"Why, he's just a fool!" said Eric vehemently. "He's missed the whole point."

"This may help business," said Thompson. "It should certainly bring the daughters in."

"You should feel flattered, Eric," said Irina Lanski, flinging the paper aside. "It reads exactly like the fin de siècle reviews of Ibsen."

"You've got some work to do, Eric," said Thompson. "As I expected, Cornelius McLaughlin paid Murray a little visit this morning, and we've got to purify the play, or else."

"Who's Cornelius McLaughlin?" asked Eric.

"He's an ex-traffic cop who is now the official guardian of the town's morals. He is also, I believe, the Mayor's father-in-law."

"Cousin," said Fineman.

"Pardon me, cousin. Anyhow, he's the boy who tells you what you can't do in Boston. And here it is." He handed Eric a sheet of paper on which were typed the required excisions and alterations.

"But this is crazy!" said Eric agitatedly. "If we do all this it'll change the meaning of the play."

"Could be. But it's what we've got to do."

"But it's ridiculous! Listen to this: the word 'whore' may not be used. Why can't I say 'whore'? The Bible says it."

"Well, I'll take your word for it. But the Bible is one thing and Boston is another. In Boston there are no whores in modern dress. And we haven't time to get new costumes."

"Costumes?" said Fineman nervously. "There's no kick about the costumes."

"Take it easy, Murray. Just a figure of speech."

"Oh," said Fineman dubiously.

"May I see that, please, Eric?" said Irina Lanski.

He handed her the civic censor's demands. "What if I refuse to make these changes?" he said to Thompson.

"Then I'll make them. That will be a violation of my contract with you, and you can complain to the Dramatists' Guild. They'll write me, demanding an explanation, and by the time I get around to answering we'll be running in New York and the whole thing will be an academic question."

"Ach, but this is preposterous!" exclaimed Irina Lanski, getting up and pacing the room in a fury. "Here we sit in a world city, with a half-dozen great universities and colleges, art museums, publishing houses, a fine library, a famous symphony orchestra, a great tradition of literature and learning and culture, and we, we people of the theater, we permit the wonderful art we live by to be kicked around like a shabby vagabond by a little, ignorant, filthy-minded police official. It makes me want to vomit!"

Thompson stood up and applauded. "Lanski for President! What do you want me to do—fight City Hall?"

"Yes, fight City Hall! And fight the Cathedral! I am a good daughter of the Church but when I see art attacked, when I am denied my American right of free speech, then I say, fight! Fight in every way that is possible. Appeal to the press, rouse the civic organizations, hold mass meetings, distribute handbills, go through the streets with sound trucks, invoke the courts. Fight for the rights that the law and the Constitution give you."

"Yes, that's what I say!" said Eric, fired by her words and her vehemence.

"Well, that's a fine program, folks," said Thompson, "and in my next incarnation I'll put on a hair shirt and mount the barricades. But right now I'm trying to get this show into New York. We either make the changes or they shut us down while we're out holding those mass meetings, and that adds another twenty thousand to our cost. If you ask me, that's a high price for a couple of whores."

"It's the principle of it!" said Eric.

"With me it's the dough. When does he want these changes in, Murray?"

"Well, he said for the matinee but I can stall him along until tonight I guess."

318

"All right, go ahead."

"Okay," said Fineman, starting for the door. "Anyhow, by the middle of next week you can start sneaking the cuts back in, and nobody will know the difference."

"Get busy, will you, Eric?" said Thompson. "I've got to dress and get around to the theater. I've excused Ginny from the matinee and I want to do a little work with Lily. Meet me at six, and we'll go over the cuts, so that I can give them to the cast before tonight's show."

"How is Ginny?" said Eric, feeling guilty for not having asked sooner.

"I haven't called her, but she'll be all right, especially after she reads her notices. It was mostly nerves anyhow. Here at six!" He went into the bedroom.

"What can I do?" asked Eric as he and Irina Lanski left the suite.

"Nothing," she said. "Not if Tommy won't fight. And, of course, we can't expect him to fight alone. For that, united action is necessary. But everybody is too busy being ruggedly individual to find time to unite for the common defense. So you had better make the changes, or else Tommy will do it, just as he said. He knows very well that we are not going to protest to the Dramatists' Guild and that they could do nothing if we did."

The cast was waiting for Thompson on the stage of the Mayflower. Now that the strain of their first public appearance was over the actors were beginning to relax. The reviews, too, were reassuring; the critics, almost without exception, had praised the acting highly. Unlike Eric, who had concentrated his attention on what was said about the play, the actors had turned immediately to the last two or three paragraphs of the reviews, which, according to custom, were devoted to a discussion of the performances. A few were indignant about O'Fallon's scathing denunciation of the play, but, on the whole, they paid little attention to the gibes and strictures that had wounded Eric and there was a general feeling that the tone of the press was distinctly favorable.

Thompson briefly discussed the reviews and the first night performance and made the cast feel that he too was pleased by the play's reception. Then he ordered the curtain lowered and rehearsed Lily until it was time for her to dress. It was all strictly professional and impersonal; even had they been alone, the girl's nervousness would have prevented her from thinking of anything but her performance.

At the end of the rehearsal Thompson went to the box-office. Though he had expected little sale for the matinee, he could not escape the sinking feeling induced by the sight of batches of unsold tickets in the racks. There had been little demand for future performances either. The box-office men were not very hopeful about the outlook. In their opinion, the reviews were not sufficiently enthusiastic to create an immediate public interest. It all depended, they said, on "word of mouth," the spreading of favorable reports by members of the audience—an imponderable factor that took time to operate.

Thompson delayed the rise of the curtain for a few minutes on the chance that there might be a few late ticket-buyers. The interior of the theater presented a depressing sight. A hundred or so spectators were clustered in the front rows; the rest of the lower floor was empty. In the balcony, too, there were whole sections of unoccupied seats. Printed slips inserted in the programs informed the audience that Lily was appearing in Virginia's stead, so that there was hardly a murmur when McCarthy appeared before the curtain to make the required announcement. Virginia's name was so little known that the audience felt no particular disappointment.

The performance was a listless one. Not only were the actors let down after the excitement of the night before, but the smallness of the audience and the weakness of its response offered them no stimulus. Nor did Lily's performance. Thompson, to whom the nervousness and unsureness beneath her outward calm were apparent, was thankful that he had resisted the impulse to entrust the part to her after Emily Crandall's withdrawal. Undoubtedly she had great talent; in a summer theater or amateur company she would have seemed quite brilliant. But in scenes with such expert actors as Florence Fulham and Reginald Olmsted her immaturity and technical deficiencies became painfully evident.

All in all, it was a wasted performance. Thompson wished that he had canceled it instead of letting Fineman, who was worried about every dollar, persuade him not to. He did not want to go back to see Lily, but his failure to do so would have a devastating effect upon her. She was using Virginia's dressing-room, and Thompson, as always, entered without knocking.

"Just a minute!" said Pearl, as Lily quickly got into her dressing

320

gown. Pearl started to leave, but Thompson motioned to her to stay. He had no wish to be left alone with Lily.

"I just came back to tell you that that was all right, kid," he said, patting her head.

"Oh, no, it wasn't! I was just awful!" Her tears began to flow.

"Well, I think you were damn good, if that means anything to you."

"I just couldn't seem to get started. Please don't hold it against me. It was just doing it the first time, that was all. I'll be better next time."

"You were all right today," he insisted. "I wouldn't say it if I didn't mean it. You've just got the jitters, that's all. Did you have any lunch?" She shook her head dismally. "I thought so. Well, get the hell out of here, and get yourself a good dinner, do you hear?"

"All right, I will."

In the mirror he could see her eyes imploring him to have dinner with her. He said quickly, "Well, I've got to run. We have to get in some changes tonight, and Eric is waiting for me at the hotel." Since, for once, he was telling the truth, he was annoyed by her obvious disbelief. "I'll see you later. And don't let anybody tell you you weren't good."

Claire, who had watched the performance from the balcony, was waiting for him on the stage. "I hope you didn't tell that girl she was good," she said in the taxi.

"What do you think I told her, that she stank?"

"You didn't have to tell her anything."

"I'll be glad to have your ideas sometime on how to handle actors."

"Yes, I know," she said. "Actors aren't in my department. All the same I told you that she'd never be able to play that part."

"Who are you arguing with? She's not playing it, is she?"

"Did you get the figure for the matinee?"

"Yes, I did. It's a dollar-fifty more than I looked for."

"It's not so funny when you have to pay the bills," she said plaintively.

Thompson's eyelids flickered angrily. "Well, just say the word and we won't bother taking it to New York."

"Nobody's suggesting that," she said hastily, afraid he might mean it and that she would not only lose her investment in the play but have an empty New York theater on her hands. Even more, she dreaded the suffering he could inflict upon her when his anger was aroused. "Do you want to have dinner in my suite?" she asked as they got out.

"I can't. I have to work with Eric on those cuts, so that we can get them in tonight."

"You have to eat, don't you?"

"We'll probably eat while we're working. Join us if you want to."

"No, thank you!" she said. "I prefer to eat by my lonely. Maybe while you're cutting you could do a little work on his hair." It would have been better to keep quiet, but she had to find some relief for her pent-up emotions. Their arrival at the elevator cut the conversation short. She got out at her floor without saying anything more. As Thompson walked down the corridor to his suite he debated the advisability of provoking an out-and-out quarrel and breaking with her entirely; but she would be in a repentant mood when next he saw her, and he too would have cooled off.

Eric arrived promptly with a sheaf of papers. After the morning conference he had carefully reread all the reviews. Though he flamed with a fierce hatred of O'Fallon and bristled again at the disparaging comments of some of the others, he found much that was heartening. He called up his mother, but she could tell from his voice that he had a cold and was much more concerned about his health than about the reviews. Then he went to work on the changes ordered by the censor. It was a grim task; each specification threw him into a fresh rage. Only by the exercise of all his will power could he bring himself to comply with the absurd demands. It was after five when he finished, with a groan of relief. He called Virginia's room repeatedly, but her line was always busy. He left for Thompson's suite deeply disappointed. He would have been more unhappy about it had he known that it was Mollison who had kept her on the telephone for an hour.

Thompson ordered dinner and began immediately to read Eric's revisions. He was not altogether satisfied. Eric, in his resistance to police interference, had not gone far enough in meeting the censor's demands. Thompson was sullen and impatient, and his temper was not improved by Eric's stubborn opposition to further changes. They argued with increasing heat, and only the waiter's arrival prevented an open quarrel. Eric's stomach had been queasy all day; he had had nothing but coffee and toast; now he ate ravenously. By the end of dinner Thompson had won every point; but he had not had time to outline his ideas for a new ending to the play, and on their way to the theater he told Eric they would have to meet again after the performance.

Some of the actors were waiting on the stage, already dressed. McCarthy hastily summoned the others from their dressing-rooms.

322

Virginia, wearing a dressing gown, was the last to appear. "Well, if it isn't Pappy O'Fallon's white-haired boy!" she said, pointing at Eric.

The actors laughed, but Thompson called them sharply to order. Seeing that he was in no mood for frivolity, they settled down quickly. When he explained what had to be done, they sighed and groaned. Weary as they were, it was not easy for them to learn new lines and cuts an hour before the curtain. With the opening night out of the way they had expected some relaxation before resuming the rehearsals that were an inevitable part of a tryout engagement. First the substitution of Lily at the matinee and now the introduction of new material demanded a continued concentration that put an added strain on frayed nerves and tired brains. However, they had to obey. Resignedly they scribbled the new lines in their parts and, under Thompson's direction, went over and over them, trying frantically to absorb them before the curtain went up.

The house was barely half full. However, it was not as bad as it seemed. The theater management having taken a firm stand on the issuance of passes, most of those present had paid for their seats. Many were there as a direct result of Kendall Petrie's favorable review and were sympathetically expectant rather than skeptically cautious, a psychological difference of great importance to the reception of any play.

Eckstein, Irina Lanski, Anthony Weir, and Frederic Haig had all gone back to New York. Eric sat alone in the vast emptiness at the back of the theater, not wishing to be near either Thompson or Claire. The performance was stumbling and uncertain. The tired actors, trying desperately to remember their new lines, lost their timing and the pattern of their characterizations. The changes themselves appeared to Eric to destroy the meaning of the play, and the response of the small audience seemed pitifully weak. Physically exhausted, emotionally depleted, and unaccustomed to appraising audience reactions, he felt that it was going very badly. It was torture to watch and listen. Actually the audience was far more appreciative than the previous night's. The applause at the end made up in enthusiasm what it lacked in volume.

Eric hurried backstage and knocked on Virginia's door. Pearl asked him to wait a few minutes while Virginia changed, and by the time she was ready some friends of hers had come back, and then Thompson, so that Eric had no opportunity to say anything to her beyond asking how she felt.

He went back to the hotel with Thompson. Refusing a drink, he ordered a pot of coffee to keep himself from falling asleep. He marveled at Thompson's capacity for alcohol and work, as the director, glass in hand, paced the room, acting out the new ending he had conceived. Eric, out of stubbornness and sheer fatigue, finally agreed with great reluctance to test the new ending at the next night's performance, on the understanding that if it did not go well it would be abandoned.

On Thursday the company rehearsal lasted all afternoon. The new ending did not require many verbal changes but called for a considerable alteration in stage mechanics which had to be worked out with great care. Thompson had edited the voluminous notes that had been made at the opening-night conference and introduced a hundred refinements and modifications of detail. Eric took advantage of a moment when Virginia was not on the scene to ask her to have dinner with him, but she had an engagement. She had many friends in Boston—former schoolmates, family connections, and acquaintances from her previous theatrical visits—and had more invitations than she could possibly accept. Seeing his keen disappointment, she suggested that they visit the Gardner Museum together on Sunday. She was dining in Brookline and spending the night there, but she had the afternoon free. His anticipated happiness made it hard for him to concentrate on the rest of the rehearsal.

The evening audience was not much larger than Wednesday's, but the performance was far smoother and the play went well. Eric had to admit that the new ending was an improvement. It was less melodramatic and achieved his purpose without too violently assaulting the sensibilities of the audience. Thompson was not yet satisfied, and on Friday he rehearsed the company again, tirelessly experimenting with one modification after another in an effort to find just the right solution. The spirit of the company was good. The actors had supreme confidence in Thompson and, realizing the value of his suggestions, worked hard and diligently. The Friday night house was better, the sale for Saturday night heartening. The box-office men reported a modest demand for the following week's performances and were a little more optimistic than they had been after the opening.

Thompson was on the whole encouraged. The week's receipts would be far below what was required to meet the operating costs and the heavy expense of the dress rehearsal; but he had been prepared for that—and for far worse! He knew from bitter experience how disas-

324

trous public apathy can be, not only financially but in terms of disappointed hopes and shattered morale: the agony of performing to a handful of indifferent spectators and of seeing months of careful preparation and hard work go for nothing. As long as people were coming in and, apparently, liking what they saw, there was no reason to despair.

On Saturday he found a note from Lily in his morning mail. It was unstamped and had evidently been left by her at the hotel desk. It read: "I'm so lonely. Please find a little time for me after the show tonight, or tomorrow sometime. Oh, please, please do!" There was no salutation and it was signed simply "L."

He tore the note to bits and cursed Lily and himself for the thousandth time. Busy as they all had been with rehearsals and performances, he had plausibly avoided her since the Wednesday matinee. Sunday was a day of rest, and he could think of no way to make her believe he did not have a free moment between the Saturday night curtain and the Monday afternoon rehearsal. Besides, even to attempt to convince her he would have to talk to her, either on the telephone or at the theater—he did not want to risk writing—and he shrank from the prospect of what was sure to be a painful scene: the faltering voice, the tears in the large blue eyes, the words of meek reproach. No, he could not face it. Nor could he bring himself to ignore the note completely and behave as though he had not received it—especially not with another whole week in Boston ahead. The best course was to leave for the weekend, on the pretense of business in New York. He could see the play that evening with what promised to be a well-filled house and leave on the midnight train. But he hated sleeping cars and the thought of arriving in New York at seven o'clock Sunday morning was a dismal one. Remembering that Claire had sent for her car and was planning to drive to Poundridge, he decided to go with her. It would mean missing the evening performance, but it would serve the double purpose of evading Lily and making things up with Claire. He put off consideration of how to get through the next week and went down to lunch with Claire. She was delighted to hear that he wanted to go with her; they arranged to leave as soon as the matinee was over.

He did not go backstage before the performance, sending back word to McCarthy to hold the cast on the stage after the final curtain. He sat at the back of the house, but he could not keep his mind on the play. After fifteen minutes he got up and walked out, suddenly realizing how tired and stale he was. Even leaving Lily out of it, he was glad to get away from the theater for a few days. He spent an hour or more in the box-office, watching the steady progress of the sale for the evening performance.

At the end of the performance he went backstage, carrying his overnight bag, in accordance with his carefully prepared plan of campaign. He saw Lily's eyes go to the bag and felt he had scored his first point. Unwittingly Virginia helped him out. "Hey, Duce, you're not walking out on us, are you?"

"Yep. Just one jump ahead of the sheriff. Pete," he said to the assistant stage manager, "see if Mrs. Weir's car is out front, will you, and tell her I'll be right out. Oh, here! May as well put my bag in too."

"Yes, sir," said Peter Quirt, taking the bag.

"Well, since Ginny has guessed my secret, there's not much more for me to say," said Thompson to the cast. "I've got a lot to do in New York, and so I'm driving down with Mrs. Weir. As some of you may have heard, we're opening there, come a week from Wednesday." Virginia groaned, and everybody laughed. "Sorry I can't watch the performance tonight, because we'll come damn near selling out and I know it will be a good show. Mack will be in general charge, and you will agree that I couldn't leave you in worse hands." This provoked another laugh.

"Will you put that in writing?" asked McCarthy.

"If you all feel that you'd like to rehearse tomorrow, I'm sure that he—" Hoots and catcalls drowned him out. "The noes seem to have it. All right, that will give you a chance to catch up on your church-going. Morning and evening services, and lots of time in between to do your laundry."

Peter Quirt returned. "The car is out there, sir."

"Thanks. There'll be a company call on Monday at one. And I guess the same on Tuesday. I want to get everything cleaned up by then, because the show we play Tuesday night is the one I want to open with in New York. I guess that's all, unless anybody has a question, a complaint, or a good blue story."

"Don't get your feet wet," said Florence Fulham, "because we all love you and need you." The other actors applauded heartily.

"Okay, I'll buy a pair of rubbers in Providence," said Thompson, pleased. "And here's a little something for you, Miss Fulham," he said, giving Florence a kiss.

"Oh, thank you, kind sir!"

326

As the actors were leaving the stage Thompson turned to Lily. She had stood motionless throughout his talk to the cast, not laughing or giving any sign of hearing what was said. "Get a good rest over the weekend," he said, patting her cheek, and then in a whisper, "Sorry about tomorrow." She did not reply, walking quickly off the stage. He had avoided her eyes, but he could feel the intensity of the pain and reproachfulness in them. He gave McCarthy some instructions, then, on a sudden impulse, went to Virginia's dressing-room and walked in.

"Is that you, Pearl?" asked Virginia, who was pulling her dress over her head.

"Yes, Miss Ginny," said Thompson.

"Oh, it's you, is it?" said Virginia, squirming into her dress again. "Well, come right in, won't you? I didn't hear your knock."

"My father used to have a sign in his office that said, 'Come in without knocking; go out the same way.'"

"Why, you're just a chip off the old block, aren't you?"

"I thought I might as well kiss you good-by, too," he said.

"Well, that's a constructive idea." She stood quite still, and he kissed her on the lips. "An old Thompson custom."

"You're a fine upstanding wench," he said. "And very good in the show."

"Every man to his taste."

He laughed. "I've got to run. See you Monday."

She stood looking after him for a moment, then turned to the mirror. Her cheeks were flaming beneath her make-up. She pressed her hands to them. "Don't be a goddam idiot," she said in a loud voice to her reflection.

The door opened and Pearl came in. "I'd o' swore I heard you talkin' to somebody," she said, looking around in perplexity.

"Pearl, you'd better lay off those chocolates. They're beginning to beat against your eardrums."

XXIX.

Virginia's doctor had urged her to get as much rest as possible. All week she had obeyed his instructions, going straight from the theater to bed. On Saturday night some friends came back and coaxed her to come to their home for a drink. The play had gone very well indeed, with the large audience, and she felt stimulated and in the mood for a little gaiety. So she accepted the invitation, intending to stay only an hour; but by the time she got back to the hotel it was after two. She hung the Do Not Disturb sign on the doorknob and told the telephone operator not to call her before noon. But she was keyed up, her head buzzed with a thousand thoughts and fancies, and it was nearly five when she fell asleep.

She was awakened by a pounding at the door. She half opened her eyes, closed them again, turned over, and tried to go back to sleep. The pounding continued, and, muttering curses, she threw back the covers and stumbled to the door. "Go away, whoever it is," she said angrily.

"It's me. Open the door," said a familiar voice.

Wondering if she could be dreaming, she unlocked the door and peeped out. Hugh Mollison was standing there. "Well, for God's sake!" she said.

"Hi!" he said. "Hope I didn't wake you up."

Half asleep though she was, she heard the elevator door open. Afraid that someone might come along the corridor, she checked an angry retort and opened the door wide. Mollison stepped into the room. She quickly closed and locked the door and switched on the lights. Mollison took her in his arms and kissed her. "Hello, Push-face, I'm glad to see you."

328

She freed herself, sat on the bed, and yawned noisily. "What time is it?"

"I don't know. About eight-thirty." He pushed her clothes off the chair beside the bed and sat down.

"What makes you so late?" she said petulantly.

"I took the sleeper after the show and just checked in. I tried to call you but the woman wouldn't connect me. You don't seem very happy to see me."

"I didn't have a grand levee on my calendar. I just got to sleep about ten minutes ago."

"I didn't sleep at all. I was over a flat wheel and there was a yowling baby across the aisle."

"You look like something the cat brought in," she said, eying him with disfavor. He was unshaven, his clothes were crumpled, his breath alcoholic.

"I feel worse than that," he said, yawning and rubbing his bloodshot eyes. "Why don't we both get some sleep?"

She stood up with alacrity. "That's a corking idea. Phone me when you wake up."

"I'll just nudge you," he said, starting to undress.

"I think we'd do better solo. This is pretty narrow for two."

"We've been in narrower ones," he said, loosening his tie.

Seething with anger, she got back into bed. When she woke up she was startled to find him beside her; it took her a moment to account for his presence. He was sound asleep, breathing heavily. She put on a dressing gown, opened the draperies, and sat by the window, glancing occasionally at Mollison, trying to think of the best way to deal with this unexpected situation. It was almost two; she had arranged to meet Eric at three to go to the Gardner Museum with him. She dreaded calling it off, knowing how disappointed he would be (she had been looking forward to it herself). To get away from Mollison was impossible; to take him along unthinkable. She strode angrily to the bed and shook him vigorously. He merely groaned and turned over. Clenching her teeth, she began pinching him and pulling his hair. "Come on, Huge, snap out of it!" she said sharply.

"Look out of there!" he said, flailing his arms and sitting bolt upright, his eyes still shut. He opened them slowly and looked at her in surprise. "Oh, it's you! I thought somebody was trying to murder me." He rubbed his upper arm.

"Get yourself up out of there," said Virginia. "It's two o'clock."

"What of it? We've got all day and all night."

"All night? Aren't you taking the sleeper back?" This was going to be worse than she had feared.

He nodded. "Tomorrow night. Or maybe I'll wait and take a day train Tuesday. I hate sleepers."

"What do you mean, Tuesday?" she said incredulously.

"Well, Tuesday. You're old enough to know what Tuesday means. I want to see the show tomorrow night. That's one reason I came up. The other was I wanted to see you."

"Look, Huge," she said in desperation. "Just try to follow me, will you? Before Tuesday comes Monday, see? And that is a night on which there is a performance of Give Them All My Love at the Stuyvesant Theater, which by the latest reports is situated in New York. That's point one. Point two is that, according to Darwin, one body cannot occupy two places at the same time. Q.E.D. Which, translated freely, means Quick Exit Desirable."

He yawned and stretched. "I've got an understudy."

"You mean that George Hamlin character?"

"George is a pretty good actor."

"There are two schools of thought on that point. But you know damned well that the cash customers aren't shelling out to see any George Hamlin."

"Then let the management refund. They can afford it. I haven't missed a performance since the show opened. What the hell am I— a galley slave?"

"No, a sharecropper, who only gets ten per cent of the take," she said.

"All right, let them dock me for one performance. With my tax situation, it costs me buttons."

"Suppose what you wittily call the management takes it into its little head to gripe to Equity."

"Not a chance. They need me more than I need them, and they know it."

"Please go back," she begged. "I'm asking you please to."

"Sorry, but I'm sticking."

"All right then," she said grimly. "In that case I won't go on tomorrow night. I can work up a beautiful case of laryngitis at the drop of a voice."

"Good! That'll give us a chance to do the town together. We'll take in a peepshow and then maybe dig up a crap game afterwards."

330

He rubbed the back of his neck. "God, I feel logy. Think I'll take a shower."

"Wait a minute, Huge!"

But he was already in the bathroom. She lighted a cigarette and thrashed around the room, trying to hit upon some expedient for getting rid of him. At last she decided there was nothing to do but locate Thompson and appeal to him for help.

"I feel a little better," said Mollison, coming out of the bathroom.

"Then why not toddle back to your room and take off that Rip Van Winkle make-up? Better put on your clothes first though."

"What's the hurry?" he asked, sitting on the bed again.

"I'd like a little privacy, if you don't mind," she said, her eyes blazing.

"Well, why didn't you say so?" Not daring to provoke her further, he dressed with the celerity of an actor, who is used to making quick changes. "How long will you be?"

"I'll phone you when I'm ready."

"Well, don't make it too long. I'm beginning to get hungry. Shall we eat downstairs?"

"Yes, all right." She opened the door for him, locked it quickly behind him, and called Eric's room. He answered almost instantly. She visualized him sitting by the telephone, waiting for her to call.

"Hello, Eric," she said. "Listen, Puppchen, I'm afraid I'm not going to be able to make it this afternoon."

"You're not?" His hurt voice made her want to cry.

"No," she said glibly, hating herself for her mendacity, "my throat seems to be tightening up again, and I think I'd better have a treatment before it gets worse. So I'm popping right around to old Doc Sawbones."

"Couldn't we go afterwards?"

"Gosh, I don't see how. It's almost three now and my friends from Brookline are picking me up at five. I'm terribly sorry about it, Eric, but there's that play of yours that goes on tomorrow night."

"Yes, certainly. You're sure it's nothing serious?"

"Oh no," she said, glad that he did not know how serious it was. "The squirt gun will fix me up fine. And if you don't hate me too much, I'd like a rain check and we'll go to the Gardner later in the week."

"Yes, of course. Any time you say," he said, trying unsuccessfully to make it all sound casual.

"Good boy! I'll see you at Philippi, otherwise known as the May-flower, tomorrow."

She blew her nose and then put in a person-to-person call to Thompson at his New York hotel. He was not there and was not expected. Next she called Claire's house at Poundridge. She waited tensely, wondering what to do if she could not reach him. Luckily he was there. "Hello, Tommy," she said. "This is Ginny. Remember me?"

"Faintly," he said.

"Well, that's exactly how I feel." She spoke truthfully, for the sound of his voice made her feel weak.

"What's the matter—has the theater burned down?"

"Oh no, I'd like that! This is something really grim. Big, boyish Huge blew into town a little while ago."

"Did he? That's nice."

"Think so? Well, I guess it all depends upon where you sit."

"Why? Is he stinko?"

"Not yet. But that's not what's worrying me. He's given birth to the quaint notion that he's staying over to see tomorrow night's show."

"The hell he is!" said Thompson.

"I thought you'd like to know."

"You're darn tootin'! Can't you talk him out of it?"

"Not in the present condition of my vocal cords. Hence the S.O.S."

"Well, let me think a minute." There was a long pause. "How about Fineman? Do you think he can handle it?"

"I don't know. Murray is a fine braw lad, kind to animals and all that, but I don't think he ever majored in psychology."

"No. I guess you're right. I suppose I'd better sashay up there myself."

She sighed with relief. "I feel like an old clinging vine, asking it of you, but this one is really too hot for me to handle."

"Don't apologize. This is what God made managers for. All right, I'll see what kind of a plane I can get out of La Guardia and shoot up as fast as I can. Think you can hold the fort till the Northwest Mounted arrive?"

"I've simply got to leave here at five, Tommy. Some people are giving a dinner party for me in Brookline. They'll never forgive me if I don't show. It was all arranged weeks ago and I just can't wriggle out of it."

"Well, don't worry about it. I should get there by seven at the latest, and I guess he'll still be right side up by then."

"I hate myself for doing this to you."

"I'd have paddled you if you hadn't. Does he know I'm not in Boston?"

"Not from me. And I'm sure he hasn't talked to anybody else."

"All right, go to your dinner party and leave Little Rollo to me. How do you feel, by the way?"

"Better since hearing the sound of your strong right arm."

Immeasurably relieved, she bathed and dressed quickly, wondering what Thompson saw in Claire. But then, she reflected, it was always hard to understand what people saw in each other. Perhaps he was wondering what she saw in Mollison. She had begun to wonder about that herself.

Her next move was to avoid being seen with Mollison. If they ate in the hotel dining-room or as much as walked through the lobby together, it was more than likely that they would run into some member of the cast, or, worse yet, Eric. She remembered a little Italian restaurant near the hotel where they were not likely to meet anyone they knew, especially at this hour. She hurried down to the drug-store and called Mollison.

"Where the hell are you?" he demanded. "I've been calling your room."

"I had to buy a few things in the drugstore. Listen, do you mind if we eat at Guiseppe's? I'm getting awfully sick of the Marlborough's incomparable cuisine."

"I don't care where we eat as long as it's soon."

"All right. Come right over. It's—"

"I know where it is. I played Boston before you were born."

She made a few purchases to corroborate her story, then went to Guiseppe's, which was almost empty. Mollison arrived a few minutes later, looking more presentable. He had had a few more drinks but was still fairly sober. They ordered dinner immediately. He had time for only one whisky before the soup was served. Virginia ordered a bottle of wine to keep him off spirits, and the substantial food, too, helped to steady him.

"This was a good idea," he said, leaning over and kissing her. "What'll we do when we're through?"

The moment had come to take the next hurdle. She braced herself. "I'm afraid I'm booked."

He looked at her sharply. "What do you mean, booked?"

"I've got to go out to Brookline for dinner and overnight."

333

"Oh, well, what the hell! Call up and tell them you can't make it. There's a booth over in the corner."

She shook her head. "Can't. They're in town," she invented rapidly, "attending some recital or other, and they're picking me up at the hotel at five."

"All right, leave a note for them at the desk. Tell them—oh, I don't know! You can think up something. You're much better at lying your way out of things than I am."

"Thanks, chum. But I don't want to lie myself out of this, as you so charmingly put it. It's Meg Kimball, whom I adore and haven't seen in years, and she's invited a lot of my old friends. I'd feel like a heel, standing her up at the last minute, and what's more, she'd never forgive me."

"And what about me?" he said plaintively. "What am I supposed to do with myself between now and tomorrow morning?"

"Well, one thing you could do is take a nice six o'clock train and be in your nice bed in New Canaan before midnight."

"Let's not go all over that again. It seems to me that when I come all the way up from New York just to see you—"

"And go to all the trouble of kicking in my door to notify me of your arrival."

"I only decided to come on the spur of the moment. There wasn't time to phone or wire. I thought you'd be glad to see me."

"I'm delighted to see you. But I'm not going to insult Meg."

"It seems to me she insults pretty easy," he said. "All right then, take me along."

"I'm afraid that isn't practicable."

"Why not?"

"I don't think they're expecting you."

"What of it? People like that must have an extra fork. If not I'll borrow one from the hotel and take it along."

"I guess I haven't quite made my point. It's not a question of cutlery but of people's ideas of correct behavior."

"Oh, pardon *me!* I guess I'd better brush up on my Emily Post. I've been to dinner parties where I've been treated as a celebrity. Who are these people anyhow?"

"Just some illiterate natives who think La Vie de Bohème is the source of an opera by Puccini and not a mode of existence."

"You've been going into that finishing-school act of yours an awful lot lately. And I don't care for it."

334

"I'm sorry I don't give satisfaction," she said. "Maybe you'd like to give me my two weeks' notice."

He gave her a pained look. "There was a time when you'd break any engagement to be with me."

"There was a time when I was a virgin. Times change."

"You bet they do. And people too."

"And God fulfills Himself in many ways. Lest one good custom should corrupt the world." She looked at her watch. "I've got to go pack an overnight bag."

"The least you could do is get back tonight. Don't tell me you can't get out of staying over."

"I was rather looking forward to it. I've been holed up in that Marlborough bedroom for a week and the idea of a change appeals."

"I see."

They walked back to the hotel in silence.

"I think I'll go into the bar for a while," said Mollison. "What about tomorrow?"

"Well, we're rehearsing at one."

"How about lunch?"

"Swell, if they get me back here in time. I'll phone you in the morning. I'm sorry about all this mix-up, Huge, but it just can't be helped."

"Uh-huh," he said and went to the bar.

Thompson arrived at the hotel a little after six, having caught a four-thirty plane from La Guardia Field. The clerk handed him a note from Virginia, telling him where she would be in case he wanted to get in touch with her. He looked in at the bar, but Mollison was not there. If the actor had gone out he would have no way of tracing him. He called Mollison's room. Fortunately he was in and still able to talk coherently.

"Hi, Hugh," said Thompson. "When did you blow into town?"

"This morning. How did you know I was here?" asked Mollison, suddenly suspicious.

"They told me at the desk when I came in. Are you alone?"

"No. I've got a couple of bottles with me."

"Well, why not move on over here? I've got a case."

"All right, I will," he said after a moment's hesitation. He had been sitting around in his pajamas, a bottle beside him, grimly determined to drink himself into a stupor. But he hated being alone and welcomed the prospect of companionship, especially Thompson's. Besides, sooner

335

or later, he would have to justify his presence in Boston. He dressed and went down the hall to Thompson's suite, a little on the defensive and not knowing whether to assume a truculent or a conciliatory attitude. To his relief, Thompson greeted him with great cordiality, apparently taking his presence there quite as a matter of course.

Thompson's nonchalance was not entirely assumed. He saw at a glance that Mollison was still manageable. Indeed, as they settled down to drink he looked forward to an evening of pleasant relaxation—just what he needed after the week's grinding work. He much preferred Mollison's company to Claire's; though the actor was emotionally and intellectually adolescent, he was also good-humored, amusing, and, most important of all, undemanding. They had had many drinking sessions and got on well with each other. Thompson had not the slightest objection to Mollison's drinking as long as it did not interfere with his performances. It was only for secret and pathological drinkers, like Anthony Weir, that he felt contempt.

He let Mollison do most of the talking—not only because it kept down the actor's consumption of alcohol but because it helped heal his badly bruised vanity. Mollison talked mostly about himself, and the more he talked the better he felt. Thompson listened with an appearance of the deepest interest, subtly flattering him and smiling appreciatively at anecdotes he had heard a dozen times. Gradually bringing the conversation around to The Clouded Mirror, he described the play's reception and dwelt on the excellence of Virginia's performance.

"Yes, I hear she's great," said Mollison, his face clouding. "I wish I could see her." This was the moment to tell Thompson he intended to stay for the Monday performance—he had not taken seriously Virginia's threat not to appear—but they were having such a pleasant time together that he could not bear to introduce a discordant note.

Ignoring Mollison's remark, Thompson looked at his watch. "Say," he said, "if you're meeting Ginny or something, don't let me keep you."

"No," said Mollison, unhappy again, "she's off somewhere, with some of those ritzy snobs she's always running around with, though Christ knows why."

"You mean you've got the evening on your hands?" said Thompson, feigning surprise.

"Looks that way."

"So have I. Well, hell's bells, why don't we make a night of it?"

336

"Suits me fine," said Mollison, delighted not to be left alone.

"How about going around to the Four Arts Club, for dinner and a little serious hoisting?"

"The Four Arts! I haven't been there in years."

"Neither have I. But I guess some of the old-timers aren't completely ossified yet."

The cool night air refreshed them, and they decided to walk.

"Tommy," said Mollison, breaking a long silence, "Ginny is giving me the gate."

"You're crazy!" said Thompson. This time he was genuinely surprised; and not only surprised but strangely excited.

"No, I'm not. I've seen it coming for a long time. For a while I figured it was because she thought I ought to marry her. But now I'm sure she wouldn't marry me if she could."

"She's probably just on the downbeat, that's all. They're all like that. Just baby her along a little and she'll snap right back."

Mollison shook his head. "I'd like to believe it, but I'd only be kidding myself. She thinks I'm not good enough for her any more. Well, maybe she's right. But the goddam thing of it is that I feel the same way about her that I always did—only more so!"

Thompson went on trying to reassure him, yet contemplating, with secret delight, the realization of the actor's fears.

The Four Arts Club was an informal gathering place for writers, artists, publishers, newspapermen, and professional entertainers. It occupied an entire floor of a building, over a bar-restaurant, from which meals and drinks were sent up. There was a central dining-room, connecting at one end with a cardroom and at the other with a lounge.

The single, long table was well filled. Thompson and Mollison were heartily welcomed. Everybody there knew them, either personally or by reputation. There were many who had seen Mollison in Give Them All My Love, and their effusive compliments bolstered his ego. Before long he was joining heartily in the general banter. After dinner he allowed himself, with the customary show of reluctance, to be persuaded to entertain the club members in the lounge. With a well-known band leader as accompanist, he stood at the piano and gave imitations of the vaudeville favorites of his youth. He was a first-rate mimic and, encouraged by roars of approval, put on a very good show. For an hour he was the center of admiring attention, and the back-thumping and handshaking that rewarded his performances were balm to the wounds Virginia had inflicted.

337

On the way back to the Marlborough Thompson clapped Mollison on the shoulder. "That was a great show! I don't think I've ever seen you any better."

Mollison beamed. "Well, they're a great bunch of guys. I was having the time of my life. Glad you thought of going around there. How about stopping somewhere for a little nightcap?"

"I can't. I'm rehearsing at one, and I've got a lot of work to do before I go to bed." Then, as though it were an afterthought, "Oh, what train are you taking back?"

Mollison was overcome by embarrassment. After the wonderful evening Thompson had provided it was not easy to tell him of his intention to stay over. "Well, I don't know," he said. "I sort of wish I could catch tomorrow night's show here. I haven't seen anything of it except for that lousy run-through. I think Ginny would like me to stay too."

He watched Thompson's face covertly. The director showed no sign of disturbance. "I'm sure she would," he said. "And so would I. You know how glad I always am to get your reactions. Too bad it can't be done."

Mollison summoned his courage. "You don't think George Hamlin could go on for me—just for the one performance?"

Thompson wrinkled his brow and ran his hand through his hair. "Well, I don't know, Hugh. It would scare the hell out of me to send him on without a rehearsal. I'd be glad to shoot down there and work with him tomorrow, but the trouble is I've got this rehearsal here, and I hate to give that up."

"No, no, you can't do that!" said Mollison hastily, feeling that he was behaving like an ingrate to this friend who had saved him from an evening of sodden despair. "Well, I guess I can pick up a train in the morning."

"I think Doc is taking the twelve-something," said Thompson, improvising rapidly. "Why don't you ride down with him? He's always good for a laugh or two."

"He sure is!" said Mollison, brightening. "What'll I do, call him?"

"No, I'll take care of it; and I'll have him call you, in the morning, in plenty of time."

"Okay. Oh, wait a minute! Ginny said something about getting back in time for lunch."

"Well, she won't have much time. The rehearsal call is for one."

"Yes, I guess I'd better skip it and go back with Doc. Well, in case

338

I don't see you in the morning, thanks again for a wonderful evening."

The instant he got back to his room Thompson called Winternitz. "Hello, Doc. Hope I didn't wake you up."

"Another frustrated hope, my boy," said Winternitz. He was a chronic insomniac and had just dropped off to sleep.

"I thought I'd better tell you that you and a ham named Mollison are taking a noonish train to New York."

"Just a moment, while I put my interpreter on." He listened resignedly to Thompson's explanation, knowing that he would not get to sleep again for hours and not at all happy at being pressed into service as Mollison's bodyguard.

"Keep feeding him and talking to him and goosing him up," said Thompson in conclusion. "Do anything that's necessary to get him on tomorrow night."

"I'll send him a wire informing him of his mother's death. That has never yet failed to make an actor go on and do his best."

Before going to bed Thompson sent a reassuring night telegram to Claire—he had with difficulty dissuaded her from coming back with him—and another to Virginia, which read: "I have landed and have the situation well in hand. Don't phone or come back to the hotel before twelve. Your loving Uncle Tommy."

XXX.

When Eric arrived at the theater for the Monday rehearsal Virginia was already there. Thompson's telegram had been comforting but not very informative, and she had thought it best not to go to the hotel at all. After satisfying Eric about her health, she again apologized for disappointing him and suggested that they have lunch on Thursday and visit the Gardner Museum afterwards. It was the only time she had free. All the while she was talking to him she kept an eye out for Thompson. As soon as he came in she excused herself and hurried over to him. He drew her aside and told her that Mollison was on his way back to New York with Winternitz.

"You're a wonder boy!" said Virginia with genuine admiration. "What is the secret of your success, Mr. Machiavelli?"

"Hard work and complete abstinence from intoxicants," said Thompson.

Eric watched them from a distance, wondering what they had to talk about in private and what it was that made her look so joyful. Thompson was in a jolly mood, wasting a great deal of time clowning and telling anecdotes, so that the rehearsal lasted until nearly five.

The Monday night audience was not very large, but Thompson was well satisfied with the performance and its reception. He went straight back to the hotel in expectation of a call from Winternitz. At half-past eleven the telephone rang. He was annoyed to hear Lily's voice.

"Can you see me?" she asked tremulously.

"I can't leave. I'm expecting a long-distance call."

"I'm in the hotel. Couldn't I come up for just a minute? Please say yes."

"Why sure," he said. He assumed that she was calling from one of the house telephones at the reception desk. If he refused she might begin to weep and attract the attention of people in the lobby. Besides, it was impossible to put off seeing her much longer. Angry and troubled, he paced the room, all his self-satisfaction dissipated. The telephone rang again, and this time it was Winternitz.

"Hello, Doc. Did you get him on all right?"

"When has Winternitz failed to get anyone on?"

"How was he?"

"A delicate study in equilibrium. What you might call a staggering performance. But no disturbing incidents, except for one second-balcony customer who was inebriated by the fumes emanating from the stage."

"Nice work, Doc. I guess the worst is over, but I think you'd better stay in New York and keep baby's nose clean till I get back."

"Well, you knows best, boss."

The door buzzer sounded. "I'll give you a little kiss when I see you. Phone me again tomorrow night, will you?"

He opened the door for Lily. "What are you doing out without a coat?" he said, looking at her in surprise.

She reddened. "I've moved over here." As his brows contracted she went on volubly, "I couldn't stand that Bay State Hotel another day. My room was right on the street, and I haven't been able to get one night's sleep."

"Why didn't you ask them to change your room?"

"They didn't have any other one." She went to him and put her arms around his neck. "Please don't be angry at me. I've been so lonesome."

"I'm not angry," he said sharply. "How about a drink?"

"No, thank you."

"Well, I think I'll have one, if you don't mind."

She sat down while he mixed a highball. He was furious, well aware that she could not afford to stay at the Marlborough and had moved in only to be near him. Yet he could not very well complain, for she had every right to live where she pleased. He sat at the far side of the room and drank in silence.

"Please talk to me," she said. "It's days since you've said a word to me."

"Well, I'm doing a job here and I've had a few things on my mind."

"I know that. I know there are lots of things that are more important to you than I am. And I've tried not to bother you—oh, you don't know how hard I've tried! But now that I'm here, couldn't you just be a little nice to me?" She went over to him and sat on his lap. "I just want to be near you, that's all."

Mechanically he set down his glass and put his arms around her. She clasped his neck and, murmuring endearments, covered his face with kisses. His sensual nature could not long resist the enticement of her young body, and he soon surrendered to her passionate longing. She wanted to spend the night with him, but at two o'clock he made her go back to her room, on the excuse that he still had work to do. He was thoroughly bored with her, yet he had enough pity in him to prevent his telling her the brutal truth. Only a few days remained before their return to New York and once there it would not be so hard to shake her off.

The play continued to go well. The indications were that the week's business would be quite good, until on Wednesday afternoon it began to rain. Not only was the window sale for the Wednesday night performance affected, but the advance sale for the remainder of the week fell off sharply.

Eric and Virginia had arranged to lunch, on Thursday, at a famous sea-food restaurant near the wharves. But Thursday was a raw, gusty day, with the rain coming down in sheets, so they decided to stay in the hotel.

The dining-room was not crowded, and they had a leisurely lunch at a secluded table. They discussed the theater and books and pictures. Eric's habitual reticence made it hard for him to talk about himself, particularly since he thought his own life lacking in interest; so he encouraged Virginia to tell of her travels and of the things she had seen and done.

"I certainly envy you all that," he said. "I've never been anywhere or seen anything—except Grant's Tomb and a few Army camps."

"Well, I guess I have been around a little. And I won't say it hasn't been fun. When I think of Venice and Salzburg, of Chartres and Vézelay and Bruges, of the sun at Juan-les-Pins and the snow peaks of Chamonix, of the high tide breaking over the sea wall at Dinard and skiing at Cortina d'Ampezzo, of bouillebaisse at the Vieux Port in Marseille and pheasant stuffed with sauerkraut in Strasbourg, of the little Flemish and Dutch rooms off the Rubens Gallery in the Louvre and the cloister of Saint Trophime in Arles—well, just talking about it like this gives me goose pimples and little wiggles running up and down my spine. But when you get to adding it all up, I'm not sure that I wouldn't swap every bit of it for what you've had."

Eric laughed. "Growing up on the wrong side of the tracks in a one-horse town? Working in a factory? Lying awake nights, wondering how your family would eat if you happened to break a leg— or if your play turned out a failure? Is that what you mean?"

"Well, I don't know about the factory part of it. I don't think I'd ever be much of a hand at a Diesel engine or a cyclotron. Cyclotron, is that right? But the rest of it, yes."

"You're not serious, are you?" said Eric in astonishment.

"But so very definitely serious!"

"But why?"

"Because you've had something that I've never had and never can have, now. Roots, a place where you belong and are at home, loving-kindness and warmth. That funny old room you told me about where you've slept all your life. That nice mother and that nice sister who's going to have a baby. How is she?"

"She's fine," said Eric. "She and my mother are coming to New York for the opening. They'd love to meet you, I know—if you wouldn't mind, that is."

342

"Mind! Don't talk like a crazy fool. I'd adore it. Promise?"

"Yes, of course."

"Good! Only I know, without meeting them, that you wouldn't trade them in for a fistful of cathedrals and a ton of caviar."

"Well, no, I guess I wouldn't."

"You know bloody well you wouldn't! Well, that's what I mean. I was handed everything—and nothing. Everything except what really mattered. A great big gold platter full of emptiness. Snuff and tobaccy and excellent jacky, and scissors and watches and knives, but nothing that ever made me feel I belonged anywhere or that anybody cared. My father is an amiable and dishonest old fuddy-duddy and my mother is a high-powered bitch, and I've never meant any more to either of them than they have to me. I'm just the accidental product of a careless moment. Nobody ever wanted me and nobody ever knew what to do with me. I was brought up by butlers and stable boys and middle-aged Lesbian schoolteachers. So I had to learn to stand on two sturdy little feet that have carried me around the world without taking me anywhere. And here I am, at an age that I am not revealing, with neither kith nor kin, nor chick nor child, nor where to lay my head. For God's sake, stop me, will you? I'm beginning to sound like Little Orphan Annie or one of the less successful creations of the late Charles Dickens. Will you be kind enough to give me a swift kick in the pants or order me another brandy or both?"

"You have a wonderful career and a million friends," said Eric, deeply moved by her frankness and sincerity.

"Yes, cocktail friends, dressing-room friends, tell-them-about-the-French-priest-who-made-a-pass-at-you-Ginny-dear friends. And if you call memorizing lines in a thing by a Nutmeg State industrial worker a career!" She leaned over and patted his hand. "A good thing, mark you, but decidedly not my own."

"What do you want?"

"Well, that is what my barrister calls a leading question, I believe. But better tell the doctor everything, Miss Upton. Well, laughable though it may seem, what I really daydream about is tiny garments and a bony shoulder to cry on."

Eric felt himself flushing. "Well, maybe you'll get them yet."

She shook her head. "Hélas, non!"

"Why not?"

"Because I'm spoiled and selfish and man delights me not—no, nor

343

woman either! But shut up, Ginny, will you? Because Ginny is awful sick of the sound of your voice."

"I'm not."

"All the more reason for turning it off in time. How's about you, little brother? What do *you* want?"

"That's not an easy question."

"Are good ones ever?"

"No, I guess not. All right then. What I want is to know the truth—"

She craned her neck. "Pardon me, is Pilate in the house?"

"Well, let's say to *try* to know the truth and to try to express it in my work. To be as honest as I can, with myself and with others. To fight the destructiveness and possessiveness that's in me and develop creativeness and self-reliance. To make myself live what I believe, which is that life and not death is the true meaning of life. Is that any kind of an answer to your hard question?"

She nodded several times. "Is good. I like."

There were tears in her eyes. With a sudden rush of boldness Eric said, "The tiny garments and the shoulder would fit in too—though not necessarily a bony one."

She sat making crisscross marks on the tablecloth with her ring. "How old are you?" she asked at last.

"Almost twenty-seven. Why?"

"I feel like your grandmother."

"Why?" he asked again, puzzled and a little hurt.

She shook her head. "Don't know. Just do."

"Do I sound as infantile as all that?"

"Oh, God, no!" she said, putting her hand on his. "Please don't think I meant it that way, because I didn't at all."

"Then what?"

"I don't know. It's just that I've always felt like everybody's grandmother, I guess. I can't remember ever feeling really young, or in fact like anything but a little old lady. So rub that hurt look off your big, brown eyes and go on being that nice, charming person I think you are."

Before Eric could think of an answer, a bellboy entered the dining-room, paging Virginia. She beckoned to him.

"Telephone for you, Miss Upton," said the boy. "Mr. Mollison calling from New York."

With difficulty Virginia kept her composure. "Well, just say that—" she began, trying to think of some excuse for not talking to Mollison. But, as far as Eric was concerned, the damage had already been done; she might as well take Mollison's call, now as later. "I'll take it in my room. Just ask the operator to hold it until I get upstairs."

"Yes, miss."

"Will you excuse me, Eric?"

"Yes, of course," he said, tight-lipped.

"Don't get up, please. You stay here and finish your brandy." She looked at her watch. "My God, it's about time I gave you a break! It's nearly five." She extended her hand, which he took automatically. "Thank you for just about the best time I've had in I don't know when. And forgive me for being such a bore."

"You know very well I wasn't bored."

"It's sweet of you to say so anyhow. We're friends, aren't we?" she said, pleadingly.

"I hope so."

"Well, hold on to that," she said, seeing that she could not make him unbend. "And let's break bread again before too long."

Eric watched her go. She turned in the doorway to wave and smile. He slumped into his chair, brooding unhappily. He had believed every word she had said and had been warmed and thrilled by her apparent confidence in his sympathy and understanding. Yet her relationship to Mollison seemed inconsistent with everything that he conceived her to be and with everything that she had expressed. A few moments before it had all seemed so clear to him; now he was troubled and confused. Had she merely been playing a game with him, using her histrionic talent to create an interesting character, or was she sincere and yet bound to Mollison in some way he did not understand? In any case, he told himself, it was better to face the facts, no matter how painful they might be, than be lulled into self-deception and false hopes.

XXXI.

The bad weather continued for the rest of the week. Fineman estimated that the resultant loss in receipts would amount to several thousand dollars. On Friday Thompson instructed the actors to revert to the original text, confident that with only three performances left the police officials would not be likely to interfere. He wanted the company to have time to feel thoroughly at ease in the version that was to be played in New York.

Since no further changes were to be made, Eric decided to stop over at Coltertown for two days on his way to New York. He had worked so steadily on the play and had watched so many performances that it seemed utterly flat and meaningless to him. He had not been home in more than a month and wanted to make sure that his mother would keep her promise to come to New York for the opening.

Everything at home seemed quite as usual. He thought he saw a great decline in his father, but then Kenwood always seemed worse in the winter months. The ending of the baseball season deprived him of his chief occupation, and the inclement weather kept him indoors, so that his irritability at times became almost unbearable.

Amelia had read all the Boston reviews, but she was interested only in the direct references to Eric. The praise had been outweighed by the numerous allusions to the play's outspokenness and particularly by Daniel O'Fallon's denunciation of it as immoral and indecent. Some of her acquaintances, who had seen O'Fallon's review, had made malicious little comments, and she had indignantly defended her son against the critic's charges. Though she said nothing of all this to Eric, he guessed what was troubling her.

His father questioned Eric closely about his returns from the play.

346

Eric estimated that his royalties for the two weeks' engagement in Boston would come to about nine hundred dollars—a very substantial sum and almost as much as he would have earned, in four months, at the Ainsworth plant—but against that had to be charged the five hundred dollars he had received as advance royalties. Under Kenwood's cross-examination he had to admit that if the play failed in New York he would not only be without any source of income but would actually have less money in the bank than he had had when he left the factory. He had to listen, with all the patience he could muster, while Kenwood rebuked him for having frittered away the past two months.

Eric evaded his mother's tactful questions about his break with Sylvia. Amelia did not press them, but she did tell him that Lydia Jethrow had let it be known that during her vacation Sylvia had met a well-to-do and well-connected man, who could be regarded as a prospective husband. Eric was pleased to hear it, for he wished Sylvia well. He was amazed to find how remote their long intimacy seemed and how untouched it had left him.

On Sunday he bought all the New York papers and was delighted by the attention given to the forthcoming opening. One paper carried a lively caricature of Virginia, Olmsted, and Florence Fulham in a scene from the play, and the others had scene photographs. There was also a chatty interview with Florence and a very amusing piece by Winternitz on Thompson's career as a producer. Amelia was proud to see Eric's name in print again, but she thought the caricature repulsive.

Eric went out to the La Pointe farm for noonday dinner. Dorothy's confinement was only about six weeks off, and he was startled by the increase in her bulk. She too had been disturbed by O'Fallon's review and bluntly expressed the hope that the play was not as bad as it sounded. Eric, half amused, half annoyed, by her prudishness, pointed out that she would soon be able to judge for herself, since she was going to the opening with Amelia.

It was years since Amelia had been away overnight and she was uneasy about going to New York. Kenwood could not be left alone, and the problem of finding someone to stay with him was not an easy one. She sounded out several of her friends, but they all found convenient excuses for declining. As a last resort she asked Cousin Elizabeth, and the old woman, always anxious to be useful, agreed. She was very nervous about it (as was Amelia), for she was in terror of Kenwood. However, since Amelia would be away less than twenty-four hours, she felt she could manage it.

On Monday Eric set out once more for New York. Depressed by his family's skepticism, he almost wished he had not gone home. It was more than five months since his first meeting with Thompson, and the fate of his play was still undecided. Everyone had assured him that the Boston reception gave no indication either of success or failure, for while the out-of-town response was frequently duplicated in New York, it happened, just as often, that plays which delighted Boston, Philadelphia, or Baltimore were frowned upon in the metropolis, or the other way around. Usually everything hinged upon the opening night. The long agony of composition, the long process of planning, of revising, of casting, of rehearsing, of tryout, culminated in one fateful performance that could connote anything from utter futility to triumphant fulfillment. And the verdict, in the opinion of many skilled observers, depended largely upon the judgment of less than a dozen men, whose business it was to review plays for the daily press.

In theatrical circles dramatic criticism was a subject of persistent and virulent controversy. In the past months Eric had read in the drama sections of the New York newspapers numerous articles and letters dealing with the function of the critic in the theater. Authors and managers who had suffered at the hands of the critics denounced them in harsh terms; the critics, according to their natures, replied petulantly, facetiously, or apologetically; and playgoers frequently joined in, siding sometimes with the critics and sometimes with their attackers.

The argument had no focus, for there were as many points of view as there were controversialists. Some contended that the critic should confine himself to reporting the reactions of the first-night audience; some that he should record his own impressions, regardless of the audience's response. Others thought that criticism should be designed to guide the theatergoer in his choice of plays; still others, that it was the duty of the critic to uphold the dignity of the drama and to judge plays by high standards of excellence. Eric inclined to the latter view, remembering that Anatole France had defined criticism as the adventures of a soul among masterpieces. His own tastes and criteria had been developed by reading the dramatic essays of Lamb, Hazlitt, and Coleridge, and of such late nineteenth- and early twentieth-century critics as Bernard Shaw, Max Beerbohm,

348

Francisque Sarcey, C. E. Montague, Henry James, William Winter, Georg Brandes, William Archer, and James Huneker, as well as some more recent writers. But he had seen enough of the New York theater to understand the difficulty of measuring it by the yardstick of perfectionism.

One point on which there was general agreement was the direct and immediate relationship between the newspaper reviews and the popularity of the play; while instances could be cited of plays that had failed in spite of favorable reviews and of others that had become great successes in the face of critical condemnation, there could be no doubt that, in the main, good reviews meant a long run and bad ones an early closing. But there was great difference of opinion as to whether this was because the critics represented a fair cross-section of popular taste or because newspaper readers tended to regard a published review as a weighty and authoritative pronouncement rather than as the expression of one man's point of view. Why, it was frequently asked, should a huge investment of money, time and creative effort be jeopardized by the hastily formed judgment of an individual, who might lack the training or perception to make a valid appraisal or whose opinion might be colored by prejudice, spite, or the fact that his dinner or his wife had disagreed with him? A curtailment of the power of critics was loudly demanded—though how this was to be accomplished was never very clearly stated. In fact, many of those who complained most bitterly about the undue influence of the press were responsible for further increasing the prestige of the critics by widely publicizing favorable reviews of which they happened to be the beneficiaries.

Whatever the rights or wrongs of the situation, Eric knew that a few columns of type in the Thursday newspapers could mean the difference between the realization and the defeat of all his hopes. It was a terrifying thought, and he reflected how odd it was that, in seventy-two hours, the fate of his play and perhaps the course of his life would be determined by the quick comments of eight or ten men whose names were barely familiar to him and of whose personalities he knew nothing. With a kind of grim amusement he tried to visualize them, at that moment, as they went about their private or professional business, hardly aware of his existence and certainly giving no thought to him as he speeded toward New York to await their judgment.

Unable to bring himself to go back to the bedlam where he had stayed during rehearsals, Eric went to a hotel that was only a block from the theater. He had to pay twice as much for a room, but if the play succeeded he could afford it; if it did not, he would not be in New York long enough for it to make much difference. He called Virginia's apartment and then, learning from her cousin Marion that she was out, he went around to Pinelli's in the hope of seeing her there; but he could not get a table and decided not to wait.

After dinner he went to the Farow, where the stagehands were assembling the production. Since the laborious process of setting up and lighting had to be done all over again, Thompson had put off the opening until Wednesday, so that nothing would be skimped and the crew would not be too tired to handle the first night smoothly. Eric did not stay long. To pass the time he went to a movie, but was unable to give it even the slight attention it required.

On Tuesday the company was called for a technical run-through, partly to keep them fresh in their lines, mostly for the benefit of the stagehands, all of whom, except the three heads, were unfamiliar with the production and had to learn how to operate it. It was a tedious affair, but Eric, for want of anything better to do, sat through it, while Thompson patiently corrected the numerous blunders and delays.

In the evening there was a preview performance to give the stagehands an additional rehearsal and to permit the actors to accustom themselves to the stage conditions and acoustics of the Farow. The entire house had been sold to a Zionist organization, which had resold the tickets, at greatly advanced prices, as a means of raising money for its activities. There were hundreds of benefit performances every season, and they were important in the economy of the theater. Many managers booked as many benefits as possible, for the guaranteed income often helped to carry a play along until it began to pay its own way or cut down the losses if it failed. Fineman, after Emily Crandall's withdrawal, had tried unsuccessfully to book the numerous benefits he had refused while she was still in the cast. He had felt no need for this insurance with her in the play; without her, he was anxious to have it. The organizations, however, were attracted by a popular star but had little interest in a work by an unknown author, with no big names in the cast.

Except for the money they brought in, these benefit performances

350

were looked upon with great disfavor by everyone in the theater, particularly the actors. The ticket-buyers came not as theatergoers but as more or less reluctant contributors to a charitable cause. Many of them watched the performance with boredom or with the resentful feeling that they were not getting much for their money.

The preview at the Farow was no exception. The audience arrived late and was noisy, restless, and inattentive throughout. Some did not understand the play, some were shocked by it, some wanted only amusement. The raggedness of the performance did not help matters either. There were still many technical slips that tended to destroy the illusion, and the actors, feeling that they were not giving pleasure, soon stopped trying to please. Besides, they were conserving their energies for the next night and did little more than walk through their parts. There was almost no applause at the end, and the departing spectators were loud in their dissatisfaction. Eric was confused and disheartened. It did not seem possible that this was the same cast and production he had seen in Boston. In spite of all he had learned in the past weeks, he was still too inexperienced to understand how sensitive actors are to the mood of the audience and how drastically their performance can be affected by it. Thompson passed him on his way backstage and, seeing his disconsolate look, said, "What's the matter, Eric? You don't look happy."

"I'm just hoping it won't be like this tomorrow night, that's all."

Thompson laughed. "You've just seen the worst performance that this play will ever have. I'm glad they got it out of their systems, because maybe they'll be good tomorrow."

Eric was by no means reassured and brooded dismally over what would happen to his play if the next night's performance should be no better.

It was now mid-November. Of all the long days of anxious waiting that Eric had known since Irina Lanski had first summoned him to New York in early June, the day of the opening was the longest and most agonizing. He had nothing to do, nowhere to go, he could not read or think, and the hours, the very minutes, dragged by with excruciating slowness. He idled away the morning in his room, working out the puzzles in his newspaper and carefully composing telegrams to the cast and to Thompson. He went out to lunch, but he had no appetite and left his sandwich half eaten. He ordered flowers for Virginia and then stopped in at Pinelli's and reserved a table for six o'clock, for he wanted to show off the famous restaurant, with its theatrical celebrities and its caricatures, to his mother and sister. Then he walked past the Farow. Except for a few people who were picking up tickets for the evening's performance, there was no activity there. Backstage he found no one but the old doorman. Thompson had not called the company, for he wanted them to be well rested for the opening. With time still on his hands, Eric went to Irina Lanski's office. Her reception room was crowded, and he did not wait. To his surprise, Myra Leech stopped typing long enough to extend her hand and wish him good luck.

Though the train from Hartford was not due until five, he was at the station at half-past four. At last the gate opened, and presently he saw Dorothy far down the platform. To his amazement and consternation, she was accompanied not by Amelia but by Cousin Elizabeth. He watched them in a frenzy of bewilderment and anxiety as they moved slowly along in the dense crowd.

"Hello," he said, taking Dorothy's bag and another that he recognized as his mother's from Cousin Elizabeth. "Where's Ma?"

"She couldn't get away," said Dorothy tersely.

"Is she sick?"

"No, no, she's all right. She just couldn't get away," Dorothy replied, putting a finger to her lips.

"It's all my fault, Eric," said Cousin Elizabeth quaveringly. "I feel just awful about it."

"Is it far to where we're going?" asked Dorothy.

"No, just five minutes." It was evident that Dorothy did not want him to question her in the old woman's presence, and he led the way to a taxi. They had to walk very slowly, for Dorothy was hampered by her unwieldy body and by Cousin Elizabeth, who clung to her arm, frightened and confused by the crowds and the noise. It was years since she had been out of Coltertown and almost half a century since her last visit to New York. She huddled in the corner of the taxi, gasping, as it wove through the traffic, clutching at Eric with her palsied hand.

Eric had engaged a double room just down the corridor from his own. After he had tipped the bellboy he whispered to Dorothy to come to his room as soon as she could and left the two women alone. As he closed the door, he caught a glimpse of Cousin Elizabeth seated in an armchair, breathing heavily and shakily removing her rusty, antiquated hat. Eric left his door open and walked nervously around the room, impatiently waiting for Dorothy and speculating on what had prevented his mother's coming.

It was fully fifteen minutes before Dorothy appeared.

"What happened?" said Eric as he closed the door.

"Well—" said Dorothy. She stopped and sank into a chair. "Just give me a minute to catch my breath."

"Are you all right? Can I get you something. How about a drink?"

"Oh no, nothing like that! Just a glass of water maybe."

Eric brought a glass of water from the bathroom. She sipped it slowly. "I hope I never have to live through another day like this," she said and began a circumstantial account of the day's happenings.

It had been arranged that Dorothy was to leave Cousin Elizabeth at the Kenwood home and drive with her mother to Hartford. Kenwood had protested at having the old woman in the house overnight, but Amelia had stood firm and at last he had grudgingly acquiesced. When the two women arrived Cousin Elizabeth went into the house. Dorothy, not wishing to see her father, waited in the car. Amelia had her hat and coat on, ready to leave, and Kenwood was in his wheel chair, listening to an adventure serial. He scowled as the old woman came in, barely acknowledging her greeting. She looked at him in terror, shocked by his twisted figure, haggard face, and glazed eyes. When she had last seen him he had still been a robust and vigorous man. Amelia took Cousin Elizabeth aside and carefully instructed her in her simple duties, among which was the removal of the radio, at Kenwood's bedtime, from the dining-room to the bedroom. To make sure that Cousin Elizabeth would know how to perform this operation, Amelia took her over to the radio and showed where it was plugged into the baseboard. The old woman, in her eagerness to get it right, bent over to look at the outlet and stumbled. Instinctively she grasped the small table for support, and the radio crashed to the floor, smashing a tube.

Kenwood flew into a wild rage and leaped from his chair, screaming obscenities at Cousin Elizabeth and quite prepared to kill her. After two staggering steps he collapsed and lay there helpless, clutching at the carpet and shouting imprecations. Dorothy, hearing the uproar, squirmed out of the car as Cousin Elizabeth came out of the house, trembling violently and wide-eyed with fright. Dorothy made her sit on the porch steps and succeeded in calming her a little and in getting an account of what had happened. Afraid that if she went into the house she would only aggravate her father's rage, Dorothy helped Cousin Elizabeth back into the car, and the two women sat there, hoping that Amelia would come out to them.

Presently she did. She had managed to get Kenwood back into the wheel chair and had given him a sedative, which worked quickly, since he was already exhausted by his outburst. But it was obvious that she could not go to New York. It would not have been safe to leave Cousin Elizabeth with Kenwood even in the unlikely event that she could have been persuaded to re-enter the house. Amelia insisted, however, that Dorothy go, as planned, for she knew how much her daughter had been looking forward to the trip. Besides, she could not bear to let Eric go through this crisis in his life with no member of his family near him. At the same time she was worried about letting Dorothy make the trip alone; so she suggested, on the spur of the moment, that Cousin Elizabeth go along. She would not be very helpful in an emergency, but she was better than no one. Dorothy demurred, but there was no time for debate; if they were to go at all, they would have to leave at once; so she had yielded to her mother's urging. As for Cousin Elizabeth, she was so shaken and so full of guilt she would have agreed to anything. There was another delay while Amelia ran into the house to get her packed bag for Cousin Elizabeth. They reached Hartford just in time to catch their train.

"Well, that's the whole story," said Dorothy. "Only I guess maybe we shouldn't have come either."

"Of course you should have come. I'd feel even worse if you hadn't. But do you really think that Cousin Elizabeth wants to go to the show?"

"I'd be afraid to leave her here alone. She'd be scared to death. So if you think she shouldn't go, I'll stay with her and you can tell me all about it afterwards."

"I should say not!" said Eric.

"Are we going out somewhere to eat?"

"No, just downstairs." It would be absurd to drag Cousin Elizabeth to Pinelli's.

"That's good. Will I have time to lie down for a little while?"

"A half-hour or so. I'll knock on your door at six-fifteen. The curtain doesn't go up until eight, but I want to go backstage first."

Dorothy went back to her room, and he sat, utterly disconsolate. For days he had been imagining how it would be with his mother

354

here. He had seen himself watching her reactions to New York (where she had not been in many years), to the lively scene at Pinelli's, to the first-night audience, and, of course, to his play, and backstage afterwards, when he introduced her to his friends, particularly Virginia. Overwrought as he was anyhow, he almost wept with disappointment. He called Coltertown to inform his mother of the safe arrival of Cousin Elizabeth and Dorothy and to inquire about his father. Kenwood was in bed and sound asleep.

"I only wish you were here," said Eric despondently.

"Well, so do I, son. But I guess it just wasn't meant to be. But my thoughts will be with you, every minute, just as though I was sitting right there next to you. And maybe you'll call me again when it's all over and tell me how things went."

"It'll be quite late. I hate to wake you up after all you've been through today."

"I won't be asleep. I'll just be thinking of you and praying for you."

"All right then, I will."

"Well, God bless you, son, and may it be all that you want it to be."

"Thanks, Ma."

He blinked away a few tears, feeling a little better for having talked to her. He knocked on Dorothy's door. The women were waiting for him. Dorothy's inexpert make-up only accentuated her dowdiness; Cousin Elizabeth, in Amelia's best dress, which hung loosely on her shrunken figure, looked even more pathetic than she had in the faded housedress in which she had arrived.

Since the dining-room was almost empty, the clatter of Cousin Elizabeth's fork against her plate did not attract too much attention. She could make nothing of the menu and asked Dorothy to order for her. Dorothy, scandalized by the prices, ordered sparingly, and Eric ate almost nothing, though he did have two cocktails. They had little to say to each other, and it was only seven when they finished their coffee. The curtain had been announced for eight in order to give the critics more time to meet their deadlines; still it was too early to start for the theater, which was only a block away. They sat in silence until Eric, unable to endure it any longer, said, "Well, I guess we may as well go."

355

XXXII.

The sidewalk in front of the Farow was blocked by the crowd that had come to gape at the arriving celebrities and Eric had difficulty in steering his companions through into the space under the marquee that the police were keeping clear.

"Hey, buddy, where are you going?" asked one of the officers. Eric and the two frumpy women did not look like first-nighters to him, and they had to show their tickets before they were permitted to enter. Murray Fineman and Samuel Rothberg, the company manager, were in the lobby. They wished Eric good luck, looking in some surprise at Dorothy and Cousin Elizabeth as he introduced them. They entered the auditorium, almost the first to arrive. He turned the women over to an usher and waited until they were seated before going down the side aisle to the pass-door. He had noticed that not only Fineman and Rothberg but the box-office men were wearing dinner jackets. It had not occurred to him that evening dress might be required; he wondered if he would look conspicuous and out of place in his tweed suit. He had no dinner jacket, but he could have rented one. He wished that he had thought of it or that someone had warned him.

He went straight to the star dressing-room, which Virginia was occupying. The assignment of dressing-rooms often called for delicate handling, for actors were always extremely jealous of their prestige and quick to take offense if they thought that someone was being preferentially treated. The importance of Virginia's part and the frequency of her costume changes entitled her to the stage dressing-room, but, in view of Florence Fulham's seniority and reputation, as well as her special relationship to the Farow Theater, Virginia had generously told Thompson that she would be willing to surrender the room to the older actress. Though he had not accepted the suggestion, he had told Florence of the offer and, deeply touched, she had expressed her gratitude to Virginia. "Tommy told me how sweet you were about the dressing-room, darling. But you have every right to it and I'm very happy up there in my cozy little cubbyhole. My starring days are over, and I'm not a bit sad about it. Besides, I don't think I could ever face sitting in that room again and living with all those memories. But thank you, just the same, for being such an angel."

Eric entered the little reception room, where Pearl was busy removing the cards from the dozens of flowerboxes and packages that filled the room. He assumed that his own modest offering was somewhere among them. "Evening, Mr. Kenwood," said Pearl, "I'll tell her you're here." She knocked on the inner door. "Mr. Kenwood to see you, Miss Ginny."

"Yes, all right!" called Virginia.

He entered eagerly but stopped with a sinking feeling as he saw Hugh Mollison seated beside the chaise longue on which Virginia was stretched, smoking a cigarette. She was dressed and ready to go on.

"Hi, Eric," she said. "I think you boys know each other."

"Yes, sure," said Mollison without the least embarrassment. "Well, this is the big night."

"Yes, it is."

"Sit you down," said Virginia, moving her feet to make room for him on the end of the chaise longue. "If you'd like a quick one, Pearl can rustle it up for you."

"No, thanks." He had rehearsed the things he wanted to say to her, but they would have to go unsaid now, for Mollison showed no sign of leaving.

"Did your mother get here all right?" asked Virginia.

"No, she didn't. Something came up at the last minute and she couldn't get away."

"What a shame! And what a disappointment for you both."

"Yes, it is. But my sister's here."

"Well, that's nice. At least the homefolks are represented. All I've got out there is a fat cousin."

"And the press," said Mollison, scowling slightly at the reference to Marion Sweet.

There was a knock, and Gladys Kaye's voice shouted, "Fifteen minutes, Miss Upton!"

357

"I didn't hear you!" called Virginia, trying to control her nervousness. "Why did she have to bring that up?" She swung her feet to the floor. The men rose too. "Tommy wants us on the stage. Well, gents, it's nice to have known you. Drop in sometime and take pot-luck—assuming that I live through this night's proceedings."

"Good luck, Butch!" said Mollison, stooping to kiss her.

"Prenez garde à la peinture!" she said, quickly averting her lips and offering him her cheek. "And now, like the good book says we should, I turn the other cheek."

Eric brushed it with his lips. "Good luck, Ginny," he said. "And thanks."

"You can say that twice in spades," said Virginia with deep sincerity, pressing his hand.

"That goes for me too," said Mollison warmly.

"On your way, men," said Virginia, pushing them out of the room and closing the door.

"Good luck, Mr. Kenwood," said Pearl, shaking Eric's hand. "We'll all be pullin' for you."

Eric walked onto the stage. To his annoyance, Mollison went along. Most of the actors were already there, and Eric wished them luck, shaking hands that were as clammy as his own. When Thompson appeared in a baggy business suit and a soft-collared shirt, Eric felt better.

"Beat it, Mollison," said Thompson. "You're in the wrong theater."

"Blessings on you, little man," said Mollison, blowing him a kiss as he left. A moment later Virginia came on.

"Everybody here?" asked Thompson.

"Yes, sir," said Peter Quirt.

"Well, lads and lassies," said Thompson, speaking slowly and quietly, "this is it! I wouldn't know how to give you a fight talk even if I thought you needed one. We've done all we can do, and it's in the lap of the gods now. So just speak the speech as it is written, neither saw the air with your hands and all that sort of thing, and let's hope that joy will come in the morning. Up to now I've had a fine time. And if I've cracked the whip too hard and bellyached too much, excuse it, please." There was a strong murmur of protest. "Well, I'm glad you feel that way. Because I think you're all wonderful and I'm madly in love with all of you."

358

"And a Happy Easter to you, Mr. Thompson," said Virginia. The actors applauded, and Thompson motioned them to silence, jerking his head toward the unseen audience on the other side of the curtain.

"That's all, Mack," he said. "It's all yours."

"Places, everybody," said McCarthy. "Will you let me know when to go?"

"Yes, Murray will give you the word. About eight-five, I think. Good luck, Eric. I'll still think it's good, no matter what the jury says."

"Thanks, Tommy. I'll never forget all you've done."

"Skip it! That's how I get my fun, when I'm not in bed." But he was pleased by the genuineness of Eric's thanks.

Eric started for the stage door, not wanting to use the pass-door with the audience in the house. "Did you get your wires?" asked the doorman.

"No." There was a pigeonholed mail rack next to the call board, and under his initial he found a dozen telegrams. He stuffed them into his inside pocket, and, afraid that he would be late for the curtain, hurried up the alley, which for once had been thoroughly swept and washed. A long line of taxis and private cars was discharging the first-nighters, who entered the theater, while the onlookers stared and murmured recognition. The house was well filled now, though many of the spectators were still crowded at the back. Eric's seat was in the middle of the seventh row and half-a-dozen people rose resignedly to permit him to squeeze through. His sister and Cousin Elizabeth were waiting anxiously for him. Dorothy moved over so that he could sit between them. In the midst of all these well-dressed and habituated theatergoers the two women looked more incongruous then ever. Dorothy felt conspicuous and ill at ease; Cousin Elizabeth sat frightened and silent, trying vainly to control the trembling of her hands. She had never seen a play and was puzzled by the absence of a screen, failing to understand Dorothy's attempted explanations.

As Eric settled into his seat he was seized by claustrophobic terror. He suddenly realized that it was only his inexperience that had led him to seat himself in the middle of that audience, and it was all he could do to keep himself from pushing his way back into the aisle and running out of the theater. He tried to divert his panic by looking around for familiar faces, and there were a few: well-known actors whom he had seen on the stage or screen and others whom he could not place. He had been told that the critics always occupy aisle seats, and he peered around, wondering which they were, but apparently they had no distinguishing marks. He did see Claire and Anthony Weir seated across the aisle, and two rows in front, Frederic Haig, accompanied by a blond youth with a weak, handsome face.

He looked at his watch. It was seven minutes past eight. The lights were still full up and the audience still coming in. He was thankful there was no orchestra, for he was sure that he could not possibly have sat through even five minutes of that lugubrious tinkling. Another two minutes passed, and he began to be afraid that something had gone wrong backstage: a mechanical mishap, or the sudden illness of one of the actors—Virginia, perhaps! At ten minutes past eight the lights began to dim, and his throat tightened. The man behind Cousin Elizabeth leaned forward to ask her to remove her hat. She was too flustered to understand, and Eric had to help her, his own hands almost as uncontrollable as hers.

The lights were out now. The curtain rose amid friendly applause for Arthur Eckstein's effective setting. Almost every entrance was greeted with applause too, the volume depending upon the actor's reputation and the number of his friends in the audience. Virginia was generously received, but a real ovation was reserved for Florence Fulham, whose return, after so long an absence, to the very stage she had once dominated appealed strongly to the characteristic sentimentality of the sophisticated first-nighters. So loud was the applause that she had to invent some stage business to keep her occupied until she could make herself heard.

Eric sat with half-closed eyes, digging his nails into his palms and swallowing his bitter spittle, far more conscious of Cousin Elizabeth's quaking and of the acute discomfort of Dorothy, wedged in her narrow seat and squirming as the child leaped, than he was of the play. In his misery he was unable to see that the play was having its best performance before its best audience. The mechanics were flawless. The cast, tuned to concert pitch, played with vibrancy and brilliant precision; every point was cleanly and sharply made. The audience sat, quiet and attentive, aware that they were seeing a play that was far removed from the mediocrities to which they were accustomed.

The first act curtain was vigorously applauded; but the house lights came up quickly, and before they were at the full the audience had begun crowding the aisles.

"It isn't over yet," said Eric as Cousin Elizabeth began putting on her hat.

"Then what are they all leaving for?" she asked suspiciously.

"It's the intermission. They're just going out for a smoke."

With a sigh of resignation she put her hat back in her lap. It was long past her usual bedtime and she found it hard to keep awake, particularly since she had not understood one word of the play. Dorothy's face was flushed and she was breathing heavily.

"Are you feeling all right?" asked Eric anxiously.

"Yes, I'm all right," she said rather petulantly, fanning herself with her program. "It's so hot in here, that's all."

"Maybe you'd like to go out and get some air?"

Dorothy looked at the congested aisles. "No, I guess I'd better stay right where I am. Goodness, do they have to smoke that bad? You'd think they could wait until it's over."

As Frederic Haig came up the aisle with his pretty companion he saw Eric and, smiling, held up his clasped hands in token of approval.

"I wish I could get some water," said Dorothy.

"I'll try to get you some," said Eric. He sidled into the aisle and joined the long, creeping procession. More than half the audience was trying to crowd its way to the tiny lobby and the sidewalk, and those who had seats near the stage could make almost no progress. At the rear the ushers were shouting, "Outside, please! Kindly step outside! No smoking in the theater!" Murmuring apologies, Eric elbowed his way downstairs to the lounge. There was a line waiting at the water-cooler. By the time his turn came the warning bell for the second act had already begun sounding and the spectators began moving back to the auditorium. He hastily filled a collapsible paper cup and, holding it close to him to prevent its spilling, started on the long journey back. He had heard no comments on the play, had not even thought to listen for any. The fear that Dorothy might faint, or perhaps give premature birth, drove everything else from his mind. As he moved slowly down the aisle the lights began to dim, and he saw that he could not get back to his seat before the curtain was up. An arm reached out from an aisle seat and pressed his. It was Irina Lanski's. "It's going well," she said, but he hardly heard her. The curtain was up and the six people in his row stood with ill grace while he stumbled past them, balancing the flimsy drinking cup.

"What took you so long?" said Dorothy, eagerly draining the insufficient contents of the cup and then crumpling it. "What'll I do with this?" A man in the row in front of them looked back in annoyance. Eric snatched the cup from Dorothy's hand and threw it under his seat. His temples were throbbing, and he sat rigid, averting his aching eyes from the brightly lighted stage and hearing only a meaningless gabble as the long minutes dragged on. Dorothy was shifting uneasily, and Cousin Elizabeth's head jerked as she tried desperately to keep awake. He hated them both, hated his mother for not being there, hated the audience to whom all this was merely an evening's diversion, hated the critics for their power to destroy him, and hated himself for his childish inability to control his emotions.

He exhaled slowly as the curtain fell to the accompaniment of loud applause. Before it was down he saw a dozen men scurrying up the aisles and assumed, rightly, that these were the critics rushing off to write their reviews. But he was too numbed to care what they did or said. The only thing that mattered was that it was over at last.

The house lights were kept down for the curtain calls, and most of the audience stayed to applaud the actors, who were recalled again and again. They stood bowing and smiling, thrilled by the warmth of the applause, for it was evident that, whatever impression the play had made, the cast had won hearty approval.

Then the lights came up, the exit doors were thrown open, and again the aisles were choked.

"Can we go now?" asked Cousin Elizabeth.

"Yes," said Eric, "but I want to go backstage for a minute first."

"Do you have to?" said Dorothy.

"Well, I'd like to. I want to see Ginny and some of the others."

"Who's Ginny?"

"Miss Upton. The one who plays Rhoda."

"Well, I hope she's nothing like the part she plays," said Dorothy, unable to conceal her shocked disapproval of the play.

"No, hardly," said Eric. He had not expected her to like the play, but she could have had the graciousness to keep quiet about it.

"Go where?" asked Cousin Elizabeth. "Where do we have to go now?"

362

"Up there on the stage, for just a minute," said Eric.

"Well, my goodness," she said shrilly, "how are we going to get up there?"

"Don't worry about it; I'll show you. Only there's no use trying to push through that crowd. Let's just sit here until it thins out a little."

"I'll be glad when I can get a breath of air," said Dorothy. "This place is like an oven. Why do they have to have it so hot?"

"We'll be out in a few minutes," Eric repeated wearily.

When the aisles began to clear he led them around the back and down the side aisle to the pass-door, where twenty people were waiting to get through. Eric held back the heavy, counterweighted iron door while Dorothy helped Cousin Elizabeth up the steep, narrow steps. Then he guided them carefully, past the switchboards and the stacked props, onto the stage, where Thompson and Claire stood, surrounded by a large group of chattering friends.

Thompson caught sight of Eric and waved to him. "Hello, Eric. Folks, this is the author!" What with the strain of the evening and the numerous drinks he had had as he watched the performance from the rear of the theater, he was louder and less self-possessed than usual. He rattled off a string of unintelligible names. Eric confusedly acknowledged the introductions and murmured thanks for the compliments he received. He felt awkward and self-conscious in the midst of these glib, smart people, and he could see Claire's disapproval of his appearance. Indeed, he was not a prepossessing figure, with his hair rumpled, his tie askew, and his coat pocket bulging with telegrams and the bulky theater program.

Thompson waved to some friends who had just come onto the stage. "Are you coming to the party, Eric?" he said.

"What party?" asked Eric.

"Well, Claire will tell you about it," said Thompson, moving off to greet the newcomers.

"Yes, do come," said Claire in angry embarrassment. She had not intended to ask Eric to her first-night gathering. It was customary for her to invite forty or fifty people to supper after the opening of a new Leroy Thompson production, though in this instance she had hesitated about doing so, having small hope of the play's success and reluctant to spend the money. However, it was expected of her, for the play's backers looked forward to meeting the principal members of the cast and the other theatrical celebrities whom she always invited. Besides, she could deduct the outlay as a business expense on her income-tax return, and that brought the cost down considerably. For a time she had played with the romantic notion of having the party in Oscar Farow's old studio at the top of the theater, but the difficulties of bringing up the food and drink, to say nothing of the guests, in the rickety elevator, decided her against it. So, as usual, she had engaged a private dining-room in a fashionable East Side restaurant. The author of the play was invariably invited as a matter of courtesy and of business policy, and Thompson had assumed that she had asked Eric. But her dislike for him was so great that she had not done so, and she was furious at Thompson for placing her in this awkward position.

"Well, I'd like to come," said Eric, "but I have my sister and my cousin with me."

Claire had not noticed Dorothy and Cousin Elizabeth. She stared in angry amazement at the quaking old woman who looked like a scarecrow in her loosely hanging dress, and at the plain, shabby country girl with her grotesquely distended belly. She was outraged at what she thought Eric's audacity in hinting that she invite these two freaks to her party, though he had had no such intention.

"Oh, well, perhaps you can come around afterwards," she said, turning away quickly and entering into a conversation that excluded him entirely.

"I don't want to go to any party, Eric," said Dorothy. "I just want to get to bed. And Cousin Elizabeth should be getting to bed too. She's not used to all this excitement."

"All right," said Eric desperately. "Just let me say a word to Ginny before we go."

He led the way to Virginia's dressing-room. At least fifty people were trying to crowd their way into it, and more were arriving every moment. It was impossible to wait, for the two women seemed on the verge of collapse, so, resignedly, he piloted them to the stage door. More and more people were streaming in by way of the alley, and he had to plead with the crowd to open a lane for them to pass through to the sidewalk. Cousin Elizabeth shrank from the honking of the taxis and the glitter of the electric signs and clung in terror to Eric's arm. He had a hard time persuading her to cross the avenue and almost had to carry her over. When at last he got them up to their room, he suggested food or a hot drink, but they wanted only to go to bed.

364

Eric left them and threw himself headlong on his own bed. His nerves had given way completely, and he lay shaking and gasping and overwhelmed by a feeling of loneliness. It seemed to him that he was always lying alone, in an unfriendly room, waiting for some decision over which he had no control and from which there was no appeal. Dismally he reviewed his carefully made plans to take his mother and sister somewhere for supper after the performance and, when Dorothy went to bed, to sit up talking to Amelia. Then he remembered his promise to telephone her. She was eagerly waiting for the call, but he had no real news. His impressions of the play's reception were blurred, and he could not keep his unhappiness out of his voice. When he hung up he felt he had succeeded only in adding to his mother's misery without in the least diminishing his own.

It was only half-past eleven. The first newspaper reviews would not be out for hours. However, there were several midnight radio commentators who reviewed plays, and he called the desk to ask for a portable radio; there was none available. He wondered whether he should go to Claire's party after all. It was obvious that she did not want him, but he hungered for a little gaiety and conviviality; besides, Virginia was sure to be there. He persuaded himself to swallow his pride and go. Then it occurred to him that Claire had failed to tell him where the party was being given. He flushed with mortification, for he knew that the omission was not accidental. Once again he tried to puzzle out the reason for her unrelenting hostility. He could not know that she had transferred her intense dislike for The Clouded Mirror to its author and unconsciously held him responsible for what she was sure would be a very unprofitable investment.

He was hungry, and, as it was too late for room service, went to a lunch counter and had a hamburger and coffee. He took the early editions of the morning papers back to his room, though he knew that the reviews could not yet possibly have appeared. The papers, however, did carry reprints of the reviews of a play that had opened the night before, and he read the scathing criticisms, wondering if they were a foretaste of what was in store for him, and if so, how he could survive it. For want of anything else to do, he read his telegrams. Thompson, Winternitz, Irina Lanski, Arthur Eckstein, and James Duncan had all sent him their good wishes, and so had several members of the cast. Virginia's message read: "I've never wished so hard for a play to succeed, Eric dear." He read that one over and over, though he had memorized it on the first reading.

Shortly after one his telephone rang. He answered it with the eagerness of a solitary prisoner who welcomes even the sound of the executioner's key. It was Winternitz.

"I got tired of dredging the Reservoir for you," he said, "so I decided to risk a nickel. Where are you? I mean where were you?"

"I've been right here," said Eric.

"I mean, why weren't you at the Tour d'Argent?"

"The Tour d'Argent? Oh, you mean the party? I don't know. I just didn't feel like it." He was afraid that Winternitz would laugh at him if he told him the truth.

"Well, it was even more brilliantly funereal than usual. Just the backing filling itself. But I have tidings for you."

Eric's heart leaped. "Are the reviews out?"

"Whom do you think you're talking to—a news vendor? A personage of my importance does not depend upon such vulgar sources of information." He had called the drama editors of the morning papers, and they had told him the substance of the reviews. They all had reservations about the play, but they were all on the favorable side, and one was decidedly enthusiastic. The radio reviews had been quite good too. "You're not in the White House yet," said Winternitz, "but you're not in the doghouse either. I thought I'd just let you know, so that you could put off hanging yourself until afternoon. It's not that I want to dissuade you from so definitive a solution of the problem of living. It's just that I have an aversion to cutting down bodies before lunch. Why, I can't say, but I attribute it to some intra-uterine quirk."

Eric thanked him profusely for his thoughtfulness. He breathed more easily now. At least he had not been annihilated; at least there was hope. He was eager to see the papers and decided that at three he would go out again for the later editions. Long before that, he fell into a deep sleep.

XXXIII.

He awoke at seven and went out for the late editions of the morning papers. Winternitz had faithfully reported the tenor of the reviews. All of them found faults in the play and dwelt upon its somberness and immaturity; but, without exception, they recognized the quality of Eric's writing and the excellence of his characterizations. One of them referred to him enthusiastically as a new playwright of great potentialities. He was pleased with the general tone of approval, though considerably disturbed by what seemed to him an undue emphasis upon the play's shortcomings. Irina Lanski telephoned while he was rereading the reviews. She cheered him further by telling him that they were far better than she had expected. She was very optimistic about the play's prospects. She had talked to many of the first-nighters, and most of them had been favorably impressed.

He took the newspapers to Dorothy's room, but she had little interest in them. Her one thought was to get home as soon as possible. She said that she would read the reviews on the way and give them to Amelia. Cousin Elizabeth was afraid that they would miss their train and could talk of nothing else. Eric took them to the station, got them settled on the train, and bade them good-by with profound relief.

He went from the station to Thompson's office. Claire was just leaving and, as usual, greeted Eric coldly. Thompson was friendly and in good spirits. "Well," he said. "It looks as though you got away not only with murder but with incest."

There was a heap of newspapers on Thompson's desk. "Are those the afternoon papers?" asked Eric.

"Yes, help yourself."

One or two were rather unfavorable, though not nearly as bad as Daniel O'Fallon's in Boston. The others, while qualifying their praise, gave the play serious consideration and recognized it as something out of the ordinary. The cast and production were unanimously acclaimed, Virginia coming off particularly well and receiving high commendation for her first appearance in a tragic role.

While Eric was still reading the reviews Winternitz came in with Albert Pepper, who represented an advertising agency. "Well, Eric, my boy," said Winternitz, "I hope you are as gratified as I was to read of the discovery of a uranium deposit in Nigeria."

Pepper had sketched a layout for a large newspaper advertisement that was to appear the following day, and Winternitz had typed up a dozen excerpts from the reviews. Thompson went over the material carefully, suggesting cuts and substitutions. Unlike many producers, who plucked words and phrases out of their context to give a false impression of a critic's opinion, Thompson never permitted the use of distorted or misleading quotations. Fortunately more than enough had been said in praise of the play and the performances to justify the claim that this was a production well worth the attention of the theatergoing public.

During the discussion Fineman came in and offered Eric his congratulations, which Eric took as an indication of optimism, for he knew that this man of business judged plays solely in terms of their box-office receipts.

"Have you been around to the Farow?" asked Thompson.

"Yes, I just came from there. It's not socko, no line or anything like that, but there's plenty of life there. The boys are busy every minute, people coming to the window, and the phone ringing. I think if we just nurse it along we're going to be okay."

He looked over the advertising layout and protested the cost, suggesting that the size of the display be reduced. Thompson overruled him. "This is no moment to be saving nickels," he said. "If we're going to hit them, let's give them a good wallop right between the eyes."

"Murray is a fascinatingly different character," said Winternitz. "Instead of imbibing Scotch, he exudes it."

Fineman shrugged. "All right, all right! It's not my lettuce."

After lunch Eric walked past the Farow. Four or five people were lined up at the ticket-window. He entered the lobby to give himself the satisfaction of watching them make their purchases. Fineman, who was in the box-office, beckoned to him to come in, and he

368

gladly complied, eager for a glimpse of its mysteries. The space was so narrow that he had to squeeze against the wall to be out of the way of the treasurer and his assistant as they answered the telephones and thumbed through the packets of varicolored tickets in the pigeonholes. He stood there, fascinated, for an hour or more, studying the faces that appeared at the window and wondering how these people, who were coming to see his play, would respond to it. As he often did in trains or restaurants he tried to picture their private lives—their backgrounds, occupations, personal relationships, emotional problems—with no other clue than an inflection, a gesture, the choice of a word, an oddity of dress or manner. They were all there on the same simple errand, yet, in the few moments that the transaction required, each revealed his personality. In turn, they were timid, suspicious, arrogant, jocose, wistful, confused, garrulous, impatient, businesslike. Yet in spite of individual differences, collectively, they constituted that curious entity "the public," to whose common emotions, tastes, and opinions his play must make some appeal if it was to succeed. Each ticket purchaser, no matter what his qualities or deficiencies, became the occupant of a judgment seat in a court of last resort and these men and women, whose foibles and quirks Eric now observed with such cool objectivity, would tonight or tomorrow night be members of that fateful tribunal.

Anxious to find out whether Dorothy and Cousin Elizabeth had arrived safely, Eric went back to his room and called his mother. She had been waiting to hear from him, for Dorothy had talked only of the discomforts of the trip and her intense dislike of the play; but the tone of Eric's voice was instantly reassuring, and she was happier yet when he told her that he was planning to come home for Thanksgiving, which was only two weeks off. He called Virginia's apartment, but, as usual, she was out. She had gone to a beauty salon, her cousin told him, and was going from there to dinner. He clipped out all the reviews and carefully reread them, then, overcome by drowsiness, stretched out on the bed and slept blissfully for two hours.

When he returned to the theater the line at the box-office extended halfway across the lobby. At the gate to the alley Virginia stood, surrounded by a dozen clamorous adolescents, who waved autograph books and fountain pens. She was too occupied to see him, and he waited until she had finished, then hurried after her down the alley.

"Hi, Sophocles!" she said. "How does it feel to be an author?"

"It feels fine. And you should be feeling pretty good too."

"Well, I must say the boys were nice and tactful about me. Just respect for my gray hairs, I guess. Or maybe I remind them of that childhood sweetheart back in Omaha."

She invited him to her dressing-room. As they entered the little reception room, which was filled to suffocation with cut flowers, she said, "Do you mind waiting here in the funeral parlor a minute while I get out of my clothes?"

A few minutes later Pearl asked him to come in. The inner room was filled with flowers too, and on the dressing table were heaps of telegrams and letters, many of them still unopened. Virginia, in her dressing gown, was seated before the mirror, her hair enveloped in a towel to protect it while she made up. "Sit you down," she said, "while I try desperately to correct old Ma Nature's mistakes."

"Thanks for that nice telegram," said Eric.

"And thank *you* for the lovely flowers. I've been a pushover for daffodils ever since I made the acquaintance of Bill Wordsworth at the age of seven plus."

Pearl moved in and out of the room, so that their conversation was necessarily casual. They talked about the reviews and the first-night audience, and Virginia said she had missed him, at the party. Eric told her, not without humor, how Claire had managed to keep him away. "I wish I could figure out what I've ever done to her that makes her dislike me so."

"Consider yourself honored," said Virginia. "I can't think of anybody whose dislike I would rather have—*and* have, when you get right down to it. There is one roly-poly of a tootsie whose effect upon me is definitely emetic. If you are ever looking for a first-rate tearoom hostess, who has been ruined by overexposure to money and high life, just run your finger down the W's and when you get to Weir, stop."

While she talked she was busy with her make-up, and Eric watched the complicated process closely. She covered her face with a thick coating of beige grease paint, daubed her cheeks with rouge and worked it in skillfully with her forefinger. Then, closing her eyes, she patted her face with a huge powderpuff and removed the excess powder with a rabbit's foot. Next, with a tiny brush, she shaped her lips carefully with liquid rouge. She darkened her eyebrows, rubbed blue eyeshadow on the lids, and, holding a little pan of mascara over an alcohol burner to liquefy it, meticulously beaded each eyelash. She added a touch of rouge to her earlobes and a tiny dot to the inner corner of each eye, and finally a drop of belladonna to dilate the pupils.

"Well," she said, surveying herself carefully in a hand mirror, "if that doesn't make them run out screaming, I don't know what will."

"You look beautiful from out front," said Eric. "But I like you better in your natural state."

"Don't be funny. Nobody has ever seen me in my natural state since my second semester in kindergarten. I was named Virginia because my parents thought it was Greek for Medusa." She removed the towel and shook out her glossy red hair.

Pearl came into the dressing-room. "Sorry, Mr. Kenwood, but it's time for us to get dressed."

"Hate to have you go, Eric, but Pearl is easily shocked."

"Who, me?" said Pearl. "I guess it would take a couple of good earthquakes to shock anybody's been around the theater all the years I have."

"Can you have a drink with me after the show?" asked Eric.

"Gosh, I wish I could! But I am bespoken by a pair of night-club addicts who are slowly but relentlessly boring each other to death."

The actors were moving into their places. They welcomed Eric with congratulatory smiles. A new air pervaded the stage. The long weeks of anxious uncertainty were over. The cast had come off well in the reviews, and, what was more important, there was every indication that the play would have a good run. Not only had they been accorded the praise that they craved, but the chilling shadow of economic insecurity had lifted. They felt warmed by the radiance of success.

Eric did not want to sit through the play again. He asked McCarthy if he could watch the performance from backstage. The stage manager found a place for him behind the proscenium arch, where he would not be in the way. Standing there in the darkness, he could look past the portal of the false proscenium to the lighted stage. When the curtain rose he was surprised to see that the spectators in the front rows, on the far side of the auditorium, were also visible. The audience, of course, saw only the small playing area and the actors who were on the scene, but the whole stage was alive with activity as the stage managers and crew performed their duties.

371

They moved with the precision of a corps de ballet, the actors tiptoeing into position for their entrances, the carpenters and property men, wearing felt overshoes to deaden their footfalls, swiftly and expertly changing the settings on the offstage platform and rolling the platforms on and off the moment the curtain fell, McCarthy and his assistants signaling warnings and cues to the curtain men, electricians, and sound operator by means of an elaborate system of lights. Everything was timed to the split second, and every mechanic played a part that was as clearly defined as an actor's. There was no confusion, no lost motion, no faultiness of execution.

Several times during the play Virginia had to hurry to her dressing-room to make a costume change; but in one scene she had so little time that the change had to be made on the stage. As she came off the lighted scene into the semi-darkness, Eric was amazed to see her pull her dress off over her head and stand there, for a moment, wearing only panties and a brassière, while Pearl helped her into the other dress. Actors and stagehands were moving around in every direction, but no one seemed to pay the slightest attention to her.

From time to time Eric looked out at the spectators in the front rows, watching their expressive faces, their changes of mood and variations in attentiveness. It was a vivid demonstration of the power of the stage to rouse the emotions and to create an all-absorbing illusion. Momentarily, at least, this heterogeneous crowd was completely under the spell of a fiction produced by painted mimes, standing before painted scenery, and speaking the lines he had written. Though they knew it was all make-believe, the onlookers were as profoundly moved as they would have been by reality, perhaps considerably more moved, for the arts of the stage gave shape and intensity to characters and events that, in actuality, might seem prosaic and formless. As he stood there in the darkness, hearing his words spoken, watching those faces, and feeling the emotional impact of the invisible hundreds in the theater, Eric had the deep satisfaction of knowing that his was the power to entrance, to stir, to exhilarate. Creation was a lonely joy, and not without pain, but public appreciation linked him to his fellow men and made him feel strong and secure.

He had nothing to do now, and he spent the next days in pleasant idleness, enjoying the sweet taste of success. He lunched or dined with Irina Lanski, Winternitz, or his friends in the cast, paid long visits to the art museums, attended afternoon symphony concerts and recitals. Every evening he went around to the Farow, watching scenes that he particularly liked, sitting in the dressing-rooms, eavesdropping in the lobby and the lounge for comments on the play.

The only disturbing element in this happy life was the elusiveness of Virginia. She seemed never to be free. When she was not at the hairdresser's or posing for magazine photographs, she was busy with her social engagements. Eric asked her to spend the Sunday after the opening with her, but she had accepted an invitation to go to Long Island for the weekend and left immediately after the Saturday night performance.

It was not until the following Friday that she was able to spend some time with Eric. Lunching at Pinelli's, they had little opportunity to talk to each other, for people kept coming to their table to congratulate Virginia. Eric was included in the congratulations, and he was not displeased to find he was now an accepted figure in the theatrical world. Producers and agents shook his hand, newspaper columnists questioned him about his plans for the future, actors smiled upon him as a creator of parts; and he was aware that at distant tables people were pointing him out. It was a new life and an exciting one, but he wished that he could be alone with Virginia.

After lunch they made a tour of the exhibitions in the Fifty-seventh Street art galleries. Here again Virginia kept running into friends or talking to the dealers, many of whom knew her well. He walked back to her apartment with her, but she did not ask him in. He left her at the door, with the feeling that she was rather glad to be rid of him. She had been aloof and impersonal all afternoon, lacking her usual exuberance and vivacity. He brooded over her coolness, wondering if he had done anything to offend her or if she was beginning to be bored with him. He reflected ruefully that there was little room for him in a life that included her exacting professional duties, her social engagements, and, above all, the ever-present Mollison, and he told himself that for his own salvation he had better become reconciled to occupying a minor place on the fringes of her busy existence.

He decided he had better go home for a while and put his thoughts and emotions in order, not only in relation to Virginia but to the new pattern of his life. Besides, there were many things that demanded his attention: leaves to be raked and burned, stormdoors to be put up, the car to be serviced for the winter months. So on the Saturday before Thanksgiving he left for Coltertown.

XXXIV.

Eric was mistaken in thinking that Virginia's aloofness had anything to do with her feelings for him. She was preoccupied with the problem of putting into effect her resolution to break with Mollison. It was not easy, for he lived entirely in his emotions and was impervious to argument or logic.

She had tried to rearrange her living conditions so that it would be difficult, if not impossible, for Mollison to be alone with her. With Marion Sweet in the apartment, he could no longer spend the night there. Further, the part-time maid, who had formerly come mornings so that the afternoons would be clear for Mollison, now came on at one and stayed until Marion got home from her classes. There was therefore almost no time of the day or night when Virginia was alone in the apartment.

She continued to see Mollison frequently, but mostly at restaurants or after-theater parties. Mollison's protests against these evasive tactics grew louder until one night he refused to accept her suggestion that they go to a night club and insisted upon going home with her.

Virginia mixed drinks and tuned in on a dance band at full volume, in the hope of waking Marion.

"Do we have to have that?" asked Mollison.

"It's Freddy Colombo's band, and he may come up with some Gershwin."

Mollison took a long pull on his drink. "Nice place you've got here. I've kind of forgotten what it looks like."

"I'm sorry, Huge. But I've sort of been opening in a show."

"That so? First I've heard of it. Does it play matinees every day, including Sundays?"

374

"I can't go on forever saying no to people who think they want to see me."

"How's that?" he said. "I can hardly hear you, way over there, with that goddam thing on. This sofa used to be big enough for the two of us, but I guess I've put on a little weight."

Virginia crossed the room and sat beside him. "Anything to make Buster happy."

"Ha! Ha! Now I'll tell one."

"Want me to run you up a little snack? There's some Camembert stinking up the refrigerator."

"No, I don't. I just want you to quit stalling."

"Do you have to be unpleasant? Or are you just doing it because you think it amuses me?"

"I could think of a lot of answers to that."

"Well, don't bother," she said. "Oh, did I tell you who was out front tonight?"

"No. And I don't give a damn."

"Well, that disposes neatly of that."

They sat for a long time in silence. Mollison drained his glass, got up to refill it, and then sat down beside her again.

"For Christ's sake, Ginny!" he said with sudden vehemence. "What is it?"

"What is what?"

"What! What! What do you suppose? This! You! Everything! The whole business!"

Unwilling to meet the issue squarely and yet knowing that she could not go on parrying much longer, Virginia was struggling unhappily for an answer when Marion appeared in the doorway, blowzy with sleep and most unattractive in an old flannel dressing gown.

"Ginny, would you mind turning down that thing a little," she said in her deep voice, nodding distantly to Mollison, whom she detested as much as he did her.

"Oh, I'm awfully sorry, darling!" said Virginia, jumping up. "I didn't realize that it was on so loud. Please forgive!" She switched off the radio.

"You don't have to turn it off," said Marion. "Just keep it low."

"No, I hate the damn thing! How about a little drink, now that you're as good as up?"

"No, thanks," said Marion with a noisy yawn. "Good night."

"I forgot all about Marion," said Virginia, when her cousin had gone back to her room. "Poor baby!"

"Baby hippo, I guess you mean," said Mollison. "When is she going to move her fat ass out of here?"

"I honestly don't know, Huge."

"I thought you just lent her the apartment while you were in Boston."

"Well, that was the idea, but she hasn't said anything about leaving, and I guess she just can't face going back to that grim dorm. Nor can I blame her."

"You mean she's staying indefinitely?"

"Well, indefinitely, yes. But that doesn't necessarily mean the same thing as definitely."

"I see. So here she sits, is that it?"

"Well, what do you want me to do? After all, she's my cousin and—"

"Oh, sure, sure!" he said, "and like the feller says, blood is thicker than water. You always *were* strong on family feelings."

"You know that's not what I mean. Only I happen to like her—however hard it may be for you to understand—and I don't quite see myself asking her to get out. Do you?"

"No, not if she means more to you than I do."

"Jesus, that is certainly the most irrational conclusion that anybody has arrived at since Don Quixote was a pup."

"Well," he said, "I don't claim to be an Einstein, but when you rub something under my nose I can smell it." Suddenly he put down his glass and went over to her. "God, Ginny, don't do this to me. I can't take it."

"I'm not doing anything to you," she said, tortured.

He knelt beside her, put his arms around her, and covered her face with kisses.

"Don't, Huge," she pleaded, trying to free herself. "Suppose Marion gets up again." She was horrified to find that he had actually become physically repulsive to her. "Where are you going?" she asked as he got up and walked to the door.

"I'm going to lock the door."

"No, don't!" she said in alarm. "How do you think that would look? You might have a little consideration for me."

He stood staring at her, his hand on the door, then walked slowly back to her. "Who is it—that four-eyed bastard Kenwood?"

376

"Who is what?" she asked, amazed that he could be so intuitive and yet so wide of the mark.

"Hanging around, always hanging around," said Mollison. "Giving you the eye and looking down his snotty little nose at me as if I didn't belong. Well, maybe I can't give out with the poetry and the philosophy, but I'm still man enough to take a poke at him, and, by God, I will, the next time he gets in my way."

"You're as crazy as a coot, Huge," she said, not taking his bluster too seriously, but glad, nevertheless, that Eric was in Coltertown. "It's nothing like that at all."

He paid no attention to what she said. "So we're washed up, is that it?"

"No, it isn't," she said desperately. "Of course, we're not washed up. You and I could never not be friends. You know that damned well."

He laughed bitterly. "Friends, huh? Well, that'll be nice. What do you say we go skeet-shooting on Decoration Day? Or is that the day you're planning to tell Marion about the birds and the bees?"

She went to him and put her hands on his shoulders. "Sit down, Huge, and let's talk as if we were a couple of people."

"Talk! Talk! Talk!" he said, flinging her off roughly. "I'll buy you a lecturer and a couple or three authors for Christmas." He put on his coat and hat.

"Don't go yet!" she pleaded. "Not like this! Please!"

"Kiss Marion good night for me," he said and left.

Virginia went to the window and saw him come out of the house. He did not look up but walked down the street with his head lowered. When he had disappeared around the corner she threw herself on the sofa, her hands locked under her head, and lay there staring at the ceiling. The sordid quarrel had made her feel unclean. She was worried about Mollison too; but what she felt was a guardian's sense of duty to a wayward and irresponsible charge. She knew now, surely, that he could never touch her emotions again.

She did not hear from him next day and thought she had better not call him. During the intermission at the Farow she called the Stuyvesant and, disguising her voice, asked what time the performance would be over. The box-office man's routine answer assured her that everything there was proceeding normally.

On Wednesday there was still no word from Mollison. Because of the Thanksgiving Day matinee, the usual Wednesday afternoon performance at the Farow had been canceled, for business did not warrant giving three matinees. At the Stuyvesant, however, where Give Them All My Love was still playing to capacity at all performances, there were matinees both Wednesday and Thursday. Virginia had planned to go to a musical comedy that she wanted very much to see, but, uneasy about Mollison, she went to the Stuyvesant instead. She waited until the curtain was up before asking the ticket-taker, who knew her, to let her in. Every seat was occupied, and she joined the standees at the back of the theater. Mollison was already on the stage, and Virginia was alarmed by his wavering and uncertain performance. He hardly knew what he was doing and was getting through it only by force of his long years of stage discipline. Fortunately the unsuspecting audience took his fuzziness and hesitation as part of his characterization and heartily enjoyed it.

Virginia did not know what to do. To go backstage would look very strange indeed; besides, there was no telling how Mollison might react to her presence. She saw that Murray Fineman was watching the performance closely, evidence that the management, at least, knew what was going on. Fineman had not seen her come in, and she slipped out before the curtain fell on the first act. She did not want to discuss the matter with him. He was anything but subtle, and her position was a difficult one. If Thompson had been available she might have brought herself to talk to him, but he had left for Florida several days before to spend a few weeks with his parents.

That night Virginia had trouble getting through her own performance, with Mollison continually on her mind. During the intermission she called the Stuyvesant again to make sure that the performance was being given there.

She went straight home from the Farow without stopping to remove her make-up, afraid Mollison might call and involve Marion in some embarrassing discussion. Her cousin was already asleep. Virginia took off her make-up and went to bed; but her troubled thoughts kept her awake for hours. She had hardly fallen asleep when she was aroused again by the insistent ringing of the downstairs buzzer. She sprang out of bed, put on her dressing gown, and went out into the hall, unable to decide whether or not to answer. To make matters worse, Marion stumbled sleepily into the hall. "Oh, you're home." She looked at her wristwatch. "Heavens, it's nearly three!"

"Is it?" said Virginia as the clamor continued. "I guess I'd better answer that damned thing."

"You're not going to let anybody in at this hour, are you?" said Marion nervously.

"I'm afraid it's that or listening to it ring all night."

Suddenly the ringing stopped. They waited tensely for a few minutes, but it was not resumed.

"Well, that seems to be that," said Virginia.

"Don't you think you ought to call the police?"

"No, of course not! Burglars don't go around ringing doorbells. You go back to bed."

"Well, if you think it's all right."

"Certainly, it's all right."

Marion went back to her room. Virginia, knowing well that this was not the end, went into the living-room. Three minutes later the telephone rang, and she picked it up quickly.

" 'Lo, Ginny, that you?" said Mollison thickly.

"Yes, hello."

" 'Lo, Ginny, this is me. Been ringing—ringing your doorbell. Couldn't find my key. Funny thing, couldn't find it. Looked everywhere. Couldn't find it. Whassa matter, didn't you hear me ringing your doorbell?"

"I must have been asleep."

"Yeah, funny thing about that key."

"Where are you?"

"What's that? Where am I? Oh, sure, sure. Right here in the drug-store. Right around the corner in a drugstore. I'll be right over, right away."

"Look, Huge, you'd better go to your hotel and get some sleep. It's awfully late and you've got two shows tomorrow."

"Okay, I'll be right over."

"No, I said it's awfully late and—"

"Yeah, sure is. Later'n hell. Okay, I won't be a minute. I'm in a drugstore, right around the corner," he said and hung up.

Marion was standing in the hall as Virginia hurried back to her bedroom. "What is it? Is anything wrong?"

"No, nothing's wrong. Please do me a favor and go back to bed. If I need anything, I'll call you."

"All right, but be sure to call me if you do need me."

"Yes, I promise you I will."

379

She was just slipping her dress over her head when the buzzer began sounding again. She pressed the latch button and, opening the door, stood there waiting while he stumbled up the three flights of stairs.

" 'Lo, sweetheart," he said, kissing her. "Hope I didn't wake you up."

"No, it's all right. Come on in."

She steered him into the living-room and closed the door.

"Funniest goddam thing about the key," he said, plumping down on the sofa. "Turned my whole goddam room upside down, looking for it. I need a little drink. But don't you bother, sweetheart. No, don't you bother one little bit. I'll get myself my own drink." He tried to rise but collapsed again.

"No, you stay right there and let me get it for you."

"Well, that's awful sweet of you, honey—awful sweet. Sure I didn't wake you up?"

"Yes, quite sure."

"Tha's good. One thing I wouldn't want to do is wake you up." He reached out an uncertain hand for the glass and took a long swallow. "Ah-h! I needed that." He winced. "Feet hurt. Two shows today, hard on your dogs. Min' if I take off my shoes?"

"No, of course. Here, let me help you," she said as he fumbled aimlessly at the laces. She knelt and took off his shoes.

"Much obliged, honey," he said, stroking her hair. "Damn sweet of you." A look of cunning came over his face. "Got a funny story to tell you. This'll kill you when you hear it. Funniest damn story you ever heard." He sat chuckling and shaking his head.

"Well, what's the story?"

"What? What story? Oh, yeah, sure! Funniest story you ever heard. Well, Fineman—you ever know Fineman? Murray Fineman!"

"Yes, I know him."

"Listen to me, will you? Why, sure you know him! Murray Fineman, Tommy's gen'l manager. 'Course you know him!"

"What about him?"

"Well, after the show—this'll kill you—Murray Fineman, see, he goes around to the hotel with me. Wants to keep me company, see? Sweet guy, Murray. So we go upstairs and we have a little drink, coupla little drinks and Murray says, 'Hugh,' he says, 'how's about going to bed? Two shows today, two shows tomorrow, two shows Saturday. Little man, you had a busy day. Need lots o' sleep.' Well,

380

I don' wanna go to bed, see? I got a date with you and I don' wanna go to bed. Only I play it foxy and tell him, 'Sure, Murray, good idea, time to go to beddy-by.' " He simulated a loud yawn, then laughed again. "So Murray watches me get undressed, see? 'Goo' night, Hugh,' he says. 'Goo' night, sweet prince,' I say. You know, book about Jack Barrymore. But he doesn't get it. Well, what the hell do you expect? He's nothing but a gen'l manager. Nice guy, but just a gen'l manager. D'you ever see Jack Barrymore?"

"No, I'm afraid not."

" 'Course you didn't! What the hell am I talking about? Way before your time. Greatest goddam actor I ever saw!" He pulled himself to his feet and gesticulated vaguely. " 'Oh, what a rogue and pleasant slave I am!' No, that's not right. 'Oh, what a rogue—' Ah, to hell with it! I used to know the whole thing." He sank into the sofa again. "Mos' won'erful acting I ever saw. What was I starting to tell you?"

"About how, when Murray left, you got up and got dressed again and came around here."

He looked puzzled for a moment, but then his face cleared. "Oh, I *did* tell you that! Good old Murray! 'Oh, that this too, too solid flesh would melt!' Wouldn't mean a thing to him. Box-office, that's all he knows. Sweetheart, know what I'd like?"

"Coming up," said Virginia, taking his glass.

"How'd you guess it?" He yawned, this time genuinely sleepy. "One more drink and then whaddye say we go to bed?"

"In a little while," said Virginia, giving him the drink. "I'm not sleepy yet. Why don't you put your feet up?"

"That's a good idea. Should have thought of that sooner. Two shows a day and walking around looking for a drugstore." She put a pillow behind him, and he leaned back against it. "Feels good. Boy, I'm tired. Must be getting late." He yawned again. "Why don't we go to bed?"

"In a little while." She saw that there was no possibility of getting him to leave, so she got up and turned off the lights.

"Good idea," he said. "Damn theater lights ruin your eyes. I'm getting as blind as a bat. Where are you, honey? Where's your hand?"

She sat beside him and gave him her hand. He raised it to his lips and kissed it and then kept holding it. He rambled on for a while, then sank into an exhausted sleep. Virginia went to the bedroom for a quilt and, wrapping herself in it, spent the rest of the night in an armchair, dozing off occasionally but waking with a start every time Mollison moved. At nine she heard Marion in the kitchen and went in to have breakfast with her.

"I'm sorry about all this, tootsie," said Virginia, seeing how troubled her cousin was, "but it's just one of those things."

"Maybe I shouldn't be here," said Marion.

"No, no, please! This is the pay-off, honestly it is. You've been a life-saver to me, so please don't walk out on me now."

She went back to the living-room. Mollison was still sound asleep, breathing heavily. She did not know what to do. She had to be at the Farow for her matinee; she could not leave Mollison in the apartment, yet was afraid of waking him, not knowing how he would behave. If his wife had been in New Canaan she would have called her, distasteful though it would have been, but Cecilia had gone to Wisconsin with the two children, to spend the holiday with her family. And Thompson was in Florida. There was no one to whom she could appeal for help but Fineman; and it was not easy for her to call him, for though her relationship to Mollison was no secret, she shrank from bluntly telling this businessman that the actor had spent the night in her apartment. She put it off, fearful that Mollison would wake up, yet half hoping that he would. The hours dragged by, and she had just decided to call Fineman, after all, when he called her, embarrassed and apologetic.

"Sorry to bother you, Ginny," he said, "but I'm trying to run down Hugh. You wouldn't know where I could find him, would you?" He had gone around to Mollison's hotel when the actor failed to answer the telephone. No one had seen him go out, but the chambermaid had reported that the room was in wild disorder. He had indeed turned everything upside down in his search for the key that Virginia had made him return to her.

"Yes, he's right here," said Virginia, too agitated to care how it sounded.

"Boy, I'm glad to hear it," said Fineman. "Is he all right?"

"He's asleep on my living-room sofa at the moment. It's anybody's guess what he'll be like when he wakes up."

"Is it all right if I come around?"

"Yes, I wish you would, Murray. In fact, I was just going to call you."

"I'll be right over."

Marion, who was going to have Thanksgiving dinner with some classmates, was hovering about, not wanting to leave Virginia alone. Virginia persuaded her to go. A few minutes later Fineman arrived with Winternitz.

"I hate to chase you out of your apartment, Ginny," said Fineman, "but I think we can handle him easier if you're not here."

"I think maybe you're right," said Virginia, eager not only to avoid another encounter with Mollison but to escape a situation that she found extremely painful and humiliating.

She was out in five minutes and the two men set to work to rouse Mollison, no easy task. It took them a good half-hour to overcome his resistance and get him to his feet. He was sodden and sullen and looked about in bewilderment, unable at first to understand where he was and how he had got there.

"How'd you know I was here?" he asked suspiciously. "Ginny call you?"

"No," said Fineman, "you told me last night you were coming here."

"Oh." He did not believe Fineman but was not sure enough of himself to call him a liar. "Where *is* Ginny?"

"She had to go to the Farow early for a rehearsal," said Fineman glibly. "Flossie Fulham's got a sore throat and the understudy may have to go on at the matinee." He looked at his watch. "You've got a matinee yourself."

"Have I ever missed a performance since the crummy show opened?"

"No, you have not. And there's not many actors you could say as much for."

"All right then, shut up about it!"

They got him into a taxi and back to his hotel room, waited while he bathed and shaved, and made him drink three cups of hot coffee. It was after two when they arrived at the theater. It took him so long to make up that the curtain was nearly fifteen minutes late. He got through the first act well enough, giving a listless performance but making no serious errors. However, during the intermission, he locked himself in his dressing-room lavatory where he had a bottle concealed. By the end of the play his speech was thickening again and he had to be prompted repeatedly.

Winternitz succeeded in persuading him to stay in his dressing-room between performances and sat with him trying to keep him amused while his dresser went out for coffee and sandwiches. Fineman, feeling that things were rapidly getting out of hand, reluctantly put in a call to Florida.

Ten days after the opening of The Clouded Mirror, Thompson had gone to Jacksonville to spend several weeks with his parents, whom he had not seen in over a year. His father, who had had a long and very successful career as a surgeon in Syracuse, had retired from practice five years before and settled in Florida. Thompson was on good terms with his parents, particularly his mother, who, because of his disfigurement, had always favored him, and he looked forward to seeing them.

For weeks, he had been working at top speed. Now that the play was successfully established, he felt the need of a vacation. The performances were running smoothly and his staff was well qualified to handle the business and publicity details. He was planning to put a touring company of Give Them All My Love in rehearsal in mid-December and to open it in Chicago in January. There was no doubt that the play would be a success there. Its fame had spread and Chicago was awaiting it. For the star part he had engaged John Ettrick, who, though not as well known as Mollison, was an excellent comedian and a great favorite with Chicago audiences. Rehearsing a second company was a simple but rather tedious task, and Thompson wanted a few weeks' relaxation before undertaking it.

He felt, too, an urgent need for solitude. Without clearly understanding why, he had a sense of impending crisis and wanted to put his thoughts and feelings in order. When Louise Henry's plane crashed, he had been able to survive only by encasing his wounded spirit in a hard, impervious shell of cynicism and calculated coldness. For more than four years he had been living in a vacuum, finding such satisfaction as he could in his work and in the indulgence of his appetites and allowing himself to feel nothing. But lately he had become increasingly conscious of his emotional emptiness and disturbed by the feeling that he was only half alive.

It perplexed him to find that he could not think of Lily without shame. Though she was a silly and shallow girl, who enjoyed wallowing in soupy romance and took a masochistic delight in enacting the role of a tragic heroine, his self-esteem had suffered severely. Proud of his self-mastery, he felt that his behavior had been lacking in taste and in judgment. Yet that, in itself, hardly accounted for his obsessive self-criticism; and, puzzling over it, he came to the surprising

384

conclusion that he was judging his conduct in terms of what Virginia's appraisal of it might be.

This strange reference to Virginia seemed to apply also to his feelings about Claire. After the Sunday at Poundridge when he asked Virginia to replace Emily Crandall, he saw Claire—unconsciously at first, but then more and more consciously—as he fancied she appeared to Virginia. His dissatisfaction with the whole relationship grew, not because of any change in Claire or any disillusionment on his part, but simply because he could not endure the thought that Virginia might see him as cheap, venal, or insensitive.

He was just sitting down to Thanksgiving dinner when Fineman's call came through. The news was disturbing but not unexpected. Ever since Mollison had told him of his fears about Virginia, he had been waiting for something like this to happen; somehow it strengthened his belief that he was approaching a climax in his life. He felt exhilarated by this call to action, for his idleness was already beginning to bore him. He told Fineman that he would try to get to New York by morning; that, in any case, the Give Them All My Love company should start rehearsing at eleven with Mollison's understudy, George Hamlin. Then, afraid that Claire might do something to worsen matters, he asked Fineman to try to keep the news from her until he arrived in New York.

Fineman and Winternitz kept Mollison under constant supervision until curtain time; but once the evening performance had begun they could no longer control his frequent visits to his dressing-room. By the third act he was so unsteady that he had to play most of his scenes sitting down and had to be constantly prompted not only by the stage managers but by his fellow actors. The audience could not fail to notice that something was wrong. There was little applause when he appeared for his solo curtain call.

Virginia learned from Fineman that Thompson was on his way back. Exhausted by the preceding night's experiences and by the day's two performances, she decided not to subject herself to another unpleasant session with Mollison. She felt she had fulfilled her responsibilities and was under no further obligation to minister to his weakness and his inability to face reality. Thus she found a logical, if not altogether satisfying, answer to her self-accusations of ruthlessness.

When she got home she tacked up a notice on her letterbox to the effect that the doorbell was out of order. Then she stuffed out the telephone bell with paper to deaden the sound, told Marion not to get up no matter what happened, and went to bed. She was awakened, shortly after one, by the buzzer, and sat up, holding her hand to her thumping heart. After five minutes it stopped, and she was not disturbed again.

Because of the heavy holiday travel Thompson had trouble getting space on a plane and did not arrive in New York until three the next afternoon. He went straight to the Stuyvesant, where everybody's nerves were on edge. The company had been rehearsing all day with George Hamlin. Claire had got wind of what was going on and had come in, leaving a houseful of guests at Poundridge. Her presence had not helped matters; but with Thompson in charge again there was a general improvement in morale.

From Fineman, Thompson got the disquieting news that Mollison had disappeared. He had not spent the night at his hotel, Virginia had not heard from him, and Winternitz was making the rounds of the actor's usual haunts. It was a disturbing state of affairs, not because Mollison was likely to come to any harm, but because he might become involved in some incident that the newspapers would get hold of and play up. To notify the police would be to invite publicity too. So there was nothing to do except continue the search quietly. Cecelia Mollison arrived at the theater shortly after Thompson. He had telephoned her in Wisconsin from Jacksonville, and she had come on by plane, leaving the children with her family. She took the situation with her usual calmness and called several places the others had not thought of. Mollison had either not been there or had gone on somewhere else.

Thompson rehearsed the company until after six. Hamlin knew the part well but was so overwhelmed by the responsibility of actually playing it that he could hardly concentrate. Thompson had dinner with Claire and Cecelia, and when they got back they found Winternitz tired and discouraged. On the chance that Mollison might arrive, Thompson waited until eight o'clock before telling Hamlin to get ready to go on.

At ten minutes after eight Mollison appeared, unshaven, glassy-eyed, and slobbering. Though hardly able to stand or to know what he was saying or doing, the discipline of the theater was so deeply ingrained that he had automatically found his way to the stage door at performance time. He staggered in, announcing truculently that he intended to go on. Humoring him, Thompson guided him to his dressing-room and sat with him while he fumbled helplessly with powder and rouge.

386

When he got up to go to the wash basin his knees gave way, and his dresser and Thompson helped him into an armchair, where he slumped with sagging head and drooping lids.

The audience groaned when the stage manager announced that, because of illness, Mollison would be unable to appear and that those who wished refunds could obtain them at the box-office. There was a great buzz of conversation as the spectators tried to make up their minds whether to go or stay, then some started to leave, and, before long, nearly a quarter of those present were crowding into the aisles and lining up at the box-office. It took fifteen minutes before the hubbub subsided sufficiently for the performance to begin.

Meanwhile Cecelia had engaged rooms for Mollison and herself at Doyle's Sanitarium, a small private hospital in the East Seventies, run by a doctor who specialized in the care of well-to-do alcoholics. Mollison had been there several times before. To get him out of the theater without attracting attention was not easy. When the refunds had been made and the street was relatively empty, Fineman and the dresser hurried him up the alley and into a waiting limousine. He resisted going, dimly aware that the performance was on; but Cecelia assured him that it was only a rehearsal and that she was taking him for a drive to clear his head.

Thompson went out front. He was not surprised that the play was not going well. Hamlin was a competent actor and played creditably, but the audience had come to see Mollison. Many of them were suburbanites or out-of-town visitors who had had their tickets for weeks, or even months, and had been looking forward to a great treat. The feebleness of their applause at the final curtain was expressive of their disappointment and dissatisfaction.

After the performance Fineman, Winternitz, and Claire went to Thompson's apartment for a solemn council. "Well," said Thompson, "we'd better try to make up our minds where we go from here."

"It would serve that souse good and right if we filed charges against him," said Claire with shrill indignation.

"That's a wonderful idea," said Thompson. "We file charges, Equity suspends him, the newspapers have a field day, we give the poor bastard a black eye and make an enemy of him for life; and then where the hell are we?"

"You mean we're just going to let him get away with this?"

"Look, I'm interested in keeping the show running. Let's leave poetic justice to Euripides."

387

Since Fineman and Winternitz agreed with Thompson, Claire did not persist in her vindictiveness. "How much did you have to refund, Murray?" she asked.

"Over a thousand smackers."

"Good heavens! And that George Hamlin certainly turned in a nice performance, didn't he? What a ham he turned out to be!"

"He's an understudy," said Thompson. "Nobody ever claimed he was Edwin Booth."

"You seem to have an alibi for everybody tonight," she said pettishly.

"Well, as somebody said to somebody, you're only interested in art and I'm only interested in business."

Claire bit her lip. "So you're just going ahead with Hamlin, is that it?"

"For tomorrow's performance, yes."

"And then what?"

"I'm going to try to talk Johnny Ettrick into taking over until we get Hugh back on his feet."

"Say, that's a hell of a good idea!" said Fineman.

"What do you think, Doc?"

"Compared to Hamlin, emphatically yes," said Winternitz.

"Compared to closing the show. Nobody knows how soon they can get Hugh back in circulation or how dependable he'll be when he does get back. I'm for playing it safe and announcing Ettrick for four weeks. You can dream up something about a long-deferred vacation, Doc."

"A generous tribute to my imagination, Tommy."

"What about the Chicago company?" asked Claire.

"Chicago will be good in February or even in March," said Thompson. "We're up against a situation, so let's not waste time blowing soap bubbles."

"How long will it take you to get Ettrick ready?" asked Fineman.

"If we start Sunday he ought to be able to open a week from Monday."

Fineman whistled. "Phew! Another whole week with Hamlin. It'll be murder."

"Murder is exactly what it would be. We'll have to close the show for a week."

"Close for a week!" exclaimed Claire, panic-stricken. "Why?"

"Because we can't get away with Hamlin," said Thompson calmly. "The customers won't take him, and I don't blame them. We'll have

388

to refund at every performance and we'll give the advance sale such a wallop that it'll never come back. Once you get them staying away, they stay away by the millions. If we're going to do this, and I don't see what other choice we have, we've got to make a clean job of it. Build up Ettrick for all he's worth and close until he's ready. Anyhow, to get him ready in ten days I'll have to rehearse day and night and that leaves no time for performances."

Claire argued and protested, appalled by the prospect of disrupting the run of the play and of the heavy loss that would result. Winternitz heartily supported Thompson; Fineman too had to admit reluctantly that there seemed no alternative.

"What if Ettrick won't do it?" said Claire when she was forced to yield.

"I haven't figured out the answer to that one," said Thompson. "But I'm hoping I can sell him the idea."

Claire did not leave with Fineman and Winternitz, and Thompson saw that he was in for a scene. She wasted no time in beginning it. "Well," she said the moment they had gone, "I hope you had a good time humiliating me in front of Murray and Doc."

"Is that what I did? I wasn't aware of it."

"I know that you're this great genius who has to have his own way in everything and that you think I'm just a fool who doesn't understand anything except how to sign checks. But if I do say so myself, I know my way around the theater and I've shown pretty good judgment about it too; and I'm getting sick and tired of always being insulted in front of your employees."

"I wish I knew what you're talking about. We had an important decision to make and I expressed my opinion, that's all. If you take it into your head to get insulted because I don't always agree with you—"

"Oh, don't play so dumb about it!" she said angrily. "You know damn well what I mean. It's not a question of agreeing or disagreeing. There are ways of doing things. You can disagree with somebody without a lot of smart cracks and snide remarks."

"We're in a tight spot here, and I guess I was more interested in trying to think of a way out of it than in following the book of etiquette."

"Who the hell is talking about etiquette? It's your whole attitude, acting so sarcastic and superior, treating me like some little stenographer or like some moron who doesn't know beans when the pot's

389

open." She launched into a recital of her grievances, citing numerous examples of his derogatory treatment. He made only a feeble attempt to justify himself—the sooner she got rid of her accumulated resentment, the sooner she would go.

Her tirade was interrupted by a telephone call from Virginia, who was anxious for news of Mollison. No one had thought of informing her. Thompson told her briefly what had happened; and guessing from his manner that he was not alone, and that it was probably Claire who was with him, she soon hung up, satisfied that Mollison was in Cecelia's competent hands.

Claire, who had listened hostilely, began a new line of attack. "Well, it's nice and considerate of her to be so interested in poor Hugh," she said.

"Oh, so now it's poor Hugh! A minute ago he was the louse of the world. And why wouldn't she be anxious to find out about him?"

"Yes, why wouldn't she? Considering that she's responsible for the whole thing."

"Responsible for what? For Mollison not being able to handle his liquor?"

"You know very well that none of this would have happened if she hadn't walked out on him. So why put on this act of defending her?"

"You're way ahead of me. You mean I ought to be sore at Ginny because she happened to decide that she's through with Hugh?"

"Well, it's perfectly obvious that if she had stuck to him he wouln't have cracked up like this."

Thompson stared at her in astonishment. "Are you suggesting that in order to help us out of a jam she should go on sleeping with a guy she no longer cares for? What do you think she is, some kind of a call girl?"

"Oh, you can always twist anything anybody says to make a person look in the wrong. She wasn't so finicky about sleeping with him, for God knows how many years, and flaunting it in everybody's face in the bargain—going around with him in public and even spending weekends under the same roof with his wife."

"And you had plenty to say about it too. I've heard you sound off by the hour about what a disgrace it all was. But now that we're having a little trouble at the Stuyvesant you're telling her off for not being willing to make a whore of herself."

"Well, of course you'd stick up for her or anybody else just as long

390

as you could put me in a bad light. But even if I am a nitwit and heaven knows what else, we'd all be a lot better off if you'd taken my advice about not producing that damn Kenwood play."

"Christ!" said Thompson, wrinkling his brow, "you move faster than a pea in a shell game. What's The Clouded Mirror got to do with what we're talking about?"

"Everything. We've had nothing but trouble since you got mixed up with it. First all that business with Emily Crandall—"

"What the hell has Emily Crandall—!"

"Let me finish, please! Then your insisting that Ginny play the part. And then, of course, she has to fall for that uncouth hick of an author and leave Mollison flat. What she can see in that corn-fed baboon is more than—"

"Wait a minute!" said Thompson, paying serious attention to her for the first time. "Are you trying to tell me that Ginny and Eric—"

"All you have to do is use your eyes. He's always mooning around after her as though she were Cleopatra or somebody. And they're always at Pinelli's or what have you. Just last week I was taxiing through Fifty-seventh Street and I saw them coming out of one of those art galleries as chummy and dreamy-eyed as a couple of honeymooners. They're so damn superior, both of them, so arty and high-brow. Where they belong is in the little theater movement, not on Broadway where people are looking for good entertainment and not for a bunch of snooty debutantes dishing up a lot of dirty, morbid psychology."

Thompson now saw clearly what was at the root of all Claire's complaints. The Clouded Mirror was not a smash hit, that is, a play that did capacity business over a long period and brought in huge profits. On the basis of mail orders, window sale, and agency demand, the indications were that Eric's play could be kept running for a good many months to substantial business, but at a margin of profit too narrow to recoup either the heavy production cost or Claire's equally heavy investment in the Farow. So, while Eric was getting his very handsome royalties and Thompson was enjoying the prestige and satisfaction of having made a distinguished production, and the actors were being well paid and highly praised, Claire was in the exasperating position of having a play in her theater that was doing well enough to warrant its indefinite continuance but not well enough to bring in more than a small trickle of profit. Oppressed by her financial worries, she was irritated by the satisfaction that everyone took in the play's reception, and her ever-growing animosity to all those involved had extended even to Thompson.

Having given vent to her feelings, she was, as usual, eager for a reconciliation. There was no one in her life who was as close to her as he, and he still attracted her strongly both physically and emotionally. So she began to relent, hinting that she had let her wounded feelings distort her judgment and had been needlessly vehement. She even hoped that he would invite her to spend the night and was quite prepared to leave her guests in Poundridge to their own devices. Thompson, though readily accepting her apologies, remained aloof and impersonal. At last she gave up and drove despondently to the country.

Next morning, when Thompson called John Ettrick's hotel, he was disturbed to learn the actor was away for the holiday weekend and would not be back until Sunday night or Monday morning. He was anxious to get things settled with Ettrick, but there was nothing to do but wait.

Cecelia called, and her report was not encouraging. Mollison had had a bad night, had developed a bronchial cough, and there was danger of pneumonia. A whole series of X-ray examinations and laboratory tests was being made; until the results were known, there could be no definite diagnosis. Thompson offered to come to the hospital, but visitors had been strictly forbidden. In consultation with Winternitz he prepared a carefully worded press release to the effect that Mollison had bronchitis and that the play would close for a week, with the expectation that the star would be able to resume performances at the end of that time. They thought it best not to make any mention of Ettrick until he assented. Winternitz telephoned the announcement to the dramatic editors for Monday release. They were all well aware of the true state of affairs, but since the statement was colorably true they agreed to publish it without comment.

Thompson, after working for an hour at the Stuyvesant with George Hamlin, stayed only long enough to watch the stampede to the box-office when the announcement of the substitution was made. He thought it politic to telephone Claire but declined her invitation to come to Poundridge that night. He did agree to come up for Sunday lunch, knowing there would be other guests.

After the Saturday night performance Thompson informed the cast of Give Them All My Love of the enforced lay-off. The actors took

392

the news glumly. The play had been running to capacity business for nearly a year, and there had been every indication that it would run for at least another year. Now they faced the likelihood of a sudden termination of their employment. They could not believe that Mollison would be able to return in a week, or that, even if he did, he could be depended upon. Thompson tried to convey to them that he had other plans for keeping the play running, but since he did not think it wise to mention John Ettrick they did not find his vague hints very comforting.

Virginia was waiting for him at the Farow. He wanted to see her, for both business and personal reasons, and had sent around a note asking her to have a drink with him after the performance. He thought that Mollison's collapse might have brought about another change of heart in her, in which case he would have to take into account the probability of the actor's speedy rehabilitation. There was something else on his mind too. Though he had dismissed as absurd Claire's conjecture that it was a growing interest in Eric that had drawn Virginia away from Mollison, he had not been able to get it out of his thoughts and he wanted to be reassured by her.

"Where shall we go?" he asked her.

"I was taught always to leave that to the gentleman."

"Well, I don't feel up to any Saturday hot-spot. Couldn't we just go around quietly to your place?"

"I'm afraid we might find my fat cousin holding hands with the bishop. How about your little air-conditioned pied à terre? That is, unless you think we might wake up some blonde." She thought it might be easier to leave his apartment than to get him out of her own.

"They never check in before two," said Thompson.

"Oh, good! Then I'll beat it when the whistle blows for the graveyard shift to come on."

They went to his suite. He ordered supper and a bottle of champagne.

"What are we celebrating?" asked Virginia.

"I always order champagne when I'm feeling lousy. I have a theory that when you're gay you don't need it."

She nodded approvingly. "I like that. I've always been against Christmas, Mother's Day, and Be-Kind-to-Department-Stores Week. I like giving presents when I jolly well feel like it, not when the National Association of Manufacturers tells me to."

"Why, we're as like as two peas!"

"I wouldn't get carried away if I were you. Tell me, what's with the Stuyvesant? I understand that Georgie Hamlin is not the people's choice."

"He's doing the best he can. It just happens that that isn't very good. We're laying off next week."

"Well, I can see why," said Virginia, genuinely worried. "Only then what? Do you really think Huge will be ready to go back in a week?"

"Not a chance. He's really shot." Pledging her to secrecy, he told her of his plan to substitute Ettrick until Mollison was in condition to return.

"Oh, that's a wonderful idea!" she said, momentarily relieved. But her face clouded again. "Only what does that do to your Chicago company?"

He shrugged. "All I can think of now is how to keep the show running here."

The waiter arrived with the supper table and poured the champagne.

Thompson raised his glass. "Here's to the best performance of the year!"

"And to the best sport of the year!" said Virginia with a rush of emotion. She reached across the table and put her hand on his. "Tommy, I can't tell you how rotten awful I feel about all this."

"No reason in the world why you should."

"Oh yes there is; there's every reason. If I hadn't been so tough with poor Huge none of this would have happened—to him, to you, to the show and everybody. What's more, everyone knows it. I suppose, from the gallery, I must look like a first-class selfish, heartless, double-crossing bitch, and sometimes I look that way in the mirror on the wall too. Only what is a girl supposed to do when she comes to the end of something? Yes, if I were dutiful and self-denying I could sit like Patience on a monument. But you might just as well say that if I were Velázquez I could paint the Surrender at Breda. Whoever is to blame, I'm the way I am: too demanding to be satisfied with memories or to feel that just being sorry for someone is enough. Maybe that's hateful, but there seems to be nothing I can do to change myself—and I'm not sure that I'd want to if I could. There! That's the longest speech I've ever made or ever hope to make."

He was conscious of an affinity such as he had never felt for anyone but Louise Henry. "It was a good speech," he said, refilling her glass. "But you don't have to convince me. I'm no little white lamb myself."

"That's gallant but untrue, I'm sure!"

Half mischievously, half seriously, he took direct aim. "Claire seems to think that Eric is the heavy."

She flushed and could not keep her anger out of her voice. "Oh, does she? Well, it's nice to know what other people talk about when they're lying down."

"Just for the record, we happened to be sitting up."

"I've always envied women with speculative minds. Just my frustrated desire to be brainy, I suppose."

"Claire doesn't like Eric very much."

"And so she wishes him the worst fate she can think of, is that it?"

"She's a great one for putting two and two together."

"Yes, I have no doubt. And making it add up to nineteen. Well, since we're keeping the record straight, I *do* like Eric very much. In fact, I'm not sure that I'm not a little bit in love with him."

"Well, you see! Woman's intuition and all that."

"Woman's goddam nosy vulgarity. Eric has nothing whatever to do with Huge, or with anything else for that matter."

"You haven't asked him to marry you or something?"

"No, come to think of it, I haven't. But if he were ten years older I damn well might—not that it's anybody's business."

"Ten years older? That would make him just about my age."

"Would it?" she said uncomfortably. "Well, that certainly is an extremely uninteresting coincidence."

"I don't want to make it look as if I were asking a lot of questions, but why ten years older?"

"I don't know why. It's just that he always makes me feel so ancient, I guess." She looked at her watch. "My God, it's nearly two! I've really got to run."

"Don't go yet."

"Got to. I'm being driven to the country at some ungodly hour."

He tried to persuade her to stay, but the conversation had taken a turn that frightened her, and she was firm. As he helped her with her coat he kept his arms around her neck. She slipped deftly out of the embrace. "Thanks for listening," she said. "And I do hope you make out all right with Johnny Ettrick."

She thought he might try to kiss her, but he merely raised her fingers playfully to his lips. "Küss die Hand, gnädiges Fräulein." This

395

was no ordinary flirtation, and he wanted to see his destination clearly before embarking upon a course from which it would not be easy to turn back.

Sunday at Claire's was uneventful. Thompson was affable and entertaining. She did everything she could to make him feel that their bitter quarrel was merely an already forgotten lovers' tiff. She avoided any mention of business and made no attempt to monopolize him.

On Monday he had a most discouraging report from Mollison's doctor. In spite of frequent penicillin injections, the actor's cough was worse and there was still danger of pneumonia. Further, the laboratory tests had revealed a state of general debilitation. He was anemic, his blood pressure was alarmingly low, and he had diabetic symptoms. In the doctor's opinion, he would have to remain in bed for two weeks and then recuperate in a warmer climate for at least two weeks more before it would be safe for him to go back to work.

At lunch Thompson explained the situation to John Ettrick. "So I thought," he said, "that you might like to play the part on Broadway for four weeks before you go to Chicago." He did not believe that Mollison would be able to resume in four weeks but thought it better not to say so, feeling that once Ettrick was in the part he could probably be induced to continue as long as necessary.

Ettrick was not responsive to the suggestion. "Well, Tommy," he said, "I sure would like to help you out of the jam you're in, but it's quite a while since I've had to work as an understudy."

"Nobody's asking you to work as an understudy. Any star rates a month's vacation after a solid year in a show, and I'm asking another star to take over while he's away. You'll be getting the same billing and the same dough. We'll ask the critics to come in and we'll give you a great publicity build-up. You get yourself a fine set of New York notices and another set in Chicago four weeks later."

"And what if Hugh isn't able to come back in four weeks?"

"Well, four weeks is what the doctor says. But suppose it did run a week or two longer. Chicago will still be good, and, meanwhile, you'll be starring in New York in a hit show."

"That's one way of looking at it. But the way it stacks up to me, I'll be bending over a hot stove, keeping Hugh's dinner warm for him until he's ready to come and get it. It doesn't appeal."

"All right. I'll make it a six weeks' guarantee if you like."

Ettrick shook his head. "It's not a question of four weeks or six weeks. It's the whole proposition. I don't see myself standing in for

Mollison. If he's stepping out and you want me to take over for the rest of the New York run, I'll consider it, just to help you out. From my own angle, I'd rather create the part in Chicago than follow somebody in New York."

Thompson listened in consternation. "But wait a minute, Johnny! There's no question of Mollison stepping out. He's got a run-of-the-play contract. How the hell am I going to ask him to give it up?"

"No, I guess you can't. But I've got a run-of-the-play contract for the Chicago company, and I'm very happy about it. They know me in Chi, and I've always found it a great show town. So why don't we just let the whole thing lay? I know you're in a hell of a spot and I wish I could do something about it, but this is meat and potatoes to me and I've got to do what's best for myself."

Thompson argued and pleaded without success. Ettrick was shrewd enough to see that the situation was desperate and that he was in a position to drive a hard bargain. Thompson went back to his office and called Fineman, Winternitz, Claire, and Anthony Weir into hurried conference. It was not easy to make a decision. Give Them All My Love was showing a weekly profit of more than six thousand dollars. If it could be kept running for the rest of the season it would mean additional profits of at least a hundred thousand. Ettrick was the only available actor who offered a hope of even that long a continuance. To close the play for a month on the dubious chance of Mollison's return was to run the risk of killing it entirely, for even if he did come back there was no certainty that he would not begin drinking again once he was no longer under medical supervision. What it came down to was that a choice had to be made between yielding to Ettrick's demands or closing the play for an indefinite period, perhaps altogether. There was no time to be wasted either, for every idle day meant a loss of revenue and a piling up of expense. After a long debate it was agreed that Ettrick's hard terms had to be accepted. Thompson called Frederic Haig in Santa Fe, where the author was visiting friends, and told him how things stood. Haig protested at first, but after listening to Thompson's irrefutable arguments he gave in.

It was one thing to decide to drop Mollison and quite another to get him to consent to the cancellation of his contract, particularly since his physical condition did not make it easy to discuss the subject with him. For the next few days there were continual conferences involving Mollison's agent, his attorney, Cecelia, the officials of the Actors' Equity Association, and finally Mollison himself. At first the actor flatly refused to consider surrendering his contract. It was not until it had been made clear to him that if charges of drunkenness were brought against him his contract would probably be canceled anyhow that he agreed, preferring a voluntary relinquishment to an ugly and damaging blot upon his professional reputation. Tears streamed down his cheeks as he signed the release, but inwardly he was deeply relieved. Physically and psychically depleted, he had been in terror of resuming the responsibility of keeping the play going.

It was Thursday before all the legal formalities were concluded and Thompson could begin rehearsing Ettrick. Because of the delay the reopening had to be postponed another three days.

XXXV.

Eric had been at home nearly two weeks when he read the surprising news of Mollison's withdrawal from the cast of Give Them All My Love. The announcement stated that the actor's physicians had ordered a long rest. He was going, with his family, to Bermuda and would probably not resume work until the following season.

For some days Eric had been trying to make up his mind whether or not to go back to New York. He had good reasons for going. Winternitz had suggested the possibility of some newspaper interviews and radio appearances, which would help to publicize The Clouded Mirror; there were plays and art exhibitions he wanted to see and the many new friends whose society he enjoyed so much; there was the sweet pleasure of going around to the Farow, seeing the crowds stream in to attend his play, watching, from an upper box, the interested faces of the spectators, listening to the comments of those who brushed by him in the lobby, not suspecting his identity, lounging backstage in the midst of all the complicated activity that his creativeness had set in motion. Most of all, of course, there was Virginia.

There was a strong counterpull too. The concepts of thrift and industry had been so deeply implanted in him that he could not surrender himself easily to idleness and self-indulgence. Though he knew very well that in an artist's life periods of creative outpouring must alternate with periods of replenishment, he found it hard to change his ingrained habits and to resist the moral compulsion to be always at work. Even during the ten days following the opening of the play he had felt a little guilty about spending his money in New York when there was no real need for him to be there; and he had come home with the intention of collecting his thoughts and laying the groundwork for a new play.

For the first few days he was busy with household chores and the Thanksgiving dinners at home and at the La Pointes'—truly festive occasions, since for the first time in many years there was indeed much to be thankful for. The home atmosphere had undergone a salutary change; enforced penny-pinching and gnawing anxiety about the future had given way to a sense of security and a more relaxed daily life. Eric was amused and rather proud to find that he had suddenly become not only the hero but the unquestioned head of his family. Even his father, awed by Eric's weekly income of over a thousand dollars, treated him with a new deference and was far more tractable than he had been in years, offering no opposition when Eric engaged a neighbor to come in several times a week to help his mother with the washing and heavy cleaning. Amelia did protest feebly, but she was easily overruled. She was beginning to feel the effect of the long years of unrelieved confinement and worry. She was proud and happy now, for Eric's success and his solicitude for her rewarded her amply for all her sacrifices.

Eric had not seen Sylvia since mid-September or heard from her since her violent rejection of his offer of marriage. He wondered what her attitude would be if they should happen to meet. He made up his mind to treat her with cordiality and consideration, for he knew very well that everyone in Coltertown—and particularly Sylvia and her mother—would assume that his success had gone to his head and that he had no further interest in his former acquaintances. However, Sylvia was off on another visit to Great Barrington. She was in poor health and had gladly accepted her indulgent father's suggestion that she give up work for a while. To her delight, Muriel Davis, still intent upon marrying her to Alden Greer, had invited her up to the Berkshires.

When the holiday was over Eric tried to settle down to work. He had a notebook in which from time to time he had jotted down an incident, a description of a character, or merely a provocative title that suggested a starting point for a play. None of these hints seemed to lead anywhere. In fact, he found it almost impossible to concentrate, and, after staring blankly at the page for fifteen minutes, he would wander off into an aimless reverie, contemplating the revolutionary changes in his life, daydreaming about his future, and reliving the exciting experiences of the past months. Virginia was constantly in his thoughts. He reviewed all their meetings, searching for hidden meanings in things she had said, trying to understand her complex and enigmatic personality. She was so unlike anyone he had ever known and her manner of expressing herself was so stylized and allusive, he was never sure just what she was thinking or feeling—particularly with respect to himself. There were moments when she seemed very close to him, and other moments when her attitude seemed merely one of polite toleration. Blunt and direct (when he was not altogether inarticulate), he was bewildered by her evasiveness and elusiveness and by her ability to lead half-a-dozen different lives at once. Least of all did he understand her relationship to Mollison. She seemed to have nothing in common with him, yet he appeared to dominate her life. She made no attempt at concealment, yet she always spoke of Mollison in the most impersonal terms. What puzzled him more than the relationship itself, however, was his own attitude toward it. He was far too unorthodox in his thinking to be shocked by the mere absence of legality, and his sense of humor made him wonder whether his disapproval sprang from a wish to be in Mollison's position.

He longed for news of her and tried several times to reach her by telephone. He could not call her from his home without being overheard, so he used the telephone booth in the lobby of the local hotel. He was never lucky enough to find her in. Three or four times he attempted to write to her, but he had to give it up. He was too straightforward and too serious about her to be able to compose a light letter that did not seem artificial and forced. Yet to write even a restrained love letter was unthinkable. Not only might she think him guilty of inexcusable tastelessness, in view of his knowledge of her relationship to Mollison, but he might meet with a sharp and conclusive rebuff.

He had about come to the conclusion that he had better try to put Virginia out of his mind entirely, but when he read the news of Mollison's illness he decided to return to New York. Since he had several good reasons for going, he did not have to admit to himself that what really decided him was the hope that, with Mollison out of the way, Virginia would have more time for him.

New York was no longer a forbidding and impenetrable fortress. It had lowered its barriers to him, and he could walk its streets with out fear, as one who had made a substantial contribution to its con plex life and had thereby earned the right to partake freely of i pleasures and rewards. He had a recognizable face and name, a shov window for his wares, friends of position and quality, and money ir his pocket. The seedy, anonymous, bewildered country boy, who only six months before had stepped so tremblingly from the Hartford train, had been transformed into a respected and admired Broadway figure.

Heady though he found the miraculous change, he was not unaware of its attendant dangers. Bred in a stern and frugal tradition, animated by high ideals and aspirations, he knew that good fortune has the power to corrupt as well as to liberate, and that the high road of success is often a street of easy virtue. In the dazzling world of the theater, of which he was now a citizen, it was not always a simple matter to distinguish the false from the true, for poverty of spirit was only too often tricked out in the cunning trappings of artisanship. Glibness masqueraded as poetry, sleek shoddy as honest stuff, and solid artistry jogged elbows with flashy meretriciousness.

Even before he had thought of becoming a playwright Eric had been repelled by the physical aspects of New York's theatrical district, that narrow area variously known as Times Square, the Rialto, the Gay White Way, the Crossroads of the World, the Main Stem, but more universally as Broadway (though it included less than a twentieth of that famous thoroughfare). His detestation had grown with his intimacy. He could not understand what anyone found to admire in this Broadway, with its glaring, twitching electric signs, making night hideous; its shabby hotels, murky bars, and decrepit rooming-houses; its noisy, overcrowded restaurants, armchair beaneries, cruller dispensaries, chop-suey joints, and hamburger heavens; its gaudy haberdasheries selling sharp clothes, and gift shops specializing in hand-painted turtles, April Fool jokes, and books on sex hygiene; its tawdry night clubs, taxi dance halls, shooting galleries, pin-ball games, juke-boxes, and flea circuses; its hole-in-the-wall ticket agencies and cluttered drugstores foul with the stale emanations of sloppy lunch counters; its mammoth movie palaces, endlessly doling out tasteless, sticky pap that deadened the palate without satisfying the appetite; this Broadway, with its crooks, grafters, grifters, chiselers, shoestring operators, and flesh peddlers; its con men, gag men, sandwich men, pitch men, and ad men; its autograph hounds, hepcats, and queued-up broadcast audiences; its bookies, touts, fight promoters, dope peddlers, and pimps; its dark-spectacled pencil vendors and legless beggars on dollies; its pick-up girls and boys; its hoofers, song pluggers, torch singers, and strip-teasers; its quacks and shysters and fixers; its roistering sailors and out-of-town buyers on the loose; its short-change artists, gold diggers, and spit-ball columnists.

The more he saw of Broadway, the more he marveled that the noble art of the drama could continue to survive in this sullied temple. Yet survive it did, in eloquent testimony to its power and indestructibility and to the courage and creative spirit of those of its ministrants who, in spite of defeat, frustration, hardship, and temptation, kept alive their faith and their hope and labored unceasingly to maintain their artistic self-respect. It was upon these valiant devotees that Eric pinned his own hopes of survival. He had been drawn to the theater through his study of the masterpieces of dramatic literature, and, though he hardly expected to attain the heights, he was determined not to sink into the quagmire.

He spent a busy and stimulating two weeks in New York. When he was not at the Farow he was lunching or dining with friends, going to plays, concerts, and art exhibitions, or making the publicity appearances that Winternitz had arranged. He was invited to lunch at the Dutch Treat Club and the Players (in the house on Gramercy Park that Edwin Booth had once occupied), and he attended a performance of Don Giovanni at the Metropolitan Opera House—his first opera.

Christmas shopping took much of his time too. He bought a muskrat coat for Amelia, a fine radio for his father, warm clothing for the La Pointes and Cousin Elizabeth, and a crib for the expected baby. He found a Matisse lithograph for Virginia, a charming antique ring for Irina Lanski, and sent liquor, candy, or cigarette lighters to Winternitz, Myra Leech, McCarthy, and his other friends in the cast. He was appalled when he figured up what it all cost, especially when he learned that the receipts at the Farow had begun to fall off after the very prosperous Thanksgiving week. However, Fineman, Irina Lanski, and the box-office men assured him that this was only the usual pre-Christmas decline from which all plays, except a few smash hits, suffered and that business would pick up again immediately after Christmas, with every prospect of a continuance of the play's run to the end of the season. He estimated that if the play ran until June his earnings would come to something like twenty-five thousand dollars, with a good chance of a road tour the next season. So he felt that his expenditures were justifiable and took a warm delight in being able, for the first time in his life, to give pleasure to others.

He saw Virginia almost every day at the theater, though seldom alone. His secret hope that she would have more free time, now that Mollison was away, proved false. She was constantly busy with her social engagements, radio appearances, visits to the beauty salon, and Christmas shopping. Sometimes Eric had the uneasy feeling that she was deliberately avoiding him, but her excuses were so plausible and her apologies so seemingly sincere he could find no real justification for his misgivings. Twice she asked him to dinner at her apartment; but Marion Sweet was there, and the conversation was general and impersonal. Outwardly Virginia was her usual self, rattling on vivaciously about everything under the sun. It was apparent to Eric that her animation was forced; beneath her gaiety she was worried and preoccupied. From Winternitz he had heard the whole story of Mollison's collapse and of the reason for it, and he assumed, mistakenly, that Virginia was brooding over the ending of her relationship and perhaps regretting it.

Three days before Christmas Amelia called to tell him joyfully that Dorothy had given birth to a fine eight-pound boy at the Coltertown Hospital. The thrifty La Pointes had intended a home confinement; Eric, wishing his sister to have the best possible care, had insisted upon paying her expenses at the hospital. Since he was planning to go home for Christmas anyhow, he decided to leave for Coltertown next day.

He spent his last night in New York at the Farow. The house was only half full, the poorest attendance since the opening of the play. But Fineman was reassuring. "I've been checking around town," he said, "and it's brutal. The next couple days are going to be worse too; but we'll snap right back after Christmas."

During the performance Eric made the rounds backstage, wishing everybody a merry Christmas and getting a warm response, for the actors all liked him and were indebted to him, besides, for an ample Christmas and the bright outlook of a full season's work. He invited Virginia to have a drink with him after the performance. She was tired and depressed and wanted to be alone, but she did not have the heart to disappoint him and suggested that they go to her apartment.

Marion Sweet was already in bed. To Eric's delight he was for once alone with Virginia. But she was silent and moody and resisted his attempts to give the halting conversation a personal turn. At last he gave up and sat sipping his drink and wishing that he had not come. The memory of this cheerless meeting would cast a shadow over his holiday visit.

"I'm sorry I'm such a drip, Eric," she said, seeing that he was puzzled and hurt by her aloofness. "It's just that dose ole blue debbils have me in thrall."

"Maybe you'd rather I went."

"No, don't go yet. That is, not unless you want to. As the old ballad has it, you may as well be miserable with me."

"I wish I knew how to cheer you up."

"So do I. But don't give it a thought. It's nothing that twenty years or a violent encounter with a bulldozer couldn't cure. Just an attack of Weltschmerz, which, I believe, is High German for a cosmic belly-ache."

"Would it help if you talked about it?"

"And, like a whore, unpack my heart with words? No, it's just that I've come to the end of a long, blind alley and find myself smack against a blank and very unscalable wall."

"Why not back out of it and start all over?"

"Up another blind alley? No, thank you! That's just what I'm afraid of."

"Not necessarily a blind alley. There are roads that lead places."

"Only for those who think they know where they're going. And that includes me out."

"I don't believe that, because it's hard for me to believe anything I don't understand."

"Of course it is! That's because you're a Christian soldier. And I don't mean that to be a crack either. If I had your gifts and that nice purring motor that makes you tick, I'd be up and doing too instead of spiking my bourbon with great salt tears. But what you are looking at is just a somewhat overripe female with a lot of unserviceable thoughts floating on top of a lot of unorganized emotions. I sometimes wonder if women are the way they are because God hated them to begin with or because He's taking it out on them for His own botched job."

"I like women."

404

"Yes, a lot of men seem to. I never could figure out why."

"I can tell you why I like you, if you want to know."

"Please, no, if you don't mind!" she said hastily.

"Why not?"

"Because I couldn't bear it. In fact, I'm going to send you home now."

"Why?"

"Because the damn dam is about to burst. And I don't want you to get your feet wet. The American theater needs you too much."

"Ginny, dear," he said, trying to put his arms around her.

She slipped away from him. "No, don't! Please don't. Not tonight."

"Then when?"

"I don't know when. But not tonight. Have a nice Christmas and a nice visit with your family. And give the baby a kiss for me. Here it is!" She kissed him quickly and then drew away again. "I think you're wonderful. And I wish I were the girl you think I am." Her tears began to flow. "There! What did I tell you?" She opened the door. "Watch your step going out."

He took her in his arms again. "Ginny!"

"All right, there's one for you!" she said, giving him another swift kiss. "Now, please, be so kind as to get the hell out of here." She pushed him out and closed the door behind him.

He walked slowly back to his hotel, happy to have broken through her reserve at last but still unable to understand what her feelings for him were.

The arrival of Dorothy's baby and Eric's success made this Christmas the most joyous that he and his family had ever known. Even Kenwood entered into the new spirit of happy relaxation. His truculence had given way to a resigned acceptance of his helplessness, and he seemed almost eager to surrender his nominal authority to Eric.

The weather was cold and clear. Eric took delight in tramping the frozen pastures and open woods behind the house, skating on the big millpond and seeing his old acquaintances. He saw nothing of the Jethrows but heard rather disquieting news of Sylvia. Her romance —if it could be called that—with Alden Greer had come to an abrupt end. Greer had sent Sylvia a note to the effect that he was taking over an automobile agency in Seattle. He regretted leaving without seeing her again, he said. Since Lydia Jethrow was not one to keep secrets, the word spread quickly through the tight little Coltertown community that her daughter had been outrageously jilted. Actually Greer

405

had merely been carrying on a mild flirtation, mainly to humor the matchmaking wife of his partner. Sylvia, lost in her soaring daydreams, was brought down to earth with a rude shock. Her physical condition now became so disturbing that her doctor turned her over to a Hartford specialist, who ordered her hospitalized for a thoroughgoing examination.

Eric's Christmas mail was heavy. Formerly the arrival of a letter had been an infrequent occurrence, and he took a childish delight in the daily load of parcels and letters. Virginia had sent him a beautifully printed copy of Candide, illustrated with drawings by Paul Klee, and from Irina Lanski there was an early edition of Walden, inscribed to one of Thoreau's Concord neighbors. He received dozens of Christmas cards (including several from authors' representatives, insurance agencies, and theatrical publications) and notes of thanks for his gifts.

Several of his letters were of peculiar interest. An official communication from the Connecticut Civil Service Commission informed him that he had passed the examination for proofreader and that, with his veteran's priority, he could soon expect an appointment. He grinned as he read it, thinking how welcome the news would have been only a few weeks ago and how unimportant it seemed now. From Frederic Haig there was a gracious note, written in a delicate hand on monogrammed paper, inviting him to a New Year's Eve party at the playwright's Fifth Avenue apartment. Eric felt flattered and a little ashamed. He had put down Haig as foppish and insincere, and, resentful of his presence at the first-night conference in Boston, had been almost uncivil to him. Now Haig's friendliness seemed to rebuke him for his inexcusable rudeness. He hesitated about going; but, telling himself that Haig would not have asked him if he had not wanted him to come, he wrote a cordial note of acceptance. He looked forward, with excitement, to a big New York party—sure, too, that Virginia would be there.

He received a note from her, in the angular penmanship characteristic of finishing schools. She thanked him effusively for the drawing and ended with a flippant reference to their last meeting. "Sorry about the flood, the other night," she wrote, "but I am working like mad, bolstering up the levee, and think I have Old Man River under control."

Her note and her gift were sufficient excuse for a letter. Though he intended to write only a few lines, he found himself going on and on, expressing himself on all manner of subjects, in a light vein but with underlying seriousness. He tried to convey to her how much she was in his thoughts and how much she meant to him. He carefully avoided any outright declaration of love, thinking it would be rather indelicate to press her while, apparently, she was still brooding over Mollison. He had a tendency to idealize all women and was afraid of offending her sensibilities. In his inexperience and emotional immaturity he needed far more encouragement than she had given him.

Most surprising of all the letters he received was a note from Eliot Ainsworth, inviting him to an eggnog party at the Coltertown Country Club. Even when he read it a second time he could not believe it, in view of the elder Ainsworth's evasive treatment of his request for a leave of absence and his humiliating discharge from the factory by Warren. His first impulse was to write a sarcastic note of declination; on reflection that seemed petty and destructive. It would be better merely to ignore the invitation. However, the more he thought about it, the more he was tempted to accept, for his curiosity and his imagination were stirred. In the very recent days of his obscurity there was about as much likelihood of his being asked to the Country Club as there was of being offered a partnership in the Ainsworth plant. He had a lively desire to inspect the sacred precincts and to find out on what terms he would be received by the rulers of Coltertown, from whose iron economic grip he had been so fortunately delivered. In the end he sent Eliot Ainsworth a note of acceptance, carefully composed to give an air of casualness.

As he chugged up the club's wide, graveled driveway in the rusty family car, and saw the parked rows of shiny new convertibles and station wagons, he felt strong misgivings and almost turned back. Hesitantly he stood in the door of the lounge, looking at the noisy assemblage of Coltertown's elite, and again had an impulse to run away, to which he might have yielded had not Eliot Ainsworth seen him and come forward to greet him heartily.

Ainsworth led him into the crowded room. Instantly he found himself the center of attention. It was not often that a local resident achieved fame in New York, and everyone wanted to have a good look at the humble factory worker who, almost overnight, had become a minor celebrity. Eric had been in high school with a few of the younger generation, had a nodding acquaintance with a few others, and knew most of the rest by sight. To them, he was appearing, for the first time, as a person worthy of notice. Some had seen The Clouded Mirror, and even if they had not liked it had been impressed by the audience response and by the high price they had had to pay for their tickets. While Eric had none of the recognizable outward attributes of wealth and success they were all awed by the exaggerated reports of his earnings and put down his plain appearance and diffident manner to artistic eccentricity.

Self-conscious and out of place though he felt, Eric was amused by Eliot Ainsworth's complacent air of proprietorship. It was evident that his former employer regarded him as a brilliant protégé whose genius he had always recognized and fostered and for whose success he was somehow largely responsible. Warren Ainsworth, however, was as coldly hostile as ever, and Eric found himself thinking of Claire. The comparison was far from unsound, for they both compensated for their uncreativeness and inner insecurity by a false assumption of superiority.

Community sentiment and the economic facts of his own existence had always made Eric stand in awe of the ruling clans of Coltertown. As he moved from group to group, observing and listening to the mighty Ainsworths and Grahams and Manchesters and McBanes, he saw that there was really nothing extraordinary about them. In the light of even his brief experiences in New York, they seemed dull, pompous, and provincial, all cut to the same pattern and conforming unquestioningly to the commonplace standards of their narrowly circumscribed world. He found himself contrasting the wit, the grace, the charm, the imaginativeness, the cosmopolitanism, the tolerance, the idealism, of Irina Lanski, Thompson, Winternitz, Virginia, Frederic Haig, Florence Fulham, and a dozen others he had met in New York, both in and out of the theater, with the complacent stodginess of these Coltertown oligarchs, the men bragging with heavy facetiousness of their new cars, their golf scores, and their business triumphs, uttering platitudes with an air of profundity, the women, flat-voiced and unanimated, chattering about their kitchens, their children, and their neighbors, all so seemingly satisfied with themselves and the state of things as they were, so blissfully oblivious to far horizons and to the realms of mind and of spirit that lay beyond. Coltertown, as Eric was aware, had its fair share of cultivated, sensitive, creative people; but lack of means, of proper family connections, or merely of inclination kept them out of this gathering place of the powerful and the well-to-do, where money and heritage were the sole determinants of worth and quality.

Eric came away as little capitivated by the Country Club folk as they were by him. The knowledge that he need no longer fear their domination was comforting and, free of Coltertown's limitations, he felt a new affection for the little community.

XXXVI.

In spite of what Virginia had written Eric, she was far from getting her emotions under control. She was tortured by conflicts and uncertainties and unable to think clearly about her future. She was too realistic and self-centered to be deeply disturbed by the unblinkable fact that Mollison's collapse was directly attributable to her. For years he had accepted all that she had given him without making any serious effort to ease her ambiguous and often embarrassing position. If it had been his emotional interest that had faded she would have had no claim upon him and would have had to face it as best she could; now that it happened to be the other way around, he would have to do the same. Of course, it could not be shrugged off quite as easily as all that; nevertheless, she did succeed in subduing her qualms. When Mollison left for Bermuda without their having seen each other again, she felt that that chapter in her life had come to an unhappy but definite close.

It was the new, unwritten chapter that troubled her, for she had no beginning for it, not even a plan. She knew neither where she was going nor where she wanted to go. She was in her late twenties, still young, but old enough to be greatly dissatisfied with her complete rootlessness. She took pride in her professional success, but she did not have enough driving ambition or enough confidence in her talent to believe in the possibility of a life-filling stage career. She wanted security and stability and some degree of permanence, of tenure and design, things she had never known. Yet she was reluctant to surrender her independence, to make concessions and compromises. She was willful, demanding, and often capricious—qualities that endangered any relationship—and she had no desire to be otherwise. Still, there were moments when she was so oppressed by loneliness that she was afraid of growing bitter and eventually becoming hateful not only to herself but to others.

She had never lacked admirers. Even during her intimacy with Mollison she had not found it easy to hold them at arm's length. Now that he was out of her life she was fair game for anyone, and it was a tedious business to keep the male friends, who were a great convenience to her in her unattached stage, and yet resist their importunities.

Eric offered a possible solution to her problem. She had given him just enough encouragement to keep his hopes alive, not from wantonness or cold calculation but because there were moments when she almost convinced herself that she could feel safe and happy with him. Again and again she reviewed the qualities that had won her admiration and affection: his honesty, his tenderness, his loyalty, his creative gifts, his idealism, his untainted zest for life. Yet she could not bring herself to a decision; her will was paralyzed by her irrational, uncontrollable feeling for Leroy Thompson.

She had tried to overcome it, tried to reason herself out of it, but she could not, and for the first time in her life she was thoroughly frightened. She had little doubt about his intentions, and she was afraid that if he were persistent enough she would not have the power to resist him; and there was every reason why she should. The last thing in the world she wanted was to get involved in another formless, haphazard, clandestine relationship. She had had enough of furtiveness and scheming and was far from being as indifferent to gossip and social disapproval as she pretended to be. The emotional implications were even more disturbing. There was no reason to believe that Thompson was to be trusted. His amorous adventures were a matter of common knowledge, and her pride rebelled against her becoming just another name in his roster of conquests—perhaps finding herself in Mollison's unhappy position, still desiring but no longer desired.

Worst of all, there was Claire. Cecelia had been hard enough to accept; but in her case, at least, there had been extenuating circumstances: her long-standing marriage to Mollison, his joint responsibility for the rearing of their adopted children, her religious scruples against divorce. Besides, Cecelia was a sensible, robust, un-affected woman, singularly free from pettiness and malice. To share a man with Claire was unthinkable. Long before Thompson had entered her thoughts Virginia had put down Claire as a dull and vulgar woman, who reminded her of the pseudo-genteel and falsely digni-fied housekeepers of her childhood. In the past months her dislike had developed into a malignant detestation. The relationship be-tween Claire and Thompson she found both incomprehensible and intolerable. If he loved Claire, she argued, then his apparent taste and sensitivity must be a sham; if he did not love her, then he stood convicted of a kind of mercenary opportunism that was foreign to Virginia's nature. In either case, he was cheapened in her eyes. She was too self-absorbed and too critical of others to understand that Thompson, in his emotional emptiness, had been drawn to Claire by mere propinquity and physical attraction.

Unable to rid herself of her obsessive feeling, she thought seri-ously of running away. She sketched out a year in Europe: a few months visiting her many acquaintances in England and then a leisurely motor tour of France, Italy, and Switzerland. If she planned it carefully, her income, added to what she had in the bank, would be enough to see her through. She might even persuade one of her unattached friends to accompany her. There were a hundred fa-miliar places to revisit and a hundred new ones to discover. She would be constantly occupied, constantly on the move, and in time she would recover her emotional equilibrium. She knew that it was an empty answer to her problem—in fact, no answer at all, merely a rather cowardly evasion—but negativism seemed preferable to self-torture or to the possibly disastrous consequences of an impulsive decision.

However, there were some very real practical difficulties to be overcome. She had a run-of-the-play contract, and The Clouded Mirror was expected to continue for another six months. Even if she could think of a plausible excuse, her request for a release would almost certainly be refused; she had made a distinct hit in the play and would not be easy to replace. She could pretend illness, but her pride rejected that dishonorable expedient. She could, of course, simply break her contract, but even if the management did not en-force its legal right to heavy damages, she would be severely disci-plined by Equity and would perhaps seriously jeopardize her career.

In her desperate state she might have been willing to risk all that had not Thompson's enforced concentration on Give Them All My Love given her a few weeks' breathing spell.

Since his hurried return from Florida, Thompson had hardly been near the Farow. His negotiations with Ettrick and Mollison and the intensive rehearsals necessary to get Ettrick ready kept him busy day and night. When the play reopened and he was satisfied that everything was running smoothly, he and Frederic Haig left for Hollywood to discuss the sale of the motion-picture rights, for which all the major motion-picture companies had been making offers since the original opening of the play. Confident of a run of at least two years in New York, they had refused to sell. Now the situation was changed; though John Ettrick's performance was good and he had received complimentary notices from the critics, who had attended the reopening, Mollison had become so identified with the part that no substitute was acceptable to the public. The advance sale had begun to slacken, and though the play's reputation would keep it running for a time, it was unlikely that it would outlast the season. Thompson and Haig agreed, therefore, to make a motion-picture sale while the play was still doing capacity business and before interest in it began to cool. The negotiations could have been left to Haig's agents; but Thompson always enjoyed matching himself against motion-picture executives, so he decided to handle the matter himself. Since the final decision rested with Haig, he persuaded the author to go with him.

He felt, too, that by going to California he would give himself more time to examine his feelings for Virginia and to consider what he should do. This was something new for him; ordinarily if a woman attracted him he proceeded to make love to her with little regard for the consequences. But Virginia had touched him as no one but Louise Henry ever had; she had stirred emotions in him that he had believed long since dead. He felt the need of unwonted caution, afraid that a hasty move might alienate her forever, or, worse yet, lead to complications for which he was not prepared. Yet he knew that he could not delay much longer, for Virginia was obviously at loose ends. While he did not take very seriously Claire's conjectures about her interest in Eric, he foresaw the possibility that in her unsettled state she might turn impulsively to anyone.

After weighing the various offers from the motion-picture companies Thompson and Haig decided to accept one that provided for their participation in the net profits of the picture with a guarantee that they would receive not less than three hundred thousand dollars. Of this sum Haig would get well over a hundred and fifty thousand, Thompson and Claire nearly thirty thousand each, and the remainder would go to the agents and backers. In addition, Haig undertook to write the screen adaptation for seventy-five thousand dollars. Thompson, refusing an offer to direct the picture, agreed to supervise its production for a fee of fifty thousand. It was a very satisfactory deal, and they were well pleased with themselves. When the general terms had been agreed upon Haig returned to New York to make arrangements for his New Year's Eve party, leaving Thompson in Hollywood to work out the details.

Thompson did not get back to New York until the afternoon of the thirty-first. Claire had come into town for the party and, anxious to get a full account of his Hollywood trip, had asked him to dine in her apartment. She did not altogether share his satisfaction. While there was no doubt that he had negotiated a good contract, she pointed out ruefully how much better off they would have been if Mollison had remained in the play. She hinted again at Virginia's responsibility but, seeing Thompson's face darken, dropped that subject.

He left her at nine, promising to return at eleven to take her to the party. Since he had plenty of time he decided to stop in at the Farow before going to his hotel to dress. The house was packed and standing room had been sold to the permissible limit. It was hardly the play for an audience bent on festivity, and there was much coughing and fidgeting and laughter in the wrong places. Thompson looked on in disgust for a few minutes and then went around to the stage door. Everyone gave him a warm welcome after his long absence. The doorman had a handful of letters for him, and he started for Virginia's dressing-room, intending to look through them there. Virginia was on, and Pearl was standing by ready to help her with her quick onstage costume change.

As Thompson tiptoed behind the setting he almost collided in the semi-darkness with Lily Prengle, who was just coming off, having finished her brief scene. He greeted her coolly and, pretending not to notice her attempt to detain him, quickly entered Virginia's dressing-room and closed the door. He had just settled down in the little reception room when Lily entered.

"I've got to talk to you," she said, closing the door behind her.

"Well, this is scarcely the time or place," said Thompson, infuriated by this intrusion. Thanks to circumstances, he had seen almost nothing of Lily during the six weeks the play had been running in New York. He had consistently ignored her messages, and she had stopped calling. Assuming that she had at last accepted the fact that he was through with her, he had almost dismissed her entirely from his busy thoughts. Yet here she was, the moment he set foot in the theater, beginning her pursuit again. It was apparent that the only way he could really get rid of her was to give her her notice.

"I'm sorry," she said, "but this is something that can't wait." She paused for a moment, her bosom heaving, then blurted out, "I think I'm going to have a baby."

Thompson's throat contracted. The veins in his face swelled painfully. "What the hell are you talking about?" he sputtered, unable to find words that had any meaning.

"I knew you'd be angry," she said. "But I didn't do it on purpose. It just happened."

"Have you been to a doctor?" he said, forcing himself to meet this unexpected and calamitous situation.

"Yes."

"And he told you?"

"He thinks so, but he says it's too soon to be sure. He told me to come back in two weeks."

"Then what is all this?"

"I know how I feel. And I'm sure, even if he isn't."

He asked her some blunt questions, which she answered in a low voice, her eyes averted in embarrassment.

"What am I going to do?" she said.

"I'll have to think about it." He kept looking nervously at the door.

"Don't worry, Ginny won't be off for a while yet. I know you don't want her to find me here. But I just had to tell you."

"Have you told anybody else?"

"Of course not! Don't you even give me credit for any character?"

"Well, there's nothing to be done until you're sure."

"I *am* sure. And I want to have the baby."

He stared at her in fright. "Look, you're not the first girl this has ever happened to. There's nothing to be afraid of. And you're not going to help things by getting hysterical about it."

"It's not hysterical to want a baby. It's a natural thing for a woman. And I do want it. I've thought it all out. If you'd just be willing to marry me—"

"You're proposing a shot-gun wedding?" he said harshly.

She became suddenly voluble. "No, I'm not. I know how you feel about me. You've made it plain enough. I wouldn't want to be married to a man who doesn't care for me, who hates me, though I don't understand what I've done that makes you feel that way. I'm just asking you to do it for the looks of things and for the baby's sake. I won't bother you or even come near you. I'll go away somewhere and have the baby and divorce you the minute it's born, or even sooner if you want it that way."

"Thanks, but I'm lacking in the paternal instinct."

"You wouldn't ever have to see it or do anything for it. I'll work and take care of it myself. I'll sign any papers or whatever you want, so you won't be responsible for it." She clutched his sleeve. "Oh, please, please! It's nothing but a five-minute ceremony for you, and to me it means everything in the world."

He moved away from her, finding even her touch offensive. "How do you know I'm the father?" he said, instantly wishing it unsaid.

Her eyes widened in reproach. The color mounted slowly to her cheeks. "Is that the kind of a girl you think I am? Well, I guess maybe I deserve it, for trusting you and believing in you."

"All right, all right, I didn't mean it that way," he said, wanting to placate her and yet too ruffled to make a fitting apology. "We'll talk it over again when I've had time to think about it." Again he looked involuntarily at the door.

"Yes, I know. Ginny! All right." She opened the door and then, with a flash of spirit of which he had not believed her capable, said, "Maybe I'll decide to have the baby anyhow!"

She was gone before he could find an answer. He sat on the chaise longue, stunned by the unforeseen blow, ashamed of his brutality, and furious at his failure to handle the situation with tact and authority. For the moment he forgot about Virginia, and he was startled to see her come hurrying in, followed by Pearl.

"Hi, Tommy," she said as she rushed into the inner room. "Did you bring that pack of laughing hyenas out there from Hollywood?" Pearl closed the door and helped her out of her dress. Virginia's heart pounded as she made her quick change. She had not

415

seen Thompson for weeks and was appalled to find how the mere sight of him affected her. She tried to think of something to say to him on her way out; she could have spared herself the trouble, for he had gone.

Her agitation made it hard for her to concentrate on her performance, and each time she went back to the dressing-room she hoped and dreaded he would be there. When she came back after the final curtain call Eric was waiting for her. To her surprise he looked almost handsome in his new dinner jacket.

"Well, if it isn't Beau Brummel in person!" she said. "You look very sweet."

"I'm glad you think so," said Eric, flushing.

"Only, if you'll allow me to say so, your man did a rather butterfingered job on your tie."

"I never can seem to get it right," said Eric, unwilling to admit that it was the first time he had ever tried.

"Well, let's see what the feminine touch can do." She pulled open the lumpish knot and deftly retied it. "There! Now you really look like an old smoothie. When did *you* blow into town?"

"Just this afternoon. I was out front for a while, and I wondered if anybody is taking you to the party."

"Not unless you are."

"That's good!" said Eric, delighted. "Do you have to go home first?"

"No, my wardrobe's right here. So why don't you settle down with a good book while Pearl tries to squeeze me into it? Or maybe you'd like to go out for a drink."

"No, I guess I can wait until we get to the party."

"Well, if it's anything like the one Freddy threw last year, we'll be up to our fannies in champagne ere the cock crows."

She went into the inner room. Eric leafed through a theatrical magazine, too excited to pay any attention to its contents. At last the door opened and Virginia came out, wearing a strapless, tight-fitting, cream-colored evening-gown, completely devoid of ornament. Eric got up and stood looking at her in dazzled admiration. "Why, you look beautiful!"

"It's just a little number I picked up in Gimbel's basement," she said, reveling in his undisguised worship. "Remind me not to breathe, will you? And if you see the damn thing starting to slip, just clear your throat loudly."

416

"You won't have a girl friend left by mornin'," said Pearl, putting Virginia's long ermine cape around her shoulders, "because you're sure gonna steal the show right away from them all."

"Well, I never did care much for women anyhow. And while I'm up, Pearl, may I wish you a happy New Year?"

"A happy one to you, Miss Ginny, and I hope that's just what it will be. And to you too, Mr. Kenwood."

"Thanks, Pearl, and the same to you," said Eric, shaking her hand warmly. He liked her directness, her humor, and her dignity.

When they arrived at Frederic Haig's tenth-floor Fifth Avenue apartment, Virginia was directed to Haig's bedroom, which was serving as the women's cloakroom, and Eric to another bedroom, daintily furnished, which, he learned later, was occupied by the blond youth whom he had seen with Haig at the opening of his play and who was nominally the playwright's secretary.

Eric put down his coat and went along the hall to the enormous living-room overlooking Central Park, where Haig was receiving his guests. He greeted Eric as warmly as though they had been life-long friends, expressed the greatest pleasure at seeing him there, and complimented him gracefully upon the success of his play. It was all part of a social technique, as carefully thought out as an accomplished actor's performance, yet Eric found himself captivated by it; he could never display such ease, tact, and charm. Haig turned away apologetically to greet some new arrivals, and Eric timidly entered the living-room to wait for Virginia. The large room had been cleared of most of its furniture and was already crowded with couples dancing to the music of a small orchestra. Waiters were circulating with trays. Eric had his first taste of champagne.

Virginia came in, and Eric was struck anew by her distinctiveness and beauty. He asked her to dance with him, but just then the music stopped. As the dancers dispersed, momentarily, he and Virginia were caught up in a swirl of her acquaintances. She knew everyone, and in introducing Eric she rattled off a roster of famous names from the theatrical, literary, and musical worlds. He was proud of all the attention that Virginia was receiving, yet he was disturbed by it too. He felt, as he had so often before, that he had little to offer in competition with her brilliant friends and admirers.

When the band began to play again he led Virginia off to dance. To have her in his arms, to be acutely aware of her warm breath, the feel of her delicate skin, and the fragrance of her hair was an al-

417

most unendurable joy. He wanted to tell her that he loved her, but all he could do was murmur apologies for his clumsy dancing. Virginia, accommodating herself nimbly to his awkward shuffling, assured him that he danced divinely, her eyes roving about meanwhile in search of Thompson. She wondered uneasily why he was not there, dreaded to see him enter with Claire, and hoped that he would not come at all.

Suddenly there was a flourish from the band. As the waiters who had been standing by extinguished the lights, there were loud shouts of "Happy New Year!" and much embracing and smacking of lips. Eric drew Virginia close to him and kissed her fervently. She responded warmly but without passion. Then she was snatched from his arms and had to submit to a whole series of hearty salutations.

When the lights came up Eric wanted to resume the dance; but Virginia, wiping her lips, said, "I've got to get that mustachy taste out of my mouth. Let's see if we can't exhume a haunch of high venison somewhere."

They went into the dining-room, where there was a buffet and a bar, catered and staffed by a celebrated Park Avenue restaurant. Eric stared in amazement at the display: caviar in ornamental nests of ice, Strasbourg pâtés, smoked turkeys, Parma hams, sturgeon and Nova Scotia salmon, cheese from France and Italy and Stilton flavored with wine, steaming chafing dishes containing creamed mushrooms, sautéed turkey livers, gratinée of crabmeat, Norwegian fishballs, and curries of chicken and lamb, lobster, chicken, vegetable, and fruit salads, ices in decorative forms, pastries, layer cakes, and meringues. At one end of the room a bartender was opening champagne and filling trayfuls of glasses, while another mixed drinks for those who preferred spirits.

"I always enjoy these homey little picnic suppers," said Virginia. "What are you going to have?"

"It's a little hard to decide," said Eric.

"Well, if you don't mind, I think I'll just have the businessmen's lunch."

They moved around the long table, Virginia heaping her plate, not because she was hungry but to have an excuse for not dancing. They went into Haig's study and joined one of the groups that were sitting around talking and drinking. Presently Claire came into the room and bustled over to them. She was flushed and excited. "Has anybody seen Tommy?"

418

"Why, have you lost him?" someone said.

"He was supposed to pick me up at my apartment, and when he didn't show up by midnight I phoned him, but there was no answer. I thought maybe he'd come on here, by himself."

"Well, you're not the first girl he's stood up," a man said.

"It's not funny. I'm afraid something may have happened to him, with a lot of drunks driving around like crazy."

She moved away. Virginia had said nothing and sat picking at the food on her plate, bitterly resentful of Claire's undisguised air of proprietorship, and agitated by the suggestion that Thompson had met with an accident. Haig came over to ask her to dance and she accepted with alacrity, welcoming any activity that might erase the horrible image of Thompson lying maimed in a hospital or even dead.

Eric watched her go, childishly disappointed. Every man there seemed to want to dance with her. Once on the dance floor, she shifted from partner to partner. She kept looking toward the door, more and more anxious as the minutes went by. Then, suddenly, he was there, just as John Ettrick came up to ask her for the next dance.

"Sorry, old man, but this one is mine," said Thompson, taking her in his arms without a word of salutation.

"I'll get you yet, Thompson!" said Ettrick as the music started and they danced away.

"Every bloodhound in town is out on your trail," said Virginia, feeling that she must say something. "What did you do, lose your collar button?" Her knees were quaking; she could hardly move her feet.

"I fell asleep," he said, bringing out the obvious lie with an air of finality that precluded further questioning or comment.

Indeed, there was no need for questioning. It was evident that he had been drinking hard. He reeked of brandy and had all that he could do to control the trembling of his lips. The stain on his cheek was an ugly purple. She was thoroughly frightened, not only by the force of her emotion but by the undeniable way in which he took possession of her. He held her in an unbreakable grip, laying his cheek against hers, pressing his fingertips into her flesh, crushing her breasts against his starched shirt front. There was no tenderness in his voice, no softness in his eyes, no apparent awareness of her personality. She tried to think of something to say and opened her lips once or twice, but her throat was tight and parched

419

and no words came forth. He said nothing, did not even look at her, just clutched her to him and danced. Drink had not yet impaired his natural agility, and he moved with grace and precision. There was nothing for her to do but follow mechanically. She swept along, with half-shut eyes, waiting for the music to end. When it did she said, "I'd like to sit down now, please," and tried to slip away.

But he grasped her wrist tightly. "No," he said, almost impersonally. "I feel like dancing."

Before she could protest there was a shrill cry of "Tommy!" Thompson automatically dropped her wrist as Claire came rushing up.

"What's the matter?" said Thompson, turning toward her, with a slow scowl.

"Oh, Tommy, darling!" she said, laughing and crying and throwing her arms around him, "I'm so happy! I've been so worried about you!" She covered his face with kisses and then, as the music started, said, "Come on, let's dance!" and dragged him away.

Virginia, choking back her sudden nausea, hurried out of the room. As she entered the dining-room she encountered Eric, who was carrying a plate of ice cream and cake. "Eric," she said, seizing his arm, "take me home, will you? I'm sick of this goddam party."

"All right," said Eric in bewilderment. "Just let me take this to Flossie Fulham."

"To hell with Flossie Fulham!" said Virginia, snatching the plate roughly out of his hand. "Hurry up and get your coat and meet me in the hall."

She pushed him out of the room ahead of her and hastened to the cloakroom for her cape. Eric was waiting for her at the entrance door, unsteadily struggling into his coat.

"Shouldn't we say good-by?" he asked foggily. The countless glasses of champagne that had slipped down so easily and had seemed so innocuous were beginning to have their effect.

"No, no!" said Virginia impatiently. "Let's just get out before I stifle to death."

The elevator was a long time coming. She kept looking apprehensively at the door of the apartment. It opened just as the elevator operator was closing his door, and Virginia heard a jangle of voices, Thompson's among them. She exhaled sharply and glanced at Eric, who was still too confused by their abrupt departure to have taken any notice.

The doorman offered to get them a cab. Virginia, afraid that Thompson might appear at any moment, said, "No, thanks, I want to get a little air."

"Let's go around to Madison," she said to Eric. "It'll be easier to get a cab there." It was hard for her to walk quickly in her high-heeled shoes. She relaxed a little once they turned the corner. They had to wait a long time for a cab and she was thoroughly chilled, for the cape gave her little protection against the frosty air, heavy with the threat of snow. Inwardly she was quivering too, with anger, disgust, and fear.

"Don't you feel well?" asked Eric anxiously.

"I'm all right. Just the heat and the noise and the stink of all those people. I just had to get out."

"You're shivering," said Eric, "and your hands are icy."

"I'm all right!" she repeated sharply.

Eric leaned back and closed his eyes; the jolting of the cab aggravated his dizziness. Virginia's temples were throbbing, too. Her capacity for alcohol was far greater than Eric's, but, in an effort to deaden her anxiety about Thompson's absence, she had been spiking her champagne with brandy. It was only a short ride to Virginia's apartment, but they were both thankful when it was over.

As they entered the apartment they were greeted by loud snores. "The Maid Marion!" said Virginia. "She saws ten cords every night."

She closed the door of the living-room to shut out the noise and dropped her cape to the floor. Eric picked it up and hung it over a chair while she switched on the lamp beside the long sofa in front of the fireplace and put a match to the fire that was already laid. As she stood up her eye caught an exquisite cloisonné vase on a carved teakwood stand, a Christmas gift from Thompson. Angrily she swept it off the mantle and kicked it under the sofa out of sight.

"Why did you do that?" asked Eric, startled by her vehemence.

"It reminds me of somebody I hate, if you must know."

He wondered if it was Mollison but did not dare ask. Virginia went to the cellarette for a bottle of brandy, filled two glasses, silently handed one to Eric and drained the other with a deep shudder. Eric's head was spinning, but he recklessly tossed off his drink too.

Shivering, Virginia held out her hands to the blaze, then poured out another drink and gulped it. "I'm freezing," she said.

"Maybe if I put my arms around you," said Eric in a choked voice.

"Sure, if you want to," she said tonelessly, staring into the fire.

He sank down on the sofa beside her and, trembling, took her into his arms. He held her very close, conscious of the thumping of his heart and feeling the beat of hers too. She leaned against his shoulder and her hair brushed his cheek. His lips found hers, and she submitted passively as he kissed her mouth, her eyes, her hair, her shoulders, her throat. "Darling!" he kept murmuring over and over. "My darling! I love you, darling!" As his kisses became more importunate she began to respond recklessly and at last with unrestrained passion.

Suddenly she freed herself from his embrace. "All right!" she said, "let's start the New Year wrong." She switched off the lamp and, standing in the firelight, unfastened her dress and let it fall to the floor. She had nothing on beneath it.

"What's the matter?" she said with desperate, hysterical flippancy as Eric moaned in ecstasy. "Didn't you believe that I was really a redhead?" He did not even hear her.

When he left, the sky was beginning to lighten. It had been snowing for hours. There was no sign of a taxi. Plodding mechanically through the thick, wet, blinding flakes, he arrived at his hotel without clearly knowing how. His clothes were sodden and his feet stiff with cold.

He fell asleep instantly and did not wake up until midafternoon. Before his eyes were fully open he reached for the telephone and called Virginia. There was no answer. He got up and looked out of the window. There was a foot of snow on the roofs of the parked cars, and it was still coming down hard. Suddenly he remembered that Dorothy's baby was to be christened next morning and that she had asked him to be its godfather. If he did not leave at once, the storm might prevent his getting there in time, and his sister would never forgive him. Resignedly he dressed and packed, pausing twice to make futile calls to Virginia. There were no cabs on the street, but he was not far from the station. He found a florist shop in the arcade and sent Virginia a box of flowers, with a loving message. Just before his train left he called her again. There was still no answer.

422

XXXVII.

The telephone awakened Thompson in the late afternoon. It was Claire, anxious to know how he was feeling. He assured her that he was all right, his thick speech belying his words. The snowstorm had kept her in town, and she asked him to have dinner with her, or, if he preferred, she would come to him. He declined, telling her that he wanted to sleep, and cut short the conversation.

He did not need her call to tell him that he had come home in bad condition. His head was splitting, his stomach was queasy, and when he got out of bed he could hardly keep his balance. He would have liked nothing better than to go to sleep; but, though his recollection of what had happened at the party was extremely hazy, he remembered vividly his conversation with Lily and was obsessed by the necessity of doing something about it.

He ordered coffee; while he was waiting for it he bathed and shaved, nicking his face several times and plastering it with bits of toilet paper to stanch the blood. Somewhat revived by the coffee, he dressed and prepared to set out to visit his brother in White Plains. One glance out of the window convinced him that driving was out of the question—even had he been capable of driving—and that he would have to go by train. His reason told him that he need not go at all in this weather and feeling as he did. His business with his brother could easily wait a few days, or a few weeks, and could perhaps be more privately discussed in New York. But his compulsion to get it settled at once overcame his logic. Afraid that Claire might call again, he told the operator that he did not want to be disturbed until morning. He had to wait a long time for a taxi, and it took half an hour to get to the station through the snow-clogged streets.

His brother Andrew was a surgeon who had set up practice in White Plains and was beginning to establish a reputation throughout Westchester County. He was on the staffs of two hospitals and had good connections with many of the wealthy, suburban residents. There was only two years' difference in age between the brothers, and they had always been on excellent terms. In fact, Thompson was deeply indebted to Andrew for restoring him to sanity and productiveness following the death of Louise Henry.

Subsequently, however, Andrew had married the young widow of a colleague. She disliked Thompson and made no effort to conceal the fact that he was not welcome in her home. The daughter of a famous Johns Hopkins' pathologist, she was socially ambitious and bent upon advancing her husband's career. She was humorless and priggish, and Thompson's raffishness, loose talk, and reputed loose behavior offended her sense of propriety. Andrew valiantly defended his brother, but he was very much under his wife's spell; in spite of himself, he began to see faults in Thompson of which he had not previously been conscious. The brothers inevitably had drifted apart, though there was no outward change in their relationship.

Thompson had another long wait for a taxi on the cold station platform at White Plains. He arrived at his brother's house weak and chilled. His visit could not have been more inopportune, for the Andrew Thompsons were just sitting down to a rather formal dinner. Their guests were Hilda Thompson's parents, up from Baltimore to see a newly arrived grandchild, and two correct, stiff suburban couples. Hilda, furious though she was, had to insist, of course, upon his joining them at dinner and went off to supervise the reorganization of her carefully planned table.

The dinner was a chilly and uncomfortable affair. Everyone was in evening dress, and Thompson's rumpled clothes and scratched face were very much out of place. Besides, his bloodshot eyes and blurred speech, which testified to his previous night's dissipation, made him the object of general disapproval. He ate little and took almost no part in the conversation—which would have seemed insufferably dull to him regardless of his condition.

As soon as dinner was over Andrew, to everybody's relief, took his brother to his study.

"Sorry to be the skeleton at the feast," said Thompson.

"It's all right," replied Andrew grudgingly. "Only next time just give us a ring and let us know you're coming. Hilda's proud of her housekeeping, and these little things are important to her."

"You're so right. I'll take a refresher course in etiquette as soon as the next semester begins." As Andrew received this pleasantry in stony silence, Thompson came to the point. "I guess you want to know what the hell I'm doing here."

"Well, it's just that I think Hilda had planned a couple of tables of contract. Of course, if you'd like to cut in—"

"No, thanks. I'll just spill the bad news and then beat it."

"What bad news?" asked Andrew.

Thompson told him, bluntly and briefly. Andrew got up and walked around, disturbed and angry. "You goddam fool! How the hell did you ever get yourself into a mess like that?"

"Well, if you'd like me to, I'll draw a diagram for you."

"For Christ's sake, haven't you any judgment or self-control?"

"That's a fascinating question, and I'll put it on the agenda for our next meeting. But what interests me right now is getting out of this jam."

"That seems simple enough to me. All you have to do is go down to City Hall and get a marriage license."

"If vaudeville ever comes back you've got a great future," said Thompson.

"What's so funny about getting married and having children?" said Andrew, righteous in his new paternity and anxious to stave off what he knew would come next. "It's about time you stopped bumming around like an old goat and knocking up girls. Maybe if you tried living a normal life and taking on a few responsibilities it would be good for what ails you."

"Maybe. But what I want to know is whether I can depend on you to help me out of this."

"Certainly not!" said Andrew indignantly. "Why, you must be crazy if you think I'm going to jeopardize my career and my family life and everything that goes with it just because you haven't learned how to keep your pants buttoned."

"I'm not asking you to do anything about it personally. All I'm asking is that you send me to the right place. What's so unusual about that?"

"I don't know any people like that; and if I did I wouldn't do anything about it. Suppose something went wrong and the girl died.

Or somebody started talking and my name got dragged into it. I'd be ruined professionally, and maybe even lay myself open to criminal prosecution. No, thanks, I'm not having any of it! You got yourself into this and you can damned well get yourself out. Why, if Hilda ever found out that I even discussed this with you I'd be in the doghouse for keeps."

"All right," said Thompson sardonically, "I'll promise not to tell her." He went on pressing his brother, who, though he continued to hurl insults and bitter reproaches, reluctantly agreed at last that he would discuss the matter further after he had had time to consider all its implications.

"There's no hurry about it anyhow," he said. "Pregnancy symptoms are sometimes hysterically induced, and the whole thing may be a false alarm. And even if it isn't, there's always a chance of miscarriage in the early stages. Or you may think it over and decide to marry her after all."

"That's a gag that doesn't improve with repetition."

"Well, all I'm saying is that there's no rush. So keep your shirt on and stop acting like a nervous woman caught in the middle of traffic with a full bladder. And if you have to talk to me, ring me up, for God's sake, and I'll come to New York. I'm going to have one hell of a time as it is, explaining to Hilda why you had to come tooting up here in a blizzard with as unattractive a hangover as I ever saw."

Thompson wanted to call a taxi, but Andrew had his butler drive him to the station. He left without saying good-by to Hilda or her guests, asking Andrew to make some suitable excuse. It was still snowing heavily, and the trains were running late. Tired of waiting, he took a local that dragged along, making frequent stops. Each time the door of the superheated car opened, he felt a chilling blast. By the time he got back to his hotel he was thoroughly spent.

However, his trip helped ease his mind. He was sure that Andrew, in spite of all his protests and recriminations, could be depended upon to help him out of his difficulty. The next step was to persuade Lily, and of his ability to do that he was not quite so sure. The chances were that her expressed determination to have the baby was just brave talk; once convinced that he had no intention of marrying her, she probably could be made to see the impracticability of her wild resolve. Yet she might persist in the romantic role of a wronged woman, heroically bearing her child in defiance of con-

426

vention. He cursed himself for his clumsy and undisciplined behavior of the night before. If, instead of lashing out at her, he had treated her with tenderness and sympathy, she would have been amenable to whatever he asked. Unless he could undo the damage and win her back to tractability, he would have to give up all thought of Virginia. If his relationship to Lily came to a definite end, however sordid and unsavory, Virginia might condone it as something over and done with. But he could not expect her to give herself to him, knowing that another woman was carrying his child. Nor could he hope to keep the knowledge from her. It was the sort of secret that was bound to be discovered sooner or later, and when she did find out, she would not be likely to forgive the deception. He had to pin his hopes upon overcoming Lily's intransigence.

As a result of his trip to White Plains he had a bad attack of influenza. His doctor ordered him to stay in bed for three days, and indoors until the weather moderated. He obeyed willingly; he was feverish and generally depleted, and he had a good excuse for keeping away from the Farow. As long as there was the slightest doubt about Lily's condition there was no point in having any further discussion with her. Perhaps by the time he was faced with certainty her sense of injury would have abated a little and she would be easier to win over. Meanwhile he would have to mark time as far as Virginia was concerned.

Claire stayed in town all week and came to see him every day, bringing him delicacies, waiting on him, trying to keep him amused. She was tactful, efficient, and gay, and her attentions did lessen the tedium of his confinement. But his gratitude was tempered by the sardonic reflection that he was being offered a baited hook. As he put it to himself, she was deliberately staging a preview of marriage.

From various remarks of Claire's he reconstructed his behavior at Haig's party. Undoubtedly he had made a rather unpleasant exhibition of himself, trying to rush out coatless after Virginia and Eric and becoming abusive and quarrelsome when he had been prevented from doing so. Claire, happy in her role of the understanding woman, dismissed his conduct as an excusable New Year's Eve aberration and seemed to attach much more importance to Virginia's precipitate departure with Eric. He wondered uneasily whether she might be right about Virginia and Eric after all.

The weather was very bad all week. Before the twenty-inch snowfall could be cleared away there was a sharp drop in the temperature, and a bitter north wind coated the pavements with a film of ice and froze the snow heaps into rough hummocks that made the streets almost impassable. Theater business was seriously affected; The Clouded Mirror played to half-empty houses.

Thompson had daily reports of the box-office receipts. On Friday Fineman paid him a visit. "We'll be way under our stop on the week," he said dourly. "If we get thirteen we'll be lucky; and the advance sale is way off too."

He was referring to the clause in the theater contract which gave the management of the Farow the right to terminate the engagement if the weekly receipts were less than fifteen thousand dollars for two consecutive weeks. It was this clause that Thompson had complained about when Anthony Weir had submitted the contract.

"What do you expect in this weather?" asked Thompson. "We're not hit any worse than anybody else. We're healthy, and as soon as the weather breaks we'll snap right back."

"Yes, I guess so. I just wish we had a lower stop, that's all."

"You were born with a bellyache and you've never got over it. Is Claire going to put her own show out, for Christ's sake, because we happen to run into a little blizzard?"

"I didn't say that. All I'm saying is that I don't like high stop clauses with an in-between show like this one."

"All right," said Thompson, "come back on May first and I'll listen to you cry. Meanwhile you'd better order another eight weeks' tickets. And tell Doc to run a couple of extra ads next week."

He did not resent Fineman's chronic pessimism, for it often acted as a useful brake upon his own exuberance. But he saw no occasion for alarm. The theatrical business was as sensitive as a barometer to climatic conditions. The state of the weather was immediately registered at the box-office. Blizzards, rainstorms, and heat waves always had to be counted among the normal hazards of this most precarious of all businesses.

Claire tried hard to conceal her uneasiness about the play's business. She did not want to say anything that might disturb their harmonious domestic interlude.

428

XXXVIII.

The weather in central Connecticut was even worse. The La Pointe farm was snowed in and the christening had to be postponed until the end of the week. Eric lamented the conscientiousness that had made him hurry home. He could just as well have stayed in New York and been near Virginia. To be separated from her now was acute torture. He was racked by an uncontrollable longing, which made the days and nights seem endless. He went about in a daze, reliving over and over again the delirious hours he had spent with her. It was impossible to call her from his home, and he trudged through the snow several times each day to the telephone booth in the hotel lobby. Either there was no response or it was Marion Sweet who answered, to tell him that Virginia was out. He tried to dispel the sickening fear that she was deliberately evading him, arguing that his calls had been merely ill timed and that she had no way of calling him back. Unable to endure the suspense, he wrote her a long, incoherent letter, pouring out his love in wild, extravagant terms. Somewhat relieved by this emotional discharge, he resigned himself to awaiting her reply.

Completely possessed though he was by his passion, he yet succeeded in bringing happiness to his mother by effecting a reconciliation between his father and the La Pointes. Kenwood had received the news of his grandchild's birth in sullen silence, but Eric, noticing that he listened attentively to every reference to the baby, ventured to hint that Dorothy might be induced to bring the child to see him. Kenwood, after a show of resistance, gave in. It was much harder to persuade Dorothy. Finally she yielded to the combined entreaties of Eric and Amelia, but not until Kenwood had agreed to include her husband in the reunion. The La Pointes stopped in on their way home from the christening. When they arrived, they were self-conscious and on the defensive, but Dorothy was so shocked by the alteration in her father's appearance that she softened and gave him an impulsive, pitying kiss. And the good-natured Leon, entering into the spirit of the occasion, shook hands cordially with his father-in-law. The baby was put in Kenwood's lap, and as he peered at it with his half-blind eyes and touched a trembling hand to its cheek, Amelia wept silently. They all sat down to coffee and cake, and Eric had the joyful feeling that the air of the house was cleansed at last of the poisonous hatred that had so long polluted it.

From Dorothy, Eric learned that Sylvia had just undergone a surgical operation for the removal of an ovarian tumor. Fears that the growth might be malignant had been unfounded, and she was making a normal recovery. Eric thought of writing her a note or sending her flowers but decided against it. She might find his attention unwelcome or might think he was patronizing her.

He kept himself busy as best he could over the weekend, confident that Monday morning would bring a letter from Virginia. None came. He did not know what to make of her continued silence. He wondered whether his overeffusive letter, with its frank expressions of physical desire, had offended her. Or perhaps she was ill or had met with an accident. Half-demented with anxiety, he tramped down to the telephone booth again. Marion Sweet told him that Virginia was spending the weekend in the country and was going straight from Pennsylvania Station to the theater. This time, Eric was sure that Virginia was intentionally avoiding conversation with him. He spent the day in feverish speculation, finally deciding that if no letter came next morning he would go to New York to find out the reason for her incomprehensible behavior.

Early next morning, however, Dorothy telephoned to tell them that Cousin Elizabeth had died peacefully in her sleep. Amelia cried a little, but the death was neither a shock nor a tragedy. Cousin Elizabeth was past eighty, and her growing feebleness had long been evident. Eager as Eric was to leave for New York, he felt that he must wait until after the funeral. An abrupt departure now would be hard for Amelia to understand. Besides, he thought it better to let Virginia know that he was coming, so that she could no longer put him off with excuses. He wrote her a restrained note, telling her that he was bewildered by her strange silence, that he hoped he had done nothing to offend her, and that it was imperative that he see her when he arrived in New York on Thursday. It meant another two days of agonized waiting, but there was no help for it.

To his surprise he was very deeply affected by the death of Cousin Elizabeth, not so much emotionally as philosophically. He had a strong belief that life was meaningful and purposeful, that every human being in some way fulfilled an immanent creative purpose. Even his father's life, now coming to a miserable end, had a clearly definable pattern that illustrated the general principle, if only in reverse. But in a life such as Cousin Elizabeth's, it was hard to find any design or any logical progression. In background and qualities she seemed no different than a hundred of her neighbors who had known the ordinary human fulfillments, even if unhappily. But experience seemed to have passed her by completely. Orphaned in early childhood, she had known no ties or intimate relationships and had lived out her long existence in genteel, useless drudgery, unneeded but tolerated, and as untouched by catastrophe as by any of life's satisfactions. She had injured no one, gladdened no one; neither her departure from earth nor her long sojourn upon it had had the slightest apparent effect upon the life of anyone else. For Eric, whose every hour was filled with stormy desire, creative fancies, or probing self-examination, and who longed for more tentacles with which to grasp life's riches, the emptiness of the dead woman's four-score years had a deep fascination. If he could find a clue to its significance or to its lack of significance, his understanding of human behavior and of life in general would be vastly enlarged. He knew that to progress as a writer—and as a human being—he must go beyond the mere projection of his own subjective processes and must learn to use them as a key to larger meanings. Specifically applying this generalization to his immediate problem, he felt that, somehow, a better understanding of Cousin Elizabeth would make it easier for him to understand Virginia.

His bewilderment about Virginia's attitude was not diminished by a telegram he received from her late Wednesday night. It read: "Please help me by giving me a little time. And don't blame yourself for anything. The fault is all mine."

He puzzled and puzzled over this rather cryptic message, weighing every word, searching for nuances and hidden meanings. Had she telegraphed because she was afraid that a letter would not reach him in time? Or was it a convenient device for not writing a letter

431

and for availing herself of the impersonality of a telegram, particularly a telegram that she knew had to be telephoned? In so far as she absolved him from blame the message was reassuring: his fear that he had offended her was evidently groundless. Yet what did she mean by saying the fault was all hers? Was she referring to her failure to answer his letters or was she implying that she had misled him by her impulsive surrender and regretted it? In the latter case, why did she ask for time? Obviously she was in a state of doubt or indecision and did not want to be subjected to pressure. But the nature of her problem and of her feeling for him remained a complete mystery.

What was certain was that she did not want to see him now. Unwilling to force himself upon her, he postponed his visit to New York and refrained from writing, sure that she would not welcome another tempestuous letter; any other sort would have failed to express his feelings. He resigned himself to waiting, wondering how long he could endure the separation and the silence.

XXXIX.

The temperature moderated over the weekend, and a thaw set in, accompanied by a cold, sleety rain that turned the streets into rivers of slush. Business at the Farow was worse than it had been the week before, and Fineman was unhappier than ever. He pointed out to Thompson that even if things picked up sharply at the end of the week, there was no possibility that the receipts would reach the required figure of fifteen thousand dollars. Thompson refused to be worried, confident that once the weather improved there would be a rush to the theaters again; the next five or six weeks were normally the best of the year. Should the current week's income drop to twelve thousand dollars—which was improbable—the loss for both the production and the theater would be inconsequential. He offered to bet Fineman a hundred dollars that the play would still be running in May, and was amused when Fineman refused to take him up on the ground that he was unwilling to bet against a production of which he was general manager.

On Wednesday, tired of being confined to his apartment and bored by Claire's continued ministrations, Thompson spent most of the day at his office. Virginia was constantly in his thoughts. He was tempted to go around to the theater or, at any rate, to call her, but it would be better to go on marking time until he had further news from Lily. In a day or two now, Lily would be visiting the doctor again; then he would be able to force a show-down. Meanwhile he avoided communicating with her too, not wanting to play into her hands by revealing his anxiety.

During the ten days that Claire had him to herself she had done everything she could to win him over. His docile submission to her wifely attentions filled her with high hopes of success. But whenever she tried to bring the conversation around to the subject of marriage, he deftly deflected it, and when he was well enough to go back to his office she knew he had eluded her again.

Defeated and disheartened, she was preparing to leave for the country when Anthony Weir called her. "Are you doing anything this evening?" he asked.

"I was just about to go to the country. Why?"

"I'm going down to Philadelphia to see that new show, Jack Sprat, that opened there Monday night, and I thought you might want to come along for the ride. They tell me it's taken the town by storm, and it looks terrific."

"Well, I don't know," said Claire. She had no particular desire to make the trip, but she had heard of this sensational opening and, always interested in success, was curious to see the phenomenon. Besides, even a trip to Philadelphia with Weir was better than sitting alone in the country, eating her heart out. And something in her brother-in-law's manner indicated that he thought it important for her to go. After some hesitation she consented.

They had dinner on the train and went straight from the station to the theater where Jack Sprat was playing. The house was completely sold out and hundreds of people were being turned away. The audience began laughing almost the moment the curtain was up, roared all the way through, and applauded thunderously at the end.

The play was what is known as a "sleeper": an unheralded production of which nothing much is expected but which turns out to be an instantaneous success. It was the work of two Hollywood writers, unknown to the theater, and was produced by two young "shoestring operators," who had had the utmost difficulty in scraping together the production budget, low though it was by current standards. The director was comparatively unknown too, and there was no one in the cast whose name had the slightest box-office value. The play was a conventional farce-comedy, abounding in stock situations, mistaken identities, contrived misunderstandings, and double entendre. In short, there seemed to be nothing about the enterprise that differentiated it from the dozens of futile and hapless productions that in the course of every season crept in and out of the Broadway playhouses or failed even to survive a tryout. Yet there was a slickness and a boisterous rowdiness about this particular play that caught the fancy of people out for a good time. It was apparent to everyone, long before the first performance was over, that it would be a smash hit. The reviews and the reports of the first-night audience started a rush to the box-office. Within forty-eight hours after the opening every seat had been sold for the entire two-weeks' engagement.

"Well, what do you think?" asked Weir when he and Claire were on their way back to New York.

"It's a funny show, no doubt about that. But is it corny!"

"I don't think anybody expects that they'll be studying it in the colleges, if that's what you mean. All the same, I'd like to have a piece of it."

"Well, who wouldn't? Too bad we didn't get in on it."

"How was anybody to know? The boys were peddling it, up and down the street, begging for dimes and nickels and vest buttons. They opened with forty dollars in the bank and a stack of unpaid bills."

"It's too bad," said Claire with a sigh.

"Not as bad as it sounds. We can still get in on it."

She looked at him in surprise. "How do you mean?"

"They want to book the Farow."

"You mean for next season?"

"No, I mean for a week from Monday."

She stared at him uncomprehendingly. "But—!"

"Let me give you the picture. They figured they might have some-

434

thing, but, of course, they couldn't be sure. So they penciled in six weeks beyond Philadelphia—Baltimore, Pittsburgh, Cleveland, and so on—to allow themselves plenty of time for rewriting and maybe recasting. But after Monday night they saw that they don't have to worry about any of that and now they want to get into New York in a hurry, so they can take advantage of the season and build up an advance that will send them breezing right through the summer. Besides, if they want to they can put out a second company in eight weeks and cash in double by playing the same territory they've got booked now. The booking situation is tight in New York now, and anyhow they're sore at the booking office for pushing them around and making the terms very tough. So they'd like to book an independent house, and the Farow is just right. They've had me on the phone, ever since yesterday morning, but I told them it was entirely up to you. I didn't say anything to you about it because I wanted you to see the show first and form your own opinion. So that's the whole story."

Claire listened intently, drinking in every detail, her eyes glistening avidly at the rich prospect that suddenly opened before her. "Well, it all sounds very pretty," she said, "but we happen to have a show in the Farow."

"You don't have to have. There's no chance of their making their stop this week. Naturally I checked on that with the box-office boys before I went into this. That'll make two consecutive weeks under the stop, and according to the contract you can give them their notice Saturday night and wind them up next week."

"What are you talking about, Tony? You know very well that I can't do that to Tommy—take advantage of a technicality in the contract just because the bad weather has slowed up business for two weeks."

"I thought you'd take that stand. But, frankly, I don't see it. There's no technicality about it. Everything was open and above-board. I put that stop clause in the contract to protect your interests, because that's what I'm supposed to do as your lawyer and business adviser. Tommy tried to argue me into reducing it, and I refused, so he knew exactly where he stood and where we stood. I don't see in what way you're taking advantage of him. It seems to me that he took advantage of you, insisting upon doing a play that no one except himself had any confidence in. And now that it turns out that we were right about the play, where has he got any kick

435

coming if we make use of the protection that we thought was necessary?"

"That's not altogether the way it is," protested Claire. "It isn't as if The Clouded Mirror were a flop. It's done pretty good business all along and showed a profit every week until these last two weeks, and that was only because of the blizzard. It'll come right back next week, I'm sure, and maybe finish out the season."

"All right, let's look at some figures," said Weir, taking out a pencil and scribbling on the back of an envelope. "The production cost came to over a hundred thousand and you've put about as much into the theater. This is the show's eighth full week and it's earned back about ten per cent of the production cost. The theater's profits have been even less. You've got about five good weeks ahead —provided we don't have another blizzard—and then after Washington's Birthday you'll begin to slide off. Maybe you can drag it out until the end of May, but not without some losing weeks that'll cut into the profits. Giving yourself all the breaks, the show may earn back thirty per cent of its cost, most of which will go to the other backers. I've looked into the chances of a movie sale and they're absolutely nil. The play is censorable and the Cathedral has blacklisted it. So the production will wind up about seventy per cent in the red. The theater, which is all your investment, will be even worse off. And what's more, you'll be shelling out overhead all summer on a dark house and be gambling on booking in a paying production next season. So unless you're prepared to put in another fifty thousand—which I certainly don't recommend—you may just as well hand the theater back to the mortgagee."

"And lose all that money—seventy-five thousand, or whatever it is?" said Claire, horrified.

"Well, I don't see how you're going to get around these figures. Now, look at it from the Jack Sprat angle—"

"What's the use of going into that when you know I can't—"

"No harm in discussing it, is there? Make your own decision, but get the facts first. I may not know anything about high art, but I do know a thing or two about show business. That show is a natural if ever I saw one. A one-set show with eight people in the cast. And no star problems either. You could replace the whole cast overnight and nobody would know the difference. If it doesn't run two years to capacity business I'll give you back my interest in the theater. With no stagehands your operating costs go down too, and I figure

436

that at capacity you'll show a weekly profit of three thousand, so that at the end of the year you'll not only pay off your entire investment but be fifty thousand ahead. And at the end of the second year you'll be having headaches about your income tax. So there it is. The rest is up to you."

Claire sighed. "If it was anybody else but Tommy!"

"Well, my dear," said the lawyer paternally, "that's something I can't advise you about. All I can do is present the business angle to you. The personal element is something you have to figure out for yourself. I've always felt that people should try to keep their business lives and their personal lives apart, but maybe that's just a cold-blooded lawyer's point of view. Now, of course, where it's a matter of husband and wife, I can see—"

"Yes, I know!" said Claire sharply. "I understand your point of view. It isn't just personal with me either. We're in business together and this might mean the end of it. That has to be considered too."

"Well, I know that Tommy is inclined to be a little temperamental—he wouldn't be the genius he is if he didn't have some of that in him. But I can't believe that he'd be so unreasonable as not to take into consideration all that you—"

Claire was too agitated to listen to any more and cut him short. "When do they have to know?"

"I told them I'd give them a definite answer by Friday noon at the latest. They'll have to cancel their other out-of-town bookings by then and make a firm deal for New York."

"Well, that gives me a little time to think it over."

"Yes, you have twenty-four hours at least. And if you want to talk it over further—or if you want me to talk to Tommy—"

"No, no!" she said hastily, knowing what Thompson thought of Weir. "You'd better leave that to me. I just want a little time to get it all clear in my mind, that's all."

She lay awake all night, torn by indecision. The more she reviewed Anthony Weir's arguments, the more incontrovertible they seemed. She had to admit that there was no logical reason for refusing to follow his advice. But much as she loved money, and eager as she was to avail herself of this golden opportunity, she could not bring herself to the point of taking a step that would very probably alienate Thompson forever. It was all very well for Weir to say that she should keep her business life and her emotional life apart; but

437

the fact was that the two were closely interwoven, and in her present predicament she could not foster one without detriment to the other. If she were sure of Thompson, she could have persuaded herself to sacrifice her financial interests, but she had not needed Weir's barbed reminder to convince her that her hold upon him was most insecure. Why, then, should she recklessly throw away a solid economic certainty for a tenuous emotional relationship with a dubious future?

She debated the chances of persuading Thompson to agree voluntarily to the closing of The Clouded Mirror. After all, he was a practical theater man and he had all the rewards that could be expected as producer and director of the play. Since there was no likelihood that the production cost would ever be recovered, he had little to gain from a continuance of the run. He could afford to do that much for her, after all she had done for him. Indeed, she told herself, carried away by her own argument, it would be a sort of test of strength of his feeling for her. When she got that far, she realized that it was precisely that test she was afraid of making. If it failed she would be forced to choose between losing him and losing a fortune. She cursed the perverse fate that had posed this dilemma.

At last she hit upon a compromise that seemed to promise a workable solution. In return for his voluntary withdrawal of the play, she would offer him an ownership interest in the Farow Theater—ten per cent, fifteen if necessary. She knew that he had resented her failure to make such provision for him when the theater corporation was organized and had often regretted her niggardliness. At one stroke she could dispel his feeling of injustice and compensate him for the closing of The Clouded Mirror by giving him a share of the certain profits that the theater would reap. The more she thought of it, the more feasible it seemed. Anthony Weir would object strenuously to what he would consider a needlessly quixotic gesture, but she had the right to do as she pleased with her own property. If she could book in the new play and keep Thompson happy too, she would consider it a very good bargain. Enormously pleased with herself, she could hardly wait for eleven o'clock, when she could expect to find him at his office.

In all her self-debate she gave no consideration whatever to the effect that the summary closing of The Clouded Mirror would have

438

upon others than herself. The fact that the general level of theatrical entertainment would be lowered by the substitution of a trashy play for a fine one, that a hundred thousand theatergoers would be deprived of the chance to attend a play they were interested in seeing, and that the economic consequences for Eric, the actors, and the stagehands would be drastic, did not enter into her calculations; indeed, she would have been amazed had anyone suggested that it should. She had been enriched by the skill and creativeness of authors, actors, and directors, yet she felt no responsibility to them, to the public, or to the theater as an institution. Since she held the purse strings, it seemed to her only proper that she should use her economic power as she saw fit, regardless of the effect upon the art of the theater and upon those who sought to keep it alive.

Thompson did arrive at his office a little before eleven, entering, as usual, by the private door to avoid being seen by unwelcome visitors who might be waiting in the reception room. He rang for his secretary, who gave him several telephone messages and then said, "Lily Prengle has been waiting out there for you for about an hour."

The dreaded moment had come, and he steeled himself to face it. "Lily Prengle?" he said nonchalantly. "What the hell does *she* want?"

"She wouldn't tell me. Something she has to see you personally about, she says. I told her you might not be in, but she insisted on waiting. Want me to send her away?"

"No, she's a little pest and she'll only keep coming back. I may as well get rid of her now."

"Shall I tell her to come in?"

"In a few minutes. All right, that's all for now," he said as the secretary opened her notebook.

Though he had carefully rehearsed his approach to Lily, he wanted a few minutes to collect himself and to dispel his annoyance at her indiscretion in coming to the office. There was nothing extraordinary about a member of one of his casts coming in to see him, but he was anxious to avoid anything that might attract the notice of his staff. He lit a cigarette and paced the office, like an actor waiting for his entrance, getting himself into the mood of the scene he was about to play. He intended to be all sympathy and kindness, not pressing her too hard at first, gradually winning her over to an

439

acceptance of what he wanted her to do. He crushed out his cigarette, told the receptionist to send her in, and rose to greet her, glancing quickly at her face for some clue to her feelings.

"Hello, Lily," he said warmly. "Have you been waiting long?"

"A little while," she said tonelessly. She was pale and rigid, her nervousness intensified by her long wait in the outer office.

He pulled out a chair for her. "Sit down. I'm glad to see you. I'd have been around to the Farow long before this but I had a rotten attack of flu and just got out."

"I didn't know when you'd be around, so I thought I'd better come here."

"Well, I'm glad you did," he said, trying to put her at her ease and at the same time to delay hearing the expected bad news. "I've been wanting to tell you how sorry I am about the crummy way I behaved. I was feeling pretty lousy that night—must have been the flu coming on, I guess—and before I knew it I was sounding off like some goddam half-witted lout. Anyhow, there was no excuse for it, and I want you to know I didn't mean it."

"It doesn't make any difference now," she said impassively.

"Well, it does to me," he said, puzzled by her words and by her manner. "I don't like to think of myself as a complete heel; and I don't like anyone else to have that impression either. You look pale and tired. How are you feeling?"

"Not very well," she said, her lips beginning to tremble.

He braced himself for the next question. "Have you been to see the doctor?"

"No."

"Well, isn't it about time you did?" he said, keeping his irritation under control.

"I don't have to. There's nothing to see him about."

Thompson stared at her, unable to accept at once the full implication of what she was saying. "You mean to say—?"

"Yes. And I know you're glad to hear it. But I'm not glad. I wanted to have a baby."

"You mean you were lying to me the other night?" asked Thompson, still unable to take it in.

"No, I wasn't lying. I believed it. And so did the doctor. It was just a mistake, that was all. Anybody can make a mistake."

The blood rushed to Thompson's face, flooding the dilated capillaries in his cheek. The tension had snapped, but instead of happy

440

relief he felt only insensate rage. For nearly two weeks he had been a prey to constant anxiety, scheming and planning to get himself out of a situation that might seriously affect his whole life. He had made a ridiculous exhibition of himself at his brother's house, antagonizing his sister-in-law beyond remedy, inviting his brother's contempt—and now his derision—and all for nothing, all because he had allowed himself to be misled by a silly, hysterical girl. The sight of her sitting there, with her pale face and thin hands and humorless, large eyes, infuriated him and he poured out a torrent of abuse, calling her vile names and accusing her of fantastic crimes. It was all that he could do to keep himself from striking her. She sat staring at him in horror, so overwhelmed by the flood of calumny she could not speak or move. When he stopped, panting for breath, she rose quickly and said in a choking voice, "I'd like to get out of the play."

"The sooner the better!" he said. "And keep out of my way too!" She was gone before he finished speaking. He sank into his chair, exhausted by his outburst and already beginning to regret it.

Lily managed to keep herself under control until she was out of the office, but, once in the corridor, she broke down and leaned against the wall, sobbing violently. It was there that Claire found her as she stepped out of the elevator on her way to see Thompson.

"Why, Lily," she said, "what's the matter?" As the girl did not answer she put an arm around her. "Come into the office and calm yourself down."

Lily wrenched herself free. "No! No! I never want to go in there again—or see him again!"

Claire looked at her sharply. She disliked Lily intensely, and, accustomed as she was to the volatility of actresses, was not in the least disturbed by her hysterics; but this emotional protest, which obviously referred to Thompson, suddenly aroused her sharp suspicion. There flashed through her mind a whole chain of incidents: Thompson's insistence upon engaging Lily instead of Suzanne Merchant; his enthusiasm for her during rehearsals; his consideration of her as a replacement for Emily Crandall. She wondered if she had been foolishly blind all these months and was determined to find out.

"Well, come and have a cup of tea or something," she said soothingly. "You'll make yourself sick, going on this way."

"No, I'm all right!" said Lily.

"You can't go out on the street like this," insisted Claire. "Come along with me."

441

Welcoming any sympathy, Lily submitted. Wiping her eyes, she docilely accompanied Claire to the elevator. They went down to the bar on the street floor of the building. It was almost empty, and they sat in an unoccupied corner. Claire ordered a whisky for Lily and made her drink it, talking to her with motherly gentleness, to which Lily responded like a hurt child. Warmed by the drink and only too eager to find an outlet for her pent-up feelings, she could not long resist Claire's womanly invitation to confide in her. Soon she was pouring forth the miserable story. Claire listened with mounting hatred, longing to slap the pretty, piteous young face but maintaining the appearance of friendly understanding and commiseration.

"I guess I shouldn't have told you," said Lily when the last detail had been wrung from her. "But I've been so lonely and so upset that I just had to talk to somebody."

"Of course, you did, you poor girl!" said Claire, patting her hand. "And you can trust me not to breathe a word of it to anybody." She offered to take her home. Lily declined, much to Claire's relief, for she did not know how much longer she could control her insane jealousy of this little nonentity who had succeeded in arousing Thompson, even momentarily, to a degree of passion that she had never known.

She put Lily into a taxi and then hurried to a telephone booth and told Anthony Weir to go ahead with the negotiations for booking Jack Sprat into the Farow. This done, she went back to her apartment and gave way to her own outraged feelings. As soon as she felt able to go out again, she left for the country. Her impulsive act of revenge gave her a sense of savage satisfaction, and she tried not to contemplate the emptiness that lay ahead of her.

XL.

Still weak from his illness, Thompson was so depleted by his emotional orgasm that he had to go home to bed. It took him a long time to steady his shaken nerves and overcome his self-disgust sufficiently to permit him to examine his altered situation with respect to Virginia. Lily was no longer an obstacle, and though the problem of Claire still had to be faced, he was not troubled by it. He could give her up without a pang. The severance of their business relationship might be an inconvenience, but only a temporary one. He was confident enough of his position in the theater to believe that he would have no difficulty in financing his productions—and without emotional entanglements or the galling officiousness of an Anthony Weir. A straight business arrangement, free from personal complications, would be far more satisfactory.

Everything impelled him toward Virginia. His feeling for her went far beyond physical attraction. Her personality, her character, her outlook on life, her talent—all aroused his admiration and stirred his imagination. She held for him the promise of a companionship and an understanding such as he had never known. He was nearing forty and was beginning to tire of his vagrant, rootless life. He viewed with distaste the prospect of going on as he had for so many years, drifting in and out of one empty relationship after another, allowing himself to be drawn into a senseless episode with some Lily Prengle. In another ten years he would be jaded, cynical, and incapable of forming any enduring or meaningful tie.

Yet he hesitated. Virginia, he knew, was not to be cheaply had. Every woman he had known intimately, even Louise Henry, had been under his domination and had offered no real challenge to his egotism. Virginia was of different caliber. Like himself, she was

443

proud, self-centered, critical, and demanding. She was fully capable of standing up to him and would not tolerate infidelity, indifference, or high-handedness. He would have to be prepared to make unaccustomed concessions and surrenders, to give at least as much as he took, and to measure up to a high standard of performance. He thought well of himself and did not doubt his ability to meet her expectations, but to do so he would certainly have to give up some of the independence he cherished so fiercely. It was not enough to tell himself that she was worth it; to succeed he would have to school himself persistently in an unfamiliar self-discipline. Still shaken by his narrow escape from Lily, he decided to give himself a few more days to think it all through. He could not hope to win her until he had rid himself of all doubt and weakness of purpose.

The improvement of the weather brought out the theatergoing public in large numbers. The Thursday night house at the Farow was very good, and so was the outlook for the remainder of the week. While Thompson was looking over the preceding night's box-office statement on Friday morning, McCarthy telephoned.

"I didn't want to bother you last night," said the stage manager, "but I thought you'd want to know that Lily didn't show for the performance. And it looks like she's taken all her things out of her dressing-room. Did she give in her notice or something?"

"Oh yes," said Thompson glibly. "It's all my fault. She told me two weeks ago that she wanted to get out—some family complication or something, I forget what—and I just clean forgot to tell you. Sorry, Mack. I'll see my analyst about it tonight."

"Well, wouldn't you think she'd have said something to me about it?"

"Well, between you and me, she's a little on the goofy side."

"You can say that again!" said McCarthy. "It didn't really matter though. Glad Kaye went in and nobody knew the difference."

"All right, I'll look around for somebody. Think Glad can carry on until next week?"

"Oh, sure! Matter of fact, she could go right on doing it and save you a salary."

"No, I'd better get somebody. I don't like to be short-handed."

He was thankful that Lily had left so abruptly, a step she would not have dared take had she been more familiar with the customs of the theater and the terms of her contract.

Fineman also came in to tell him of Lily's strange departure. "Yes,

444

I know," said Thompson, cutting him short. "Mack just called me. She told me she wanted to quit and I said it was all right with me. It must have slipped my mind and, of course, she wouldn't have the brains to tell anybody."

"All notices are supposed to be in writing," said Fineman, not believing a word of Thompson's story. "We can hold her for two weeks' salary."

"Tell it to the district attorney. Well, we weren't so bad la night."

"No," said Fineman, wondering what was behind Lily's behavior but telling himself that it was none of his business. "And we look all right for the rest of the week. But even if we sell out we'll still be under the stop."

"How does next week look?"

"Looks very good right now, provided we don't get another blizzard. The advance took a big jump yesterday and again this morning."

"Then what the hell are you worrying about?"

"That's what I'm paid for," said Fineman. "Another thing. I ran into Joe Gillian last night—you know Joe, he's with the Platt-Kahn agency."

"Oh, sure! Who's he sleeping with now?"

"I forgot to ask him. But he was down in Philly, Wednesday night, catching that new Jack Sprat show, and he says Claire and Tony Weir were there too."

"You pick up the most fascinating stories. Have you ever thought of bringing them out in a book?"

"I just thought you might be interested, that's all. They tell me that show is a sure winner, and I thought Tony Weir might be looking it over as something for the Farow. You know that legal mind of his."

Thompson shook his head. "Murray, you're going to wake up some morning and find that you've scared yourself to death."

"I wouldn't be surprised. Well, that's all I've got to say," said Fineman, walking out of the office.

Thompson stroked his lip thoughtfully. He was not nearly as uninterested in Fineman's news as he had pretended to be. When he had talked to Claire on Wednesday morning she had told him that she was going to the country. She had said nothing about a trip to Philadelphia, nor had he heard from her since. That was rather un-

445

usual too; ordinarily if she had been to see a tryout she would have called him next morning and spent an hour telling him about it. Furthermore, he shared Fineman's opinion of Anthony Weir's mental processes. The lawyer would not hesitate to avail himself of any technicality in order to gain a business advantage—even when there was no personal animosity involved. Still, he could not believe that Claire, avid for money though he knew her to be, could be induced to take a step that was so certain to antagonize him. He reached for the telephone, intending to call her, but thought better of it. If she had a secret intention she would not be likely to divulge it over the telephone. If she had not, there was certainly no point in putting it in her mind. Besides, there was nothing he could do about it now. If the theater management were to give the required week's notice of closing, it would have to do so on Saturday night, after it became certain that the receipts had not reached the stipulated figure. The notice, of course, was not irrevocable; if it were given, he had confidence in his ability to persuade Claire to withdraw it between Saturday night and Monday night, when notice of closing would have to be given to the cast. He decided to dismiss the whole thing from his mind. He did not go to the Farow that night but spent most of the evening at the Stuyvesant, where there were disturbing indications that the play might not even last out the season.

On Saturday he had a late breakfast in his apartment. There was nothing to take him to the office, and he had a ticket for the matinee performance of Tristan and Isolde at the Metropolitan Opera House. Just as he was about to leave Fineman called him.

"I don't like what's going on at the Farow box-office," he said. "The boys are pushing the sale for next week and making it tough for anybody who wants to buy ahead."

"Did you say anything to them?"

"Well, I hinted around, but they're playing them close to their chest and not talking. I think they got their orders from higher up."

"Maybe this is just one of your blue days."

"Maybe. But it don't look kosher to me. Are you coming around this afternoon?"

"No, I'm going to the opera. I like music with my hard-luck stories."

"What about tonight?"

"I think I'll stay home and read some scripts. Unless you need somebody to hold your hand."

"Well, I'll give you a ring after we count up, just to let you know what the score is."

"I'm looking forward to it."

He was beginning to believe that Fineman's suspicions were not unfounded. But he could accomplish nothing by going around to the theater or by talking to Claire now. In a few hours he would know how things stood; then it would be time enough to take whatever action seemed necessary. In spite of his determination to let nothing interfere with his enjoyment of the opera, he found it hard to keep his mind on the performance. He dined alone and then, settling down with a cigar and a brandy bottle, thumbed through the pile of playscripts on his table in an unsuccessful attempt to find one that would capture his interest.

At ten o'clock Fineman called. "I'm down here in the lobby with Doc. Is it all right if we come up?"

Fineman's tone and the faces of the two men when he opened the door for them were enough to tell Thompson that the blow had fallen.

"Here it is," said Fineman, handing him a sheet of paper on which was typed a formal notification that the theater management elected to exercise its right to terminate the engagement of The Clouded Mirror at the end of the following week. It was signed by Cleveland Dean, the house manager of the Farow.

"Well, let's try to figure out where we go from here," said Thompson with assumed calmness.

"Where is there to go?" asked Fineman. "We're out on our fannies and that's all there is to it."

"I may be able to talk Claire out of it."

Fineman shook his head. "Not if they've cooked up a deal with the Jack Sprat show. And you wouldn't be getting the notice unless they have. Tony Weir is too smart a cookie to stick out his neck if he didn't have an ace in the hole."

"Well, I'm going to try anyhow." Fineman was probably right, but Thompson was unwilling to admit it.

"Oh, sure, it don't hurt to try," said Fineman. "Only I'm laying ten to one you don't get to first base with it."

"Meanwhile you'd better get busy and see if we can find another theater."

"I've been checking around all week, and it looks like we haven't got a Chinaman's chance." Thompson was a little annoyed that

447

Fineman had anticipated him in everything; yet he could not help admiring the realistic pessimism that had motivated him. "Anyhow, to make the move will cost us five grand, easy, and that's a lot of meatballs."

"As much as that?" said Thompson.

Winternitz chimed in. "We'd have to do a lot of display advertising to let the customers know where we are, and you know what that runs to."

"Well, I may want to do it anyhow. I like this show and I'm not lying down on it unless I have to. Try to keep it out of the papers until Tuesday. No matter what happens, I'd rather have the cast hear it from me first."

Winternitz nodded.

"What about the theater, Murray? Can you get them to lay off too?" asked Thompson.

"I guess I can wangle it. I figure they won't sign the Jack Sprat contract till sometime Monday. It wouldn't be legal before we got the notice."

They went on examining every aspect of the situation. The more they discussed it, the more unlikely it seemed that the closing of the play could be prevented. Nevertheless, when the two men had gone Thompson called Poundridge. The telephone rang and rang, and at last the butler answered sleepily, to say that Claire had retired at nine, instructing him not to disturb her.

Thompson called her again next morning at eleven but was told that she was still asleep. She was obviously trying to avoid talking to him, but that very fact made him feel that she was afraid he might induce her to change her mind. He was sure that she had yielded reluctantly to Weir's persuasion and was now suffering from misgivings. In that case there was still a chance that he might be able to counteract the attorney's influence. He ordered his car for twelve-thirty, breakfasted, and drove out to Poundridge. He was afraid that Claire might have guests and that it would not be easy to talk privately to her. However, he found her alone in the living-room, having her after-lunch coffee and reading the Sunday papers. Though she was half expecting him, she was flustered by his arrival, hastily putting down her cup so that he would not see the trembling of her hand.

"You feeling all right?" he asked. "You look a little jittery."

448

"I've got a very bad headache," she said stonily, "and I was hoping to spend the day alone."

"Sorry, but I got a little billet doux from the theater last night, and I just wanted to be sure that it's all a mistake."

She tightened her lips. "There's no mistake about it."

"You mean you're really giving me the bum's rush?"

"I've got a chance to book in a hit show and I can't afford to turn it down the way I'm fixed with the theater."

"Oh, pardon *me*," he said, "I didn't realize that you were in financial difficulties."

She flushed, stung by his sarcasm, and angered to be on the defensive in spite of her firm conviction that the right was all on her side. "I didn't say I was in financial difficulties. I have a right to run my own business in my own way, and do what I consider best for myself."

"I was under the impression that we were in business together." Then, as she did not answer, "Or am I wrong?"

She was finding it harder and harder to keep herself under control. "I don't care to discuss it any further," she said, rising. "I'm sorry, but I'll have to ask you to excuse me. I'm not feeling at all well and I've got to lie down." She wanted to escape before her feelings carried her away.

But Thompson intercepted her. "Wait a minute! You can't just run out on me like that! What the hell am I around here, an office boy?"

She could contain herself no longer. "I'll tell you what you are if you really want to know! A dirty, lousy, stinking bastard!"

Thompson stared at her, completely dumfounded. "What is this anyhow?"

"That's right!" she said shrilly. "Play dumb! Try to make a monkey out of me, the way you've been doing all these years! But, oh no! No more! I've had all I'm going to take! Christ, what a heel *you* turned out to be! Screwing little extra girls in the ladies' room!"

"Of *your* theater!" said Thompson sardonically. Now that he knew that she had found out about Lily, everything appeared in a different light.

"Yes, of *my* theater!" she screamed. "And I want you out of it— and out of my life too! And what's more, get the hell out of my house!" She spat in his face, shoved him violently aside, and rushed out of the room.

449

Thompson wiped his face, put on his coat and hat and got into his car. He was singularly unaffected by the sordid scene. If Claire had shown signs of grief or had sadly reproached him, he might have had some feeling of remorse and offered explanations and apologies. But her vulgar rage had merely cheapened her in his eyes; he felt nothing for her but contempt. She was using Lily merely to justify herself for stooping to a shabby piece of business chicanery, which violated the spirit of their relationship far more than his witless escapade had done. She had saved him the trouble of disentangling himself from her; and he congratulated himself upon gaining his freedom at such small cost.

Nor did he feel any anger toward Lily for having given him away. In view of his inexcusable heartlessness, he could hardly blame her for what she had done. The more he thought about the situation, the more grimly amusing he found it, for it all sprang from the childish perversity that had made him deliberately ignore Anthony Weir's recommendation of Suzanne Merchant. If he had acceded to Weir's request, as he could so readily have done, he would have made a firm ally of him instead of an implacable enemy who had eagerly seized the opportunity to revenge himself. And, of course, he would never have become involved with Lily. The closing of The Clouded Mirror would mean little to him, either financially or professionally. It would, however, mean a great deal to Eric and the cast, and it distressed him that they were the helpless victims not only of the cupidity and petty spite of Claire and her brother-in-law, but of his own vanity and recalcitrance.

He spent all day Monday trying to find another theater for The Clouded Mirror. But it was the height of the season, when theaters were in great demand, and those that were available either preferred to gamble on a new production that might turn out to be a hit or demanded guarantees that he could not meet without the risk of substantial losses. Having exhausted every possibility, he instructed Winternitz to prepare a Tuesday morning press release, announcing merely that the play would close on Saturday night. He was tempted to put the blame upon the management of the Farow, but, like most theatrical people, he did not like washing his dirty linen in public. Once the news was out, tongues would begin wagging and eventually the responsibility would be put where it belonged.

Under the Equity rules the producer could terminate the engagement by posting a week's notice on the call board (except for actors having run-of-the-play contracts, who had to be given individual notices). Since the notice had to be posted before the end of the Monday night performance Thompson sent word to McCarthy to assemble the cast on the stage ten minutes before the rise of the curtain. He was unwilling to have the actors learn the bad news from a cold, businesslike announcement and wanted to break it to them himself, painful though the task was.

The actors were waiting for him when he walked onto the stage, some dressed and ready to go on, others still in their dressing gowns. They had not seen him since New Year's Eve and, having no foreboding of what awaited them, greeted him warmly and plied him with questions about his health. He looked quickly at Virginia, uncertain whether her welcoming smile was genuine or assumed. With his back to the curtain he scanned the semicircle of faces before beginning.

He wasted no time on meaningless preliminaries and came to the point at once. "This is a tough moment for me," he said. "I have some very bad news to tell you. We've been under our stop for the past two weeks, due to the weather of course, and the theater has given us notice, effective Saturday night. And that means, I'm sorry to say, that we have to close this week."

The actors were stunned and could only murmur their incredulity. Florence Fulham was the first to find words. "But what does it mean? I thought we were a hit." There was a chorus of agreement.

"Not according to our theater contract," said Thompson. "If we go under our stop for two consecutive weeks, they have the right to give us a week's notice."

"Even with a blizzard like that, when nobody goes to the theater?"

"That has nothing to do with it. They've got the legal right and they're exercising it."

"But haven't you an interest in the theater yourself?" asked Reginald Olmsted. "I'm sure that's the general impression."

"It may be, but it happens not to be correct. I'm a member of the board of directors, but I have nothing whatever to do with decisions like this." He saw their doubting looks and was a little hurt. Yet he could hardly blame them, since they knew how intimate he and Claire were. It was impossible to tell them the whole truth, but if he wanted to retain their trust and respect he had to offer some explanation.

"I give you my word," he said, "and I think you all know me

451

well enough to believe me, that if there was any way I could prevent it we would not be closing. I liked this play from the minute I read it, and I put in six months' hard work on it. I didn't expect it to be a smash, and I'm well satisfied with the way it got over and very grateful to all of you for your fine performances. In fact, I'd like to go on record as saying that, although I won't make a nickel out of it, I'm as proud of this show as any I've ever done. But that's not the angle from which Mrs. Weir, who owns the theater, and Tony Weir, who's her business adviser, look at it. The theater's just about breaking even, and there's nothing in it for them to keep the show running. They've got a chance to book in a show, called Jack Sprat, that's just opened in Philly and looks like a sock, and so that's why they've given us notice. I've tried to argue them out of it, but they've made up their minds and there's nothing in the world anybody can do about it."

"Jack Sprat!" exclaimed Florence Fulham. "Why, Irina Lanski told me she saw that in Philadelphia and it's nothing but a cheap farce!"

"That may be, but it's standing them up, and it looks good for two years in New York."

"Can't we move to another theater?" asked McCarthy.

"If we could I'd do it in a minute. But Murray and I have been working on that and there's not a chance."

"May I say a word?" said James Lawless, the oldest member of the cast, a man of seventy.

"Sure, go ahead."

"Well, I just want to say that I think it's an outrage," said the old actor, trembling. "This is a fine play and the public wants to see it. We've played to good houses, and they've shown us their appreciation. And now we're being turned out in the street—twenty-five people thrown out of work because of a few days' bad weather. I say it's not right—contract or no contract. You know what conditions are in the theater today, and how hard it is for an actor to find a job. Maybe it's worse for me—an old man, who's trying to keep his head above water and stay out of the Actors' Home. But we all have our living to make and responsibilities we have to meet. Hard luck and failure—we're all used to that and expect it. But not when a play's a success, when the critics praise it and the public is supporting it. Hasn't an actor any rights or any protection?

452

That's what I want to know!" His voice rose in excitement. The other actors were stirred to angry applause and cries of assent.

Thompson raised a warning hand. "Sh! There's an audience out there. And it's past curtain time." He turned to Lawless. "I agree with everything you say," he said with deep sincerity. "This is the hardest thing I've ever had to do to any company. I've tried everything I could think of to keep running, but I haven't been able to swing it. So unless somebody else comes up with a workable idea, I'm afraid we're licked."

"Can we have a chance to talk it over among ourselves?" asked Florence Fulham.

"Yes, of course. Only you realize there isn't much time."

"Maybe we'll be able to think of something before the show is over. When can we talk to you again?"

"Well, I'll come back after the performance if you like."

"All right, please do."

Thompson went out front and watched part of the performance. The house was well filled and the audience attentive and responsive. He had been deeply touched by the scene backstage and was even more moved to see how discipline and artistic integrity triumphed over disappointment and anxiety. Technically the performance was as smooth and flawless as always; only to Thompson was the crushing effect of the heavy blow visible. He felt tears rising and could watch no longer. He went to a newsreel theater but paid little attention to the screen. His quickened emotions and the mere sight of Virginia had put an end to his irresolution. He went back to the Farow with clarity of feeling and firmness of purpose.

Again he confronted his cast, and it hurt him to see the set, tense faces.

"We've asked Reggie to speak for us," said Florence Fulham.

"All right, Reggie, go ahead," said Thompson.

Olmsted cleared his throat a little nervously. "Well, we've been rather talking things over among ourselves, and there's a general feeling that we would like to go on if it's at all possible."

"So would I."

"Yes, quite. And I do think I should say, at the very beginning, that we all understand your position. We all realize that you're more or less the victim of circumstances, just as we are."

"Well, I'm happy to hear it," said Thompson genuinely.

453

"Of course, we haven't had too much time for discussion, but there are two definite suggestions that we'd like you to consider. The first is that we're all agreed to take a substantial cut in salary—subject, naturally, to Equity's approval—if that would make it possible for you to come to terms with another theater."

"That would be a big help if there were any theater that would be willing to take us. But no theater owner wants to take a chance, at this time of year, on a show that's being forced to move. I'll try again and keep trying all week, but I can tell you that it's about a fifty-to-one shot. What's your other proposition?"

"Well, it's hardly what I'd call a proposition," said Olmsted. "It's rather in the nature of an emotional appeal. We thought of presenting a sort of petition, signed by us all—and by you, we hoped—to Mrs. Claire Weir and Anthony Weir, setting forth the hardships and all that sort of thing and asking them if they wouldn't—"

Thompson interrupted him. "I don't want to cut you short, but that's hopeless. They couldn't reconsider now if they wanted to. The contract for the new show has been signed, it'll be advertised in tomorrow's papers, and tickets go on sale here in the morning." He had obtained this information from Fineman and Winternitz in the course of the day.

There was nothing more to be said. The disappointed actors went to their dressing-rooms. Virginia was almost the first to leave, anxious to get away before Thompson had a chance to talk to her. She had taken no part in the general discussion and had agreed to join in any action that would ensure the continuance of the run only out of consideration for her fellow actors, to whom it meant so much. For her own part the news of the closing was far from unwelcome; it meant that her obligations were at an end and she would be free to go away if she chose. She could no longer delay taking some decisive step, for the strength of her feelings frightened her. When Thompson had walked onto the stage her knees had almost given way, and she had been so intent upon maintaining an appearance of composure that she had not heard half of what had been said.

He came to her dressing-room while she was removing her makeup. Pearl left the room, as etiquette demanded, when the producer entered. In her agitation Virginia could think of no reasonable excuse for asking her to stay.

"It's been a hell of a time since I've seen you," said Thompson. She busily rubbed cold cream on her face, not daring to look at him even in the mirror. "I'm sorry you were sick. Are you all right again?"

"Yes, except I'm a little down about the show." He could feel that her tension matched his own. It heartened him to know that whatever she felt for him, it was not indifference.

"Who wouldn't be?" she said. "Poor Eric! Does he know about it?"

"Not yet. I didn't see the use of getting him all stirred up until I was sure," he said, trying not to show the pique he felt at her reference to Eric. "Can you have a drink with me?"

Terror engulfed her. "Not tonight, if you don't mind," she said hastily. "I'm off my feed and I'd just like to get a little quiet shut-eye."

He rose abruptly. "Well, maybe tomorrow night."

"Yes, maybe."

"Get a good sleep."

And he was gone. It was all that she could do to restrain herself from calling him back. With trembling hands she finished removing her make-up and got into her dress. As she came out of the alley her heart stopped. A taxi was waiting, and Thompson stood beside it, smoking a cigarette.

"Thought I'd save you the trouble of looking for a cab," he said.

"Thanks," she replied almost inaudibly, getting in. Her eyes widened as he threw away his cigarette and got in beside her. "Am I dropping you or are you dropping me?" she asked with attempted nonchalance.

"Neither," he said, closing the door. "I want to talk to you." He gave the driver her address. As the cab rolled away she leaned back in silence, her hands tightly clasped.

XLI.

As day after day went by without further word from Virginia, Eric began to find the uncertainty intolerable. He felt he could not go on much longer waiting for the telephone to ring and living in a state of suspense from one day's mail to the next.

On Tuesday morning he drove to the neighboring resort and spent the whole day skating on the lake, thinking his problem through and coming, at last, to a firm decision. He would go to New York and ask Virginia to marry him. Anything, even a flat refusal, would be better than this paralyzing inaction. But he was unwilling to believe that she would say no as flatly as all that. If she knew her own mind as well as that, it would have been simple enough for her to have said so long before. He could not think her shallow enough, cruel enough, or wanton enough, to torture him deliberately. She was putting him off, pleading for time, he told himself, because she was not sure enough of her feeling to commit herself definitely. If he could only get that assurance from her own lips he would at least have a tangible hope to sustain him until she made up her mind. And just to see her, to hear her voice, to touch her hand, would in some degree assuage his aching desire.

He pondered the revolutionary change in his way of living that marriage to Virginia would bring about. It would mean that he would have to live in New York—since it was inconceivable that she would be willing to abandon her career and bury herself in the country—and to accustom himself to an entirely new mode of life. It was a rather frightening prospect, for his shy and introverted nature shrank from the hurly-burly of New York life and he doubted his ability to keep up with Virginia's smart and sophisticated friends and to accommodate himself to the social whirl of which she was so much a part. And, if he did succeed, what effect would it have upon his work? Perhaps it was her own doubt about his adaptability that was troubling her. If so, he was ready to assure her of his willingness to mold himself to her pattern, for no concession or sacrifice seemed too great a price to pay for her.

When he arrived home in the late afternoon, physically tired but buoyed up by his resolution, his mother told him that a New York operator had called several times. He was sure that the call must be from Virginia, and his eagerness to talk to her overcame his hesitancy to use the home telephone. When the connection was completed he was deeply disappointed to hear Irina Lanski's voice.

"I've been trying to get you all day," she said. "Have you seen the New York papers?"

"No," said Eric, alarmed by her obvious agitation. "Is anything wrong?"

"Yes, there is, I'm sorry to say. The Clouded Mirror is closing Saturday."

The news was so unexpected and so shocking that he could not take it in. "I don't understand."

"The theater gave Tommy a week's notice and so he has to close. It all came about very suddenly. I only heard it myself this morning."

"But—but why?" he stammered. "What happened?"

Briefly she gave him the essential facts. "It's an outrage," she concluded, "but there is nothing anyone can do."

"I was planning to come to New York tomorrow," said Eric, unable to think of anything else to say. "What time can I see you?"

"I have a rather heavy calendar. Can you meet me at the Arlington for seven-thirty dinner? Then we can talk at leisure."

"Yes, all right."

In spite of Irina Lanski's explanation he could not understand what had happened. Everyone connected with the play had assured him that it would run all season. Now, with almost no warning, its career was coming to a swift end. He had written a good play and it had been well received, yet a mercenary theater owner, who had contributed nothing, had the power to close it arbitrarily and deprive him of his well-earned satisfactions and rewards. It was baffling and frightening, and he felt a surge of hatred against the pushing, small-souled woman who was robbing him of prestige and security and demolishing his well-grounded plans.

457

For now, even assuming Virginia's willingness, he would have to give up any thought of immediate marriage. He had estimated that a full season's run, with a reasonable certainty of a road tour to follow, would bring him in forty or fifty thousand dollars during the next twelve or fifteen months. As it was, his total earnings would come to a little more than ten thousand dollars. Taking into account his expenditures in New York, the substantial gifts to his family and friends, and the income tax he would have to pay, he would have about five thousand left. By his standards that was still a considerable sum and enough to keep him going for well over a year if he continued to live at home. He could make it stretch even further by accepting a proofreading job in the State Education Department at Hartford, which, he had been informed, would be open to him in April. (He was glad that he had delayed sending off a letter of rejection.) But any possibility of living in New York was now precluded. Provision for his parents and his own maintenance in New York would exhaust his resources in a few months—particularly if he had to adopt Virginia's standard of living. She was well able to provide for herself, but he could not expect her to support him, nor would his pride and independence permit him to accept such an arrangement. He could ask her to wait—but for what and for how long? Meantime, what opportunity would he have to see her? A short trip to New York now and then would be all he could afford. How could he expect her, accustomed as she was to doing whatever she pleased and having whatever she wanted, to understand the limitations that his day-by-day economic problems imposed upon him? The more he thought about it, the more hopeless it all seemed.

He found Irina Lanski deeply sympathetic and as indignant as he was. "It's all that cheap, money-grubbing cosmetics peddler's doing," she said. "It is shocking and immoral that artists should be at the mercy of these bloodsucking harpies, but that is the nature of the materialistic world in which we live. Fortunately they never wholly succeed in defeating God's purpose, and, somehow or other, in the midst of all the cut-throat savagery, the sacred flame is kept burning. I know how hard this is for you and how unfair it must seem. But you must look at the positive side too. You have had your play produced, and well produced. You have made the beginning of a reputation. You have made a little money too. For a young author, particularly for a young author with integrity and ideals, I

458

think you have done rather well. You must not be discouraged because some filthy slut pulls your chair from under you. Pick yourself up, forget about your bruises, and go to work again. Are you thinking of a new play? I very much hope so."

"Well, in a way, yes," said Eric, reluctant to talk about it and wishing he could overcome his reticence and unburden himself to her about Virginia. But in response to her coaxing, he told her haltingly of the new play that was still in its early beginnings. It had grown out of his musings upon Cousin Elizabeth's empty life and was to be a tender, intimate study of a small-town woman whom opportunity passes by and who goes from youth to old age always hoping for a fulfillment that is never achieved.

Irina Lanski listened attentively and approvingly. "Yes, I like that very much. If you do a good job of writing and we find the right actress for it, it might turn out very well. I'm leaving for Hollywood on Sunday, and I'll try to find out who is likely to be available for next season. Which reminds me that I spoke today to Mike Muhlbach, through whom I work out there. I told him that your play is closing, and he asked me if you would be interested in a Hollywood writing job. He thinks he could probably get you one."

"Well, I don't know," said Eric, startled by this unexpected suggestion. "Would it pay well?"

"Well, I suppose about five hundred a week to begin with, and, of course, much more if, as they charmingly put it, you made good."

"That's a lot of money!"

She nodded. "Yes, a lot of money. Think it over and let me know how you feel about it before I leave."

By the time Eric got to the Farow the first act was half over. He went backstage and was struck by the general air of fervid indignation. As he stood in the wings he was aware that the play was going as it had never gone before. The house was packed. The announcement of the closing had brought a great rush to the box-office of those who had been planning to come at some future date. Those who had bought tickets in advance hastened to exchange them for the current performances. The atmosphere was electric. The actors, stimulated by the enthusiastic response of the large audience and seething with a sense of injustice, threw themselves into the performance like a band of valiant zealots dedicated to a lost cause. For most of them the immediate future was bleak indeed. Virginia, Florence Fulham, and one or two of the others did not

459

have to worry about money; for the rest the financial problem was grave. There would be few new plays opening after mid-March, and those that were scheduled for the next six or eight weeks were already in rehearsal or well along with their casting. Consequently there was little hope of new employment until late summer, when activity for the next season would begin. That was a long way off. Meanwhile the unemployed actors would have to support themselves and their dependents as best they could, by finding radio jobs or some other form of work unrelated to the theater. Yet so great was their professional pride and their loyalty to the theater that, in spite of the dark days that lay ahead, they were determined to finish their present engagement in a blaze of glory.

Virginia caught a glimpse of Eric in the wings and was prepared to find him in her dressing-room at the end of the act. "Hello, Eric dear," she said, pressing his hand warmly, "I'm glad to see you."

"I'm glad to see you," he murmured. It took all his will power to resist the impulse to crush her in his arms and kiss her passionately.

"It's a rotten shame about the play! Did you hear them out there? They love every word of it. And it's been like that all week." She spoke with simple sincerity, unlike her usual high-strung levity.

"It's quite a blow," said Eric, so overwhelmed by her nearness that he found it hard to say anything.

"Oh, I know! We were all sunk when we got the news. But it's ten times worse for you and your beautiful play. It's all the fault of that droopy, pudgy Weir woman—werewolf, I almost said! If thoughts could kill she'd be surrounded by calla lilies right now." Then, before he could answer, she said quickly, "Well, I'd better go make my change. There's a second act coming up—for a few nights more anyhow."

"Can I see you after the show?"

"Not tonight, please, darling!" She saw his hurt look and put her hand on his shoulder. "Please don't think I'm being difficult, because I don't mean to be. It's just that all this, everything that's happened, has knocked me higher than a kite. So bear with me, won't you, and give me just a few days more."

"Yes, of course. Whatever you say."

"Just a few days, that's all—just till the end of the week. And don't hate me for being such a pig."

"That's something you don't have to worry about—as you very well know!"

Her eyes filled with tears. "Well, I'm glad to hear it—though I really don't deserve it. I've got to go now." She started for the inner room, then came back, kissed him quickly, and went in, closing the door behind her.

In the alley Eric met Thompson, who was on his way back-stage. "Hello, Eric," he said, clapping him on the shoulder. "Well, we've had a tough break."

"Yes, we certainly have." He noticed that Thompson, too, had dropped his habitual half-satiric manner and spoke with unwonted sobriety.

"I was going to call you in the country, but I still had hopes that we might be able to work out something. No dice though."

"What about a tour?"

Thompson shook his head. "You couldn't book a workable route on this short notice. Anyhow, we'd be licked before we started with only ten weeks in New York behind us. If we'd run out the season, we'd have had something to work on, but as it is we wouldn't have a chance. No, I'm afraid we're washed up. It's just show business, that's all."

"It's pretty hard to understand."

"Not when you've been at it as long as I have. But don't let it get you down. Write yourself a new one and give me a crack at it, and maybe next time we'll get the breaks. How long are you going to be around?"

"Until the end of the week anyhow."

"Well, I'll be seeing you."

Eric went into the theater and joined the standees to watch the second act. He had not seen the play since New Year's Eve. The house had been crowded that night too, but this audience in no way resembled the inattentive holiday-makers. These people had come because they were eager to see the play, and they followed it with excited interest. At the end there was prolonged applause and the actors were repeatedly recalled.

He went to his hotel in a far happier frame of mind than he had known for weeks. The play was closing, it was true, but not ignominiously. On the contrary, the emotion of the audience and of the actors was a tribute to the quality of his work and to his stature as an artist. The backstage friendliness and Thompson's expression of confidence gave him a sense of fellowship and the feeling that he had won not only the affection and respect of his

461

brother-craftsmen, but a solid place in the world he had chosen to make his.

Virginia's tenderness, too, gave him new hope. He accepted her earnest plea for time as proof of her seriousness, and he could not doubt that she cared deeply for him. Indeed, he was almost pleased to be put off, for he wanted much more from her than mere love-making, and needed time to review his whole situation again and find a way to make a permanent relationship possible.

But no matter how much he thought about it, he could not escape the economic facts that barred the way to an immediate marriage to Virginia. He considered the alternatives of spending the next six months writing a new play, in the hope that it would have a suc-cesssful production in the fall, or of going to Hollywood to try to accumulate enough money in six or eight months to give him security. Either of these expedients would entail nearly a year's delay and almost complete separation from Virginia. Could he ask her to wait so long on so doubtful a contingency? He tried to per-suade himself that if she cared enough for him she would wait; but he knew that he was merely trying to rationalize away his fear of a refusal. At any rate, all he could do was to tell her frankly what his situation was.

On Friday his thoughts were dramatically diverted from Vir-ginia by the arrival of a letter which his mother had forwarded. It was from Sylvia Jethrow, who was in Atlantic City, recuperating from her operation. Written in a sprawling, unsteady hand and blurred with tears, it was a tumultuous outpouring of penitence and passion. She asked his forgiveness for her savage rejection of his offer of marriage. It had all been due, she said, to the long illness, which had tortured her nerves and clouded her reason. Now that she was able to think clearly, she had reread his letter again and again and was shocked to discover how cruelly she had misunder-stood and misjudged him. If he only knew what agonies of re-morse she was suffering he would surely find it in his heart to excuse her. All she asked was an opportunity to make amends. Her ordeal had had a sobering and maturing effect upon her; he would find her greatly altered: no longer a peevish and irresponsible schoolgirl but a woman, ready and eager to assume the obligations and duties of adult life. She had awakened to a full appreciation of his fine quali-ties: his strength, his courage, his brilliance, his integrity. It must have been her unconscious knowledge of his worth that had made her cling to him during all the years of their furtive intimacy. She did not regret that circumstances had prevented their earlier marriage, because now she felt ready to enter into the kind of marital relationship that theirs should be. If she were not so sure of herself and so convinced that they could have a lifetime of happiness together, she would give him up rather than run the risk of making him unhappy. As it was, she had had to steel herself to write this letter: it was not easy for a sensitive girl to throw away all her defenses. Only because she believed he had meant everything he had said when he asked her to marry him did she venture to expose herself in this fashion. Her whole life hinged upon his reply. She ended with a flood of endearments.

Eric read the letter in amazement and consternation. It was more than three months since he had heard from Sylvia, and he had accepted her previous letter as final. He was unprepared for her complete reversal of feeling and staggered by her assumption that he still wanted to marry her. Logically her scornful rejection of his proposal had destroyed any claim that she might have had upon him. Nor was he touched by this new effusion. The more he read it, the less indication could he find of any change or growth in her. The picture she drew of her martyrdom of pain, her spiritual regeneration, and her all-consuming love was the product of a feeble imagination, overstimulated by romantic novels and movies, rather than of an honest self-examination. Further, he was too realistic not to suspect that her change of heart might have been influenced by the defection of her Great Barrington admirer and by his own success.

But he could not dismiss the letter as easily as all that. He still felt a certain sense of responsibility toward Sylvia. Whatever her faults, she was neither frivolous nor wanton. Her long intimacy with him had undoubtedly been based upon the expectation of marriage and had, perhaps, robbed her of other opportunities. That was the very reason he had asked her to marry him when his fortunes had been at their lowest ebb. If she was unduly eager to have him, now that he had made his mark (he could not help wondering whether she knew that his play was closing!), he had, perhaps, been unreasonable in asking her at a time his prospects seemed hopeless. It was easy to see how his refusal of her, now, would be regarded. Coltertown was a small community, and they were both well known there. As usually happens, the reports of his income were highly exaggerated; it was believed that he was well on the way to a great fortune. In the eyes of the townspeople, it would seem—Lydia Jethrow would see to it!—that he had offered to share his beggary with Sylvia, only to jilt the faithful girl when he found himself rolling in wealth. Once this false interpretation had been given currency, it could never be explained away. (How often, he wondered, had he accepted similar conclusions about people without taking the trouble to inquire into the facts?) The prospective loss of his reputation for integrity troubled him almost as deeply as did the immediate problem of finding the least painful way to make Sylvia understand that he no longer wanted to marry her.

On Saturday night he went around to the Farow again. Since Wednesday he had forced himself to stay away, afraid that, once there, he would be unable to resist the temptation of going back to see Virginia. Besides, he was unhappy enough about the play's closing without subjecting himself to a nightly reminder of its imminent end.

The theater was filled to capacity and many people had been turned away. It was a very special occasion, for the audience, aware that it was watching the demise of a play that deserved a better fate, behaved as though it were attending a protest meeting rather than a theatrical performance. Every scene was vigorously applauded and at the end there was a thunderous demonstration of approval and indignation. The actors were recalled twenty times to the accompaniment of cheers and cries of "Bravo!" When McCarthy ordered the house lights up, the spectators still refused to leave their seats and continued to stamp and clap. The curtain rose once more, with the entire cast lined up behind the footlights. The actors, deeply moved, many of them in tears, bowed again and again. At last, Reginald Olmsted stepped forward and, motioning for silence, addressed the audience.

"Ladies and gentlemen," he said, "I hope you will forgive me for assuming a function that rightfully belongs to Mr. Leroy Thompson, the producer of this fine play, or to Mr. Eric Kenwood, its gifted young author. But I know that I am speaking for them, as well as for all of us here on the stage, when I tell you that we are profoundly touched, profoundly grateful to you for this generous expression of your approval. Every member of the cast has felt it a privilege to appear in this play and regards its untimely closing not only as a personal loss, but as a distinct loss to the theater and to the intelligent theatergoing public. Your warm demonstration

464

convinces us that you share our feeling. And so, kind friends, we, one and all, say thank you, thank you, thank you, and bid you a sorrowful good-by."

The actors applauded in fervent agreement, the curtain fell for the last time, and the audience crowded into the aisles. Eric, choking with emotion, dashed out through the lobby and hurried backstage. The work of dismantling the production was already in progress. The electricians' long ladders were going up, the carpenters were unlashing and stacking the flats, the property men were putting dust-covers on the furniture and stowing small props in wooden cases. They would be working all night, getting the production out of the theater, so that the Jack Sprat production could move in next day, preparatory to the Monday night opening.

Virginia was at her dressing table, removing her make-up, and when she saw Eric her tears began to flow again. "Eric, dear, it's awful sad!"

"The audience seemed to think so too."

"I've never seen anything like it. None of us ever has. I'll never forget it."

"I won't either. Well, I want to go around and say good-by to everybody before they get away. I just stopped in to ask if I can take you home."

"Not tonight, Eric," she said, and he was surprised to see that she looked almost panic-stricken. "When do you go back home?"

"Well, I don't know. I thought tomorrow sometime. But I can stay over if—"

"No, no!" she said hastily. "Let's say tomorrow then."

"What time? I have a lunch date with Irina Lanski, but I can break that if you—"

"No, don't do that. After lunch—let's say, after lunch."

"All right. Shall I call you or shall I just come around?"

"It doesn't matter. Well, call me. Yes, better call me." Her voice was muffled and she blinked away the tears, not looking at him.

"All right, I'll run along then," he said. "Good night, darling."

"Good night, Eric dear!" She rose impulsively and, putting her arms around his neck, kissed him. "Don't be downhearted, please don't!"

"I won't." He kissed her again, and then she freed herself and pushed him toward the door.

"Go away, before I make a crying fool of myself!" she said.

465

Eric made the rounds of the dressing-rooms. The cubicles looked cold and bleak with the valises and tin make-up boxes packed, the clothes hooks empty, the dressing tables bare, the little personal knickknacks no longer visible. Everyone had kind and affectionate words for him, but the emotion that the brave last hours had engendered was already beginning to fade and the bonds that held them all so strongly to a common enterprise would soon be dissolved. The fine teamwork, the collective effort, ended in nothing, led nowhere. All that remained was a score of unrelated individuals, a handful of unemployed actors going their separate ways, worried about the future, each preoccupied with the problem of finding a way to make ends meet. On Monday they would once more be haunting the offices of producers and agents, scanning the theatrical columns for announcements of new productions, watching the pennies, and wondering how long it would be before the dollars would begin to come in again. The art of the theater and their own growth as artists were secondary considerations now. The important thing was to find a job.

On the way out Eric stopped to shake hands with his friends among the busy stagehands. "Good luck to you, Mr. Kenwood," said Harry Baumrucker. "And I hope we'll see you right back here, next year, with a new one." And McCarthy, who was superintending the job of taking the production down, hugged him and wished him luck too.

For the last time Eric walked up the dismal alley. The audience had long since departed and the front of the house was dark. A theatrical transfer truck was already parked at the curb, waiting for the first load of scenery. To Eric it seemed like a hearse, arriving with indecent haste before the corpse was cold.

He went to his room, but sleep was out of the question. He was seething with the excitement of the past hours and with anticipation of tomorrow's meeting with Virginia. The fact that she was no longer putting him off made him believe that she was ready to give him a definite answer—a favorable one even! He felt that he had been attaching too much importance to his economic difficulties. Virginia was no Claire or Sylvia, to whom dollars and cents were always a matter of primary concern; if she cared enough for him, it was unlikely that she would be influenced by any mercenary consideration. He began to be a little ashamed of his own preoccupation with money matters, and to feel that he had been unimaginative and

466

guilty of false pride. If a man and a woman really felt they belonged together, they could surely find some way of surmounting material obstacles.

Having put himself into this sanguine state, he sat down to write to Sylvia. He wanted that troublesome problem settled before he talked to Virginia. It was not an easy task. He wanted to make his answer unequivocal and yet spare her sensibilities, in so far as that was possible. Whatever he said, however, would be sure to be misconstrued. If he were sympathetic, he might sound patronizing; if logical, heartless. Since nothing he wrote could satisfy, the less said the better; still, a brief reply to her long letter would make him seem cold and indifferent. He made three or four starts but found each time that he was putting either her or himself in the wrong. At last he told her the simple truth that he had fallen in love with someone else and that their marriage, therefore, could bring satisfaction to neither of them. Assuring her of his affection, he ended with the hope that they would one day find a new basis for friendship.

He reread several times what he had written. Though he was not altogether satisfied, it was the best he could do. Forgetting Sylvia, he lay for hours, rehearsing what he would say to Virginia next day.

XLII.

While Eric was dressing a bellboy brought up a special delivery letter. He recognized Virginia's hand and tore open the envelope with a sense of foreboding.

"Eric darling," he read, "this is the hardest letter I've ever had to write. By the time you get it, Tommy and I will be on our way to Jacksonville, where his parents live and where we're going to be married. I know I should have told you, but the truth is that I just didn't have the courage. Please don't hate me for it, and please, please, believe that I'm not just saying it, when I tell you that you are well rid of me. I'm not half the girl that you think I am and could never live up to what you believe me to be. When you found that out, as you would all too soon, it would make you unhappy and me even unhappier. So it's best this way, truly it is. I'd rather give you this momentary pain than the lasting pain of disillusionment. It's been so thrilling knowing you and I'm so grateful for all the happy hours I've spent with you—including that beautiful night—and for all I've learned from you. I loved being in your fine play and am heartbroken that it couldn't go on. Will you let me be in another, one of these days? Please do! Anyhow, write another one soon. I think you are a wonderful writer and a wonderful person, and I hope that you will have all the happiness and all the good fortune that you deserve. And I *do* love you, in my fashion, my dear. So try to find it in that warm, generous, understanding heart of yours to forgive me. But don't forget me! I want and need your friendship and I'd be desolate without it. And since there's no way of saying it in English, I'm ending this inadequate epistle with an earnestly hopeful au revoir!"

Eric's first reaction was one of savage bitterness. He felt that he had been cheated and made a fool of. He raged against himself, too, for having been so blind. It was obvious enough, now, that it had always been Thompson upon whom Virginia had set her heart. He recalled a dozen incidents that would have given him a clue had he been less naïve and less absorbed by his own infatuation. Her veiled self-justification of her break with Mollison, her way of bringing Thompson into the conversation, her strained manner when he had encountered the director in her dressing-room—all these should have been sufficient indications of the state of her feelings. And, above all, her strange behavior on New Year's Eve: her precipitate flight from the party, the confused scene of Thompson's attempted pursuit and her panicky fear that he would follow her, and, finally, her hysterical surrender, in a sudden reflex of jealousy and frustration, to Eric himself. He saw it all with painful clarity. She had kept him dangling, not because, as he had fatuously believed, she had any doubt about the true state of her feelings, but because Claire stood in her way and Eric presented the possibility of a second choice—a sort of emotional consolation prize. But with Claire out of the way—and

468

Irina Lanski had intimated that her action in closing the play was either the cause or the result of her estrangement from Thompson —the path was clear for Virginia, and she had summarily dismissed Eric from her thoughts. He writhed in the agony of wounded pride, telling himself that he had been played with and hoodwinked. Thompson, too, with his hearty friendliness, had just been playing a part in the elaborate game of deception. Eric's heated fancy evoked an image of Thompson and Virginia lying intimately together, reviewing the whole episode of their courtship and laughing with condescending pity at his own gullibility. Hatred for them both possessed him. He picked up Virginia's letter, meaning to tear it to bits.

Instead he read it again. His insight and judgment began to get the better of his rage. Pondering what she had written and thinking back over all the hours they had spent together, it was impossible for him to believe that she had deliberately conceived and executed a campaign of deception and chicanery. Undoubtedly she had been less than honest with him; her conduct had been motivated by a selfish regard for her own feelings rather than by consideration for his. (She freely admitted her lack of courage too.) But that was very different from the cynical callousness that he had at first attributed to her. She was probably right in saying that he had overidealized her; he could hardly blame her for not conforming to a standard of behavior that was, perhaps, superhuman. She had neither his ethical training nor the sense of obligation and responsibility that circumstances had implanted in him. She had told him that her conditioning had made her self-centered and accustomed to having her own way, and he had no right to complain when she demonstrated what he had chosen not to understand. Perhaps she was wiser than he in perceiving that two people with such divergent philosophies of life would find it impossible to reach an adjustment.

This rational conclusion did little to ease the ache of losing her or to lessen his desolate feeling of emptiness. It was time to leave for his engagement with Irina Lanski, and he resisted the impulse to call it off. Anything was better than being alone with his grief. She, at least, was a friend of whom he could be sure. As he was about to leave he noticed on the writing desk his letter to Sylvia, ready to be mailed.

He stared at it, wondering if he would have written it had he known what he knew now. He had refused Sylvia upon the ground that he loved someone else. It was still true, but since his love was now hopeless, was it still a valid excuse? What was more important, was he still sure he wanted to refuse? Virginia, in accordance with her finishing-school code, had tried to soften her rejection by saying that she was not good enough for him. Might it not be that she really believed he was not good enough for her, that she found him too immature, too inexperienced, too lacking in the qualities that would make him acceptable in her world? Perhaps he had been aiming too high, deluding himself with the belief that he could keep pace with her sophistication and cosmopolitan tastes—as Thompson undoubtedly could! Sylvia was more on his level: a small-town girl with small-town ways and a background very much like his own. She would make no demands that he could not meet, had no interest in a career, and could be depended upon for all the domestic virtues. Life with her would not be exciting, but it would be based solidly upon the normal and traditional family foundation. In his present deflated and lonely state it held a not unwelcome promise of security and permanence. He must avoid the danger of hurling himself into Sylvia's arms on the rebound, but he was by no means as sure as he had been, the night before, that he wanted to put her entirely out of his life. Uncertain what to do, he slipped the letter into his coat pocket.

Irina Lanski was alone in her apartment. They sat down immediately to a salad, cheese, fruit, and a bottle of Beaune. Eric was dejectedly silent, hardly touching his plate.

"I don't want to be a Job's comforter," said Irina Lanski, "but I think you should find a little consolation in that ovation at the Farow last night."

"Oh, were you there?"

"Of course I was there! You don't think I would have missed it, do you? I had some English friends with me, and they were deeply moved by the play. They think it would be well received in London, and so do I. So, if you don't mind, I'll send a script to my English representative."

"Yes, certainly."

"I've had an inquiry from Scandinavia too. And some of the better community theaters here are sure to want to do it. And I've been talking to a publisher about bringing it out. There'll be no money to speak of, but at least the play will be kept alive, and, for a serious author, that is very important, I believe."

"Yes, I think so too," said Eric, a little heartened by the prospect of seeing his play in print.

She looked at him searchingly. "I don't want to be prying, but I can't help feeling that something is troubling you—something besides the play, I mean. Of course, it's none of my business, so if you think I should keep my mouth shut, don't hesitate to say so."

He welcomed the opportunity to unburden himself. "I had a note from Ginny this morning. She and Tommy are on their way to Florida to get married."

She nodded. "I thought it might be something like that. In fact, I rather expected it."

"You knew they were thinking about it?" he asked in surprise.

"Well, one can never be sure about these things. But I know them both quite well, and there were little indications that made me suspect. Perhaps I should have warned you, but, after all, it is as your agent that you employed me, not as a meddler in your private life."

"You knew how I felt about Ginny too?"

"Well—!" she said with a deprecatory gesture.

"Good God!" said Eric, flushing with mortification. "Did I make it as obvious as all that?"

"No, no!" she said, putting her hand on his arm. "You mustn't take it that way. It is only that I am an old woman whose own life is behind her and who has nothing better to do than to observe those who are still young and capable of emotional experiences. But not coldly, not cynically, believe me. I have known what it is to suffer, as you are suffering now, and I know how little words can do to ease the pain. But God has implanted in us a will to live that is stronger than any pain, and in time even the deepest wounds heal themselves."

"I can believe that with my mind, but I'm afraid it doesn't help much."

"Not today, perhaps, or tomorrow. But you have something in you that I never had, that few people have—the power to create. You can pour your emotions into a mold of your own making and weave a poem out of your unhappiness. For the tender-minded and the pure in spirit, life can never be easy, but at least their feet are not rooted in the earth and theirs is still the victory."

"I wish I could tell you how much I owe you—in every way!"

"Nonsense! You don't owe me anything. Don't you think it means something to me, in this grimy business of mine, to find someone

471

who is young and idealistic and endowed with your gifts?" She looked at her watch. "I'm afraid I must send you away now. I still have some packing to do."

Eric rose. "When will you be back?"

"In two weeks or so. You haven't told me if you want me to do anything about a Hollywood job. Have you thought about it?"

"Yes, I have. Do you really think they'd pay me all that money?"

"Yes, I'm sure of it. They are always looking for new blood. And no wonder! Blood ages fast in Hollywood."

"Would I be able to hold the job and still write the plays I want to write?"

"If you did, you would be the first that had ever accomplished it."

"Then what do you think I should do?"

"I think that you must make that decision yourself."

"Well, then, I guess my answer is no."

"I was hoping it would be—though I can ill afford the loss of commissions!" She extended her hand. "Good-by, Eric, and God bless you!"

Impulsively he embraced and kissed her. "Good-by, Irina dear!"

He walked back toward his hotel, heartened for the moment at least. At the corner, he turned out of his way for a last look at the Farow Theater. On the big electric signboard over the marquee The Clouded Mirror had already come down and Jack Sprat was going up. A truck was parked in front of the alley, and the transfer men were unloading the scenery of the new production and carrying it down the narrow, littered passageway.

The sidewalk was strewn with handbills that had been intended for insertion in the programs of other theaters. Eric found one that had not been trampled and picked it up. On one side were excerpts from the reviews of his play; on the other, a photographic cut of a scene from the play, showing Reginald Olmsted, Florence Fulham, and Virginia. Eric gazed at it for a long moment, then, folding it carefully, slipped it into his coat pocket. As he did so, his hand came in contact with his letter to Sylvia. He hurried back to the corner and dropped the letter into a mailbox. An hour later he was on his way to Coltertown.